WITHDRAWN

D1087293

GRAVE LANDSCAPES

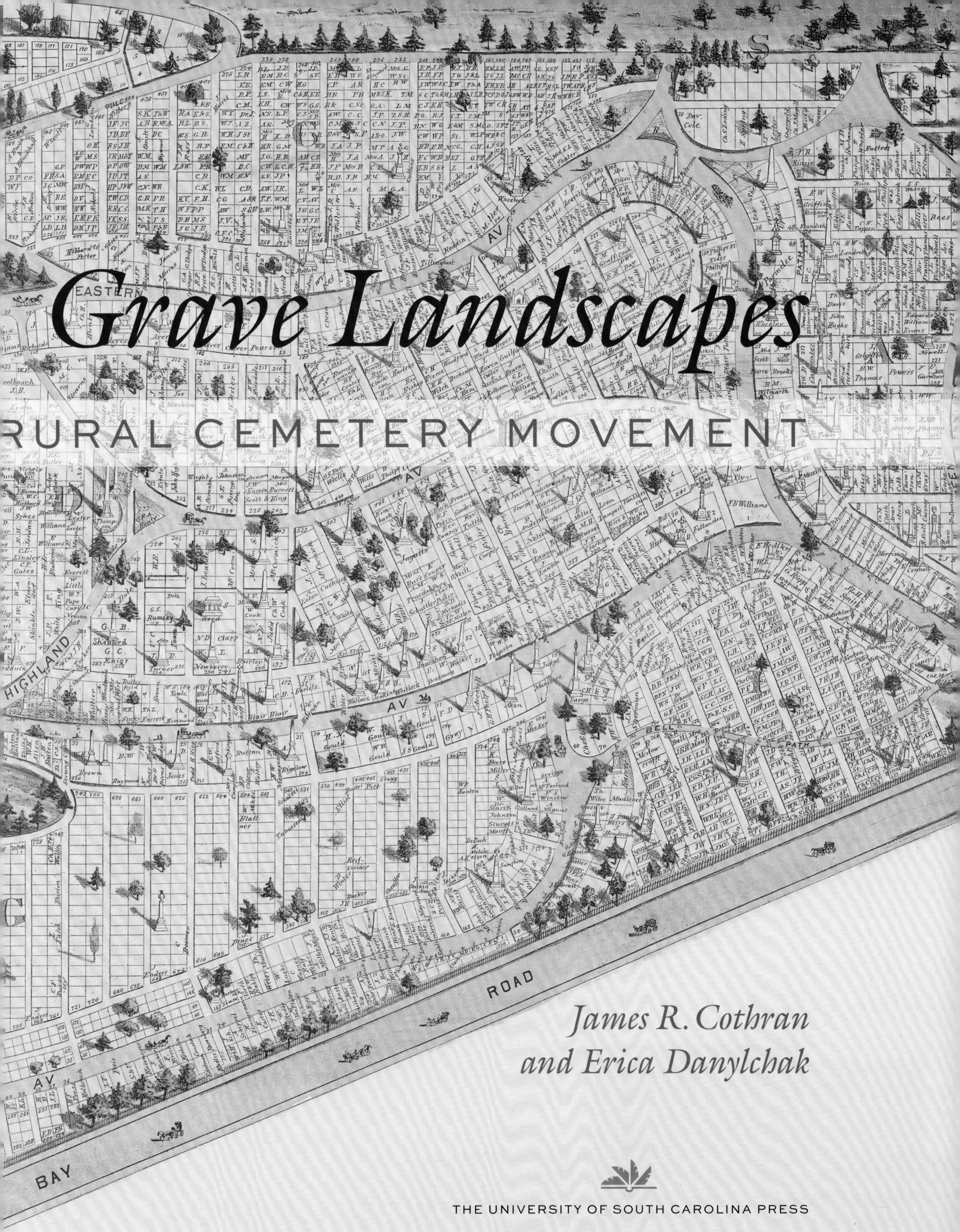

Grave Landscapes

RURAL CEMETERY MOVEMENT

*James R. Cothran
and Erica Danylchak*

THE UNIVERSITY OF SOUTH CAROLINA PRESS

© 2018 University of South Carolina

Published by the University of South Carolina Press
Columbia, South Carolina 29208

www.sc.edu/uscpress

Manufactured in China

27 26 25 24 23 22 21 20 19 18
10 9 8 7 6 5 4 3 2 1

Library of Congress Cataloging-in-Publication Data
can be found at http://catalog.loc.gov/.

isbn: 978-1-61117-789-5 (cloth)
isbn: 978-1-61117-799-2 (ebook)

Previous: 1878 bird's-eye view of Graceland Cemetery.
The southern part of the site is pictured at right. Green
Bay Road runs along the western boundary of the
cemetery. Published by Charles Rascher, Chicago
History Museum, ICHi-27725.

To students of historic landscapes and their teachers

CONTENTS

ILLUSTRATIONS

In early nineteenth-century America, as the Industrial Revolution lured throngs of workers to ever-more-congested cities, urban burial grounds became increasingly overcrowded. Graves were stacked one atop another, and graveyards were blamed for the diseases seizing cities. A society, under the influence of Romanticism, was spurred toward reformation. In Boston, Jacob Bigelow, physician and botanist, and other members of the Massachusetts Horticultural Society envisioned a different type of American burial place—a rural cemetery removed from the city and embellished with carefully selected trees and shrubs and poignantly consoling monuments.

The establishment of Mount Auburn Cemetery outside of Boston, Massachusetts, in 1831 set a far-reaching precedent that was emulated again and again by cities across the country. These rural cemeteries reflected a belief in the consoling benefits of nature on an increasingly frenzied society and grieving individuals. These burial landscapes featured a recurring and specific set of design characteristics to foster contemplation, moderate fear, and refresh the soul—monumental gateways, curvilinear roadways, informal groupings of diverse trees and shrubs, sinuous lakes and meandering streams, picturesque views and vistas, and commemorative sculpture.

The rural cemetery movement profoundly impacted America's landscape. These cemeteries, which drew city dwellers and tourists to their grounds to revel in leisurely promenades, propelled the movement for public parks in the United States. At a time when there were few other large-scale landscape commissions and few individuals with refined experience planning complex landscapes in America, rural cemeteries also spurred the professionalization of landscape gardening. The new professional field would ultimately take the name landscape architecture.

The term *rural cemetery* is often misunderstood. Today, using the term conjures up the image of a small family or church burial ground out in the country. However, during the nineteenth century, the term *rural cemetery* was applied consistently to large-scale picturesque burial places on the fringes of cities and towns. The term had specific connotations that reflected the motivation for their establishment. The text begins with an overview of the conditions and influences that instigated the development of the landscape type.

The extent and impact of the rural cemetery movement in America is not widely appreciated. A primary objective of the following text is to provide the reader with an understanding of how prolific and influential the movement was in nineteenth-century America. To this end, the text includes numerous cemetery profiles—not only the most famous examples but also many not typically cited in literature on historic cemeteries. The appendix also includes a selected list of 175 examples that illuminates the geographical distribution and migration of the rural cemetery movement. In addition, the text examines the influence of rural cemeteries on public parks and garden suburbs and on the emergence of the profession of landscape architecture.

Many contemporary published accounts of rural cemeteries emphasize the details surrounding the cemetery's establishment and the personal histories of those buried there. The following text focuses on the landscape characteristics of rural cemeteries and places them within a broader context of American (and European) landscape design. The text offers a practical guide to rural cemetery design characteristics and information on the evolution of the landscape type to promote the identification, and hopefully, the appropriate rehabilitation of these historic sites.

Grave Landscapes: The Nineteenth-Century Rural Cemetery Movement was envisioned by James R. Cothran, Fellow of the American Society of Landscape Architects. For years, whenever Jim traveled, he sought out the closest rural cemetery to visit. He found inspiration in the design and botanical riches of rural cemeteries and often photographed their remarkable landscape features. He also began accumulating a vast research collection about these sites and their landscapes. Jim intended to write a book that was a well-documented examination of the rural cemetery movement aimed at landscape historians, historic site curators, and landscape architects. He also wanted to create a narrative history aimed at a broader audience—anyone with an interest in historic landscapes—to encourage greater interest in historic cemeteries in general and a more widespread understanding of rural cemeteries in particular.

In 2009 Jim asked me to assist him with research for his book. I had been one of Jim's students in the Heritage Preservation Program at Georgia State University. His course on southern garden history had been my introduction to the study of historic landscapes, the concept of landscape preservation, and the examination of the rural cemetery movement. He had recognized my burgeoning interest in historic landscapes and fostered it. Ultimately, his influence on my professional interests was profound . . . and enduring.

Working with Jim for two and a half years on this project was a distinct privilege. He provided wise and steadfast guidance, always delivered in his southern gentlemanly manner. We also enjoyed sharing stories about our visits to cemetery sites and discoveries in our research. As our work together progressed, he asked me to write portions of the manuscript, knowing it would help my professional growth. Jim was an inspiring mentor and a valued friend. After Jim's untimely death in January 2012, I was encouraged to continue the project and have it published posthumously. I am indebted to Jim's wife, Lynn, for urging me to continue the work Jim had started and laid the groundwork for finishing. I am sincerely grateful to Linda Fogle at the University of South Carolina Press for her unwavering encouragement and support of my completion of the project. I am incredibly thankful to my friend and colleague Staci Catron, director of the Cherokee Garden Library, for her tireless support throughout the project including insightful feedback on parts of the manuscript. I am also sincerely grateful to Andrew Kohr, a fellow landscape preservationist whom Jim also mentored, for encouraging me to carry the project to its completion. It has truly been an honor to do so.

Many individuals generously gave their time and shared their expertise with Jim as he built his research archive. A sincere thank-you is extended to each and every one.

Special appreciation goes to the staff of the Kenan Research Center at the Atlanta History Center, including Paul Crater, Erica Hague, Josh Hogan, and Carla Ledgerwood. Sincere appreciation is also extended to the following individuals and institutions: Jason C. Escalante, Avery Architectural & Fine Arts Library, Columbia University; Heather Stone and Johna L. Picco, the Filson Historical Society; Kelly Kerney, the Valentine; Sarah Yarrito, Chicago History Museum; Lorna Kirwan and Crystal Miles, the Bancroft Library, University of California, Berkeley; Thomas Lisanti, the New York Public Library; Aubrey Parker and Muriel Jackson, Middle Georgia Archives, Washington Memorial Library; Virginia L. Ellison and Faye L. Jensen, South Carolina Historical Society; and Jenny Liddle, National Trust.

A special thank-you is extended to John Rousmaniere, Anthony Salamone, and Donato Daddario for sharing their extensive knowledge of the Evergreens Cemetery and their time to guide me on a tour through the site, of which they are careful stewards. I also thank Paul May and the Woodlawn Cemetery security team for providing direction on the cemetery grounds and information on the major monuments.

A special acknowledgment goes to several friends and colleagues who provided valuable feedback on the manuscript—Fred Mobley, Hilary Morrish, and Sonya Unsworth.

And finally, a heartfelt thank-you goes to my family for their continual love and support.

ERICA DANYLCHAK

CHAPTER 1

A Brief History of Common Burial Landscapes Prior to the Nineteenth Century ❧

Burial landscapes reflect a civilization's religious and cultural attitudes toward death and the deceased. As different religious traditions prevailed over time, the location of burial grounds and their approach to memorialization signaled fundamental changes in beliefs. The ancient pagan cultures of Greece and Rome buried their dead in natural settings outside of cities with tombs to preserve memory. With the rise of Christianity, the role of cemeteries declined in the Western world as tombs moved inside the church or huddled against its exterior walls. Memorials were reserved for clergymen and nobility; for most believers burial was transient and impersonal. Beginning in the sixteenth century, reform-minded Protestants encouraged a retreat from papist idolatry and urged permanent burial in secular outdoor spaces instead. New England's earliest urban burial grounds reflected the principles of Protestant Dissenters and bristled with tombstones inscribed with the religious convictions of their sect. The later decline of Puritanism and fragmentation within America's religious community contributed to deteriorating conditions within these burial spaces. By the nineteenth century, the shameful condition of urban burial landscapes helped provoke reform in the form of rural cemeteries.

Rural cemetery advocates recognized that burial landscapes reflected fundamental cultural and religious beliefs, and they chronicled the history of burial practices in their speeches and literature. They emphasized the virtues of ancient naturalistic landscapes while lamenting contemporary burial-ground conditions. Amidst rising alternatives to Protestantism and declining religious fervor, these reformers argued for the establishment of a new type of burial landscape that would embody the ideology of their era.

Ancient Burial Practices

In the ancient polytheistic cultures of Greece and Rome, people feared the return of the dead to disturb the living. For protection, these civilizations established outlying burial places beyond the walls of their fortified cities.[1] In the fifth century B.C.E. the ancient Roman Law of the Twelve Tables codified the practice of extramural burials with its restriction that no dead body be buried or cremated inside the city. Instead, the Romans often buried their dead along suburban roads. In ancient Athens, too, the principal cemetery was "situated on 'the sacred way,' at some distance from the city."[2]

To help prevent the dead from returning, these ancient cultures treated the tombs of the departed with reverence. Tombs sited the specific place of funerary worship, memorialized the dead, and provoked meditation. Significantly, the exact location of individual burials was marked. The tomb either contained the body or ashes of the deceased or covered a chamber where the body was buried. Cultural historian Philippe Ariès underscores the point: "There were no tombs without bodies, and no bodies without tombs."[3] The tomb served as a place of remembrance. In most cases, it carried an inscription that shared the name of the deceased, his age, his date of death, sometimes his rank or profession, his position within the family, and the relationship between the deceased and the person responsible for handling the burial. These kinds of inscriptions were meant to "transmit the memory of the deceased to later generations."[4] In fact, they became a significant source of ancient history, particularly of the Roman civilization. A nineteenth-century guidebook to America's first rural cemetery—Mount Auburn—underscores the presence and importance of memorial monuments within these ancient landscapes. It notes that the Appian Way, one of ancient Rome's most strategically important roads, was lined with burials and "crowded with columns, and obelisks, and cenotaphs to the memory of her heroes and sages; and at every turn the short but touching inscription met the eye,—Siste Viator,—Pause Traveller,—inviting at once to sympathy and thoughtfulness."[5]

Placed within a natural setting, these ancient burial places intended to quiet grief and provoke contemplation. In his consecration address at Mount Auburn Cemetery, Judge Joseph Story noted ardently that the Greeks "consigned their relics to shady groves, in the neighborhood of murmuring streams and mossy fountains, close by the favorite resorts of those who were engaged in the study of philosophy and nature."[6] They called their burial landscapes, "with the elegant expressiveness of their own beautiful language, Cemeteries, or 'Places of Repose.'"[7] The name itself implied a peaceful atmosphere and softened the associations of death by equating it with sleep.

Notably, trees were often used within these burial landscapes to provoke specific sentiments, because they often held long-standing symbolic significance from one pagan religion to another. The evergreen cypress (*Cupressus sempervirens*), for instance, had its symbolic meaning rooted in Greek mythology. After the young boy Cyparissus accidently killed his pet stag, his grief transformed him into a cypress tree. The

THE APPIAN WAY; IN ITS ACTUAL STATE, AND AS RESTORED BY M. ANCELET.

1. Tomb ruins along the ancient Roman road, the Appian Way, accompanied by a mid-nineteenth-century drawing by M. Ancelet depicting how the monuments likely looked originally. Wood engraving, 1890, Estes and Lauriat, publishers, Danylchak collection.

A BRIEF HISTORY OF COMMON BURIAL LANDSCAPES

2. Cypresses and road leading to the cemetery, Scutari, Constantinople, Turkey. Photograph ca. 1890, Detroit Publishing Company Photograph Collection, Library of Congress Prints and Photographs Division.

tree became a quintessential and widespread symbol of mourning.

The ancient Egyptians also famously buried their dead amidst nature. In his address at the dedication of America's Spring Grove Cemetery, the Honorable John M'Lean noted that the burial ground of the ancient Egyptians was "a large plain, surrounded by trees, and intersected by canals, to which was given the appellation Elisicens, meaning rest."[8] Judge Joseph Story, too, cited the Elysian fields in his dedicatory address, noting that the Egyptians had "soothed their grief" by interring their dead amidst the magnificence of nature.[9] Greek historian Diodorus, writing in the first century B.C.E., first suggested that these meadows in the vicinity of Memphis, where the Egyptians of that city buried their dead, inspired the Greek concept of the afterlife.[10]

In Greek mythology the Elysian Fields, or simply Elysium, was home to those favored by the gods after death. It promised an existence of perpetual happiness. Poets described and refined this idea of the hereafter for hundreds of years. The Greek poet Homer placed Elysium at the western edge of the earth next to the great, earth-encircling river Okeanos. In *Odes*, Pindar (ca. 522–443 B.C.E.), the Theban lyric poet, described a life in Elysium free from toil for the righteous dead on an island where ocean breezes blow and flowers of gold glow. Meanwhile, in his epic poem *The Aeneid*, the Roman poet Virgil (70–19 B.C.E.) described Elysium as a pleasant place of laurel groves, crystal streams, and verdant fields bathed in radiant light. This mythological place was invoked by supporters of burial ground reform many centuries later.

Early Christian Burial Practices

The rise of Christianity ushered in new conceptions of death and the afterlife that affected burial practices throughout Christendom. One of the key tenets of Christianity affecting change was the concept of resurrection embodied in Christ's proclamation, "I am the resurrection and the life; he who believes in me, though he die, yet shall he live, and whoever lives and believes in me shall never die" (John 11:25–26). The biblical account of Jesus's entombment and Resurrection encouraged the idea that a proper, safe burial place would increase the possibility of salvation. In the earliest days of Christianity, adherents had continued to prohibit burials near the living. But the growing importance that the Church placed on Resurrection inspired a new approach to the burial of the dead.[11] The church eventually changed its position and ecclesiastical practices required burial in consecrated ground, either in a church or adjacent to it.

An influential precedent was set when Constantine the Great (ca. 272–337 C.E.)—the first Roman Emperor to convert to Christianity—was interred in the outer porch of the Church of the Holy Apostles in Constantinople.[12] It was later under the tenure of Pope Gregory I (ca. 540–604 C.E.) that the Roman

Catholic Church allowed bishops, priests, and chosen lay members of the church to be buried within the church itself.[13] Those who had dedicated their lives to God or those who by their nobility, actions, or merits had distinguished themselves in the service of God were the only ones deemed worthy of accompanying the "body and blood of Our Lord on the altar."[14] The location of burial within the church was a matter of money—"the choicest and most expensive location was the choir, near the altar where Mass was said."[15] For those buried in the churchyard, the choicest spot was one nestled against the east wall of the church as close to the altar as possible. The practice of burial within churchyards or churches spread to England by the middle of the eighth century.[16] By the Medieval period, the dead had ceased to "frighten the living, and the two groups coexisted in the same places and behind the same walls."[17]

Meanwhile, burial outside the city became a punishment reserved for society's pariahs—those who had committed suicide, had been executed, or had been excommunicated from the Church. These extramural burial sites were not affiliated with the Church and thus offered no spiritual protection for the deceased. Bodies were often left exposed to the elements or buried in shallow graves that provided little safeguard from roaming animals.

By the early Medieval period, tombs had become anonymous, even for the most venerated deceased. Funerary inscriptions had disappeared because of the decline of writing. However, after the twelfth century, the "attitude of anonymity steadily declined in Latin Christendom."[18] The rejection of anonymity began first among the rich and powerful buried within the church. Visible inscriptions reappeared on the tombstones of the elite signaling a desire for lasting memorialization. The desire to "leave a memory behind" grew steadily throughout the Medieval period so that one of the distinguishing characteristics of the late Medieval period was the "conviction that there is a correspondence between heavenly eternity and earthly fame."[19] To perpetuate their memory, eminent people often chose vertical mural tombs with inscriptions affixed to a wall of the church. Sometimes, those with means commissioned carved recumbent figures in their likeness attached to horizontal tombs.

Interestingly, the late Medieval period saw the emergence of a macabre attitude toward death that manifested itself in visual representations on sculpted tombs of the period. Historians often cite the horrific plagues that ravaged Europe in the fourteenth and fifteenth centuries as the impetus for the period's morbid focus on the physical horrors of dying and decomposition. The outlook is evident in tombs depicting life-size sculpted images of the naked deceased with details such as decaying flesh and abdomen stitches left by embalmers.[20] American Washington Irving (1783–1859) later famously cited such morose representations as counterpoints to his Romantic philosophy. The Medieval Christian's dread surrounding death, however, was limited to the body. Adherents clung to ingrained optimism for immortality and an eternity in heaven.

During the Medieval period, most church parishioners were buried within the churchyard leading to a rapid consumption of space within these outdoor burial grounds. As a result, earthen burial became temporary and depersonalized. After the bodies decomposed over the course of a couple years, the bones were unearthed. Medieval practices saw bones placed in an ossuary—a covered cloister or gallery—or removed to the charnel house—located either under or adjacent to the church—where they were mixed with the remains of others. These practices reduced the total space needed for remains and allowed burial plots or pits within small church graveyards to be reused over and over again.[21]

The location of individuals was largely unknown in these burial landscapes. As Philippe Ariès points out in his influential study *The Hour of Our Death*, the practice of burying bodies atop one another and moving bones to other locations made it nearly impossible to track the whereabouts of specific remains. Few monuments were placed within these spaces and official diagrams of underground burial systems were nonexistent. In graveyards of the poor or those faced with relentless burials, bodies were often placed in mass graves. But the religious beliefs of the average Medieval Christian did not demand an individual grave in a fixed, marked place. Instead, he "cared only that the Church accept his body, to dispose of it as it pleased but within sacred ground so that he might be included in the regular prayers for the collective dead."[22]

Nature was not welcomed within these Medieval churchyards. Ecclesiastics rarely tolerated any substantial plantings, particularly trees, because many possessed "superstitious" associations from various pagan religions. Moreover, Medieval Christians considered nature evil—"the tainted vestiges of Eden lost in Adam's Fall or the wilderness outside the sacred walled Garden into which God thrust Man in punishment for original sin."[23] Allowing nature—even a tamed version of it—to infiltrate churchyards was deemed inappropriate. Practical considerations also precluded plantings from church burial grounds; these spaces were generally small, confined landscapes. Plantings were simply not important within the contemporary conception of burial spaces. By this time, churchyards served a functional purpose—they were temporary repositories for decomposing corpses. As a result, most churchyards were barren plots of land with trenches or mounds, perhaps peppered with weeds and grasses.[24]

Changes in England after the Protestant Reformation

The Protestant Reformation swept across northern Europe in the sixteenth century, aiming to reform Catholic doctrines and practices. In England, the rise of Protestantism—particularly Calvinism—incited an early rejection of accepted church funerary practices. Calvinist theology motivated dramatic changes related to the treatment of the deceased's body. It scorned the Catholic practice of displacing corpses so graves could be reused. Instead, Calvinism encouraged keeping the body "intact in its original place of 'rest' so that it could be identified."[25] Therefore, burial grounds associated with the churches of the

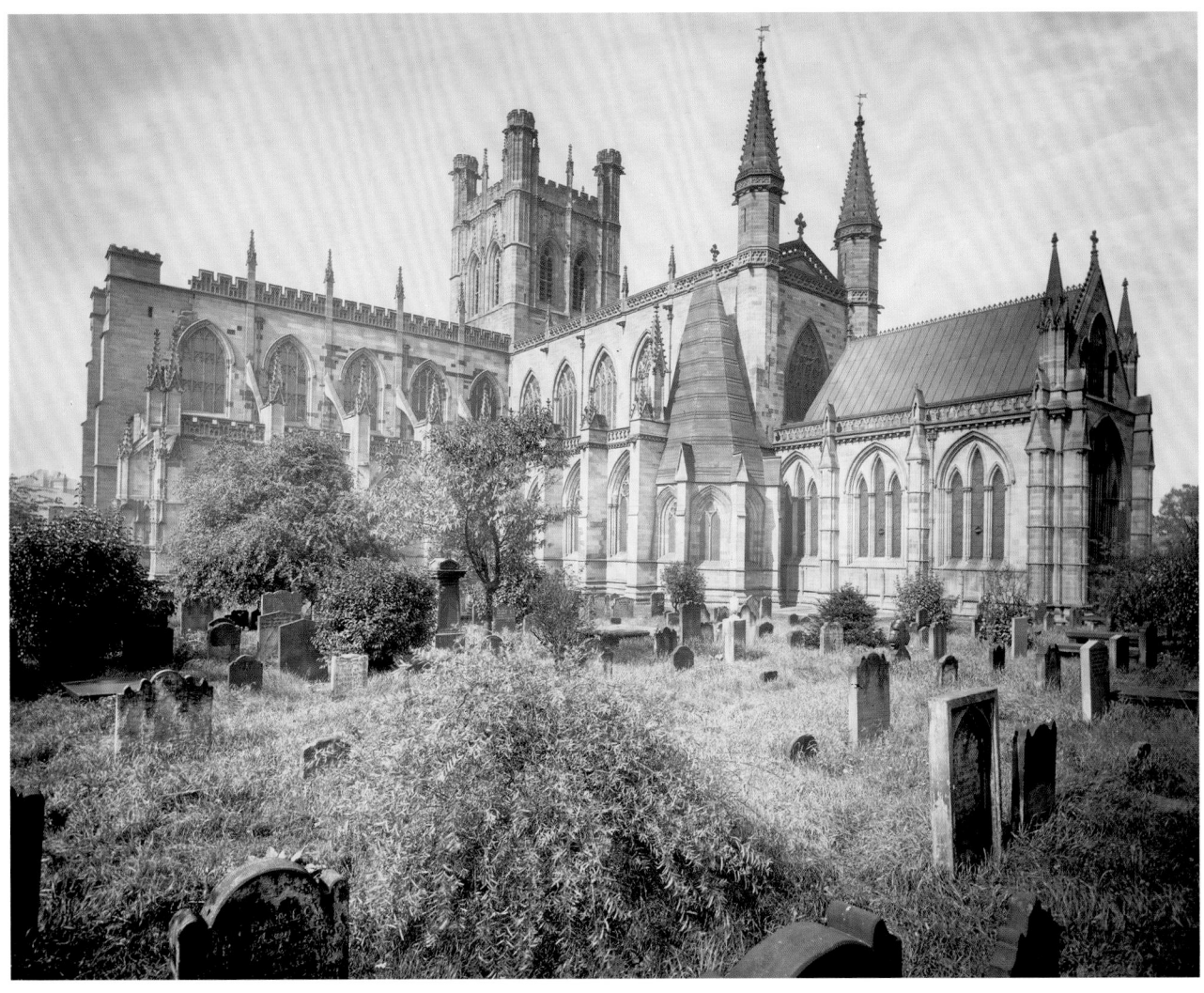

3. Chester Cathedral—a Church of England cathedral located in the city of Chester, Cheshire, England—with its graveyard populated with mural tablets. Photograph ca. 1900, Detroit Publishing Company Photograph Collection, Library of Congress Prints and Photographs Division.

Protestant Reformation seldom had a charnel house or an ossuary. Moreover, their burial grounds rarely included trenches dug to receive numerous occupants unless they were used for interring the poor or were in densely populated urban areas that put a serious strain on their restricted space.[26]

After the rise of Protestantism, "people of quality" began choosing burial in English churchyards instead of within the confines of the church. Throughout the Medieval period, nobles, merchants, and other important individuals increasingly had sought—and had been granted—burial space within the church building or cloister. But the accepted place of burial shifted, particularly beginning in the second half of the seventeenth century. The transition is important, because practices of postmortem commemoration within the church followed the migration of these more affluent dead to the churchyard. Mural tablets similar to what would have been used within church buildings to memorialize the dead began to populate outdoor burial spaces. These tablets or headstones featured inscriptions, ornate frames, and even religious scenes.[27] They signaled, too, the desire for permanency of gravesites. With the practice of perpetual burial, burial spaces soon "bristled with headstones."[28]

Although churchyards predominated in England in the late seventeenth and eighteenth centuries, the Calvinists laid important groundwork for the secularization of burial spaces. Calvinists shunned the Catholic belief that the deceased needed to be buried on sacred ground, within a churchyard or inside the church itself. Because they believed in predestination, they considered it presumptuous to expect that "all the dead were destined for 'the resurrection to eternal life.'"[29] Calvinists, therefore, called for public burial in the ground away from the church.

Bunhill Fields, north of the city of London, became an important early example of a public nondenominational graveyard used by many Protestant sects. After the Restoration of 1660, which reestablished Anglican rule within the Church of England, Calvinistic Puritans, Presbyterians, and other Independents were banned from burial grounds overseen by the High Church. These "English Dissenters" were equally averse to burial in grounds controlled by the Church of England. Instead, they chose burial within a small piece of unconsecrated ground that had previously been used for burial of heretics and plague victims. In 1665 the site known as Bunhill Fields was devoted to use by the Dissenters. It was enclosed by a brick wall and gate. Graves were sold for perpetual burial, and gravesites were marked with commemorative monuments or headstones. Although the burial ground experienced many of the same crowding issues as contemporary churchyards and presented a disorderly appearance with little vegetation, it "signaled radical Protestant's nascent impulse to create a new kind of burial place."[30]

American Burial Practices and Attitudes toward Death in the Colonial Era

Most English immigrants to the American colonies, with the exception of the Puritans, imported the churchyard model. Their burial grounds were generally located next to a church or town meetinghouse, which served a central religious function. In New York—in its early days under English rule—every church had a graveyard connected to the church building. By the early nineteenth century, twenty-three graveyards populated the area of Lower Manhattan south of city hall.[31] Outdoor burial was most common in the English colonies, while burial within churches became increasingly rare. A nineteenth-century history of Trinity Church in Manhattan, which received its parish charter from King William III in 1697, notes that a "curious privilege of former days" was burial in the church's chancel, which cost a heavy fee. It called this rare practice, however, "a relic of the old superstition concerning the sanctity of certain spots, and the benefits conferred to the souls by such a disposal of the body."[32]

America's early urban graveyards were generally small in size, which impacted the appearance and burial practices within these landscapes. Because space was at a premium, these landscapes rarely had walkways or vegetation beyond grass and perhaps a few scattered trees and shrubs. Burials and any associated memorials were randomly placed where room permitted. Long-term planning was seldom a consideration, so space was rarely set aside for family members to be buried together. Manhattan's Trinity Church adopted an interesting solution to the space constraints of its graveyard, which encompassed only a few acres. To accommodate the increasing number of interments during the eighteenth century, the level of the Trinity graveyard was raised several yards above the surrounding streets, which is plainly evident today.[33]

In America in the seventeenth and eighteenth centuries, as in England, the churchyard was no longer the site of anonymous graves.[34] Instead, over time it became "dotted with simple but often quite elegant monuments" that located the specific burial places of individuals.[35] Burial markers in America's churchyards imitated those found in England beginning in the late seventeenth century. They took the form of box tombs, slabs, or headstones. The practice of precisely marking gravesites with inscribed markers became prevalent by the end of the eighteenth century.[36]

Importantly, the Calvinistic Puritans who immigrated to New England rejected the churchyard model and set aside land for common, secular burial grounds in towns across the region. Boston's first burial ground was not attached to church property. It was established in 1630 on the estate of influential colonist Isaac Johnson. However, during the reign of Catholic King James II (1633–1701), who deliberately exerted royal political and religious control over the Puritan Commonwealth of Massachusetts, the secular burial place was converted to consecrated ground. Sir Edmund Andros (1637–1714), the King's appointed governor, ordered the construction of the Anglican King's

Chapel on part of the burial ground, displacing the graves of the colony's founding fathers. The remaining ground became a churchyard known as the King's Chapel Burying Ground. The episode illuminated the passionate difference of opinion held by the Church of England and Dissenters regarding burial practices. Meanwhile, Boston's Granary Burying Ground (originally called the South Burying Ground) was established in 1660 on unconsecrated ground that was part of the Boston Common. Like most burial grounds in the growing colonial towns of New England, both Granary and King's Chapel were located in the heart of the town's populated area. The fact that Puritan burial grounds were unconsecrated did not mean that they were neglected. On the contrary, the Puritan community was vigilant about the condition of these burial spaces, because Puritans exhibited a "tribal unity" that gave meaning to the bones of their ancestors and "thus necessitated care of those remains."[37]

In New England, Puritan beliefs heavily influenced the iconography and messages inscribed on the region's grave markers. When the Puritans immigrated to the Massachusetts Bay Colony and other parts of New England to practice their religion freely, they

4. Old Swedes' (Gloria Dei Church) in Philadelphia, Pennsylvania, with Rev. Jehu Curtis Clay standing among the gravestones in its crowded churchyard, which was established in the late seventeenth century. From a stereograph, ca. 1860, Marian S. Carson Collection, Library of Congress Prints and Photographs Division.

brought with them an influential doctrine of predestination and a harsh view of death. The Calvinistic Puritans believed that "in Adam's fall, we sinned all" and therefore all people were depraved beings who "fully deserved death and damnation from God."[38] Death was a dreadful punishment for Adam's original sin and the damned would suffer eternal torment in hell. However, Puritans also believed that God, in his infinite mercy and love, offered salvation to a select and predetermined few. Salvation was not based on good works or ritualistic expressions of penance, but was "a free gift of an inscrutable God—a gift that had been bestowed on some since the very beginning of time, and a gift that was theirs and theirs alone."[39] For these holy elect, death was a blessing. They would be released from the misery of their earth-bound existence, ascend to heaven, and experience the Glory of God.[40]

In the Puritan doctrine, no one could fully recognize his standing as one of the elect or one of the damned. All Puritans searched their consciences endlessly for signs of grace, signs that they might be among the select. This fierce searching took the Puritan on a "journey of harrowing and tearful introspection."[41] But, ultimately, the Puritan could not be confident in his salvation. In fact, "to presume such knowledge would be to presume a godlike omniscience."[42] Puritans were, therefore, wracked with an endless, agonizing uncertainty about their ultimate fate. For the devout Puritan, death was an important

5. The Granary Burying Ground, established in 1660 in the heart of Boston, Massachusetts. The obelisk in the center was a later addition, erected in 1827 to honor Benjamin Franklin's parents and relatives buried in the cemetery. Cabinet card, ca. 1900, Edwin A. Cleaveland (1838–1909), photographer, Danylchak collection.

A BRIEF HISTORY OF COMMON BURIAL LANDSCAPES

preoccupation of his thoughts that caused significant emotional stress.[43]

New England burial grounds became filled with carefully carved stones that indicated specific burial sites and reflected this theology. Memorials—frequently in the form of thin vertical markers—did not commemorate the lives or accomplishments of the individual. Instead, the inscriptions emphasized the message of *momento mori*—"remember that you must die." A *Historical Sketch and Matters Appertaining to the Granary Burial-Ground* reported that the first marker bearing a metrical epitaph at the Granary Burying Ground belonged to the wife of the pastor of the First Church who died in 1667 at the age of twenty-one. The verse on her horizontal slab began:

STAY! THOU THIS TOMBE THAT PASSETH BY
AND THINK HOW SOON THAT THOU MAYST DIE

Some Puritan markers even bore the Latin phrases *memento mori* or *fugit hora*—"hours are fleeting." The markers often showcased temporal carvings of skulls and crossbones, coffins, skeletons, and commonly the death's-head figure. Puritans shunned religious imagery—like crosses—associated with Roman Catholicism.

The Decline of Puritanism and Its Consequences

The Puritan way of death, which dominated the culture of New England during the seventeenth and early eighteenth centuries, completely lost its potency by the early 1800s. After the Great Awakening of the 1730s and 1740s, Puritanism began its decline in the northern colonies and the thought of death as a harsh eternity of suffering was "willed out of existence."[44] By

6. Gravestone featuring a death's-head motif in a burial ground in Cambridge, Massachusetts. Photograph by Frank O. Branzetti, 1940, Historic American Building Survey, MASS, 9-CAMB,11–1, Library of Congress Prints and Photographs Division.

7. Skull-and-crossbones motif on a headstone in the Old Hill Burying Ground, Newburyport, Massachusetts. Photograph by James R. Cothran, undated.

8. Winged-angel motif on a headstone in a Weston, Connecticut graveyard. Photograph by Edwin Locke, 1937, Farm Security Administration/Office of War Information Collection, Library of Congress Prints and Photographs Division.

the early nineteenth century, very few people believed in the idea of hell, except perhaps "halfheartedly—and then only for strangers and enemies."[45]

The spread of Arminianism brought a particularly dramatic change in doctrine that alleviated the tension and fear associated with the Puritan way of death. In its place, liberal preachers espoused a more optimistic view. Arminianism embraced the concepts of personal salvation through good deeds and divine grace. Those who chose to be saved would find joy and eternal life in heaven. Meanwhile, evangelical preachers consoled survivors by emphasizing heavenly reunions and evoking personal memory.

With the rise of religious alternatives to Puritanism that offered more hope of salvation, the iconography of burial markers morphed from grim images to more optimistic spiritual representations. Beginning around the mid-eighteenth century, angels and soul effigies—winged depictions of the soul ascending to heaven—often appeared on headstones. Philippe Ariès describes the evolving iconography in reaction to the religious climate: "In eighteenth-century New England, where the meaning of death was changing and the Puritans were belatedly ceasing to cultivate the fear of death, the winged death's-head was transformed into a winged angel's head by an almost cinematic process in which the face gradually became fuller and gentler."[46]

Paradoxically, just as soul effigies, angels, and other heavenly devices appeared more often on New England gravestones, "the cemeteries in which those gravestones were placed began to become overcrowded while simultaneously falling into neglect and disarray."[47] Historian David E. Stannard contends that it was after the demise of Puritanism that New England graveyards became disregarded and unkempt. With the decline of the close-knit Puritan community, the vigilance over the graves of its former members simply dissipated. The history of Boston's burial grounds supports this contention. In 1740 the selectmen of Boston were petitioned to establish a new burial ground, because the Granary was so filled with dead bodies that gravediggers often had to bury them four deep.[48] Although the Central Burying Ground was subsequently established, interments continued in the Granary as well as King's Chapel "amid complete indifference on the part of the town, and with very disagreeable results a century or more later."[49] By the nineteenth century the tombs constructed beneath the earth of these burial grounds "were exceedingly dilapidated, giving free vent to gases."[50] Meanwhile, the soil at both was "saturated with buried remains, the two cemeteries containing about 3,000 bodies."[51] Such conditions ultimately helped compel a dramatic change in America's burial landscapes.

CHAPTER 2

Changing Attitudes toward Nature and Death ❧

The seventeenth and eighteenth centuries witnessed changes in cultural and religious attitudes toward nature and death first in Europe and then in America that created both the theoretical and aesthetic underpinning for the establishment of a new form of burial landscape in the nineteenth century. In England, a growing "cult of melancholy" recognized nature's ability to provoke emotion, while religious liberalization promoted the contemplation of immorality. With the emergence of a new landscape aesthetic—the English landscape garden—elegiac commemoration found its appropriate setting. The rise of Romanticism further shaped a cultural view of death as peaceful deliverance and a vision of consoling nature as the proper environment for burial and memorialization. Conditions in colonial America forestalled the immediate importation of these ideas. However, the American Revolution, industrialization, and belated Romanticism eventually provoked the embrace of monumental commemoration, soothing remembrance, and naturalistic landscapes in America. The convergence of these ideas—along with practical considerations regarding sanitation and disease—incited calls for burial reform.

The "Cult of Melancholy"

Beginning in the seventeenth century, England experienced a growing and influential "cult of melancholy." Religious dissenters were the first to nurture melancholy sadness. It was, in fact, a "by-product of religion."[1] The ceaseless uncertainty caused by the doctrine of predestination and the intense fear triggered by brutal images of hell cultivated a melancholy humor within Puritan society. Professor John W. Draper's analysis of the Puritan elegy offers a window into the Puritan outlook. He notes that these poems often emphasized the themes of death's "omnipotence over human life" and the horror of the tomb, frequently accompanied by gruesomely realistic details about bodily decay.[2]

In the latter part of the seventeenth century, however, changes in religion affected an evolution in the English attitude toward death and the cult of melancholy. Calvinism's zealousness declined appreciably in the face of liberal theological alternatives, some of which were influenced by a growing deistic trend during the period and the discovery of scientific law. The influence of widespread education and the increasing wealth among the commercial classes, which brought improved living standards and a concomitant optimistic outlook, also dampened British religious dissent.[3] Religious liberalization, in turn, initiated a decline in the cultural fear of death. England embraced, for example, the work of the French Protestant divine, Charles Drelincourt (1595–1669), including *The Christian's Defence Against the Fears of Death*. The book contained beatific personifications of death and comparisons of death to sleep. The work, in historian David E. Stannard's words, was "intended to ally its reader's fears of death by making death a state of existence to be longed for rather than dreaded."[4]

Meanwhile, with the disintegration of militant Calvinism, the English cultivated emotionalism for its own sake, without ardent religious motives, and developed a predilection for sweet melancholy. The leisure classes particularly demanded "constant variety to escape *ennui*" and found "a new pleasure in the cultivation of the lachrymose."[5] The English found that melancholy aroused an "agreeable titillation" of the senses and they developed a fondness for "the pensive sadness of lingering memories."[6]

At the same time, nature became increasingly recognized for its power to provoke a heightened emotional response. Deism played an important role in this growing exaltation of nature. Deism identified God as the First Cause of the Universe, which he set in motion and left to be governed by immutable laws. Within this theological position, people could only know God through reason and the observation of nature. The growth of deism thus helped popularize the "pensive landscape."[7] Meditating on and within nature had the power to impart moral lessons and stir melancholy thoughts of mortality and immortality.

Contemporary literature reflected this evolving attitude toward death and nature. In the latter part of the seventeenth century, poetry began using descriptions of nature to invoke a desirable melancholy. One powerful example is M. Browne's *An Elegiack Essay* written upon the death of Rev. Matthew Mead in 1699. In the poem, the author employs an "expressive background" of nature and "finds the 'Recess' of melancholy 'sweet.'"[8]

> Gone ever, whom we *ever shall deplore,*
> *For ever gone,* whom we did all *adore,*
> MEAD, dearest MEAD, alas! Is now no more.
> Long since I heard the *News,* yet scarce wou'd give
> It *Credence,* but believ'd great MEAD did live,
> And until *now* cou'd not consent to grieve.
> But t'other Day walking a *silent Grove,*
> I found a sweet Recess, a *dark Alcove,*
> Seem'd made by Nature, fit to Contemplate
> The Turns and Destinies of Rigid Fate:
> Where on my Hand my Head supinely laid,
> *Methought I heard a Mournful Accent spread,*
> *Which Eccho-like in murm'ring Whispers said:*
> *Drop, drop a Tear for* MEAD, *Great* MEAD *is Dead....*[9]

In his analysis of the funeral elegy, Draper notes that the literary form saw the fully developed use of a "soft sensibility" and the nature description by the 1720s.

Concurrently, English clerics, writers, and architects began to suggest alternatives to prevalent forms of burial landscapes. Anglican writer and gardener John Evelyn (1620–1706), for example, was an early assailant of the "customary" tradition of burial in or around churches, especially in populous cities; these burial grounds, he said, had become "undecent, sordid, and very prejudicial to health."[10] Instead, he advocated for burial grounds amidst nature and focused early attention on the sacredness of nature and its ability to invoke spiritual melancholy. In his *Silva; or, A Discourse of Forest-Trees,* first published in 1664, Evelyn argued, "There are none more fit to bury our Dead in, than in our *Gardens* and *Groves,* or airy *Fields, sub dio;* where our beds may be decked and carpeted with verdant and fragrant *Flowers, Trees,* and *Perennial* Plants, the most natural and instructive *Hieroglyphics* of our expected *Resurrection* and *Immortality;* besides what they might conduce to the Meditation of the *living.*"[11]

This type of burial landscape was not unprecedented. Evelyn emphasized that since Antiquity groves of trees had been "consecrated to holy uses" including as shelters for the dead. Evelyn cited several examples of burial grounds amidst such groves from both biblical texts and mythology. In Greek mythology, for example, Ariadne, the daughter of Minos, King of Crete, reposed in a tomb set within a grove, because the ancient Greeks, Evelyn explained, "believed that the Spirits and Ghosts of Men delighted to expatiate, and appear in such solemn Places."[12] Meanwhile, he noted that the Book of Genesis reported that Sarah, wife of Abraham, was buried on land "conveyed to him with particular mention, ver. 3. of all the *Trees* and *Groves* about it."[13] Evelyn noted that other examples of burial grounds from antiquity were sited alongside the "most frequented *Highways*" and "planted about with *Cypress* and other *Ever-greens.*"[14]

Evelyn observed that not only did nature provoke reflection among the living within these burial landscapes but so, too, did the commemorative structures erected there. Many of the sepulchers built along the ancient roadways, he said, were "magnificent *Structures* and *Mausoleums,* adorn'd with *Statues* and *Inscriptions.*"[15] He called these memorials "a noble and useful Entertainment to the Travellers, putting them in mind of the Virtues and glorious Actions of the Persons buried."[16]

Evelyn did not stand alone in visualizing alternatives to churchyard burial. Contemporary English poets alluded to modest tombs set in gardens, harkening back to the Elysian Fields celebrated by Homer, Hesiod, Virgil, and others. Abraham Cowley (1618–1667), one of the outstanding English poets of the seventeenth century, for example, expressed his desire in verse to be buried in a modest tomb in his own garden, "'Cover'd with flowers, free from noise and pain,'" with the beauties of the landscape invoking "a heavenly paradise."[17]

As early as 1711, the eminent English architect Sir Christopher Wren (1632–1723), too, advocated for landscaped burial grounds on the outskirts of towns with commemorative monuments created by architects or sculptors. In a "Letter of advice to the Commissioners for Building Fifty New City Churches" (in London and its surroundings), Wren proposed outlying burial places "inclosed with a strong Brick Wall, and having a walk round, and two cross walks, decently planted with Yew-trees." No doubt in repugnant reaction to contemporary practices, Wren specifically noted that within such burial grounds bodies would not be buried four or five deep. Nor would they be removed to recover burial space. Neither Evelyn nor Wren was successful, however, in provoking the establishment of extramural, commemorative cemeteries amidst nature. As architectural historian Richard Etlin has noted, it was only with the beginnings of a new landscape aesthetic—the Picturesque—that "the tomb entered the garden."[18]

The Intertwined Emergence of the English Landscape Garden and the Elegiac Landscape

In the eighteenth century, English nobility and landed gentry who took the Grand Tour to study the architecture, art, and culture of Italy and France affected

9. *Pastoral Landscape: The Roman Campagna*, Claude Lorrain, ca. 1639. The Metropolitan Museum of Art, www.metmuseum.org.

the emergence of a new landscape style in England. The touring English were particularly inspired by the works of Baroque painters Claude Lorrain (ca. 1600–1682), Nicolas Poussin (1594–1665), and Salvator Rosa (1615–1673), in which the artists depicted Italian landscapes containing rivers and streams, rugged mountains, and informal groupings of trees.[19] These artists' spacious landscapes were also "scattered with the ruins of ancient buildings, to which were appended old allegories."[20] These artists also played with bright streams of light and distinctively dark shadows created by the ever-present Mediterranean sun, an effect foreign, yet powerful, to the English so accustomed to overcast skies. The work of these painters helped prompt the rediscovery of the "aesthetic, poetic, and emotional aspects" of landscapes in the eighteenth century.[21]

One of the most important examples of Baroque painting that influenced later English landscape design was Nicolas Poussin's second version of *et in Arcadia ego* (ca. 1635–1636). The painting featured a naturalistic setting and, even more important, created a model for an elegiac landscape by featuring a commemorative tomb within classical Arcadia, a mountainous region in Greece. In Greek mythology, Arcadia was the abode of Pan, the rustic god of mountain wilds, shepherds, and flocks. In ancient times, in his *Eclogues*, Roman poet Virgil had created a vision of an imaginary Arcadia, where contented shepherds peopled an idyllic landscape. His representation was enduring and influential. Poussin, in his seventeenth-century painting, portrays shepherds carefully studying the inscription on a simple tomb set against Arcadia's bucolic backdrop. One of the shepherds, kneeling next to the tomb, casts a shadow upon it; the shadow represents the spirit of the departed, in the sense of the classical *Manes*.[22] Architectural historian James Stevens Curl asserts that this painting provided a particularly powerful image for those advocating the creation of elegiac landscapes: "The memorial in a garden would not only evoke the shade of the departed, but ideas of Arcady too: most importantly, all references

10. Veue du chasteau de Versailles (View of Versailles, garden façade), illustrating the formal landscape aesthetic that had been "refined and perfected" by the French by the seventeenth century. Adam Perelle, artist (1640–1695), etched by Israel Silvestre (1621–1691), 1680s. The Metropolitan Museum of Art, www.metmuseum.org.

CHANGING ATTITUDES TOWARD NATURE AND DEATH

11. The Roman-inspired Ionic Temple within William Kent's landscape at Chiswick, outside of London, England. Chiswick was one of the earliest examples of the English landscape garden aesthetic. Photograph by James R. Cothran, undated, James R. Cothran Collection, Cherokee Garden Library at the Kenan Research Center at the Atlanta History Center.

to the horrors of decay, bones, decomposition, and the dank, unwholesome graveyard were banished. Here was the peaceful, beautiful ideal, a place fit for reflection and memories where death was civilized."[23]

In the first half of the eighteenth century, a distinctly English landscape aesthetic emerged. Until this time, gardens in England were laid out in geometrical patterns that were strictly symmetrical. They defied nature and followed the long-established formal landscape aesthetic that had been conceived by the Greeks and Romans, had spread to northern Europe during the Middle Ages, and had been "refined and perfected" by the French by the seventeenth century.[24] English landscape gardeners, however, came to reject the man-made formality so closely associated with the French to embrace the irregularity and emotional intensity of nature.

The enlightened English elite, who owned large-scale estates, began replacing their formal gardens with a naturalistic style. Informal groupings of trees and meandering drives and pathways were favored over tidy allées. Streams and lakes with undulating shorelines were prized over circular or octagonal lakes or pools and rectangular canals. Elaborate cascades were often featured at the edge of a lake or between two bodies of water. Grottos or artificial caves made of strikingly beautiful stones and shells were introduced to offer contemplative retreats within these landscapes. The English called these large-scale landscapes pleasure grounds, but the new, distinctive style came to be known as the English landscape garden.[25]

William Kent (1684–1748) was one of the first and most influential landscape gardeners to employ an informal landscape aesthetic. English writer and connoisseur Horace Walpole (1717–1797) declared that in his landscape designs, Kent "realized the compositions of the greatest masters in painting."[26] The primary design principals Kent utilized were "perspective, and light and shade." Kent broke up extensive and uniform lawns with groups of trees and juxtaposed the shimmering, sun-filled plain with evergreens and woods, which cast lengthened shadows across the light. But Walpole argued that Kent's management of water added more beauty to the countryside than any of his other design elements. Walpole explained: "The gentle stream was taught to serpentize seemingly at its pleasure.... Its borders were smoothed, but preserved their waving irregularity, . . . and when it disappeared among the hills, shades descending from the heights leaned towards its progress, and framed the distant point of light under which it was lost, as it turned aside to either hand of the blue horizon."[27] Kent also frequently punctuated his naturalistic designs with strategically placed objects, often classically inspired. Walpole noted that where objects "were wanting to animate his horizon," Kent skillfully provided visual termination with buildings, seats, and temples.[28] Kent, who began his career as a painter, thus evoked the landscape paintings of Claude Lorrain whose light-infused landscapes often featured ancient temples, towers, and aqueducts in various states of disrepair. Garden historian Miles

12. Distant view of the Temple of Ancient Virtue, designed by William Kent, erected 1736, as a "paraphrase" of the Temple of Vesta at Tivoli, but using the Ionic order, Stowe Landscape Gardens, Buckinghamshire, England. © National Trust Images/National Trust.

13. View of Congreve's monument, and Pavilion, Stowe Landscape Gardens, Buckinghamshire, England. J. C. Nattes delt 1805, Stowe. © National Trust Images/ Photographer.

Hadfield notes that Kent's style "was largely based on pictures—hence its 'picturesque' qualities."[29]

In his designs, Kent often strategically placed temples, exedra, and bridges in an inward facing landscape to display symbolic or allegorical meaning and thus provoke specific reflections and ideas. Between 1730 and 1748, Kent worked for Lord Richard Cobham at Stowe in Buckinghamshire, England. Stowe was one of Kent's most significant and famous works. At Stowe, he created the Temple of Ancient Virtue, modeled on the circular Roman Temple of Vesta, which dates to the early first century B.C. Kent's temple housed statues of the greatest poet, philosopher, law-giver, and general in ancient Greece: Homer, Socrates, Lycurgus, and Epaminondas, respectively. Within Kent's classically inspired rotunda, which was situated on a slight rise, these luminaries represented virtues the estate's owner, Lord Cobham, felt were lacking in contemporary government. Kent also designed a semicircular exedra with niches for busts of sixteen exceptional English cultural and political figures, including Shakespeare, Locke, Newton, Queen Elizabeth I, and King William III. Meanwhile, the ironically named Temple of Modern Virtue was a crumbling ruin that served as a "commentary upon the shoddy ethics of the present government."[30] The juxtaposition of these architectural features was intended to trigger consideration and stimulate "noble ideas." Stowe was inspiring because it reminded the visitor "not only of individuals, but of virtues, nationhood, liberty, and cherished ideals, all by means of buildings, monuments, man-made landscapes, vistas, and sequential episodes in a vast garden."[31]

Stowe was also an early example of an elegiac landscape peppered with commemorate monuments to individuals. At Stowe, Kent designed a modest pyramidal cenotaph honoring Cobham's friend, William Congreve (1670–1729), a comedic playwright. This memorial joined others in the garden including a small obelisk in memory of the Reverend Robert Coucher, the chaplain to Lord Cobham's Dragoons. Stowe was enormously important and influential, because it effectively and movingly demonstrated how "death and commemoration could be contained in a pastoral setting that evoked Arcady and Elysium."[32]

English poet and essayist Alexander Pope (1688–1744) was another early and persuasive advocate of placing commemorative structures in naturalist landscapes in order to stir melancholy sentiments. In his

1734 *Essay on Man,* he emphasized the "'moral utility' of commemorative statuary when engraved with instructive messages of the past."[33] He believed monuments inscribed with memorial poetry and placed within naturalistic gardens would remedy failed memory.[34] On his own estate at Twickenham, outside of London, Pope "composed a sequence of outdoor spaces, light and shady, open and closed, including a grotto, through which the visitor passed before reaching the focal point nestled in a grove of mournful cypresses—the poet's mother's tomb, complete with an obelisk erected in 1733."[35] The inscription upon its pedestal bid farewell to the best mother, the beloved woman.

> AH EDITHA!
> MATRVM OPTIMA!
> MULIERVM AMANTISSIM!
> VALE!

The landscaped gardens at Castle Howard in Yorkshire, England, set another powerful precedent for placing tombs within a naturalistic garden thus evoking the conception of the Elysian Fields. Toward the second decade of the eighteenth century, the estate's Wray Wood was laid out with what a visitor described as a "tangle of secret paths that rose and fell, twisted and crossed, leading from one circle to another."[36] Then, in 1742, a classically inspired circular domed mausoleum was completed on the estate to serve as the final resting place for the family after the local parish church and churchyard had been destroyed. Blanche Linden emphasizes that it was "the first funeral structure standing free of a church built in England since ancient times."[37] By the end of the century, England's elite were erecting private mausoleums within their landscaped estates in large numbers.

Along with executed examples of elegiac, naturalistic landscapes, contemporary English literature, including so-called graveyard poetry, reflected and fueled the growing cult of melancholy among the country's intellectual elite and bourgeoisie in the eighteenth century. The graveyard poets provoked contemplation about the meaning of death and reflected the growing opinion that the appropriate setting for burial

14. The grounds of Castle Howard in Yorkshire, England, with the Hawksmoor's mausoleum in the background. Photograph by James R. Cothran, 1998, James R. Cothran Collection, Cherokee Garden Library at the Kenan Research Center at the Atlanta History Center.

and commemoration was within a natural setting. Important examples of the literary style include Edward Young's *The Complaint: or Night-Thoughts on Life, Death & Immortality* (1742–1745) and Thomas Gray's *Elegy Written in a Country Church-Yard* (1751). The graveyard poets ultimately had a profound impact on the "flowering of the Victorian Celebration of Death."[38]

Gray's *Elegy* struck a tone of gentle melancholy and commented on the ability of the country churchyard to provoke remembrance and reflection on death. Significantly, Gray's graveyard was in nature, unlike the barren churchyards so often seen in contemporary England. It was a "place of serenity and consolation . . . imbued with the peace of evening."[39] And it was filled with tombs inscribed with poetry that allowed "communication between the living and the dead."[40]

> Yet ev'n these bones from insult to protect,
>   Some frail memorial still erected nigh,
> With uncouth rhymes and shapeless sculpture
>   deck'd,
>   Implores the passing tribute of a sigh.
>
> Their name, their years, spelt by th' unletter'd
>   muse,
>   The place of fame and elegy supply:
> And many a holy text around she strews,
>   That teach the rustic moralist to die.[41]

Meanwhile, in his *Night-Thoughts* Edward Young tempered the terror and abhorrence associated with death by cultivating hope of immortality. He encouraged "aspirations towards the 'good death'" and revealed that the contemplation of death could be a powerful "corrective to careless living."[42] For Young, the "good death" meant deliverance from the worn habits of life to the Eternal, divine end to which life is ultimately a means.

> Death gives us more than was in Eden lost.
> This King of Terrors is the Prince of Peace.
> When shall I die to Vanity, Pain, Death?
> When shall I die?—When shall I live for ever?[43]

Young's *Night the Third* became particularly influential in the movement to create naturalistic burial grounds with its description of Narcissa's death and burial, which was based upon the actual death of Young's stepdaughter, Elizabeth Lee (ca. 1718–1736). Having died in papist France, the young, beautiful Protestant 'Narcissa' was denied a proper Christian burial. In his melancholy-infused poem, Young dramatically described how Narcissa's grief-stricken husband furtively dug a grave—one probably already occupied—and buried her in midnight darkness. In reaction to the poem, reports circulated that the young Elizabeth was buried in a "little gloomy grove" in the *Jardin Royale* at Montpellier, France. A tomb memorializing Narcissa was later erected there and became a popular tourist attraction.[44]

Changing Conceptions of the Ideal English Landscape Garden

During the mid–eighteenth century in England, a deviation in the naturalistic landscape style occurred with the ascension of a second generation of designers led by Lancelot "Capability" Brown (1716–1783). (Although it did not contribute to the growing appetite for contemplative, elegiac landscapes, the new model did later impact the American rural cemetery movement by serving as inspiration for Adolph Strauch, the superintendent of Spring Grove Cemetery in Cincinnati. So, it is important to the overall story.) Following in the footsteps of Kent and others, Brown embraced an informal aesthetic, but he largely rejected the use of contained vignettes and the placement of man-made objects within the landscape. Instead, he reduced the landscape "to a few simple elements, playing one against the other."[45] He focused on the use of large bodies of water, gently rolling lawns, and dispersed groupings of trees. Moreover, he generally only employed five species of trees within his sweeping landscapes. Overall, Brown engineered large expanses of lawns dotted by serene lakes and irregular clumps of trees to create outward facing views that emphasized the element of space. Although naturalistic in appearance, these landscapes were carefully planned and demonstrated man's ability to exert control over the natural environment. This style became known as the "Beautiful."

By the end of the eighteenth century, however, the pastoral landscapes of the Beautiful provoked intense reactions from English garden critics. They found smooth lawns, graceful lines, calm waters, and carefully sited masses of trees artificial, monotonous, and ultimately boring. Instead, to inspire their admiration, "a landscape had to offer variety, irregularity, surprise."[46] They revived the style that had been developed by the first generation of naturalistic gardeners

15. Bowood House and Gardens, Wiltshire, England. Lancelot "Capability" Brown designed the beautiful park surrounding the Georgian country house to include a serene lake and spacious, rolling lawns. Drawn by J. Neale, engraving by J. C. Varrall, 1831, Danylchak collection.

16. Alnwick Castle and landscape in Northumberland, England. Lancelot "Capability" Brown completed the park at Alnwick Castle toward the end of the eighteenth century. Carte de visite photograph by Potter of Alnwick, ca. 1860s, Danylchak collection.

17. Plate No. 104 from *Liber Veritatis. Or, a Collection of Prints after the Original Designs of Claude Le Lorrain, in the Collection of His Grace The Duke of Devonshire, Executed by Richard Earlom, in the Manner and Taste of the Drawings.* Published 1775 by John Boydell, London, Danylchak collection.

and officially termed it Picturesque. They brought the landscape garden aesthetic back to one where "a rich variety of planting was employed and much was drawn from the pictures of great artists—that is, the designs were picturesque within the true meaning of the word."[47] The Picturesque balanced nature and art. It stood on the aesthetic spectrum between the Sublime—untamed, irrational, thrilling nature—and the Beautiful—controlled, artificial, serene nature.

William Gilpin (1724—1804), an English artist, author, and Anglican cleric, was important to defining and disseminating what constituted the Picturesque. In his popular *An Essay on Prints, Containing Remarks upon the Principles of Picturesque Beauty* (1768), he defined Picturesque as "a term expressive of that peculiar kind of beauty, which is agreeable in a picture."[48] Gilpin's conception of what was truly Picturesque was demonstrated in the advice he gave a landowner who wished to improve his own grounds: "Consult such pictures or prints as are applicable to the case. The *Liber Veritatis* of Claude, and the *Liber Studiorum* of Turner, will afford many examples to the purpose."[49] The proponents of the Picturesque admired Claude Lorrain's idyllic representations of the Italian countryside, scattered with ancient ruins. They also turned their attention to a contemporary English printmaker and painter J. M. W. Turner (1775–1851), who produced his own collection of engraved landscapes, both pastoral and more expressively wild, to rival Claude's earlier work.

Sir Uvedale Price (1747–1829) ultimately became the principal theorist of the Picturesque style and spread his philosophy in the 1794 publication *Essays on the Picturesque*. He described the two essential characteristics of the style—intricacy of the "disposition of objects which, by a partial and uncertain concealment, excites and nourishes curiosity" and variety "in the forms, the tints, and the lights and shadows of objects."[50] He admired, for instance, the winding lane with sudden, unexpected turns bordered sometimes by irregular, broken banks, sometimes by gently sloping land, as nature dictated. At times this lane, in its natural state, would be overhung by a dense thicket of trees and shrubs, at others bounded by a loose forest of assorted species. The Picturesque style drew inspiration from the complexity and variation inherent in the natural world.

Spread of Ideas to the Continent

Books on the English landscape aesthetic, travel accounts, and even translated graveyard poetry began to spread the English landscape garden ideology and the vogue for elegiac, commemorative landscapes to France and other European nations in the second half of the eighteenth century. In 1774 the French writer and garden enthusiast Claude-Henri Watelet (1718–1786) introduced the English landscape garden (*le jardin Anglois*) to his countrymen as an alternative to the time-honored formal gardens of France in his

Essai sur les jardins. Meanwhile, in his five-volume work *Theory of Garden Art,* published between 1779 and 1785, German intellectual Christian Hirschfeld (1742–1792) endorsed the English landscape garden and the use of commemorative monuments within them to prompt emotions, associations, and memory. The work was printed in both German and French. Young's *Night-Thoughts* also encouraged the "fashionable cult of sepulchres, melancholy, and ruins" as it was widely circulated throughout Europe in the latter part of the eighteenth century.[51] As it underwent subtle metamorphoses in translation and adaptation, it particularly emphasized "the solitary poet's personal grief as he wandered alone among the tombs."[52] Narcissa's burial in *Night the Third* especially captured the European imagination and created a widespread vogue for burial in gardens.[53]

Young's *Night-Thoughts,* which was published in German in 1751–1752, profoundly influenced Salomon Gessner (1730–1788), a Swiss poet who subsequently made his own significant contributions to the growing discourse on the desirability of placing tombs within an Arcadian landscape. It was Gessner's widely translated *Idylls,* first published in 1756, that "gave birth to

the cult of making a sentimental visit to the tomb of a loved one."[54] In Gessner's works, the tomb became "a type of family altar to which the living often returned to pay homage, shed tears, and commune with the dead."[55] The family could thus keep the memory and spirit of the deceased alive. For the visitor, such communion aroused moral inspiration and tender feelings for the dead. Notably, many of the graves in Gessner's *Idylls* were described as being within beautiful landscapes, surrounded by such plants as willows and honeysuckle. By the 1790s, Gessner's depiction of the gravesite had been adopted by those urging a new type of burial place. Meanwhile, Gessner's work significantly influenced many continental aristocrats who created celebrated gardens in years subsequent to the publication of *Idylls.*[56]

One of the most important examples of the transplanted English commemorative landscape was Ermenonville in France. The Marquis des Girardin (1735–1808) imported the informal landscape aesthetic to his estate after traveling extensively in England and receiving advice from his friends among the English gentry. He embraced the Picturesque style, the essence of which he eloquently described in his

18. *Landscape with an Antique Tomb and Two Wayfarers,* Salomon Gessner, 1768. The Metropolitan Museum of Art, www.metmuseum.org.

Essay on Landscape, which was translated into English in 1783.

> It is only by considering the effect of [nature] as a picture, that one can dispose pleasing objects to advantage; for the picturesque effect depends entirely upon the choice of the most agreeable forms, the elegance of outline, and keeping the distances; it consists in managing a happy contrast of light and shadow, in giving projection and relief to the objects, and producing the charm of variety, by showing them in different lights, in different shapes, and under different points of view; also in the beautiful assemblage of colours, and above all, in that happy negligence which is the peculiar characteristic of grace and nature… It is not then as an architect or a gardener, but as a poet and a painter, that landscape must be composed, so as at once to please the understanding and the eye.[57]

Girardin's own garden of Ermenonville was an Arcadian landscape featuring lush forests, winding pathways, and serene water features, including an arti-ficial lake punctuated with an island densely planted with poplar trees. In 1778, Girardin devoted this small island to the gravesite of philosopher and writer Jean-Jacques Rousseau (1712–1778). The Marquis was Rousseau's final patron and he wanted to pay tribute to the writer within his garden. Designed by artist Hubert Robert (1733–1808), a stone sarcophagus marked Rousseau's gravesite in 1780; it was inscribed "to the friend of nature and truth." Inspired by Rousseau's novel *Émile* (1762), a scene of mothers praying to a statue of the goddess Nature was depicted on the memorial in bas-relief. It quickly became a place of pilgrimage. Notably, the author of the official guidebook to Ermenonville remarked that the park could have easily provided Gessner with inspiration for the settings in his *Idylls,* revealing just how prominent and influential the work was during the period.[58]

Rousseau's tomb at Ermenonville, in turn, provided an influential example of a poignant burial place within nature. Rousseau's eternal resting place on the Île de Peupliers gained widespread interest in the press and was noted for stirring an appropriate feeling of melancholy. Other prominent burials with

19. View of the Isle of Poplars with the first tomb memorializing Jean-Jacques Rousseau at Ermenonville, France. The tomb was replaced in 1780 by one designed by Hubert Robert. Engraving by J. M. Moreau le Jeune, 1778, Danylchak collection.

attendant memorials were placed in private gardens in ensuing years. In his gardens at Franconville in northern France, for example, the Comte d'Albon (1753–1789) built a tomb for famous linguist Court de Gébelin in 1784. The memorial included a sarcophagus flanked by four "ruined" columns in a picturesque setting.

In the ensuing decades, Ermenonville also significantly served as a "source of inspiration and a rallying point" for reformers and writers as the subject of burial reform gripped France.[59] Hirschfeld hailed Rousseau's gravesite "as a model for a new system of burying in gardens rather than within overcrowded town churchyards and churches."[60] Hirschfeld's ideal cemetery, which he described in 1785, was a spacious landscape garden with "grand and picturesque scenes created by the play of light and shadows over the partially hidden tombs with the white stone contrasting vividly against the dark foliage."[61] The Marquis des Girardin himself delivered "a stinging condemnation of the contemporary urban cemetery both for empoisoning the living and for inspiring disgust and repulsion" and "reminded his readers that the ancients had buried their most important citizens in the beautiful countryside."[62]

In his 1784 work *Etudes de la Nature*, writer and botanist Bernardin de Saint-Pierre (1737–1814) actually proposed creating public burial grounds outside the city following the example of the ancient Romans and Greeks, as well as the Chinese and Ottoman Turks. And he promoted the use of the English Picturesque style. He called for grounds planted "with bosquets of cypresses and pines mixed with flowering and fruit-bearing trees."[63] He proposed the use of varied monuments including "obelisks, columns, pyramids, urns, bas-reliefs, medallions, statutes, pedestals, peristyles and domes" to prevent visual repetitiveness.[64] The union of this landscape and its memorials would, according to Bernardin, inspire a "profound and sweet melancholy."[65] Bernardin's concept for a public cemetery "became a standard point of reference through the remainder of the century."[66]

The Ascent of European Romanticism

The seeds of Romanticism were sown in the eighteenth century and saw early nascent expression in the rise of the English landscape garden and the emergence of the elegiac commemorative landscape. However, Romanticism blossomed into a mature intellectual, philosophical, artistic, and literary movement in the first half of the nineteenth century. Romanticism was a way of perceiving the world, primarily with strong emotions. Romanticism elevated individualism and subjectivity. It valued imagination, intuition, inspiration, feelings, and the senses over absolute reason. It was, in this sense, a reaction against the Age of Enlightenment.

Romanticism venerated nature and its proponents affected changing attitudes toward it. For the Romantic, nature had the power to stimulate human emotion and affect the human mind. In fact, for Romantic philosophers, writers, and artists, the inspiration and consolation of nature was "a paramount and universal theme."[67] The philosopher and writer Jean-Jacques Rousseau believed that "reverie amid scenes of nature inevitably produced rapturous sentiment."[68] Responses to nature were personal and ranged from delight to pleasurable fear to sweet melancholy to philosophical contemplation.[69] The individual experience of nature, therefore, transcended aesthetics to become something spiritual.

Under the decisive influence of Romanticism, the beginning of the nineteenth century ushered in an era that prominent French cultural historian Philippe Ariès terms the "Age of the Beautiful Death." During this time, the idea fully emerged likening death to a "desirable and long-awaited refuge 'where one could eat and sleep and take one's ease.'"[70] Death was seen as a "peaceful and beautiful deliverance."[71] The Romantic anticipated salvation and an infinite afterlife in heaven filled with all the things that brought true happiness on earth including love and affection. The earthly preoccupations that triggered sadness were left behind.[72] Moreover, heaven held the promise of reunion with family and friends. Death simply created a temporary separation of loved ones. In fact, Ariès argues that death was actually "desired because it was a step toward the reunions of eternity."[73]

Despite the emphasis on eventual heavenly reunion, however, those left behind did experience tremendous grief at the loss of a loved one. Beginning in the latter part of the eighteenth century, familial affection was "cultivated and even glorified" and "outweighed every consideration of self-interest, law, or propriety."[74] This elevation of the emotional bonds of the family consequently made separation at death more painful for survivors than it had before. In this atmosphere, melancholy sadness was the culturally idealized response to death.

Romantic writers heavily contributed to the growing drum beat for burial places within nature, which would offer consolation to survivors. The English Romantic poet and writer William Wordsworth (1770–1850) asserted that for those faced with contemplating death, nature offered "soothing influences."[75] In his 1810 essay "Upon Epitaphs," he called attention to the fact that, in ancient times, the dead were buried outside the walls of the city and that the Greeks and Romans often buried their dead along the roadways leading to town. He invited the reader to contemplate with him the advantage of the practice: "We might ruminate upon the beauty which the monuments, thus placed, must have borrowed from the surrounding images of nature—from the trees, the wild flowers, from a stream running perhaps within sight or hearing, from the beaten road stretching its weary length hard by. Many tender similitudes must these objects have presented to the mind of the traveller leaning upon one of the tombs, or reposing in the coolness of its shade, whether he had halted from weariness or in compliance with the invitation, 'Pause, Traveller!' so often found upon the monuments."[76]

Wordsworth, too, noted the importance of preserving the memory of the dead with inscribed sepulcher monuments. He contended that epitaphs held the power to disarm death "of its sting."[77] An epitaph properly composed to pay tribute to an individual's worth provided a sense of "satisfaction to the sorrowing hearts of the survivors."[78]

Wordsworth contrasted this scene with the modern burial landscape where monuments were "crowded together in the busy, noisy, unclean, and almost grassless church-yard of a large town."[79] These spaces offered no healing effects on the contemplative mind. As Blanche Linden points out, Wordsworth was echoing the growing aesthetic and spiritual concerns surrounding urban burial places as well as commemorative trends that developed through the eighteenth century in response to changing ideas about death and nature.[80]

Late Transformation in America

America did not immediately adopt European attitudes toward nature and death. Into the nineteenth century, America's vast, untamed wilderness often cast an intimidating shadow upon early settlements, especially since it often concealed hostile natives and wild animals. When William Bradford and his fellow pilgrims landed at Plymouth in 1620, he described what they encountered: "What could they see but a hideous and desolate wilderness, full of wild beasts and wild men? And what multitude there might be of them they knew not.... Which way soever they turned their eyes (save upward to the heavens) they could have little solace or content in respect of any outward objects. For summer being done, all things stand upon them with a weatherbeaten face; and the whole country, full of woods and thickets, represented a wild and savage hue."[81] And for the Puritan of the Massachusetts Bay Colony, the woods were a "netherworld where the faithful could become *bewildered* by evil spirits, witches, or even the Devil Himself."[82]

In the seventeenth and eighteenth centuries, American colonists attempted to either distance or tame fearful nature. Landscape designer and historian Elizabeth Barlow Rogers explains that with "a tenuous hold on the land, the seventeenth-century Puritans viewed the vast forest with its towering, centuries-old trees as wilderness to be subdued in accordance with biblical injunction to take dominion over the earth."[83] In response, early New England settlers idealized towns exhibiting man-made spatial order—clustered buildings around a central meetinghouse and outlying common or private fields. Beyond the nucleated town, pioneers often clear-cut surrounding forests and created wide open pastureland "in their battles against nature."[84] The early towns remained fairly insular, however; few roads were built through the forest to connect the dispersed settlements for few townspeople wanted to venture beyond their safe, ordered space into the chaos of the wilderness.[85] Meanwhile, early colonists constructed enclosed gardens generally adjacent to the house and defined by brick or stone walls, fences, hedges, or trellises. This pattern provided protection against scavenging animals and the elements.

Americans also found comfort in demonstrating an ability to visually manipulate nature. The gardens of the American colonies and early republic were frequently laid out in geometric patterns, following the French model. As Derek Clifford explains in *A History of Garden Design*, "the rectilinear ground plan persisted in America for the very good reason that it was a necessary demonstration of man's authority in a land which was still for the most part stubbornly wild."[86] The colonists' early inward-facing, enclosed gardens featured paths laid out in orderly patterns and often incorporated simple, generally rectangular, raised beds. The Puritan owner of the 1640 Whipple House in Ipswich, Massachusetts, for example, followed this design pattern when laying out his garden. Later, colonists began creating more elaborate parterre patterns.

By the middle of the eighteenth century, wealthy landowners along the civilized Atlantic seaboard, from north to south, were "experimenting with the geometrically organized vista garden."[87] Middleton Place, situated overlooking the Ashley River fourteen miles upstream from Charleston, South Carolina, exemplified such a garden. The main house, which sat atop a bluff, enjoyed a breathtaking view of the river and the surrounding Carolina Low Country landscape. However, the plantation's gardens, likely laid out beginning in 1741, featured rational order, geometry, and balance. Strictly symmetrical terraces descended on axis from the main house to the river. Although appreciated, nature was still kept safely at bay.

Meanwhile, pioneers moving west across the American landscape steadfastly clung to elements of the architectural style during the eighteenth century. In their gardens, they used various well-ordered elements including terraces, parterres, bowling greens, boxwood borders, and long, linear allées. The natural, picturesque landscape ideal that the English had adopted and exported was not yet embraced in America.

However, American attitudes toward nature changed dramatically after the beginning of the nineteenth century as the new country imported and adapted European Romanticism. By this time, America was experiencing widespread settlement and expansion that razed nature. This continual loss of the native landscape affected a transformation in people's attitude toward it. The Industrial Revolution, which came late to America, was also beginning to impact New England. Industrialization drew people to employment opportunities in cities and away from daily contact with nature on generations-old farmsteads. It hastened overcrowded and unsanitary conditions in cities that, in the eyes of social reformers, fostered crime and immoral behavior. In counterpoint, Romantic philosophers perceived wild nature as a cure for the ills of society created by urbanization; they believed that contact with the wilderness was "the essential source of moral, intellectual, poetic, and spiritual

20. "New Year's: guarding against the dangers of the wilderness (1681), and of civilization (1881)," illustrating changing American attitudes from the days of early settlement to those after intensive urbanization. Drawing by Thomas Nast, 1881, Danylchak collection.

energy."[88] Nature was suddenly perceived as "a pure force able to invigorate men and women sensitive enough to see it with their whole spirits."[89]

Although a few early examples of the naturalistic landscape style began to appear in America at the end of the eighteenth century, including parts of the grounds of George Washington's Mount Vernon, it was only after the turn of the nineteenth century that the style became more widely appreciated and fashionable. The principals of English garden designers and critics began to take root first in the North, particularly along the Hudson River Valley, where a movement away from traditional architectonic gardens emerged. André Parmentier (1780–1830), a Belgium-born horticulturist and landscape gardener, was a seminal figure in the development. Parmentier immigrated to America in 1824, established a nursery in Brooklyn, New York, and designed the grounds of private country estates, including David Hosack's estate (now the Vanderbilt Mansion National Historic Site) at Hyde Park, New York, on the Hudson River. According to the Cultural Landscape Foundation, this 1828 Parmentier work may, in fact, be the first landscape created in the Picturesque style in America. In the same year, Parmentier wrote an article entitled "Landscapes and Picturesque Gardens" in the *New England Farmer Magazine;* it has since been "recognized as one of the first learned discussions on the naturalistic garden" published in America.[90] Andrew Jackson Downing (1815–1852), widely considered America's first gardening tastemaker, actually considered "Parmentier's labors and examples as having effected, directly, far more for landscape gardening in America, than those of any other individual whatever."[91] Significantly, Parmentier worked and drew admiring attention just as a forward-thinking group of elite Bostonians were contemplating a new type of burial ground.

Downing, in turn, followed with persuasive commentary on landscape design in books and magazines and became, by far, the most influential individual on America's changing landscape aesthetic in the mid-nineteenth century. He rejected the formal garden aesthetic and encouraged Americans to embrace nature and the naturalistic landscape style. In 1849, he succinctly described the essence of this aesthetic and how it differed from the formal gardens of Italy and France, which had influenced the American colonists.

> In the English landscape garden, one sees and feels every where the spirit of *nature,* only softened and refined by art. In the French or Italian garden, one sees and feels only the effects of *art,* slightly assisted by nature. In one, the free and luxuriant growth of every tree and shrub, the widening and curving of every walk, suggests perhaps even a higher ideal of nature,—a miniature of a primal paradise, as we would imagine it to have been by divine right; in the other, the prodigality of works of art, the variety of statues and vases, terraces and balustrades, united with walks marked by the same studied symmetry and artistic formality, and only mingled with just foliage enough to constitute a garden,—all this suggests rather a statue gallery in the open air,—an accompaniment to the fair architecture of the mansion, than any pure or natural ideas of landscape beauty.[92]

Downing's proselytizing actually postdated the establishment of America's first rural cemetery, which embodied the naturalistic landscape style. However, his influential *Treatise on the Theory and Practice of Landscape Gardening* appeared at the same time as a widespread upsurge in rural cemetery establishment in the 1840s.

American Romanticism flourished in the moderated religious climate of the early nineteenth century and helped shape religious views. In fact, Elizabeth Barlow Rogers asserts that American Romanticism was "essentially religious, rooted in Transcendentalist belief in Nature's inherent divinity."[93] Although most Romantics experienced religious ardor, Romantics generally did not embrace traditional religious doctrines. They revered nature and frequently believed the spirit of God permeated nature. For many, nature, as an all-encompassing, immanent God, replaced the anthropomorphic Christian God. These Romantics viewed the organic and inorganic objects within nature—those things visible to the human eye as symbolic expressions of Divine truth. For Ralph Waldo Emerson (1803–1882) and other American transcendentalists, nature was, therefore, "the proper school in which to instruct the soul in ways that lead to an apprehension of the divine."[94]

Romanticism also motivated changes in the American view of death. One influential faction of American Romantics "encouraged people to consider death a natural occurrence, and to accept the coming of death as a friendly visit."[95] These Romantics placed death within the cycle of seasons and emphasized the organic reunion of the individual with divine nature. Dissolution in nature did not mean a "return to nothingness" but a continuation of existence in other, vegetable forms.[96] Those who subscribed to this Romantic conception encouraged burial and subsequent bodily decomposition in nature.

In his masterpiece "Thanatopsis" American poet William Cullen Bryant (1794–1878) reflected the Romantic preoccupation with nature and its soothing conception of death. The poem, whose title is often translated as "meditations upon death," was first published by the *North American Review* in 1817. In it, Bryant emphasizes the interconnectedness of death and pantheistic nature—upon one's death, the individual returns to and becomes one with the earth.

And, lost each human trace, surrendering up
Thine individual being, shalt thou go
To mix for ever with the elements;[97]

In Bryant's view of death, everyone retires to the same final resting place, in "one mighty sepulchre."[98] This eternal resting place—the earth—is surrounded by the picturesque elements of nature:

The hills
Rock-ribbed and ancient as the sun,—the vales
Stretching in pensive quietness between;
The venerable woods—rivers that move
In majesty, and the complaining brooks
That make the meadows green;[99]

Bryant ends his masterpiece with an impression of death infused with a comforting and sentimental melancholy. Death is peaceful sleep, devoid of fear or terror.

Thou go not, like the quarry-slave at night,
Scourged to his dungeon, but, sustained and
        soothed
By an unfaltering trust, approach thy grave,
Like one who wraps the drapery of his couch
About him, and lies down to pleasant dreams.[100]

The sentiments that Bryant expressed were later embraced by the proponents of the rural cemetery movement. His sentimental poem "The Old Man's Funeral" (1824) was even published in *The Picturesque Pocket Companion, and Visitor's Guide, Through Mount Auburn.* In the poem, Bryant's protagonist asks why the funeral goers mourn their friend. He compares the old man's death to the setting sun and the falling autumn leaves. His life has run its natural course.

"Why weep ye then for him, who, having run
The bound of man's appointed years, at last,
Life's blessings all enjoyed, life's labors done,
Serenely to his final rest has passed?"[101]

Bryant also sentimentalized the act of remembrance, which he described as "soft" like "twilight hues, when the bright sun is set."[102] A noticeable shift had taken place in the American attitude toward death and remembrance.

American short story author and essayist Washington Irving (1783–1859) accentuated and encouraged the growing American Romantic conception of death and nature and memory. Upon a trip to England, Irving recorded his observations of funeral rituals in a country churchyard in an essay published in *The Sketch Book of Geoffrey Crayon, Gent.* (1819–1820). He was particularly taken by the "solicitude shown by the common people for an honoured and peaceful grave."[103] He reflected on the practice he witnessed of people scattering flowers before funerals and planting them on the graves of departed friends. He remarked that the practice persisted from the ancient Greeks and Romans; it was once "universally prevalent" but now infrequent. He mentioned the planting of evergreens such as rosemary and holly in some remote precincts and said that there was a "melancholy fancifulness in the arrangement of these rustic offerings, that had something in it truly poetical."[104] Meanwhile, the flowers that were strewn or planted often carried particular meanings: "The rose was sometimes blended with the lily, to form a general emblem of frail mortality. . . . The nature and colour of the flowers, and of the ribands with which they were tied, had often a particular reference to the qualities or story of the deceased, or were expressive of the feelings of the mourner."[105] Irving noted that the intention of using "sweet-scented evergreens and flowers" in English graveyards seemed to be "to soften the horrors of the tomb, to beguile the mind from brooding over the disgraces of perishing mortality, and to associate the memory of the deceased with the most delicate and beautiful objects in nature."[106] He thus emphatically lamented the passing of such an "elegant and touching" custom from most cultures.

On the same journey, Irving observed a monument at Westminster Abbey with a terrifying scene of a menacing, "fleshless" skeleton aiming a dart at his victim who cowers and tries in vain to avoid death. In response, the poet was compelled to consider: "But why should we thus seek to clothe death with unnecessary terrors, and to spread horrors round the tomb of those we love? The grave should be surrounded by every thing that might inspire tenderness and veneration for the dead; or that might win the living to virtue. It is the place, not of disgust and dismay, but of sorrow and meditation."[107] The pointed question and response became a repeated refrain of advocates for rural cemeteries. John Claudius Loudon (1783–1843), a Scottish botanist and garden designer whose work *On the Laying Out, Planting, and Managing of Cemeteries* influenced rural cemetery designers throughout the United States, included Irving's quote in his seminal work. *The Guide to Laurel Hill Cemetery* showcased it as well. It encompassed, perhaps as succinctly as ever published, the motivating sentiments of the movement.

Monumental Commemoration in America

America's desire for commemoration lagged behind that of Europe's as well. Colonists in eighteenth-century America did not, generally, create monuments as a form of commemoration. It was only after the American Revolution that a collective consciousness arose to honor the heroes and statesmen of the new Republic to foster a sense of history separate from England. As Blanche Linden relates, the Revolutionary War produced "heroes for Americans, providing names and stories ready to be invoked as independence created the need for defining a common purpose, principles, and past. Thus was born the necessity for monuments."[108]

One of the earliest and most significant monuments of the young United States was the tomb of George Washington (1732–1799) on his Virginia estate. Like Rousseau's tomb at Ermenonville, Washington's tomb at Mount Vernon became a place of pilgrimage. Americans were encouraged to visit the site, which would stir remembrance of the events that led to the country's independence and inspire patriotism and devotion to the principles upon which the country was established. Idealized images of Washington's tomb appear in eighteenth-century paintings, engravings, and mourning pictures, which depict the surrounding scene as dramatically picturesque. Although it was not quite as strikingly situated in reality, these romanticized versions of the tomb and its environs spoke to a growing desire for melancholy-infused burial places.

21. Residence and tomb of George Washington, Mount Vernon, Virginia. Published by Fisher, Son & Co., London & Paris, 1840, Danylchak collection.

22. Bunker Hill Monument. Photograph ca. 1890, Detroit Publishing Company Photograph Collection, Library of Congress Prints and Photographs Division.

In Boston, a group of influential citizens noted the conspicuous absence of commemorative monuments to the Revolution and stressed the responsibility of citizens to recognize the contributions of those who made independence possible. In 1823, with the fiftieth anniversary of the Battle of Bunker Hill fast approaching, William Tudor Jr., Henry A. S. Dearborn, Edward Everett, George Ticknor, John Collins Warren, Daniel Webster, Judge Joseph Story, Jacob Bigelow, and others joined forces to plan for a monument to showcase Boston's pivotal role in the Revolution. They petitioned the Massachusetts legislature for a charter to form the Bunker Hill Monument Association with the authority to purchase land and build an appropriate monument to honor the ancestors that sacrificed to form a nation built on republican principles. In their petition, the incorporators argued:

If great actions, having for their object the public good; if individuals, renowned for their civil and military virtues, have, in all ages, illumined the history and claimed the admiration of nations;—if they have been decreed worthy of the triumphal arch, the column, the temple, or the mausoleum,—what people ever had more cause thus to cherish the memory of their statesmen and heroes than those of the United States? Emerging from the war for Independence, we have advanced in the rout of national glory with the rapidity unprecedented in the annals of empires; but, during our cheering progress in agriculture, manufactures, commerce, literature, science and the arts, we appear not to have been sufficiently mindful of the infinite obligations we are under to those who braved the hardships, privations, and dangers of the conflict, for the boasted privileges we enjoy. No monument designates the ever-memorable heights of Charlestown, or Saratoga, the plains of Trenton, Monmouth, or Yorktown.[109]

The cornerstone for a grand 221-foot granite obelisk on the battlefield site was laid on the fiftieth anniversary of the battle—June 17, 1825. The ambitious and costly project was finally finished in 1842. In the interim, Bostonians, including several of the prominent men involved in the Bunker Hill Monument Association, turned to the idea of commemorating individuals, on a smaller scale, within a burial ground.

In the post-Revolutionary era, Americans increasingly adopted classical symbols related to mourning to adorn their headstones. This appropriation of classical symbols for funerary art was contemporaneous with American architects' adoption of Roman architectural forms, which was done intentionally to associate the new nation with the strength and ideals of the Republican civilization. The urn-and-willow became the most common marker motif around the turn of the nineteenth century. Gravestone materials began to change as well; more expensive marble was introduced to graveyards in Salem, Massachusetts, for example, around 1803. The concurrent interest in classical civilizations helped stimulate the use of marble, a material closely associated with the art and architecture of ancient Greece and Rome.

Unitarianism's View of Nature and Death

At the beginning of the nineteenth century, Unitarianism became an influential Protestant denomination and created a religious climate conducive for reconsidering established forms of burial landscapes in the United States. Unitarianism borrowed some tenets from the Enlightenment as well as traditional religion to form a unique view of death. Like evangelicals, Unitarians rejected the Calvinistic doctrine of predestination. They believed in salvation by character and the "perfectibility of human beings over universal human depravity."[110] However, they placed particular emphasis on human rationality over the "feverish, forced, fluctuating zeal" associated with evangelicalism.[111] Unitarians promoted a religion "based on reason," which they considered the appropriate "ideological basis for the new republic."[112] They believed that rational individuals with the ability to exercise free will could save themselves. This belief, in conjunction with their faith in an infinitely benevolent and just God, dispelled the anxiety and terror associated with the earlier Puritan way of death.

Unitarians also emphasized the continuation of one's being beyond death. In 1827, the Reverend William Ware (1797–1852) asserted, "Death, we regard not so much as even a temporary, momentary extinction of being, but simply as the appointed manner in which we shall pass from one stage of existence to another—from earth to heaven."[113] The Unitarian theologian and author James Freeman Clarke (1810–1888) asserted, too, that upon death, "We shall find ourselves familiar and at home in another state, before we are conscious of entering it."[114] Unitarians believed that in that heavenly state, loved ones would meet again.

Importantly, some of the influential voices of Unitarianism also advanced the idea that "God is in nature." The Reverend Joseph Stevens Buckminster (1784–1812) believed that God was evident in nature's design.[115] Meanwhile, the pastor at Boston's Federal Street Church, the Reverend William Ellery Channing (1780–1812), asserted in an 1828 sermon, "He penetrates all things, and delights to irradiate all with his glory. Nature, in all its lowest and inanimate forms, is pervaded by his power."[116] These pantheistic beliefs influenced the New England Transcendentalists as well as advocates of a new type of burial landscape. It was Boston Unitarians, affected by a growing spirit of Romanticism, who founded the first rural cemetery in the United States—Mount Auburn Cemetery.

Practical Matters

Although changes in cultural and religious attitudes toward nature and death led to new perspectives on the appropriate location for burial grounds, practical issues finally provoked widespread change. Religion professor Gary Laderman argues that it was actually problems such as overcrowding, sanitation, and the unsightly appearance of urban graveyards that "contributed more immediately to a reinterpretation of the relationship between the living and the dead."[117]

In both France and the United States, burial crises immediately preceded the far-reaching transformation in burial practices that philosophers, poets, and garden designers had been advocating for over a century.

As early as the seventeenth century, in France, there were public health fears stemming from conditions of urban churchyards. But by the middle of the eighteenth century, objections and investigations had become numerous. One particularly influential admonition about the dangers of urban burials came from Félix Vicq-d'Azyr (1748–1794) who was the head of the Société Royale de Médecine in Paris as well as the queen's physician. His 1778 publication *Essay on Burial Places and Dangers* theorized that "noxious effluvia from mass graves might engender disease."[118]

23. Depiction of the conditions in the Holy Innocents' Cemetery in Paris, France in 1550. Tinted lithograph by F. Hoffbauer (1839–1922), 1891, published by Firmin Didot & Cie Editeurs, Paris, Danylchak collection.

This theory aroused international attention and was advanced by other physicians and social reformers, including John Gorham Coffin (1769–1829) in Boston, Massachusetts. In 1823, Coffin[119] emphatically remarked in a pamphlet entitled *Remarks on the Dangers and Duties of Sepulture:* "It is now admitted in many parts of Europe, that city and church burials are capable of destroying the purity of the surrounding air and water; and of producing not only single deaths, but of originating mass epidemics."[120] The miasma theory, which was the predominant theory about the spread of disease at the time, commonly held that decaying animal and vegetable matter resulted in poisonous air. This bad air, also known as miasma, caused people to become sick. In concentrated forms it could cause asphyxia and, therefore, instant death. In diluted forms, the effect was "less prompt," causing dangerous fevers.[121] Coffin stated that it was well-known that "in certain years and seasons, there is something in the atmosphere we breathe, which predisposes the human system to yellow fever, typhus, or to some other diseases that destroy life. Individuals and communities may ordinarily escape these maladies, if no local exciting cause exists. This local cause, cooperating with the atmospheric morbific tendency, is sufficient to unfold the disease."[122] For Coffin, miasma from graveyards was a powerful local instigator. It was not until the mid–nineteenth century that the miasma theory was replaced by the germ theory of disease.

Offensive examples of overcrowding, with their attendant health hazards, encouraged French reformers to rethink the location of burial grounds in relation to population concentrations. The Holy Innocents' Cemetery in Paris, for example, had been receiving burials since at least 1186 and had been the repository of about 10 percent of the city's dead annually. In 1780, the graveyard's enclosure could no longer contain the crush of remains and the basement wall of an adjacent apartment building was crushed as over two thousand partially decomposed bodies spilled through it. The French government, "alarmed at the evils caused by the exhalations from these receptacles of the dead, ordered the cemetery of the Innocents to be shut up."[123]

In 1794, the Administration of Public Works in Paris issued a report condemning the mass graves of the city's cemeteries "not only for their insalubrity but also for offering 'the disgusting spectacle of putrefaction.'"[124] The administration called for four new cemeteries in rural settings outside the city; however, no immediate plans for the extramural cemeteries proceeded. In 1796, the city's cemeteries were reorganized, with only five cemeteries remaining open to burials—those farthest from the city center and most recently opened. All the other cemeteries were closed. In the years preceding the widespread closure of the city's burial grounds, many of the mass graves in Parisian cemeteries held about 1,200 to 1,500 bodies. By 1799, the five cemeteries that remained in operation had estimates of 2,000 to 2,500 corpses in their mass graves.[125] Serious concerns about the unhealthy conditions of the graveyards deepened. The burial crisis in Paris had reached a breaking point.

CHAPTER 3

The Rural Cemetery Movement

The Cemetery of Père Lachaise in Paris, France, the first cemetery designed as a Picturesque garden landscape in the western world, was the culmination of influencers—the rise of Romanticism, a growing cult of melancholy, a desire for sepulchral commemoration, an embrace of naturalistic landscape design, and, most immediately, concerns regarding the sanitary conditions of urban burial grounds. Père Lachaise became a hugely influential precedent and helped inspire the development of similar burial sites throughout Europe and the United States—including Mount Auburn Cemetery established outside of Boston, Massachusetts, in 1831. By this time, the conditions were ripe in America for the creation of a decisive alternative to earlier urban burial grounds. In response to the contemporary cultural climate, Mount Auburn adopted a collection of groundbreaking characteristics for an American burial place that became the definitive model for America's large-scale cemeteries to follow.

The Cemetery of Père Lachaise: An Influential Precedent

While the English had developed the naturalistic garden style and first infused it with commemorative monuments, it was the French who first built a burial ground inspired by this model to service a city. In 1804, in the midst of Paris's burial crisis, Napoleon I (1769–1821) issued the Imperial Decree on Burials, which set forth regulations for cemeteries that codified sixty years of burial reform initiatives in France. The decree prohibited burials in churches and towns

and, instead, required cemeteries to be at least forty to fifty yards beyond the city limits. Communal graves were also forbidden (although this was not observed in Paris). The decree, instead, required individual graves with at least thirty to forty centimeters to each side and thirty to fifty centimeters of space beyond the head and feet of the corpse. While ordinary graves could be reused after five years, commemorative monuments could be erected in the interim. If the cemetery had ample space, land could be sold for permanent graves, which could be marked by monuments or mausoleums for individuals or families. Burial vaults could also be built on permanent parcels. The decree also stipulated that new cemeteries be established on "elevated sites, preferably exposed to the north winds" and that the properties be enclosed with walls and planted in such a way so that air circulation was not hindered.[1] The last provision was a compromise between contemporary arguments, which held that trees were needed to absorb miasmas emanating from decaying corpses, and older opinions, which held that air circulation was the best method for dispersing unhealthy air.

The decree sanctioned the cemetery of Père Lachaise—"the touchstone for all future discussions about the nature of cemeteries."[2] In 1804, the City of Paris, under Napoleon's direction, purchased the former estate of Mont-Louis, located just northeast of the city limits, for the establishment of a new form of burial ground. The estate had been a Jesuit retreat, serving as the home to Jesuit François d'Aix de la Chaise—known as Père La Chaise—from 1675 to

1709. The forty-eight acres of elevated land purchased by the city was irregular with various picturesque undulations but also had formal garden elements that remained from the retreat. Alexandre-Théodore Brongniart, the architect for the City of Paris, transformed the site into a cemetery, choosing to balance the existing formal features with informal, park-like elements throughout his scheme. For instance, Brongniart added a winding carriage road on the site's periphery that rose from the base of the hill, through a valley, around an escarpment, to the upper plain, to create a foil to the existing formal esplanade that rose from the entrance boulevard directly up to the mount. Over time, the site expanded to envelop 107 acres.

Père Lachaise set an important precedent in regards to ownership rights and significantly advanced the practice of land grants and burial in perpetuity. Until the establishment of Père Lachaise, burial spaces in France were generally rented for six to twenty years after which remains were disinterred and placed in a charnel house. At Père Lachaise, for one hundred francs a square meter, wealthy families could purchase permanent burial plots, which could be marked by a commemorative monument. Meanwhile, for fifty francs those of modest means could purchase individual graves tied to five-year renewable contracts. These gravesites, too, could be marked by an inscribed memorial. The cemetery also set aside land for the poor

24. A funeral procession entering the Cemetery of Père Lachaise. Brongniart's formal esplanade rises up the mount while winding drives ascend the site's periphery. Engraving by R. A. Rolph, "Engraved Expressly for *Grahams Magazine*," undated, Danylchak collection.

THE RURAL CEMETERY MOVEMENT

to be buried in communal graves without charge, but these graves could be reused after six years. Although not all burials were permanent here, Père Lachaise was the first cemetery in Continental Europe to allow individuals to purchase perpetual burial rights.[3]

Despite the prospect of perpetual burial, however, the French elite were slow to choose this new public cemetery as their final resting place. Instead, they chose their private estates. For at least the first decade of its existence, the Cemetery of Père Lachaise saw relatively few burials and associated monuments. It was the relocation of the tomb and remains of famous lovers Abélard and Héloïse to the cemetery in 1817 that spurred the new bourgeoisie to accept Père Lachaise as a viable (and fashionable) option for burial. The lovers' small gothic temple became famously frequented by visitors and brought greater prestige to the burial ground.

Emulating earlier private examples of Arcadian-like burial landscapes, the site of Père Lachaise became much more densely planted within its first two decades as a cemetery than it had been as a Jesuit estate. For instance, lime and chestnut trees were planted to flank the cemetery's allées, while poplars were planted to line one of the lower carriage paths. The influential eighteenth-century German intellectual Christian Hirschfeld would have approved of the use of these trees as he considered their dark, thick foliage "well suited to creating a somber and 'mysterious' shade, suggestive of the 'compassion' and 'sweet melancholy' that one would want in a funerary garden."[4] Meanwhile, carefully tended shrubs and flowers were added to family plots. One visitor in 1825 noted that the cemetery "is beautifully shaded with cypress and other evergreens, amidst the lively verdure of which the white marble monuments and tomb-stones . . . produce the finest and most picturesque effect. In some cases a solitary shrub hangs its somber tresses over a grave; while in others, the monumental marble is completely embowered by the green branches."[5] Another contemporary observer described the effect of surrounding and overshadowing the sepulchral ornaments at Père Lachaise with green glades and gloomy cypresses: "The contemplative mind is not only impressed with sentiments of solemn sublimity and religious awe, but with those of the most tender and heart-affecting melancholy."[6]

Within this "vast grove of the dead," varied commemorative monuments marked gravesites. A commentator noted in 1831, "Within this spot, there is always a sepulchral urn, a small pillar, or a cross, to tell the name and the quality of him who lies below. . . . The more ambitious monuments consist of obelisks, pyramids, temples, and marble sarcophagi, decorated with figures and *basso relievi;* while a third consist of crypts and family sepulchers in some degree similar to those of ancient Rome."[7] Deeply affecting monument inscriptions signaled that the dead were not forgotten. Meanwhile, the defined spaces of family plots—which were frequently bound by low fences—reflected the importance of family ties. Gravesites with their commemorative monuments became places of pilgrimage where the living could commune with the dead, just as Gessner had depicted in his *Idylls.* An early observer noted, "It is there the custom for surviving friends to visit the tombs of their relatives, and, as a token of recollection and respect to their memory, to weave a garland of flowers, and hang it on their monument. At every turn the eye is arrested by the tender proof of some late friendly visitation."[8]

To cater to cemetery proprietors desiring lasting commemoration, the government provided a marble sculptor at the cemetery to foster the installation of sculpted memorials. By the 1820s industrious stone cutters and architects had also set up shop surrounding the site. By 1825, there were over twenty-six thousand funerary monuments dotting the landscape of Père Lachaise. As more and more burials and associated monuments took the place of vegetation, the visual character of the site changed as art overpowered nature toward mid-century. During the American rural cemetery movement, a similar transformation occurred. In response, however, Americans took deliberate measures to re-elevate nature within their rural cemeteries. But for the French, nature had "lost its impact, and all emotion was completely absorbed by the monument."[9] Continuing its trajectory, Père Lachaise eventually became a densely monumented site—a "city of marble."

Soon after its establishment, the Cemetery of Père Lachaise became a popular tourist attraction. Guidebooks featuring maps of the site and itineraries of the most noteworthy landscape features and monuments were published. Travelers' accounts of its distinctive features also spread throughout Europe and across the Atlantic. In 1825, for example, Nathaniel Hazeltine Carter (1787–1830), a New York newspaper editor, visited the cemetery and wrote about his encounter:

Our casual attendance at the interment of General Foy, and a subsequent visit on a day more favourable for observation, afforded us a full opportunity of examining the cemetery of Pere La Chaise, which is the great repository of the dead at Paris, and reflects infinite credit upon the city, as well as upon the character of the French people. In all respects it very far surpasses any thing of the kind I have ever seen, and the design strongly recommends itself to the imitation of all great cities. Were it possible for the inhabitants of New-York, *en masse,* to pay a single visit to this cemetery, I am persuaded they would at once surrender every lingering prejudice, and be unanimously in favour of adopting a similar plan; for besides possessing all the conveniences of sepulture, on very moderate terms, a burying-ground ... has here become a great monument of national taste and national feeling, inviting the stranger, as well as the citizen who is attracted by more sacred ties, to resort frequently to its rural,

retired, and consecrated walks, where the body is refreshed by a pure air, the mind meets with themes for serious meditation, and the heart cannot fail to be improved.[10]

The New Burying Ground:
A Harbinger of Change

In America, an early alternative to the overcrowded urban burial ground model was created in New Haven, Connecticut, in 1796. The New Burying Ground—now called Grove Street Cemetery—was established, in part, as a reaction to the overcrowded conditions in the town's primary burial place, which was over 150 years old, contained over four thousand burials, and was located in the center of the community. Its congested condition became particularly apparent during yellow fever epidemics in the 1790s, which precipitated a burial crisis. At the same time, Sen. James Hillhouse (1754–1832), a leading New Haven citizen, noted that burial on family estates did not offer much

25. Cemetery procession within the heavily monumented grounds of Père Lachaise. C. Reiss del., Aus d. Kunstanst. d. bibli. Instit. in Hildbhn., ca. 1859. Danylchak collection.

THE RURAL CEMETERY MOVEMENT

reassurance regarding permanency of burial. If a family's property passed in time to another owner, the sanctity of a family graveyard was not guaranteed.

Under these circumstances, Hillhouse enlisted thirty-one local citizens to join him in incorporating a private association to purchase and maintain a ten-acre tract of land as a permanent burial place removed from the center of the city. Creating a corporate entity to purchase and manage a burial ground was a unique approach that had only become possible after the American Revolution. In 1784, the City of New Haven became one of the first entities in the United States to be granted a charter of incorporation. In the 1790s, private groups and associations were also granted the right to incorporate. The New Burying Ground was the first burial ground incorporated in the United States, setting an important precedent for later rural cemeteries. Each lot owner in the burying ground, typically the head of a family, became a member of the corporation and was thus entitled to a vote in the affairs of the association. At New Haven, it was no longer a church or a governmental authority that had control over who could be buried in the burial ground or if remains could be removed. Instead, it was a voluntary association of private individuals making decisions about the sacred space. As historian David Charles Sloane explains, "The cemetery belonged to the families who, through their investment in lots, joined with one another in securing the safety of their dead."[11]

The layout of the New Burying Ground also deviated from traditional urban burial places and signaled a growing desire by family members to be buried together. Although nine sections were created for use by religious congregations, Yale College, the poor, "Negros," and "Strangers," the rest of the property was divided into family lots. These lots were generally organized around a central monument—generally of marble, often in the form of an obelisk—inscribed with the family name. As Sloane remarks, "The landscape revolved around the family."[12] New Haven's burial lots were also systematically numbered to ensure accurate record keeping of burials and ownership.

The New Burying Ground had a consciously designed layout created by Josiah Meigs, a mathematics and natural philosophy professor at Yale College. Unlike typical urban burial grounds, the New Burying Ground had roadways, which were eighteen and twenty-four feet wide, that allowed hearses and carriages to enter the grounds. The cemetery's avenues were laid out in a perpendicular fashion similar to the traditional urban grid system. However, at New Haven, nature was welcomed into the American burial space. The cemetery association made a conscious decision to provide some improvements to the landscape. Lombardy poplars, for example, lined the roadways to provide shade and a few weeping willows dotted the landscape. The weeping willow had just recently been introduced to America. Commonly associated with mourning, the weeping willow had previously been added to examples of English elegiac landscapes. The corporation also authorized individual owners to make additional improvements to their lots, and low hedges, fences, and trees began to dot the site. Overall, the improvements were fairly minimal compared to those seen in the forthcoming rural cemeteries, but they were an early indication of a desire for change. A Scottish traveler who visited the site praised it as an improvement to the practice of "huddling so many graves in the confined space round the places of worship in a populous city."[13] He described the common result of this long-standing practice, which was all too familiar to the citizens of New Haven: "sloppy graveyards, where the mourners sink ankle-deep in a rank and offensive mould, mixed up with broken bones and fragments of coffins."[14] In contrast, the Scottish traveler called the New Burying Ground "one of the prettiest burying places I ever saw."[15] New Haven's burying ground set an important precedent, but it was the landscape at Mount Auburn Cemetery outside of Boston, Massachusetts, that stirred the country's imagination and provoked a revolution in burial ground design in the United States.

Mount Auburn Cemetery: The First Rural Cemetery

Like many growing cities during the Industrial Revolution, Boston—the commercial and cultural capital of New England—faced a burial crisis by the 1820s. Boston's population had surged from 33,787 in 1810 to 43,298 in 1820. By 1830, the city encompassed 61,392 inhabitants. A shortage of space for burials prompted the city to ban all individual graves in 1816. In the Granary Burying Ground, earthen burial continued in unmarked common graves, stacked four deep. However, within a couple years, all of the Burying Ground's available space was filled. In 1822, St. Paul's Church petitioned the city for permission to bury its dead within vaults in the cellar of its building. Other churches followed suit with similar petitions. Opposition to such crypts swelled, however, amid public health concerns and an enduring American attachment to earthen burial. In addition, many considered the vaults antidemocratic because they were an expensive burial option and, therefore, would only be available to the financially elite.

In 1823, under the command of May. Josiah Quincy (1772–1864), the city council appointed a Joint Committee on Urban Interments to investigate the issue. The committee's ensuing report recommended that the city prohibit the construction of new subterranean tombs within the Boston peninsula and adopt provisions that would ultimately exclude all urban burials. The report went further, recommending a common municipal burial ground for all of Boston's citizens outside of the city. A second committee was appointed to advance this advice and select a site for a new common burial place, but no real plan materialized. Meanwhile, in 1826, an Ordinance on the Burial of the Dead closed the Granary, Central, and King's Chapel burial grounds. Only parts of the Copp's Hill Burying Ground, established in 1659, and the South End Burying Ground, opened in 1810, were permitted to receive new burials. Interments in either would be temporary, only allowed for up to twenty years.

The increasingly untenable situation fueled innovative thinking and, ultimately, a solution. In 1825, Jacob Bigelow (ca. 1787–1879) gathered a group of prominent Bostonians together at his home to explore the idea of establishing a new kind of burial ground for Boston—one that "might at once lead to a cessation of the burial of the dead in the city, rob death of a portion of its terrors, and afford to afflicted survivors some relief amid their bitterest sorrows."[16] According to his own recollections, Bigelow presented a general concept for a burial place "composed of family burial

26. Boston faced a burial crisis by the 1820s as its urban burial grounds became densely populated. Copp's Hill Burying Ground was one of only two in the city that could still receive burials after 1826. Photograph ca. 1904, Detroit Publishing Company Photograph Collection, Library of Congress Prints and Photographs Division.

THE RURAL CEMETERY MOVEMENT

lots, separated and interspersed with trees, shrubs, and flowers, in a wood or landscape garden."[17] In addition to having a medical background, Bigelow was also a botanist. He had published *Florula Bostonsiensis*—a tome on the city's plant life—about a decade before. This vocation no doubt influenced his conception of what an alternative to existing intramural burial grounds should look like. Although Bigelow's idea won approval, no location was immediately secured and the scheme remained dormant for five years.

Then in 1830, Bigelow approached George W. Brimmer (1784–1838) about purchasing his recently acquired seventy-two-acre tract of land known as "Stone's Woods" for use as an ornamental burying ground. The property—four miles west of Boston—straddled the boundary between Cambridge and Watertown. The ample tract was removed enough from the city to possess a rural character. In fact, it had once been a popular rustic retreat for Harvard University students and local residents who nicknamed it "Sweet Auburn" after the town depicted in Oliver Goldsmith's nostalgic poem "The Deserted Village" (1770). This nickname would ultimately inspire the moniker of the future burial ground. The tract's sufficient distance from Boston would also reduce the threat of urban encroachment on the burying place while removing any threat of emanating miasmas from the population center. The burial ground would still be accessible to Bostonians, however, who could travel to Cambridge across the West Boston Bridge, which saw hourly stage runs begin in 1826. Brimmer was known to be a cultured and generous man. In fact, just a few years earlier he had assembled an art collection at the Boston Athenaeum. (The collection, however, was not open to the general public.) Brimmer agreed to the sale and offered his property for the amount he had paid for it in 1825 even though it had increased in value.

The Massachusetts Horticultural Society had been incorporated in 1829 and, following his exchange with Brimmer, Bigelow took the burial ground proposal to the officers of the Society. Bigelow himself was the corresponding secretary of the newly established organization. He and his cohorts saw an advantage in linking their project with the Horticultural Society to help overcome any public concern about the viability of the large-scale enterprise. A partnership between the Horticultural Society and the organizers of the new burial ground would also serve to underscore their commitment to creating a landscaped burial place unlike any precedent in America. In an address before the Society's membership in September 1830, Zebedee Cook Jr. (1786–1858), the vice president of the organization, presented the idea:

> The improvement and embellishment of grounds devoted to public uses is deserving of especial consideration, and should interest the ingenious, the liberal, and tasteful in devising ways and means for the accomplishment of so desirable an object; and I deem this a suitable occasion to direct the attention of our citizens to a subject I have long wished to see presented to their consideration, with an eloquence that could not fail to awaken, and with arguments that will not fail to insure the influence of all in its execution. I refer to the establishment of a public cemetery similar in its design to that of Père La Chaise in the environs of Paris, to be located in the suburbs of this metropolis....
>
> I would render such scenes more alluring, more familiar, and imposing, by the aid of rural embellishments. The skill and taste of the architect should be exerted in the construction of the requisite departments and avenues; and appropriate trees and plants should decorate its borders; the weeping-willow, waving its graceful drapery over the monumental marble, and somber foliage of the cypress, should shade it; and the undying daisy should mingle its bright and glowing tints with the native laurel of our forests.[18]

At the time of the Horticultural Society's founding, Americans were experiencing a physical and psychological disconnection from the rural countryside as they relocated to cities *en masse*. Meanwhile, the country's virgin forests were rapidly disappearing along the East Coast with continued settlement. In response, an intellectual movement was afoot to cultivate "rural" taste, which involved nostalgia for America's virgin landscape and a desire to live in harmony with nature. Cook and his horticultural associates appreciated the idea of a "rural" burial ground, which would foster familiarity with a natural landscape for those who visited it—an experience they felt would have a moralizing influence on urbanites.

Meanwhile, from its founding, the Horticultural Society envisioned the creation of an experimental garden, a concept that soon merged with the idea of creating a public burying ground. The Society perceived an advantage in connecting the two ideas and believed that "the whole would ultimately offer such an example of landscape gardening as would be creditable to the Society, and assist in improving the taste of the public in this highest branch of the art of horticulture."[19] In June of 1831, the Horticultural Society convened a meeting "of gentlemen who were favorably disposed to the enterprise."[20] The attendees unanimously agreed to a plan to purchase the Brimmer property for $6,000 as soon as enough subscriptions for cemetery lots could be obtained—one hundred lots sold at $60 apiece. It was also agreed that at least forty acres of the property would be devoted to cemetery purposes.

On June 23, 1831, the Massachusetts legislature passed an act authorizing the Massachusetts Horticultural Society to "dedicate and appropriate any part of the real estate now owned or hereafter to be purchased by them, as and for a Rural Cemetery or Burying Ground, and for the erection of Tombs, Cenotaphs, or other Monuments, for, or in memory of the dead." The act specified that the land once laid out and appropriated for burial purposes by the society would be deemed "perpetually dedicated" for that purpose. Notably, this act was the formal origin of the term *rural cemetery*, which became the standard name for the new type of burial ground that developed. The term *rural* as applied to these burial grounds held both Romantic and geographical connotations. It meant a place in nature—a picturesque, civilizing environment—and one outside of the city—not in a remote area, but one on the accessible outskirts. Meanwhile, this new burial ground was the first in the United States to adopt the moniker *cemetery*, which derives from the Greek word for "sleeping chamber." Using the word *cemetery* likened death to sleep, softening its associations and emphasizing the continuity of life. The term's use reflected the Romantic sensibilities of the age and America's more optimistic religious climate. The word cemetery had been used only sporadically in Europe prior to this time. It became widely used by American burial institutions after Mount Auburn donned it.

The founders of the new cemetery were adept at fanning the flames of public curiosity and building support for their new endeavor through public speeches and the press. Many of the speeches have actually been preserved in print "because like good

publicists anywhere the speakers carefully released texts to the press."[21] Excerpts from early committee reports were also quoted at length in New England newspapers. These passages often spoke to the moral motivation and civilizing vision for establishing the new type of burial ground. An excerpt of a report penned by Gen. Henry A. S. Dearborn (1783–1851), the founding president of the Horticultural Society, was reprinted in an article in the *Nantucket Inquirer* on July 2, 1831:

> How consoling and pleasing is the thought, that our memories shall be cherished after death; and that the spot, where our ashes repose, shall be often visited, by dear and constant friends; that they will there linger, to call up the soothing, yet melancholy reminiscences of by gone times; that the sod which covers us, will be kept ever verdant; that a magnificent forest will be reared to overshadow our graves, by those truly kind hands, which performed the last sad offices of affection; that flowers will fringe the pathways, leading to our lowly resting place, and their fragrance, mingled with the holiest aspirations ascend towards the throne of the Eternal.

The organizers also worked to shape publicity to alleviate public fears about burying loved ones in a distant location. A contemporary article in the *Daily Advertiser*, likely penned by a member of the Horticultural Society's Garden and Cemetery Committee, drew public attention, for example, to the benefit of joining the two endeavors: "Being connected with the adjacent experimental garden, [the cemetery] will be under the constant inspection of the Society's Gardener; and thus possess advantages, in reference to the care and neatness, with which it will be kept, not usually found in places of burial."[22] By August 3, 1831, subscriptions for the one hundred lots needed to move forward with the property purchase had been secured and members of the society began to plan for a formal dedication of the cemetery.

On September 24, nearly two thousand people participated in the consecration ceremony for Mount Auburn Cemetery in a heavily wooded valley outfitted for the occasion; the sacred spot was subsequently christened Consecration Dell. A temporary amphitheater was fabricated on a hillside with a platform for speakers below. The proceedings commenced with instrumental music from the Boston Band, an introductory

27. Consecration Dell, Mount Auburn Cemetery. Engraving by J. Smillie, from *Mount Auburn Illustrated*, 1847, Danylchak collection.

prayer by Reverend Dr. Ware, and a hymn by Reverend Pierpont. Then, the preeminent US Supreme Court Associate Justice Joseph Story (1779–1845), a member of the Horticultural Society, addressed the gathering.

Story's address presented the lofty, Romantic ideas of the cemetery's founders. He condemned contemporary burial practices and instead presented the rural cemetery as a just model that would serve, in part, to "moderate human suffering" and "cultivate moral sentiments and sensibilities." He remarked: "A rural Cemetery seems to combine in itself all the advantages which can be proposed to gratify human feelings, or tranquillize human fears; to secure the best religious influences, and to cherish all those associations which cast a cheerful light over the darkness of the grave."[23] The cemetery was intended to inspire "meditations on human mortality" and instigate reflection upon "the sublime consolations of religion."[24] As Story explained to his attentive audience, "Our Cemeteries rightly selected, and properly arranged, may be made subservient to some of the highest purposes of religion and human duty."[25] A cemetery may provide instruction on "the true value of life."[26] It may awaken "a new enthusiasm for virtue."[27] It may demand that the "powers given by God should be devoted to his service."[28] Story contended that after communing with the dead, the mourner should return to the world "purer, and better, and wiser."[29]

Placing burials amidst nature was not a new idea. As Story pointed out in his consecration address to the gathered public, the rural cemetery idea had roots in ancient burial practices. The aboriginal Germans buried their dead in groves. The Hebrews interred their departed in "ornamented gardens and deep forests, and fertile valleys, and lofty mountains."[30] The Greeks laid their dead to rest outside their cities "in the neighborhood of murmuring streams and mossy fountains" and called them "Cemeteries or 'Places of Repose.'"[31] But, the graveyards in the midst of America's cities were devoid of nature's comfort. "Why?" was Story's repeated refrain.

The tract of land chosen for the new cemetery was part of a glacial moraine, which infused it with a variety of surface, a key attribute sought by the cemetery's founders. Dearborn had earlier reported that a proper site would be "diversified by hills, valleys, plains, brooks, and low meadows, and bogs, so as to afford proper localities for every kind of tree and plant that will flourish in the climate."[32] An enamored visitor to the site later itemized its varied features in a letter to the editor of the *United States Gazette:* "Swelling hills, rounded knolls, deep ravines, secluded dells, opening glades, steep acclivities, primeval forests, tiny lakes, and even quite a lofty mountain, are all features of the landscape."[33] The highest elevation on the site, 125 feet above the Charles River, became known as Mount Auburn. From here visitors could view Boston to the east as well as surrounding farmland in the foreground. On a clear day, visitors could even see the Blue Hills of Milton to the south and New Hampshire's Mount Monadnock to the north. English Picturesque landscapes had often incorporated such dramatic panoramas from a mount reached by a winding pathway. Such panoramic scenes served to evoke moral meditations and a sense of awe.

Gen. Dearborn was selected to lay out the grounds of the cemetery with the assistance of civil engineer and surveyor Alexander Wadsworth (1806–1898). At the annual meeting of the Horticultural Society in September 1831, Dearborn submitted a report in which he concluded: "As the tract which has been solemnly consecrated, by religious ceremonies, as a burial place forever, is so abundantly covered with forest trees, many of which are more than sixty years old, it only requires the avenues to be formed, the borders, for some ten feet in width, planted with shrubs, bulbous and perennial flowers, the underwood cleared out, the fences, gateways, and appropriate edifices erected, to put the grounds in a sufficiently complete state for the uses designed, and to render them at once beautiful and interesting."[34] Shaping the grounds into the ornamental burial landscape the founders envisioned, however, ultimately proved to be more intensive than Dearborn initially calculated.

Prior to designing the grounds, Dearborn ordered books and maps from Europe illustrating and describing English landscape gardens as well as the Cemetery of Père Lachaise. Notably, Dearborn amassed two hundred engravings of the art, architecture, and landscape of the famous Parisian cemetery. Dearborn's library also included a copy of Evelyn's influential *Silva; or, A Discourse of Forest-Trees.* Drawing inspiration from these resources, Dearborn adopted the Picturesque style of landscape design for Mount Auburn Cemetery, which respected the existing natural and varied features of the grounds.[35]

First, Dearborn created a circulation system that followed the existing topography of the site and served both practical and philosophical purposes. He planned broad avenues about eighteen to twenty feet wide on more level portions of the ground, which allowed hearses and carriages to reach all areas of the site. He also laid out a dizzying maze of footpaths about six feet wide on more rugged terrain, where pedestrians could wander contemplatively without the intrusion of carriage traffic. An early visitor remarked,

"The whole of the surface is intersected by broad and graveled avenues for carriages, and by foot-paths, graveled in like manner, running in every conceivable direction."[36] The pathways were "so curved and winding in their course, as to make it difficult for a stranger to keep the even tenor of his way and thread the mazy labyrinth with a mind serene."[37] Instead, the journey was intended to provoke the visitor to "ponder on the ever-changing state of man's mortality."[38] Dearborn also arranged the avenues and footpaths in such a way as to reveal carefully planned sequences of picturesque views thus prompting surprise and reflection. Bigelow was subsequently authorized to have a plan of the cemetery grounds lithographed and to name the avenues and pathways Dearborn had created. Bigelow chose to assign them plant names, reiterating the central importance of horticulture to the cemetery endeavor. Subsequent rural cemetery corporations imitated the naming practice.

Although inspired by Père Lachaise, Dearborn and the Horticultural Society's Garden and Cemetery Committee sought early on to avoid the congested fate of the Parisian precedent and protect the rural character of Mount Auburn into the future. Dearborn created six-foot setbacks between burial lots and pathways. He also established three-foot buffers between burial lots. In addition, the Committee agreed to conserve forested areas on hillsides unless they granted a special request for a tomb there.

Mount Auburn also deviated from Père Lachaise with its inclusion of bodies of water, which were staples of English landscape gardens. Two major ponds and several smaller, spring-fed ones graced the early landscape of the cemetery. In 1832, the upper Garden Pond was excavated and an island formed at its center, which was connected by a bridge to an adjacent avenue. Part of this elongated, irregularly shaped Garden Pond later became known as Halcyon Lake. (The upper end was filled to create more than an acre of burial ground in 1856.) Arrangements were also made early on to excavate Forest and Consecration Dell ponds to greater depths and surround them with "embellished pathways."[39] In the late 1850s, Meadow Pond—which was originally a bog meadow covered

28. Map of Mount Auburn Cemetery illustrating the circuitous roadway system and noteworthy natural features. From *Mount Auburn Illustrated*, 1847, Library of Congress Prints and Photographs Division.

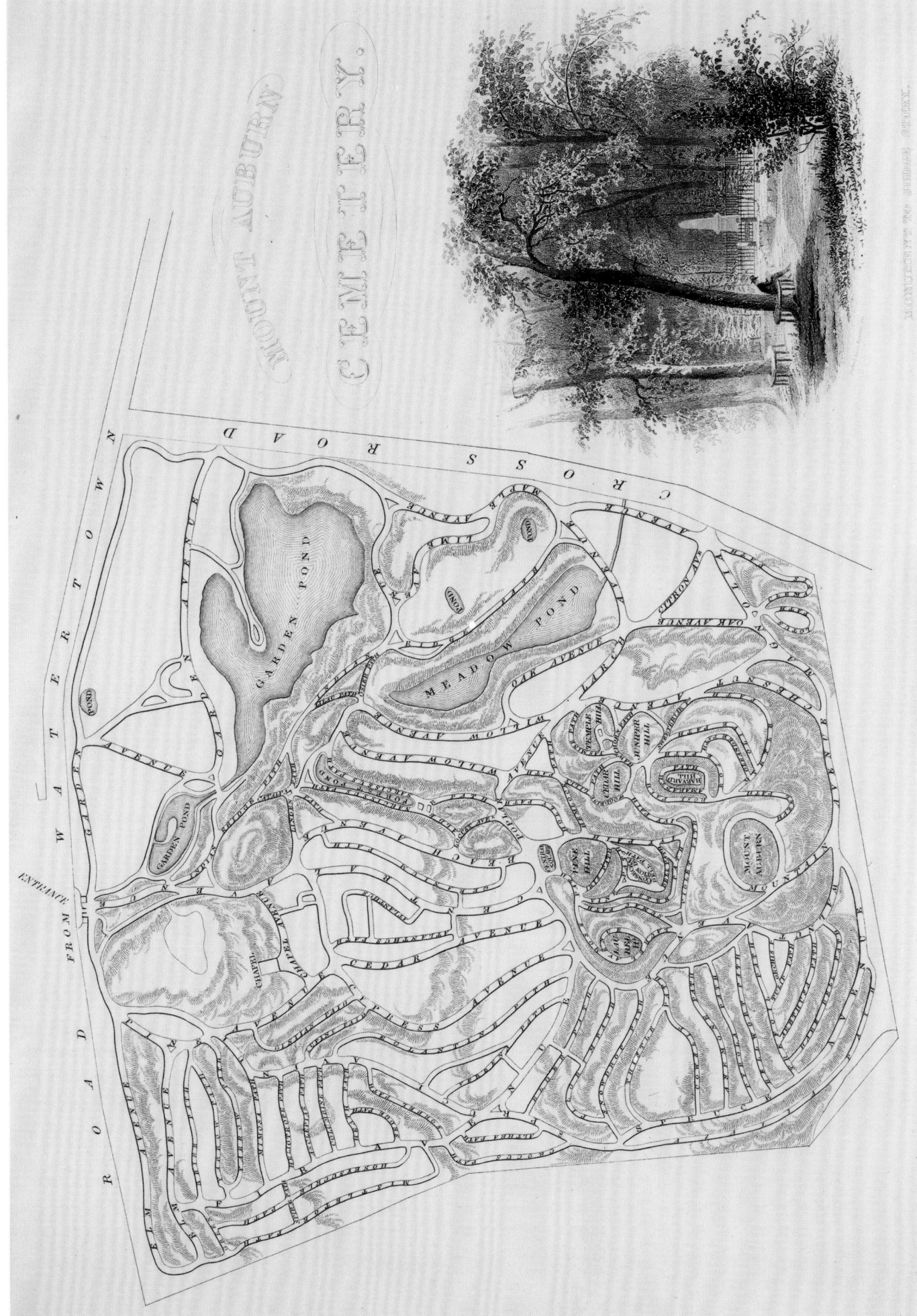

MOUNT AUBURN
CEMETERY.

MOUNT AUBURN FROM THE ENTRANCE GATE.

29. View of Mount Auburn Cemetery. Engraving by W. H. Bartlett, 1839, Cothran collection.

with grass and bushes—was improved and became known as Auburn Lake. The edges were lined with stone, the banks sodded, and a small bridge added to its narrowest part. In rural cemeteries, bodies of water were an important feature, valued not only for their aesthetic quality but also for their symbolic meaning, for folklore often held "that lakes and ponds . . . had the power to contain spirits."[40]

An experimental garden was intended to be an integral part of the Horticultural Society's endeavor on the Mount Auburn tract. Dearborn explained that it was "intended for the improvement of Horticulture in all its departments, ornamental as well as useful."[41] The garden would be a repository and laboratory for study of common, improved, and new varieties of fruits, vegetables, forest and ornamental trees and shrubs, as well as flowering and economic plants. In 1832, Dearborn laid out the paths and avenues of the intended garden in the northeast portion of the site between Garden Avenue and Garden Pond, which acted as a feature of "demarcation, rather than of disconnection" from the cemetery area.[42] It was intended that the ornamental grounds of the garden

and cemetery "be apparently blended, and the walks so intercommunicate as to afford an uninterrupted range over both, as one common domain."[43] In 1833, David Haggerston, a member of the Horticultural Society and an esteemed gardener from neighboring Charlestown who had owned a commercial garden known as Charlestown Vineyard, was appointed as the experimental garden's first superintendent. Under his supervision, 450 varieties of seeds, some imported from as far away as Asia, Europe, and South America, were planted in the garden.

However, the experimental garden soon ceased to exist. A later history of the Horticultural Society explained that it "had no funds specially appropriated for its support, and most of the proprietors of cemetery lots probably felt indifference, if not a positive aversion, to the idea of an experimental garden."[44] When Dearborn resigned as president of the Horticultural Society in 1834, the garden's fate was likely sealed. The society and the cemetery soon agreed to dissolve their ties and the experimental garden was discontinued. In 1835, an act of the Massachusetts legislature incorporated the independent Proprietors

THE RURAL CEMETERY MOVEMENT

of the Cemetery of Mount Auburn and granted each cemetery lot owner membership in the corporation. The Horticultural Society surrendered the land that had been set aside for the experimental garden. However, it would receive a portion of the proceeds of lot sales each year from the cemetery corporation for the promotion of horticultural practices; this arrangement remained in effect until 1975.

Mount Auburn Cemetery, which was founded by intellectuals with liberal religious leanings, was notably nondenominational. In a sermon delivered in 1819, Unitarian preacher William Ellery Channing had derided the pervasive "spirit of intolerance" among religious sects and called for "charitable judgment, especially toward those who differ in religious opinion."[45] This Unitarian mandate for interdenominational tolerance was followed by the founders of Mount Auburn when they decided to make the cemetery nondenominational. Most subsequent rural cemeteries followed this inclusive model. However, during the nineteenth century, they generally serviced Protestants. Catholics often continued to establish their own burial grounds, reflecting long-standing historical divisions.

Mount Auburn Cemetery was innovative as a private enterprise. Until its founding, burial grounds in the United States had largely been owned by churches or local governments unless they were small family burial plots on farms or estates. (The New Burying Ground in New Haven, Connecticut, was a notable exception.) Mount Auburn's corporate body had the right to purchase and hold real estate for cemetery purposes and to grant and convey subdivisions of that real estate to any person or persons for the "sole and exclusive right of burial." The original burial units created were family lots, measuring three hundred square feet. Purchasers of these lots were considered members of the corporation and were entitled to vote at meetings. This burial arrangement and governing structure reflected the increasing importance placed on the family unit and the sphere of domesticity during the nineteenth century. The members of the corporation would elect trustees who would then have charge of the "general management, superintendence, and care of the property, expenditures, business, and prudential concerns of the Corporation."

Mount Auburn Cemetery was heralded by its idealistic founders as being egalitarian. In an 1834 report, Judge Joseph Story explained that "every man in the community may become a proprietor upon paying the usual sum fixed for the purchase of a lot."[46] Even people of modest means could purchase—or barter for—a family lot at Mount Auburn. Originally, such lots cost $60, which was likely "well within the capability of middle-class families."[47] In fact, early deed records indicate that artisans like carpenters, engravers, and sailmakers purchased such plots. Moreover, some farmers, mechanics, and "dealers in building materials" traded their services or supplies—which could be used for improving the cemetery—for burial plots.

At Mount Auburn and its subsequent imitators, lots were sold as real estate in fee simple and conferred to purchasers by deed. The proprietor was granted associated burial rights in perpetuity, which notably deviated from the impermanence of burial "privileges" in many church graveyards. At Mount Auburn, once a lot was occupied by burials, it would pass intact to the heirs of the original proprietor unless unused space was reconveyed to the cemetery corporation. Proprietors were not allowed to sell burial rights or subdivide lots, which prevented financial speculation within the new enterprise. Professor Edward North of Clinton, New York, later commented on this concept of permanency within the country's rural cemeteries in the *Horticulturist*: "In this age of sudden changes, revolutions, and runnings to and fro, when household altars are set up to-day and deserted to-morrow, when a church is consecrated this year for sacred worship, and next year sold for a theatre or a barn; when even religious principles are pulled up every now and then, 'as children pull up the shrubs they have planted, to see if they have taken root,' it is pleasant to be permitted to organize cemeteries that carry the elements of permanency."[48]

The lot owners were also granted the right to embellish their own real estate. They were allowed to erect "tombs, cenotaphs, and other monuments" on their parcels. They were also conferred the right to cultivate trees, shrubs, and plants within their lots. (However, if any of those trees or shrubs became detrimental to adjacent lots or avenues, the corporation had the right to remove them. The proprietors, on the other hand, were not allowed to remove any trees without the consent of the corporation.) Proprietors were also conferred the right to enclose their parcels. In fact, in the early years of the corporation, proprietors were encouraged to do so. To delineate the boundaries of the lot, the corporation required that the proprietor, in the very least, place "suitable land-marks of stone or iron"

30. The Samuel Appleton family lot featuring a marble temple made in Italy, ca. 1838, and an elegant enclosure. Engraving by J. Smillie, from *Mount Auburn Illustrated*, 1847, Danylchak collection.

at the lot corners and inscribe the lot number upon the premises. Early regulations allowed lot owners to also erect "a wall or fence, not exceeding one foot in thickness . . . on the adjoining land of the corporation exterior to the said lot."[49] The types of enclosures that were subsequently constructed ranged from simple granite posts with chains or bars between them to elaborate wrought or cast iron creations, which often incorporated funerary symbols like urns, inverted torches, willow trees, and oak leaves. The corporation did require approval of fence design and materials by the trustees; wooden fences were prohibited. During the first decade of Mount Auburn's existence, about forty new fences were erected each year to enclose family lots. The average rose to seventy-one per year from 1842 to 1857.[50]

Although the cemetery was initially only divided into family plots, the cemetery corporation later made provisions for single interments. After all, common laborers and even some skilled craftsman could not afford the original cost for a family lot. So, a public lot was established to accommodate 160 permanent single graves at $10 apiece. Owners of these lots, however, were not members of the corporation and, therefore, had no voice in the decisions of the organization. Moreover, monuments and fences were not allowed in this section. In reaction to this arrangement, the Scot's Charitable Society, one of the oldest charitable organizations in the country, purchased a lot for the

burial of its own members in 1841. Although group lots later proliferated in other rural cemeteries, the Scot's Charitable Society lot was one of the few established at Mount Auburn, which continued to favor burial as a family unit.

As a nonprofit organization, Mount Auburn's corporation also set a significant precedent for future rural cemeteries. The corporation was structured so that the private funds secured from the sale of burial lots would be used first to pay off the purchase price of the land and to cover the annual operating expenses of the corporation. Any remaining funds would then be used exclusively for the "preservation, repair, ornament, and permanent improvement" of the grounds. No individual proprietor or trustee of the corporation would receive any monetary benefit. Later in 1857, the trustees adopted a plan to create a permanent fund for the maintenance and preservation of the cemetery. They agreed to put aside one-fifth of the proceeds from new lot deeds and any interest on that money to accumulate $150,000. Once that target was reached, then additional accrued interest on the fund could be used to help defray the costs of operating the cemetery and repairing the grounds. By this time, the need for such a fund had become particularly acute as maintenance needs had become more labor-intensive over time.

The fact that no individual proprietors would benefit financially from their affiliation with the cemetery helped win widespread support for the endeavor. As Judge Story explained in his 1834 report, the cemetery was set up so that no individual "has any private interest in the establishment beyond what he acquires as the proprietor of a lot in the Cemetery."[51] Many subsequent large-scale cemeteries in Europe, including Kensal Green and Highgate in England, were structured differently—as private stock companies, which paid dividends to investors. However, in the United States, the not-for-profit model dominated. When Green-Wood Cemetery was first established in Brooklyn, New York, as a private stock company, it failed to gain support; only after it amended its charter to become a nonprofit did the venture gain momentum.

From the beginning, Mount Auburn's founders intended to embellish the grounds with picturesque structures drawing inspiration from English landscape gardens, which were captivatingly punctuated by temples, chapels, and gateways. Mount Auburn's first monumental structure was a gateway that contrasted decidedly from the simple entrances to urban burial grounds. In fact, it was even more elaborate than the entrance gateway at Père Lachaise. It set the expectation that Mount Auburn would be a "place of great civic and cultural importance."[52] Once the cemetery corporation had the financial means to do so, it added additional architectural ornamentation to the landscape to enrich its romantic tableau.

In 1832, Jacob Bigelow designed the monumental Egyptian Revival gateway to the grounds. It was first built of wood, painted to look like granite. It was replaced about ten years later by one constructed of Quincy granite when money became available for the upgrade. Bigelow testified that the "outline of the gate" was inspired by "some of the best examples in Denderah and Karnac," sites of two famous temple complexes in Egypt.[53] The structure rises twenty-five feet high at the center where a ten-foot-wide entrance is framed by massive four-foot-square piers. Overhead, the cornice features Egyptian-inspired motifs, including a winged globe and lotus flowers. This visually dominant central section is flanked by lodges for a porter and superintendent, which stretch the structure to a length of sixty feet. Bigelow later reported that the "size of the stones, and the solidity of the structure, entitle it to a stability of a thousand years."[54] Over the entryway on the structure's front façade, the following inscription appears:

THEN SHALL THE DUST RETURN
TO THE EARTH AS IT WAS;
AND THE SPIRIT SHALL RETURN
UNTO GOD WHO GAVE IT. (Ecclesiastes 12:7)

Surprisingly, Christian messages often intermingled seamlessly with Egyptian Revival architecture during the rise of the rural cemetery. After Napoleon

31. The monumental Egyptian Revival gateway at the entrance to Mount Auburn Cemetery. From *Gleason's Pictorial Drawing-Room Companion*, Boston, 1853, Danylchak collection.

32. Detail of Egyptian Revival gate at Mount Auburn Cemetery. Photograph by Jack E. Boucher, ca. 1989, Historic American Building Survey, MASS,9-CAMB,70–5, Library of Congress Prints and Photographs Division.

Bonaparte invaded Egypt in 1798, a fascination with the Egyptian civilization spread to Europe and eventually to the United States. Artists and scientists who accompanied Napoleon's troops documented the exotic architecture and culture they found there. Two subsequent publications—Vivant Denon's *Voyage dans la Basse et la Haute Egypt* (1802) and the Institute of Egypt's *Description de l'Egypte* (1809)—fueled Eygptomania, including the spread of Egyptian Revival architecture, which was considered particularly appropriate for cemetery settings.

Mount Auburn's substantial entranceway, along with fencing and the presence of salaried staff, helped assure cemetery proprietors that the graves of their loved ones were safe from possible desecration. Mount Auburn set the precedent for perimeter fencing preventing people from entering the grounds outside of the public hours of operation. In contrast, town graveyards had only been surrounded by low fencing or walls, if anything, as a way to keep out grazing animals. But grave robbing had become a legitimate fear for families in the early nineteenth century as so-called "resurrectionists" supplied an ever-more demanding medical profession with cadavers for dissection and

study. Soon after its establishment, Mount Auburn was enclosed with a seven-foot-high fence of rough sawed pales. In 1844, an iron fence was added along the public road from Cambridge, on each side of the gateway structure. By the early 1850s, a more substantial timber fence replaced the earlier fencing along the less visible southern and western boundaries of the site. Meanwhile, iron fencing was added along Coolidge Avenue by 1851, which allowed views into the cemetery from this major roadway.

Bigelow, in partnership with architect Gridley J. F. Bryant (1816–1899), also designed the sixty-two-foot-high Washington Tower, a memorial paying tribute to the country's first president. The structure had been envisioned for the highest elevation of the cemetery since its founding. Towers were, in fact, a type of architectural landmark common in English landscape gardens. They often assumed Gothic Revival ornamentation. Stourhead in Wiltshire, for example, featured a 160-foot "Gothick" tower designed in 1762 by architect Henry Flitcroft (1697–1769). Bigelow's tower, completed in 1854 of Quincy granite atop Mount Auburn, was also modeled on "the general plan of some of the round towers of the feudal ages."[55] It includes

33. A glimpse of Bigelow's Washington Tower. Photograph ca. 1890–1900, Detroit Publishing Company Photograph Collection, Library of Congress Prints and Photographs Division.

prominent battlements and Gothic windows. Meanwhile, on the interior, a stone staircase spirals to the top where visitors can glimpse panoramic views of the cemetery and the surrounding countryside. More than a decade before it was even constructed, an 1843 guidebook to the cemetery celebrated the views the tower would afford:

> From the proposed tower, may be seen the city looming in the east, with its ten thousand buildings and its numerous elevated spires, steeples and eminences, its shipping and its railways to every section of the country; to the right of which, in a south-east direction, Roxbury and Dorchester with many country seats, beautiful gardens, with the blue hills of Milton in the back ground; in the south, Brookline and Brighton, with their numerous grazing hills and well cultivated farms, affording a rich treat to the eye: in the south-west, the beautiful villages of Watertown and Waltham, with the meandering of the crooked Charles, and many water mills on their southern boundary line; West Cambridge with famous Lexington on the north-west; Somerville and Medford in the north, Charlestown with its battle monument 220 feet high, its Navy yard and Dry Dock, costing one and a half millions of dollars; Malden on the north-east-by-north, and Chelsea and Lynn on the north-east, bounded by the waters of Massachusetts Bay, whose surface is dotted with the heads of many green islands and made brilliant with numerous craft, plying their sails or steam, for reaching adjacent or distant places.[56]

The inclusion of temples, pavilions, and towers atop mounts in English Picturesque gardens was intended to encourage visitors to pause and contemplate the "wide horizons, panoramic vistas, and broad rivers" which were "emblematic of infinity and the divine."[57] Mount Auburn's tower was intended to inspire similar

34. View of the front elevation of Bigelow Chapel at Mount Auburn Cemetery. Photograph by Jack E. Boucher, ca. 1989, Historic American Building Survey, MASS,9-CAMB,70-A-1, Library of Congress Prints and Photographs Division.

lingering and reflection in its visitors. The tower could also be seen from miles away allowing the cemetery to be identified from a distance, thus visually and symbolically elevating Mount Auburn's standing within the community.

Although the cemetery was established by a secular organization, its founders intended to add a chapel for funeral services to the grounds from the beginning. The Bigelow Chapel was built in 1846 of hammered Quincy granite in the Gothic Revival style, which was deemed supremely suitable for rural environments by American tastemaker Andrew Jackson Downing. The chapel was built using plans rendered by Bigelow, who later recounted in his *History of Mt. Auburn Cemetery* that his own plan was chosen in a blind competition against half a dozen plans from the principal architects of Boston. With the names of the entrants concealed, all the trustees, except one, chose his proposal. He further reported that the lone dissident subsequently changed his vote thus making the decision unanimous. Unfortunately, the first construction deviated from the building specifications, which caused the building to leak and become unstable. In the mid-1850s, it was rebuilt on essentially the same plan with more substantial stones.

Mount Auburn's founders envisioned creating a place of reflective commemoration where notable individuals would be honored for their accomplishments through distinctive monuments and illuminating inscriptions. Upon the cemetery's dedication, Judge Story asked the gathered crowd, "Who, that has stood by the tomb of Washington on the quiet Potomac, has not felt his heart more pure, his wishes more aspiring, his gratitude more warm, and his love of country touched by a holier flame?"[58] He reasoned that at Mount Auburn, too, "even a cenotaph to the memory of a man" could convey his enduring excellence through the ages. Meanwhile, Bigelow not only supported monuments celebrating the heroes of the community, region, and nation but he also encouraged "developing a cult of ancestors within each family."[59] Ultimately, both private funerary monuments and civic memorials became part of the Mount Auburn landscape.

In 1847, a monument to Nathaniel Bowditch (1773–1838), a self-taught astronomer and mathematician and father of modern maritime navigation, was raised by public subscription and created by British-American sculptor Robert Ball Hughes (1806–1868).

35. View of the Bowditch Monument at Mount Auburn Cemetery. From Gleason's *Pictorial Drawing-Room Companion*, Boston, 1853, Danylchak collection.

The life-size bronze statue was the first of its kind cast in the United States. Both the monument itself and its honoree "represented the latest advances in American industry and art."[60] It was sited prominently on elevated terrain along Central Avenue, positioned to greet and instruct incoming visitors. In fact, it was positioned next to another monument prompting consideration of America's seafaring history and accomplishments. In the 1840s, officers and members of the scientific corps of the US Exploring Expedition erected the Naval Monument in memory of their members who died in the South Pacific in 1839 and 1840. The twenty-foot cenotaph proclaimed the men heroes who promoted the worthy causes of science and philanthropy. In commemorating these maritime heroes, Mount Auburn was emulating famous landscape garden precedents. Both Stowe in England and Méréville in France, for instance, had incorporated cenotaphs dedicated to "the Great Ocean's Greatest Explorer," Capt. James Cook (1728–1779).[61]

Meanwhile, the Bigelow Chapel was built in part as a depository for works of sculpture in memory of honored dead that needed protection from the elements. In 1854, Bigelow submitted a report to the trustees that drew attention to the fact that commemorative sculpture was not uncommon in chapels and churches in Europe but was only occasionally seen in the United States. Bigelow reported that very few deserving Americans had such memorials erected in their honor in the young nation. He argued, however, that there were distinguished men in American history of "high intellect, indomitable courage, and unquestioned patriotism,—such qualities as civilized nations, in all ages, have been prompt to recognize and commemorate by lasting memorials."[62] Since Mount Auburn Cemetery had the financial resources to do so, it was fitting, Bigelow said, for the cemetery to erect such "forms of grateful remembrance of the dead" and set a powerful example for other rural cemeteries that had imitated Mount Auburn's model. Later that year, the trustees approved the expenditure of $15,000 for the commission of memorials honoring individuals important in American history. Ultimately, the chapel's niches exhibited statues of figures representing four important periods of Massachusetts history. John Winthrop (1588–1649) represented the early settlement of the colony; James Otis Jr. (1725–1783) represented the first resistance to British policy in the colonies; John Adams (1735–1826) represented the era of Revolution and the adoption of the Constitution; and Judge Joseph Story represented the peaceful era associated with the rule of law within the new nation. The cemetery became a history museum, of sorts, where visitors could learn about the contributions of those influential in the annals of the young Republic.

As a result of their encouragement of both striking civic monuments and elegant grave markers, Mount Auburn and its imitators "supplied a great impetus to the development of sculpture in America."[63] Historian

Elise Madeleine Ciregna has argued that America's rural cemeteries actually played "a crucial role in helping the first generations of native sculptors develop successful careers."[64] At Mount Auburn, one of the early figural sculptures to capture the public's admiration was *The Binney Child* monument created by Henry Dexter (1806–1876) in 1840. With its success, Dexter's stock rose and he was subsequently hired for two hundred known commissions. Meanwhile, deserving American sculptors were chosen for the statuary commissions for the Bigelow Chapel. Richard S. Greenough (1819–1904) was commissioned for the sculpture of John Winthrop. Thomas Crawford (1814–1857) was hired for the statue of James Otis Jr. And Randolph Rogers (1825–1892) was engaged for the sculpture of John Adams. After these commissions, the careers of Greenough and Rogers particularly thrived and they became "celebrated artists in their time."[65]

Before there were public art museums in America, Mount Auburn served as an extensive exhibit space where sculptural works were displayed for the public to admire. (Prior to the establishment of rural cemeteries, it was generally only the wealthiest class of Americans—those who had been on the Grand Tour of Europe—who had any exposure to academic sculpture.) Although the Bigelow Chapel eventually provided space for some celebrated works, most of Mount

36. *American Sphinx* (1872) by American sculptor Martin Milmore. Milmore was commissioned by Jacob Bigelow to create the monument to honor the Union dead. Photograph ca. 1890–1901, Detroit Publishing Company Photograph Collection, Library of Congress Prints and Photographs Division.

Auburn's art was exhibited in an "open-air gallery." By 1838, Mount Auburn already counted 125 monuments. Through the 1840s, most of the proprietors chose simple neoclassical monuments for their family plots, which were generally displayed within a niche of surrounding trees.

Mount Auburn was also the first large-scale designed landscape open to the public in the country and as such became an attraction for local, national, and even international visitors. Dearborn had anticipated that the site would become a place of "healthful, refreshing and agreeable resort, from early spring until the close of autumn."[66] For Bostonians, there were few park-like settings at the time to seek quiet refuge from the urban streetscape and frenzy of daily life. Mount Auburn quickly became an exceedingly popular place to commune with nature, to stroll along meandering pathways beneath a canopy of trees. Mount Auburn also became a celebrated place to contemplate and cultivate spirituality and virtue. It was acknowledged as a "school both of religion and philosophy."[67] Naturalist, poet, and Mount Auburn commentator Wilson Flagg (1805–1884) noted that visitors would resort to the consecrated grounds just as they would "attend service in the house of God, to indulge in serious meditation, and to ponder on those themes which are neglected by the multitude, during the hurry of business or in the idle whirl of pleasure."[68]

Improving transportation systems, meanwhile, made the retreat increasingly accessible to visitors. By the late 1830s, people could reach the cemetery on Cambridge's horse-drawn omnibuses. In 1847, the Fitchburg Railroad established a station outside the cemetery, providing access to and from the cemetery from the west. In 1856, the Cambridge Horse Railroad, a horse-drawn street railway system, extended service from Boston's Bowdoin Square through Cambridge to Mount Auburn's gateway, greatly facilitating public access. Cars ran every fifteen minutes and fares were low.

Guidebooks to the cemetery drew the attention of visitors to the most important or interesting sites within the grounds and promoted Mount Auburn as a repository of history and school of virtue. The cemetery's first published visitor's guide dated to 1839, *The Picturesque Pocket Companion and Visitor's Guide through Mount Auburn*. It included a history of the institution itself along with the text of Joseph Story's dedicatory address. It also included over fifty engravings of noteworthy monuments, accompanied by descriptions of where the visitor could find them. The monument descriptions often offered biographical information about the person commemorated, emphasizing their virtues and contributions to society. In 1850, Nathaniel Dearborn (1786–1852), a local woodcut engraver and publisher, produced *Dearborn's Guide*

37. Visitors along Pilgrim Path at Mount Auburn Cemetery. Engraving by J. Smillie, from *Mount Auburn Illustrated*, 1847, Danylchak collection.

Through Mount Auburn . . . for the Benefit of Strangers, Desirous of Seeing the Clusters of Monuments with the Least Trouble. In his volume, Dearborn curated a collection of epitaphs from Mount Auburn's monuments that promoted noble qualities like faith, philanthropy, diligence, humility, and moderation. The compact book was published annually, with at least fifty-four engravings of monuments, through the 1860s and sold for twenty cents.

Regional and national newspapers, local and national guidebooks, and published travel accounts also disseminated Mount Auburn's appeal to potential visitors, both across the United States and abroad.

Carl David Arfwedson in *The United States and Canada, in 1832, 1833 and 1834*, stated:

> I one day visited the new cemetery, planned in imitation of that of Père la Chaise at Paris, distant about four miles from Boston. It is but lately commenced, but shows already what it is likely to be. Situated on Mount Auburn, an eminence of which it bears the name, this cemetery offers to the view a variety of objects seldom witnessed in similar places.... Each step we advance in this receptacle of the departed reminds us of our equals, slumbering in repose in their silent dwellings. Above their quarters we see names written in gold. Is there no intercourse between those who inhabit this mortal city? Silence itself!—is it not a painful language? Look at these weeping willows, these cypresses—what do they not announce? And this flower, but lately planted, spreading its fragrance through the air, this rattling and crystal-like stream, this plaintive tone of a solitary bird—is not all this a language that speaks to the heart? Death inspires here no dread: on the contrary, a glance at this beautiful cemetery almost excites a wish to die.[69]

In an 1838 letter to the editor of the *United States Gazette*, E. C. Wines wrote, "It embraces an accumulation and variety of classical beauties, and presents scenes of Arcadian loveliness, both within its own enclosures and in the charming vistas you catch in every direction through the openings in its deep and overhanging groves, which certainly no spot in America can match, and which probably few places can equal in any part of the world. One can scarcely resist the impression in walking over this ground, that it was expressly designed by the Creator, for its present use."[70]

In 1841, James Silk Buckingham, in *America: Historical, Statistical & Descriptive*, maintained, "The most interesting spot, however, in all the environs of Boston, varied and beautiful as they are beyond that of any other city we had yet seen in the United States, is the Cemetery at Mount Auburn. We visited this spot, in company with one of its proprietors, on a beautiful day towards the close of September, while the rich foliage of autumn still clothed its woods, and when everything in nature was favourable to our seeing it to the greatest advantage; but, highly as our expectations had been raised by all that we had heard of this Cemetery, they were fully realized."[71]

In his 1849 *Gazetteer of Massachusetts*, John A. Hayward said of Mount Auburn: "Numerous monuments of exquisite workmanship are already erected, which add, if possible, to the melancholy grandeur of the scene. It is an enchanting spot;—a magnificent resting-place of the dead."[72] In that same year, Charles Lyell noted in his travel journal: "Oct. 29.—Went to Cambridge to visit the cemetery of Mount Auburn, where a large extent of wild, unreclaimed, hilly ground, covered with oak and pine, has been enclosed for a public burial-place. From the highest eminence there is a fine view of the surrounding country. Since I was here in 1842, a chapel has been erected of granite, in the Gothic style, and in good taste, with painted glass from Edinburgh in the windows, and a handsome entrance gate. The chapel is to serve as a Westminster Abbey, Pantheon, or Walhalla, to contain statues, busts, and monuments of distinguished men."[73]

In 1857, *Appletons' Handbook of American Travel* proclaimed: "It is the oldest and by many considered the most beautiful of American rural burying-places, embellished by landscape, and horticultural art and taste, and by a most picturesque chapel, and many elegant and costly monuments. Its walks, and lanes, and lawns make it the most delightful of all the resorts in the vicinage of the city. Cars run from the station in Bowdoin square, every 15 minutes, during the day, and until half-past eleven o'clock at night."[74] Sixteen years later J. G. Medley noted in *An Autumn Tour in the United States and Canada*, "I walked one day from Harvard to the famous cemetery at Mount Auburn, some four miles from Boston. A more lovely resting-place for the dead I never beheld, and the view of the surrounding country from the tower overlooking the cemetery, with Boston and the sea in the distance, and a charming English landscape of woods and hills around, has left me one of my pleasantest reminiscences of American scenery."[75]

With such high praise being so widely disseminated, visitors came to the cemetery in large numbers during Mount Auburn's first several decades of existence. In the beginning, anyone was allowed onto the grounds on foot, horseback, or carriage. But, it was not long before "great inconvenience was felt from the number of persons, in pursuit of pleasure, who rode or drove recklessly through the grounds to the detriment of the paths and the annoyance of other visitors."[76] As early as 1833, the trustees adopted regulations for visitors that sought to protect the cemetery grounds. Proprietors were provided preferential treatment. Proprietors, or members of their household, were the only people allowed to visit the grounds on Sundays or travel the grounds in a carriage. The following regulations were published in a guidebook to the cemetery in 1843.

REGULATIONS CONCERNING VISITORS.
The secretary will issue to each proprietor one ticket of admission into the Cemetery with a vehicle, under the following regulations—the violations of any of which, or a loan of the ticket, *involves a forfeiture of the privilege.*

No person is admitted on horseback

No vehicle is admitted unless accompanied by a proprietor or a member of his *household,* with his or her ticket.

No vehicle is to be driven in the cemetery at a rate faster than a walk.

No horse is to be fastened except at a post provided for this purpose. No horse is to be left unfastened without a keeper.

All persons are prohibited from gathering any flowers, *either wild or cultivated,* or breaking any tree, shrub or plant.

All persons are prohibited from writing upon, defacing or injuring any monument, fence, or other structure in or belonging to the cemetery.

All persons are prohibited from discharging fire-arms in the cemetery.

The gates are opened at sunrise and closed at sunset.

No money is to be paid to the porter.

No persons are admitted on *Sundays* and *Holidays,* excepting proprietors, and members of their *household,* and persons accompanying them.

The superintendent has the care of the cemetery, and is authorized to remove all who violate any of these regulations or commit trespasses. Trespassers are also liable to be fined *fifty dollars.*

Over time, Mount Auburn's landscape expanded to satisfy demand for its burial space. The original tract was enlarged by land acquisitions beginning soon after the cemetery's establishment. As Bigelow explained in his *History,* "In a year after the consecration of Mount Auburn Cemetery, the success of the enterprise being considered no longer doubtful, it was deemed desirable to secure the addition of about twenty-four acres of land."[77] Additional acquisitions were made in 1844 and 1854. In 1860 Bigelow reported that the site had increased to a little less than 130 acres. In the late nineteenth and early twentieth centuries, the corporation acquired additional adjacent parcels to the west and south, bringing the size of the modern cemetery to about 175 acres.

Expansion and Evolution
of Mount Auburn's Model

Mount Auburn Cemetery quickly captured the imagination of the country and inspired other cities to follow its pioneering model. Andrew Jackson Downing commented at mid-century that "no sooner was attention generally roused to the charms of this first American cemetery, than the idea took the public mind by storm."[78] The 1830s witnessed the development of at least ten rural cemeteries. With the exception of Akron Rural Cemetery—now Glendale—in Ohio, these earliest examples were all in the Northeast, which was far more urbanized than other parts of the country. Bangor, Maine, which aspired to challenge Boston as the industrial and shipping epicenter of New England, wanted to also match that city's cultural advancements—it established the second rural cemetery in the United States in 1834. Meanwhile, bearing enormous population pressure and attendant burial ground crises, the three largest cities in the country— New York, Baltimore, and Philadelphia—all saw rural cemeteries established on their peripheries during the decade. An 1866 history of Green-Wood Cemetery, founded in Brooklyn in 1838, emphasized the importance of Mount Auburn Cemetery in stimulating followers.

The idea of a rural cemetery in this country was first developed in Boston. Crude conceptions of such an institution may have existed elsewhere and earlier; but to Mount Auburn will ever belong the praise of having led the way in a much-needed reform. That cemetery dates from 1831, and its distinguished founder, Jacob Bigelow, still lives, and still presides over the successful institution, which has been so long the object of his care. In 1832, Henry E. Pierrepont of Brooklyn returned from a visit to the new cemetery at Cambridge, with the desire awakened that New York and Brooklyn should have a similar establishment, commensurate with their wants, and not unworthy of their greatness.[79]

Travel accounts, newspaper reports, guidebooks, and published histories of these early examples, particularly Mount Auburn and Green-Wood, proliferated and helped hasten a widespread rural cemetery movement. In its first visitor's guidebook, Mount Auburn made clear that the guide was not only for local individuals who had a kindred connection with the burial ground but that it was also for those farther afield who looked to Mount Auburn as a model and desired more information related to it. Meanwhile, between 1839 and 1866, Green-Wood Cemetery produced thirteen official publications.[80] And, in 1847, at "the pinnacle of this publishing history," both Mount Auburn and Green-Wood were featured in ornately bound, gilt-edged books, heavily illustrated with intricate line engravings of monuments and natural features.[81] With these examples of cemetery literature, and many others, Mount Auburn and Green-Wood reached beyond their immediate communities and "achieved a national significance, inspiring the construction of rural cemeteries from coast to coast and shaping the image of the modern cemetery."[82]

The 1840s saw the increasing proliferation of the new burial landscape. The South saw its first rural cemetery outside of Macon, Georgia, in 1840, and another outside of Savannah, Georgia, in 1849. However, with an economy based largely on agriculture and, therefore, fewer densely populated cities, the South established fewer large-scale examples of rural cemeteries over time than the Northeast and growing Midwest. Meanwhile, the construction of canals and the extension of railroads into the midwestern

38. View from Battle Hill at Green-Wood Cemetery with visitors in the foreground.
Engraving by J. Smillie, from *Green-Wood Illustrated*, 1847, Danylchak collection.

hinterland spurred westward migration and the exponential growth of cities in the region just as the rural cemetery model achieved widespread admiration. Rural cemeteries became a repeated feature of Ohio's settled landscape with examples created outside of Dayton (1841), Cincinnati (1844), Xenia (1845), Hamilton (1848), and Columbus (1848). Founded in 1849 in St. Louis, Missouri, Bellefontaine Cemetery became the first rural cemetery west of the Mississippi River. California did not see its first rural cemetery—Lone Mountain outside of San Francisco (1853)—until the California Gold Rush. As the West remained rather sparsely populated during the heyday of the rural cemetery movement, characteristic examples are less common in the region.

Meanwhile, back in the East, the passage of the Rural Cemetery Act by the New York Legislature in 1847 significantly fueled the creation of new large-scale cemeteries in that state. The act authorized the incorporation of cemetery associations and empowered them to purchase up to two hundred acres within their county of incorporation, to sell lots or plats within the cemetery, and to use income from those sales for the improvement or embellishment of the burial ground. It also exempted any cemetery property owned by such an association, or the individual proprietors of plots within an association's cemetery, from public taxes, rates, and assessments. Within the next few years New York saw the creation of countless rural cemeteries throughout the state including Cypress Hills in Brooklyn (1848), the Evergreens in Brooklyn (1849), Forest Lawn in Buffalo (1849), Sleepy Hollow in Tarrytown (1849), and Forest Hill in Utica (1850), just to name a few. A contemporaneous New York City law prohibiting new burials within the city limits further stimulated the establishment of rural cemeteries, particularly in Brooklyn and Queens. Brooklyn's proximity to New York City—and its sandy soil—helped fuel the founding of numerous large-scale cemeteries there making Brooklyn "the City of Cemeteries."[83]

By mid-century the rural cemetery had become a pervasively embraced landscape form. In his *History of Horticulture in America,* U. P. Hedrick remarked on the country's enthusiastic reception of the rural cemetery model: "Seldom has there been more universal acceptance of a new form of art, and seldom has progress been more rapid in making a change."[84] In 1849, Andrew Jackson Downing famously observed that not even twenty years had passed since the founding of

Mount Auburn and "at the present moment, there is scarcely a city of note in the whole country that has not its rural cemetery. The three leading cities of the north, New York, Philadelphia, and Boston, have, each of them, besides their great cemeteries,—Greenwood, Laurel Hill, and Mount Auburn,—many others of less note; but any of which would have astonished and delighted their inhabitants twenty years ago. Philadelphia has, we learn, nearly twenty rural cemeteries at the present moment,—several of them belonging to distinct societies, sects or associations, while others are open to all."[85]

Not only large cities but also small towns and villages, particularly in the Northeast, adopted the model, unmistakably displaying the cultural motivations and power of the art form. The rural cemetery was not just a burial-ground model suited to large cities grappling with health and sanitary concerns. Testifying to this fact, an 1855 history of Forest Hills Cemetery began, "Within the last twenty-five years public sentiment in this country, or in this section of the country, has made a marked and praiseworthy progress in relation to the places set apart for the burial of the dead.... The good taste and reverence for the dead which led to the establishment of Mt. Auburn, the first cemetery of the kind in the country, has extended far and wide to large towns and small hamlets." In 1857, citizens in Cambridge, New York, a small village northeast of Albany with a population of only about two thousand people with room to spare in its urban graveyards, organized a rural cemetery association and purchased fifteen acres for a new burial ground north of the village. Members of the incorporating group traveled to Albany, Philadelphia, Baltimore, Cincinnati, and Boston to tour other rural cemeteries. They then hired J. C. Sidney (1819–1881) of Philadelphia, to lay out the cemetery grounds into avenues and walks and to survey and stake out one hundred burial lots. Sidney had previously laid out Oakwood Cemetery in Troy, New York, and later designed Woodlawn Cemetery in the Bronx, New York. Although it was on a smaller scale than the country's most famous rural cemeteries, the Woodlands Cemetery in Cambridge, New York, emulated the fashionable naturalistic landscape characteristics set forth in the most significant examples.

The impact of rural cemeteries extended beyond the form given to new burial grounds. Existing burying grounds were transformed by the cultural force of the model, too. Contemporary literature urged the

TARRYTOWN CEMETERY
at Sleepy Hollow
WEST-CHESTER COUNTY
N.Y.

Mount pleasant,
October 1848

Laid out by
James E. Serrell.
City Surveyor.

Lith. of Serrell & Perkins 75 & 77 Nassau St. N.Y.

THE OLD DUTCH CHURCH

adoption of naturalistic landscape elements for all burial landscapes. For instance, after describing the landscape characteristics a rural cemetery should have, an 1855 volume titled *Practical Landscape Gardening* noted that the described features "are applicable, not only to the magnificent and expensive Cemeteries attached to larger cities, but also to the more confined village Burying-Ground, which by a tasteful arrangement of a few flowers, shrubs and trees, may be made a most beautiful place."[86] Even as early as 1841, the *North American Review* had observed the tasteful "renovation and embellishment" of existing graveyards on the model of Mount Auburn. Copp's Hill Burying Ground, which had been established in the heart of Boston in the seventeenth century, received revised treatment beginning in 1833 when city authorities appropriated fifty dollars for purchasing trees to ornament the grounds. A few years later, some of the grave stones were removed from the site so that new avenues and walks could be laid out, "thus affording opportunities for pleasant promenades."[87] Meanwhile, drawing inspiration from Mount Auburn Cemetery, architect Isaiah Rogers (1880–1869) designed a small granite Egyptian Revival–style gate for the Old Granary Burying Ground in Boston in 1840. Colonial and Federal–era burial grounds did not originally have symbolic gateways of any note, but many added the feature in response to the rural cemetery movement.

As the rural cemetery movement gained momentum, cemeteries not originally modeled after Mount Auburn often chose a naturalistic, curvilinear layout if they expanded during the latter part of the nineteenth century. The Atlanta Cemetery, for instance, was founded in 1850 outside the southeastern limits of the relatively recently settled Atlanta, Georgia. The cemetery's original six acres were laid out on a grid pattern, similar to New Haven's New Burying Ground. However, over time, as Atlanta grew, more land was added to its cemetery through a succession of seven expansions. Picturesque elements were incorporated into the successive design phases to align it more closely with the fashionable rural cemetery movement sweeping the country. In sharp contrast to its earliest

plan, the northwest portion of the cemetery, for example, included winding avenues that divided the uneven terrain into diversely shaped sections. By 1872 the cemetery had grown to its present size of eighty-eight acres and changed its name to Oakland, after the native oaks that proliferated on the site.

The rural cemetery model, as it was originally conceived, endured until after the end of the American Civil War (1865). Early rural cemetery supporters desired burial within nature. However, the long-term accumulation of monuments and plot enclosures within these burial spaces tipped the landscape balance away from nature toward art. The original rural cemetery concept, implemented over time, was unsustainable; the naturalistic landscape it intended could not be maintained. It was landscape gardener Adolph Strauch (1822–1883), working at Spring Grove Cemetery in Cincinnati, Ohio, who first introduced modified design characteristics in 1856 that sought to tip the scale back in favor of nature. As a result of Strauch's influence, the Picturesque rural cemetery evolved into what became known as the landscape lawn plan, which emulated the simple and flowing forms of the landscape style known as the Beautiful. Crown Hill Cemetery in Indianapolis, Indiana (1863), Cedar Hill Cemetery in Hartford, Connecticut (1864), and Lakewood

39. Plan and scenes from Tarrytown Cemetery at Sleepy Hollow, West-Chester County, New York, 1848, James E. Serrell, Surveyor. From the Lionel Pincus & Princess Firyal Map Division, the New York Public Library.

40. New Egyptian Revival gateway to the Granary Burying Ground. The new gateway, designed in 1840, emulated the famous and precedent-setting entrance at Mount Auburn Cemetery. From *Harper's New Monthly Magazine*, 1876, Danylchak collection.

Cemetery in Minneapolis, Minnesota (1871), implemented the revised aesthetic in their original plans. At about the same time, Graceland Cemetery in Chicago, Illinois (1860), and Woodlawn Cemetery (1863), in the Bronx, New York, used the pure rural cemetery aesthetic in their initial layouts. However, these examples adopted the modified landscape lawn approach with their expansions. While the rural cemetery model prevailed during the middle third of the nineteenth century, the landscape lawn plan became the dominant cemetery style in the last decades of the century. Spring Grove actually outpaced Mount Auburn in popularity in the 1870s to become the singular model for large-scale designed cemeteries.

At the same time that Strauch's landscape lawn plan was gaining traction, the Civil War ushered in cultural changes that affected the American attitude toward death and hastened the adoption of the modified burial ground aesthetic. Romanticism had helped shaped the American view and treatment of death in the antebellum period. Americans had embraced a close, sentimental relationship with death. However, after the bloody and brutal Civil War, Americans adopted a less romantic conception of it. The mood of the country became one of practicality and progress rather than sentimentalism and melancholy.[88] In the latter part of the century, realism and commercialism began to reshape the country's attitude toward death.[89] The landscape lawn plan, with its less dramatic, less melancholy appearance and its more efficient and business-like approach, better reflected the new era's cultural climate.

Cemetery Profiles

Mount Hope Cemetery, Bangor, Maine, 1834

With a strategic position on the navigable Penobscot River just thirty miles inland from Penobscot Bay, Bangor had become a trade and shipping hub by 1834 when the city was incorporated. Surrounded by vast forest land, Bangor also developed a significant lumber industry and became known as the "Lumber Capital of the World" by the mid-1830s. The city's leaders had visions of Bangor challenging Boston's predominance as the industrial and shipping center of New England. The emerging city also "looked to Boston for cultural standards or trends during much of its early period."[90] Boston, of course, had established the

first rural cemetery in the United States. With Mount Hope Cemetery, Bangor became home to the second.

In February 1834, the Bangor Horticultural Society was incorporated and soon sought to establish a large cemetery to venerate the dead and provide a place of rural beauty for the living. By this time, many of Bangor's old burial grounds had been abandoned; while its existing interment spaces were small, overcrowded parcels that the mayor declared had a "soul-chilling appearance."[91] Although its 1834 Act of Incorporation did not mention a cemetery, the society soon negotiated a purchase agreement for fifty acres of elevated land on the Penobscot River from Joseph Treat, a portion of which would be used for horticultural purposes and the rest for burial grounds. The society quickly reincorporated as the Mount Hope Cemetery Corporation, which secured the Treat property and set about improving the grounds according to a plan created by Charles G. Bryant (1803–1850), who was considered the first architect in Maine. On July 21, 1836, the cemetery was officially dedicated.

Bryant's original plan for the cemetery respected the dual purposes originally envisioned for the site. He reserved the highest ground for the first burial sites, which were divided into about two hundred family plots of ten to twelve gravesites each. He also planned a "Garden Lot" in the southwest portion of the site for horticultural endeavors. Over time, it became the site of a pond and burial lots improved with plantings. In 1864, the area also became the chosen location of the Soldier's Memorial, the first Civil War memorial of its kind in the country.[92] Here, a commemorative monument in the form of a dignified, twenty-foot-tall obelisk was erected at the center of a burial lot dedicated to the city's fallen soldiers. The project cost of nearly $3,500 was covered almost completely by local citizens through a subscription drive.

Over time, the 1864 Civil War burial lot proved insufficient for Maine's veterans of the conflict. As a result, in the mid-1890s the cemetery began planning for the Grand Army of the Republic lot and donated adjacent land to the Hannibal Hamlin and H. H. Beal Posts for the construction of a Grand Army of the Republic Fort. The crenellated masonry tower, which included canons and a flag, became a popular destination for visitors in the cemetery.

Even into the 1870s, the cemetery corporation continued to make picturesque improvements to its grounds. In 1871, after it expanded its land holdings,

41. Grand Army of the Republic Fort at Mount Hope Cemetery. Postcard postmarked 1911, Cothran collection.

the cemetery corporation commissioned civil engineer Charles E. Green to complete a new plan for the site. Green's plan showed Western Avenue, the main thoroughfare, lined with an allée of trees and other narrow, curving carriageways named for trees or natural features, as had been the fashionable trend in rural cemeteries. It also illustrated a pond and "numerous treed spaces" within the grounds.[93] In 1878, the cemetery corporation added another charming enhancement with the completion of a slate-roofed pavilion on a hillside ledge adjacent to a main avenue. As reported in the annual meeting minutes of the cemetery corporation, the area had been "wholly unfit for burial purposes" but now presented "a tasteful and beautiful

42. Winding drive, pond, and heavily treed areas at Mount Hope Cemetery. Stereograph by Charles L. Marston (1826–1895), undated, Danylchak collection. Stereographs became popular in the United States in the 1860s and helped fuel the popularity of photography. When viewed through a device called a stereoscope the side-by-side images on the stereocard appeared three-dimensional.

appearance, both as to the grounds and building."[94] The pavilion welcomed visitors seeking rest or shelter from sudden showers or scorching sunshine. Often disembarking from the train station across from the cemetery's Western Avenue entrance, visitors had begun flocking to the cemetery—Bangor's largest public open space—soon after it opened.

As the cemetery continued to mature, its corporation added water features and a wide variety of trees to the grounds. By the early 1900s, several ponds had been created along the stream that snaked through the northern portion of the site. The cemetery corporation also directed its attention to planting new trees, with more than one hundred specimens planted in two consecutive years to open the new century,

demonstrating that horticulture remained an important part of the cemetery endeavor.

Laurel Hill Cemetery, Philadelphia, Pennsylvania, 1836

In the midst of the Industrial Revolution, Philadelphia felt the intensifying burden of a swelling population and expanding development. Increasingly crowded graveyards stood in the path of progress and lay too close for comfort to the living. In 1835, John Jay Smith (1798–1881), a civic leader and the librarian of Philadelphia's Library Company, was compelled to find a solution to the circumstances after his own encounter with the chaotic conditions of one of the city's urban burial places. As he recounted in his diary, "In connection with the fact that on recently visiting Friends

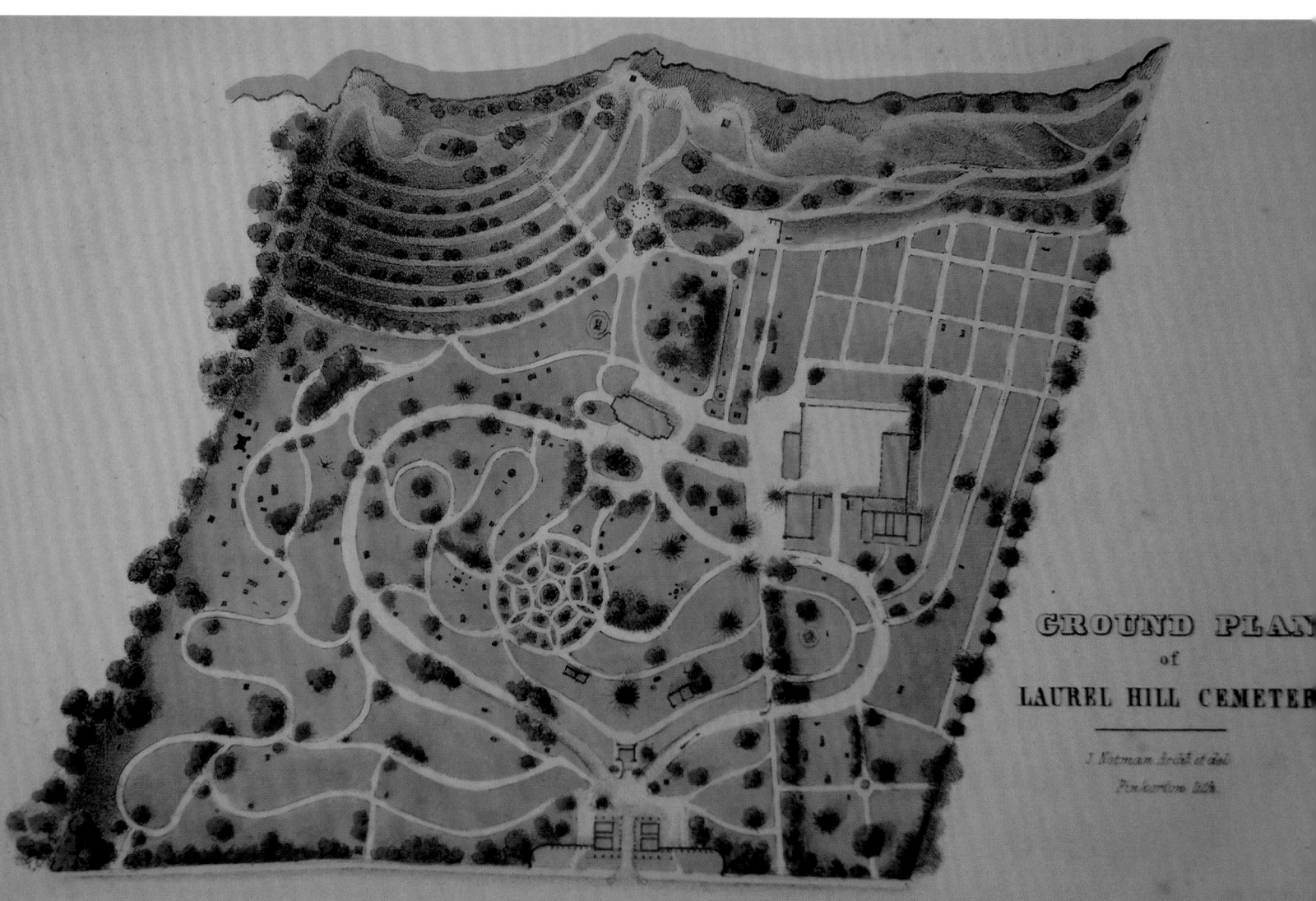

43. Ground Plan of Laurel Hill Cemetery, J. Notman, Architect. From *Guide to Laurel Hill Cemetery, near Philadelphia*, 1844. Courtesy of the Cherokee Garden Library at the Kenan Research Center at the Atlanta History Center.

THE RURAL CEMETERY MOVEMENT

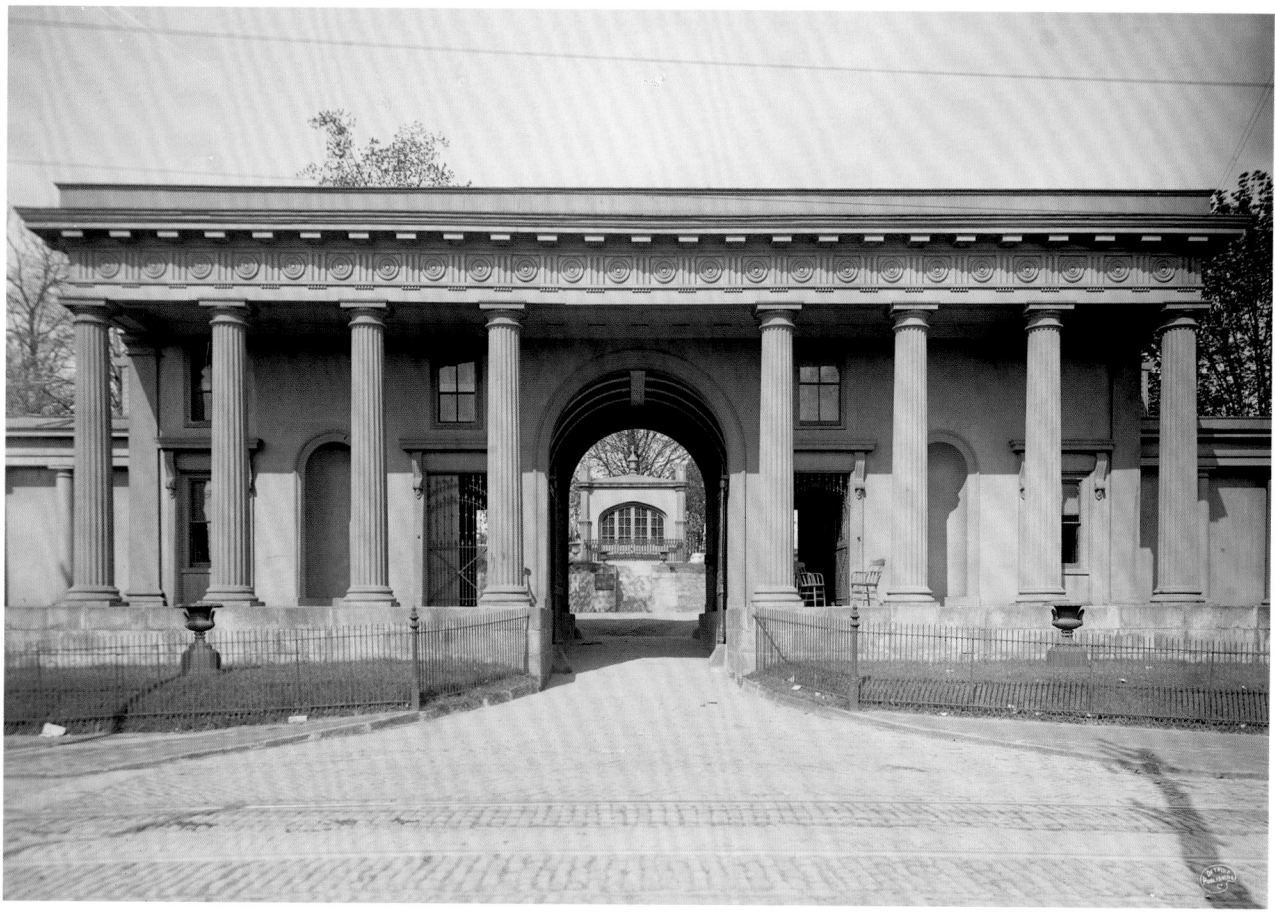

44. Entrance to Laurel Hill Cemetery. Photograph ca. 1905, Detroit Publishing Company Photograph Collection, Library of Congress Prints and Photographs Division.

gravy yard in [sic] Cherry Street I found it impossible to designate the resting place of a darling daughter, determined me to endeavor to procure for the citizens a suitable, neat and orderly location for a rural cemetery, where each individual or family might have a lot in fee simple to bury their dead."[95]

Smith subsequently gathered together "several public spirited citizens" who formed a cemetery company and established the nation's third rural cemetery in 1836 on twenty acres of land northwest of the city. The property had been the country estate of Joseph Sims and had been known as Laurel Hill. The picturesque site, on a plateau of undulating ground, rose over one hundred feet above the Schuylkill River and was about three-and-a-half miles outside the city. The *National Aegis* profiled the cemetery just two years after its founding and reported on December 12, 1838, that it "lies . . . on the romantic Schuylkill, and at a point where its banks are uncommonly bold, rocky and picturesque. The view of the river, as it is seen both above and below the burying-ground, gracefully

winding for several miles between its fertile, well cultivated, and well wooded shores, has a charming effect. In this particular it may challenge comparison with, and even assert its superiority over Mount Auburn."

Architect John Notman (1810–1865) won a design competition for the layout of the cemetery's original northern section, which was subsequently laid out according to plan by surveyor Philip M. Price over the following four years. Notman's plan was "loosely based" on the layout of Kensal Green Cemetery (1831)—London's first commercial cemetery inspired by Père Lachaise—where the site's design was arranged around an oval-shaped main drive.[96] At Laurel Hill, Notman too planned an oval-like main roadway, which encompassed a formal geometric feature, known as the Shrubbery. In the areas on the exterior of his primary drive, however, Notman planned a largely informal network of sinuous paths. Notman also incorporated existing features of the Sims estate into his plan including the carriage turn-around and the straight road that ran from Ridge Avenue to Sims's house and stables. When the house was demolished, its ashlar blocks were used to create the terraces in Section S overlooking the river. These terraces eventually became lined with above-ground mausoleums to dramatic effect.

Notman also drew upon his training as an architect to help shape the tenor of the entrance to the grounds. His design proposal for the site included plans for a massive main gatehouse, which was constructed early in the site development. The Roman Doric structure features a barrel-vaulted passageway between a gardener's lodge on one side and a porter's lodge on the other. The entrance passage was a clear and dramatic demarcation between two worlds, conducting visitors from the harried realm along Ridge Avenue into the serenity of the grounds. Notman also designed an eye-catching enclosure for the sculptural group of *Old Mortality, his Pony and of Sir Walter Scott* that appeared immediately as the visitor passed through the entrance corridor. The sculpture, fashioned by James Thom (1802–1850) and previously exhibited

in Edinburgh and London, was inspired by a scene in Scott's novel *Old Mortality* (1816). Its prominent positioning signaled the visitor's entry into an outdoor sculpture garden. In light of the circumstances that motivated the establishment of Laurel Hill Cemetery, the sculpture also signaled the cemetery company's desire to promote the idea that this new burial ground was "to be permanent."[97] As a later *Guide to Laurel Hill Cemetery* explained, "Old Mortality loved to repair defaced tombstones, so the originators of the plan of the Cemetery hope it may be the study of their successors to keep the place in perpetual repair, and to transmit it undefaced to a distant date."[98]

Smith, the cemetery's founder and president, was also an amateur horticulturalist—a fact that significantly influenced the appearance of the grounds. Smith was largely responsible for the planting scheme for the site, which substantially augmented the forest and fruit trees that were part of the Sims estate. Within a year of the establishment of the cemetery, Smith had already planted over eight hundred trees

45. View of Laurel Hill Cemetery. From *Guide to Laurel Hill Cemetery, near Philadelphia*, 1844. Courtesy of the Cherokee Garden Library at the Kenan Research Center at the Atlanta History Center.

and shrubs, including balm of Gileads, hollies, rho-dodendrons, and mountain laurels.[99] The importance placed on the cemetery plantings was underscored by the inclusion of a catalogue of the site's most "remarkable and interesting" varieties of trees, shrubs, and flowering plants—over 175 of them—in *The Guide to Laurel Hill Cemetery*.[100] In fact, the *Guide* reported that the cemetery managers sought to include "one specimen at least of every valuable tree and shrub which will bear the climate of this latitude . . . to form a species of Arboretum."[101] Meanwhile, another guidebook to the cemetery noted that after contemplating the sculptural group within the cemetery's gateway, "the visitor, looking around, will find himself in an extensive and variegated garden, redolent with flowers, and thickly planted with a luxuriant growth of trees and shrubs, through which monumental stones, obelisks, pyramids, &c., &c., are seen in all directions."[102]

Over time, the cemetery was enlarged north and south along the Schuylkill River to accommodate additional burials. In 1849, the cemetery company acquired the twenty-seven-acre estate of William Rawle, which lay separated from the northern section to the south. Steeply sloped from the southeast toward the river in its northwest corner, the southern section was laid out by civil engineer James C. Sidney and architect James P. W. Neff (1827–1855) with a combination of curving and rectilinear circulation patterns. Another ten acres was acquired from Frederick Stoever north of the original cemetery tract in 1855. Then in 1861, the rugged estate of George Pepper, which had conspicuously separated the northern and southern sections of the cemetery, became available for purchase and completed the site, which today is a National Historic Landmark.

Green-Wood Cemetery, Brooklyn, New York, 1838

The year after Mount Auburn Cemetery was established, one of Green-Wood Cemetery's future founders Henry E. Pierrepont (1808–1888) traveled to Boston to see the burial ground experiment. He returned to New York inspired to create a similar site. In 1834, while serving on a commission to lay out the streets of Brooklyn, Pierrepont recommended the acquisition of land in the Gowanus Hills for a large-scale burying ground. Then the following year, Maj. David Bates Douglass (1790–1849), a civil engineer who had surveyed New York City and its environs, advised in a public lecture that "the hills back of Brooklyn would

furnish, not only the best locality in this vicinity, but, probably, one of the finest in the world" for such a cemetery enterprise.[103] However, the cemetery proposal stalled for several years until the Depression of 1837, which substantially reduced real estate prices and created a "unique opportunity to buy land for Brooklyn's rural cemetery."[104]

In 1838, the Green-Wood Cemetery was officially incorporated by an act of the New York State Legislature and was authorized to purchase up to two hundred acres for the purpose of establishing a public burial ground in the City of Brooklyn. Douglass, with the input of Pierrepont and Judge A. G. Hammond, began to quietly conduct "a minute professional reconnaissance" to select the best possible ground for the new endeavor.[105] Ultimately, about 178 acres encompassing the Schermerhorn, Sackett, Dean, Ibbotson, and Wyckoff farms was purchased for just over $134,000.

The land chosen for Green-Wood Cemetery, on the Gowanus Heights, was "beautifully undulating and diversified, presenting continual changes of surface and scenery."[106] It included former tracts of farmland and pastureland, six ponds, and stands of both hardwood and evergreen trees. From its highest hills, the site offered panoramic vistas encompassing Jamaica Bay, New York Harbor, the East River, and the Atlantic Ocean, as well as New York City, Brooklyn, Staten Island, New Jersey, and small towns and villages in every direction. A promotional guide later noted that Green-Wood was "within sight of the thronged mart, and not three miles from [the city's] busiest haunts" but also enjoyed "perfect seclusion."[107]

Douglass subsequently surveyed the grounds and created a layout that enhanced the site's existing topographical variety. His plan produced a decidedly picturesque environment that alternated areas of spacious, sun-bathed lawns with shadowy, contemplative spaces. Formal construction began in the spring of 1839. One of the first elements added was a four-and-one-half mile-long avenue that wound its way through the most interesting sections of the site. The drive was later modified but was the basis of what became known as "The Tour," the main avenue for carriages during the first two decades of the cemetery's existence. In 1847, *Green-Wood Illustrated* provided readers and cemetery visitors with a map of the grounds that highlighted the Tour. A few years later Nehemiah Cleaveland's *Directory for Visitors* described the route at

GREEN-WOOD CEMETERY.

length and in great detail. It provided turn-by-turn directions for visitors so they could encounter the most noteworthy monuments and experience the most striking views while navigating the grounds. One of the first stops described by the *Directory* was Sylvan Water, a scenic three-acre pond surrounded on three sides by elevated ground. The guidebook noted, "The lake is beautifully hedged in by lofty trees and dense shrubbery, whose leafy coverts are tenanted by numerous and various birds. This embowered expanse, with its sweet woodland music, its flashing and murmuring *jet d'eau*, and its mirrored beauties of trees and sky, is a pleasing image of life and of repose."[108]

The *Directory* also described in detail and provided an accompanying engraving of one of the cemetery's most elaborate and celebrated individual monuments—the mausoleum of Charlotte Canda—at the intersection of the Tour and Greenbough Avenue. Charlotte was a charming socialite who died on her seventeenth birthday after having been thrown

46. (left) Map of Green-Wood Cemetery showing the route of the Tour. From *Green-Wood Illustrated*, 1847. Courtesy of the Cherokee Garden Library at the Kenan Research Center at the Atlanta History Center.

from her carriage. The concept for her richly ornamented marble monument was sketched by Charlotte herself for a beloved aunt, but appropriated by her parents for their daughter's memorial after her tragic death. The grieving mother and father asked Robert Launitz (1806–1870), a Russian-born sculptor who had immigrated to New York in 1831, to use the design to create an appropriate memorial for their daughter. Charlotte's marble monument features six rows of steps ascending to an oblong platform that stretches toward an ornate structure carved with symbolic ornaments, fleurs-de-lis, roses, lilies, acanthus leaves, and an escutcheon displaying the cypher "C.C." The structure shelters a statue of Charlotte withdrawn in a set of niches and framed by a series of Gothic arches. In marble, she dons the same party dress she wore on her fateful seventeenth birthday.

Travel guidebooks including *Appletons' Handbook of American Travel* (1857), *Morford's Short-Trip Guide to America* (1881) and *Baedeker's United States 1893* recommended the cemetery to tourists, who joined the families of the deceased in visiting "one of the most beautiful cities of the dead in America."[109] At the beginning of the 1850s, the cemetery welcomed about 100,000 visitors per year; by 1860, approximately

47. Monument to Miss Charlotte Canda. Engraving by J. Smillie, from *Green-Wood Illustrated*, 1847, Danylchak collection.

48. Visitors lounging by Silver Lake, Green-Wood Cemetery. Stereograph, undated, Cothran collection.

49. Green-Wood's grand Gothic Arch. Photograph by Erica Danylchak, 2013.

500,000 people visited the site annually.[110] One of the most famous early visitors was Fredrika Bremer, a Swedish writer who accompanied Andrew Jackson Downing to the cemetery in 1849. She recorded her impressions in a travel letter, which was later published. She noted that the cemetery was like "a young *Père la Chaise*, but on a more gigantic scale as to location and plan."[111] She further observed, "One drives as if in an extensive English park, amid hill and dale. From the highest point, Ocean Hill as it is called, one looks out to the sea—a glorious view. I should like to repose here."[112]

The extraordinary popularity of the cemetery, along with the regrading of Fifth Avenue, motivated a change in Green-Wood's main entryway from a small rustic lodge that served the keeper of the grounds to an imposing main gatehouse with symbolic stature and practical amenities. Between 1861 and 1863, a Gothic Revival—style structure, designed by Richard Upjohn (1802–1878) and his son Richard Michell Upjohn (1828–1903), was built to grace the main entrance. The design of Green-Wood's grand Gothic Arch consists of a double carriageway topped by a central 106-foot tower, which itself is flanked by flying buttresses and ninety-foot pinnacles. Each carriage opening is surmounted by an elaborately carved tympanum by sculptor John Moffitt (1837–1887) featuring scenes from the New Testament, while tracery-filled gables

reach heavenward above each scene. Asymmetrical buildings that originally housed a receiving room, offices, and restrooms flank the carriageway. These brownstone buildings are ornamented by steeply pitched, patterned slate roofs capped by delicate metal filigree along the ridgelines. Robert A. M. Stern, the dean of the Yale University School of Architecture, has identified this majestic structure as the "finest example of high Victorian Gothic Revival architecture in America."[113]

Green Mount Cemetery, Baltimore, Maryland, 1838

At a time when Baltimore was America's second-most-populated city, local tobacco merchant Samuel Walker advocated for the establishment of a rural cemetery there after visiting Mount Auburn in 1834. In 1838, the General Assembly of Maryland passed an act incorporating a new cemetery and its appointed proprietors, including Walker, subsequently purchased the former country estate of prominent merchant Robert Oliver just within the northern limits of the city. The cemetery's charter was structured to ensure financial stability and deter private profit. It was also shaped by a sense of civic responsibility prevalent during the era. The sale of lots was expected not only to cover the $65,000 cost of the land but also to generate a perpetual trust fund of $40,000. Any sums over that goal were to be divided, two-fifths for cemetery purposes, one-fifth for the schools of Baltimore, one-fifth to promote the cause of Sunday schools, and one-fifth to establish a Seamen's Home and Apprentices' Library.

Retaining the estate's name Green Mount, the cemetery encompassed sixty-eight acres of land "rolling in character and very thickly studded with shade trees and evergreens."[114] Benjamin Henry Latrobe Jr. (1806–1878), a civil engineer who had worked on the Baltimore and Ohio Railroad, was retained to lay out the site, which was described with flourish by John Pendleton Kennedy (1795–1870) during the dedication ceremonies on July 13, 1839. Kennedy, a novelist and prominent politician, pronounced:

50. Green Mount Cemetery entrance. Drawn from nature by Aug. Köllner; lithography by Deroy; printed by Cattier, ca. 1848, Library of Congress Prints and Photographs Division.

Here, within our enclosures, how aptly do these sylvan embellishments harmonize with the design of the place!—this venerable grove of ancient forest; this lawn, shaded with the choicest trees; that green meadow, where the brook creeps through the thicket begemmed with wild flowers; those embowered alleys and pathways hidden in shrubbery, and that grassy knoll studded with evergreens and sloping to the cool dell where the fountain ripples over its pebbly bed:—all hemmed in by yon natural screen of foliage which seems to separate this beautiful spot from the world and devote it to the tranquil uses to which it is now to be applied.[115]

The Proprietors of Green Mount Cemetery soon built improvements to separate the cemetery from the outside world. Not long after the dedication, an imposing stone wall, eight-and-a-half feet high, was added around the site. A massive Tudor Gothic gateway was erected in 1846. Designed by one of Baltimore's most important architects, Robert Cary Long Jr.

(1810–1849), it cost $10,500—an impressive sum at the time. Long's design for the symmetrical gateway offered a carriage entrance at its center through a Gothic arch topped by a battlemented parapet, which itself was flanked by forty-foot battlemented towers. To each side of the central passageway were pointed arch openings for pedestrians surmounted by comparable parapets. At each end of the entrance structure, small square towers with gothic arched windows of stained glass housed the cemetery offices. The gateway greeted visitors with an "impression not of magnificence, only, but also of solemnity."[116]

Robert Oliver's original home, which had been built circa 1800, stood atop a hill just within the entrance gate until at least 1848. However, between 1851 and 1856, a Connecticut sandstone chapel was built on the site, becoming the most visually prominent structure within the cemetery. It could also be seen from miles away, making it a notable visual landmark in the city. Designed by the architectural team of John Rudolph Niernsee (1814–1885) and James Crawford Neilson (1816–1900), the chapel drew inspiration

51. View of assemblage of monuments at Green Mount Cemetery. Photograph by James R. Cothran, undated.

THE RURAL CEMETERY MOVEMENT

from a monument built in Edinburgh to honor Sir Walter Scott in the early 1840s. The design for the octagonal chapel featured flying buttresses, multifoiled arch windows, stained glass, ornate detailing, and a spire rising to a height of 102 feet. The quintessentially Gothic Revival–style building cost $30,000 to build, a figure reported in an 1866 Baltimore guidebook. The money spent by the cemetery's proprietors on site enhancements certainly drew attention at the time. In 1869, *Appletons' Hand-book of American Travel* used the cost of the cemetery's grounds and improvements—a number that exceeded a quarter of a million dollars—to provoke its readers' interest.[117]

From the beginning, Green Mount served as a retreat for Baltimore's city dwellers and an attraction for visitors. People flocked to see the beautifully sculptured monuments and seek out the graves of the famous and infamous. One family plot, in particular, drew curious sightseers over time—that of John Wilkes Booth (1838–1865), the assassin of president Abraham Lincoln (1809–1865). Booth was originally buried at the Arsenal of the Navy Yard in Washington, D.C., but his mother and sister petitioned to have his body reburied in the family plot in Green Mount. The appeal was granted under the condition that the burial location never be disclosed. Although the grave is unmarked and thus protected from looters, it is likely south of the seven-foot marble shaft marking the gravesites of Booth's parents.[118] Meanwhile, the gravesites of nine governors, six mayors, fifteen Civil War generals, major philanthropists including Johns Hopkins (1795–1873), and noted artists including sculptor William Henry Rinehart (1825–1874) and poet Sidney Lanier (1842–1881) lure tourists, too. But as a centennial history of the cemetery notes, "It is probably not the assemblage of brilliant names that makes this spot in a sense the emotional center of the city."[119] Instead, it is the assemblage of memories evoked by the resting places of "a vast number of others, who did nothing spectacular, who were merely honest men and virtuous women, whose work created no flaring headlines in the newspaper, created nothing except a great and powerful city rich, not merely in money, but also in honorable tradition."[120]

Mount Hope Cemetery, Rochester, New York, 1838

Settled in 1812, Rochester grew exponentially in its first few decades of existence because of its location in a rich agricultural area with water resources to power industry and facilitate transportation. In fact, it was one of the first boom towns in the country. Even in the 1820s, Rochester faced crowded conditions in its urban graveyards, and cholera outbreaks in 1832 and 1834 hastened discussions of a solution to the growing burial crisis. In 1836, the Rochester Common Council passed a resolution to form a committee to determine the "expediency" of purchasing Silas Andrus's property on the east side of the Genesee River or any other land near the city for a burial ground. By the end of the year, Andrus's fifty-four-acre tract of land was purchased by the city for $100 per acre. It was about a mile-and-a-half south of the flourishing downtown. The new burial ground—named Mount Hope—became the first municipal rural cemetery in the country establishing a second, but less frequent, pattern of rural cemetery ownership.

Rochester's mayor, along with three aldermen and the city surveyor, formed a committee to create a plan for laying out the grounds. They first consulted Maj. David Bates Douglass who surprisingly encouraged leveling the land and removing vast numbers of trees. The committee subsequently broke with Douglass and called upon Silas Cornell (1789–1864), Rochester's city surveyor, to lay out the cemetery with respect for the natural beauty of the picturesque landscape, which had been molded into hills and valleys by glacial movement between 12,000 and 14,000 years before. One of the cemetery's main roads was positioned, for example, along a long, winding ridge that had been formed as the ice sheet receded. The Seneca Indians had also positioned a pathway along this esker's crest inspiring the name Indian Trail Avenue. The receding glaciers also left kettle holes behind, one of which became Sylvan Waters. In his dedicatory address in 1838, Rev. Pharcellus Church highlighted the varied topography that could be seen traveling on the roadways through the site: "As we slowly wind round the mount, gradually rising to its summit like life in its advancing stages, we meet abrupt declivities, deeply shaded valleys, natural arbors, towering heights with their superincumbent weight of primeval forest, narrow ridges on which you seem to poise between the deep descent of either hand, while your eye searches in vain for the bottom lands below."[121]

The primeval forest that Church referenced was populated by red, black, and white oaks as well as American beech, basswood, chestnut, sugar maple,

52. View of Rochester, New York, from Mount Hope Cemetery. Engraving published in *Picturesque America*, 1874, Danylchak collection.

white ash, and tulip trees. Even with such a rich native botanical collection, however, trees were added to the site. To celebrate the cemetery's tenth anniversary, the famous Ellwanger & Barry Nursery, located just east of the cemetery, gave fifty shade trees to Mount Hope, in part to "encourage the city to persist in its efforts to improve the already famous cemetery."[122] The specimens included European purple beech and weeping beech trees as well as Nikko firs, Caucasian spruces, and Norway maples.

Improvements to the grounds did, indeed, continue long after the dedication. The original northern entrance, for instance, was greatly enhanced with architectural embellishments and a reengineered landscape during the second half of the nineteenth century. During his tenure, George D. Stillson, a civil engineer who served as the superintendent of Mount Hope from 1865 to 1881, eliminated the marsh in the area by tunneling through the ridge that carried

Indian Trail Avenue and channeling the water into the Genesee River. This engineering feat allowed a large section near the entrance to be opened up for broad lawns, reflecting a contemporary shift in the approach to cemetery design. Strategically placed trees, in-ground burial plots, and several mausoleums also scattered the area. In 1862, a Gothic Revival–style chapel designed by the architectural firm H. Searle & Son was built in the area inside the entrance gate. In 1872, a gazebo with Moorish-style ornamentation was added as an amenity for visitors. Then in 1874, the present Romanesque Revival–style gatehouse and the accompanying stone and iron gate were designed by Andrew Jackson Warner (1833–1910), Rochester's most famous architect at the time, to replace an earlier entrance gate complex. The following year, a cast-iron Florentine fountain was installed within a circular lawn area and became a charming focal point just inside the new entrance gate.

THE RURAL CEMETERY MOVEMENT

In 1885, a *Guide for Mount Hope Cemetery* was published to direct both lot owners and "the thousands of visitors" who came to the grounds to "admire all that is grand and beautiful in nature."[123] To the west of the main historic entrance, near the Genesee, visitors could climb stone steps ascending a terraced bluff to a plateau, where they could view the river below and the city beyond. Meanwhile, to the south of the entrance, the terraced banks of Sylvan Waters invited "the tired tourists to rest awhile."[124] From Observatory Hill, visitors could obtain a birds-eye view of the cemetery's surroundings: "Broad fields, the vast nurseries, the pride of Rochester and the wonder of the world, farms yellow with golden grain, hills and valleys dotted with thriving villages, Lake Ontario, Irondequoit Bay, the Flower City, with its massive and costly buildings, broad tree-lined avenues, the extensive public buildings of the County; the glittering lines of steel with trains of cars speeding over them, form an enchanting picture."[125] The grounds undeniably offered an awe-inspiring retreat for the citizens of the city that created it.

53. Gazebo built in 1872 with Moorish-inspired ornamentation in Mount Hope Cemetery. Photograph by James R. Cothran, 2007.

54. Romanesque Revival entrance to Mount Hope Cemetery. Postcard ca. 1909, Cothran collection.

Rose Hill Cemetery, Macon, Georgia, 1840

In 1840, just seventeen short years after its city charter, Macon established Rose Hill Cemetery, likely the first rural cemetery in the South. Four years earlier, the Macon City Council feared that, even in its infancy, the city graveyard on Seventh Street would soon prove inadequate and appointed Simri Rose, Ambrose Baber, Levi Eckley, and R. W. Willis to search for a new cemetery site. The committee ultimately identified a fifty-acre tract of uneven land overlooking the Ocmulgee River about one-half mile north of the city for the new burying ground—another early example of a municipal rural cemetery.

Simri Rose (1799–1869) played a leading role not only in identifying the site but also in designing and managing its layout. Rose was a well-known horticulturist and served as the newspaper editor of the *Georgia Messenger*. He also served on the Macon City Council and had assisted James Webb in laying out the city in 1823. Rose is generally credited with personally overseeing "the clearing out and improvements" of the cemetery grounds, including the layout of drives and walkways.[126] In describing the arrangement, Rose reported, "A broad avenue from the gate terminates on a rocky bluff at the river. Carriage ways are laid out wherever necessary. One makes the entire circuit of the ground; another winds along the heads of the valleys, and presents most picturesque views. The entire length of the roads and footwalks is about 5 miles. Many of them have been constructed with great labor, being cut into steep sides of the river bank and hills, winding through every place that presents any object of attraction."[127] The City Council voiced its appreciation for Rose's many contributions by naming the cemetery after him in May of 1840 and presenting him with a free lot of his choice. Rose assumed a long affiliation with the site as its superintendent and, upon his death, became a permanent resident in a lot overlooking the Ocmulgee River.

Rose had appreciated the scenery the river offered. The river ran along the cemetery's northeastern edge for half a mile. Calling it a "prominent feature," Rose noted that its banks rose between thirty to sixty feet and were generally "rocky and precipitous."[128] Meanwhile, terraced hillsides sloped upward from the rocky

55. Modern view of the Ocmulgee River from Rose Hill Cemetery. Photograph by James R. Cothran, undated.

THE RURAL CEMETERY MOVEMENT

56. Visitors Spring at Rose Hill Cemetery. Stereograph by Henry E. Rees, 1877.
Courtesy of the Middle Georgia Archives, Washington Memorial Library, Macon, Georgia.

banks to 142 feet above the river bed at the highest point. In 1850, the Swedish writer Frederika Bremer visited the cemetery and was drawn to the water. She wrote, "I came to the banks of a river which ran in gentle windings between banks as beautiful, and as youthfully verdant as we, in our youth, imagine the Elysian Fields. On my side of the river I beheld white marble monuments glancing forth from amid the trees, speaking of the city of the dead. The trees here and there bent over the water."[129] At the end of the Civil War, a river-facing hillside was selected to bear over six hundred Confederate dead in what became known as Soldiers Square. Unfortunately, the view of the river was later marred by the intrusion of the Macon and Brunswick Railroad in the 1880s, when the company laid its tracks between the cemetery and the waterway.[130] In the twentieth century, the construction of I-16 on the opposite bank of the river further spoiled the once stunning views.

Other picturesque elements, both natural and manufactured, captured the attention of visitors. Deep, narrow dells cut across the site to the river, including one at the cemetery's center that carried a spring-fed stream toward the Ocmulgee. With its steep, heavily wooded banks, the stream was, according to Rose, "the most attractive spot for visitors."[131] To the valley, Rose added a pond of about eighty yards by twenty yards that drew water from the site's springs. Mean-

while, two rustic rock bridges provided passage across the scenic valley. To the entrance, a modest, tri-partite brick gate was constructed within the first decade of the cemetery's existence to beckon both pedestrians and carriages inside. Over time, numerous brick-enclosed terraces demarcated family burial lots, which were adorned with monuments of varied architectural forms.

Wild woodlands and manicured spaces of lawn and flowers offered striking juxtapositions to the guest. On April 17, 1853, Curtis B. Pyle, a Pennsylvania farmer and corresponding editor for a Masonic periodical, visited the "charming" site and composed his impressions. He noted that the cemetery was "shaded by a dark and somber pine-wood," yet observed that the open space was "covered with flowers."[132] He further described a "spot almost too beautiful to leave"—a cold spring of "delightful water in the heart of a wood, and where the ground was carpeted with flowers."[133] In his own description of the cemetery, Simri Rose cited the eye-catching contrast in flora at the man-made pond in the valley, which had its "banks neatly sodded with grass" and a "variety of fine roses" near it.[134] He noted, too, that several cypresses and weeping willows surrounded it.

Rose consciously used a rich botanical palette in order to create dramatic scenes such as this. He stated that it was "worthy of remark that there is scarcely a

57. Brick terraces in Rose Hill Cemetery. Photograph by James R. Cothran, undated.

tree, shrub, or wild flower, that is known in our country, that may not be found within this area of 50 acres."[135] Most notable, he said, were towering poplar, giant oaks, beech, and sycamore as well as wild honeysuckle, woodbine, and golden hypericum. Unfortunately, over time, the site lost considerable vegetation because of the demand for additional burial space. A devastating tornado in 1954 also claimed large numbers of mature trees that were never replaced. As a result, Rose Hill has undergone a "physical metamorphosis from a romantic forest to a necropolis, a transformation surely unforeseen by Simri Rose."[136]

Allegheny Cemetery, Pittsburgh, Pennsylvania, 1844

The idea for Pittsburgh's rural cemetery originated in 1834 when James Ramsey Speer (1796–1891), Stephen Colwell, Esq. (1800–1871), and John Chislett Sr. (1800–1869) sought a burial ground sufficiently large to serve the congregation of the First Presbyterian Church—the church to which they were associated. The gentlemen considered an eleven-acre site on Wylie Avenue for the church graveyard. However, news of the successful recent development of Mount Auburn Cemetery persuaded Speer to visit Boston and tour the city's newly established rural cemetery. He returned to Pittsburgh as an advocate for creating a rural cemetery to serve the citizens of both Pittsburgh and Allegheny, regardless of denomination.

A decade passed, however, before conditions compelled action. By 1844, the First Presbyterian Church, along with Trinity Episcopal Church, faced a burial crisis. An 1873 *Historical Account* of Allegheny Cemetery relayed a vivid description of the situation: "Indeed so densely populated with dead bodies had these [church burial] grounds become, that it was scarcely possible to open a new grave without desecrating the remains of some one previously interred. For more than half a century, they had been the depository of large numbers from the noted and respectable families whose names are associated with the early history of the city. They were, therefore, the object of deep interest, and the necessity for some new arrangement to remedy the increasing evil had become not only urgent but imperative."[137]

Meetings were held to discuss solutions and ultimately committees were appointed to obtain a charter of incorporation for a tax-free, nonprofit cemetery company; to identify a suitable site for the cemetery within four miles of the city that was between fifty and one hundred acres in size; and to raise money through subscriptions so that plans for development could move forward. Richard Biddle (1796–1847), a State Representative, drafted the charter, which was granted by the State of Pennsylvania on April 24, 1844.

Several rural sites were considered for the establishment of the cemetery, but ultimately the Board of Corporators purchased the one-hundred-acre farm and homestead of Col. George A. Bayard in Lawrenceville for $500,000. The farm overlooked the Allegheny River and the communities of Millvale, Etna, and Shaler Township on the opposite bank. Conveniently,

it was located within three hundred yards of the Pittsburgh and Greenburg turnpike, which would provide adequate access to the cemetery for visitors and family members of those buried there. More important, the farm site was thoroughly suitable for the development of a romantic funerary landscape as described in the 1873 account of the cemetery: "As a whole, the grounds are diversified with hill and ravine, valley, brook and lake, all so happily blended and arranged as to admit of the highest improvement, and to gratify all lovers of the beauties of nature, whether she be clothed in her summer vesture of foliage and flowers, and animated with the melody of cheerful birds, or in the snow-white winding-sheet of winter, and saddened with the moaning sounds of chilly winds passing through the leafless forest."[138]

The cemetery board chose well-known architect and original cemetery proponent John Chislett Sr. to lay out the site and serve as the cemetery's first superintendent. In addition to planning miles of winding

58. View of curvilinear road layout at Allegheny Cemetery. Photograph by James R. Cothran, undated.

59. Butler Street entrance to Allegheny Cemetery. Photograph by Joe Elliott, 2005, Historic American Landscape Survey, Pa.-3-A-3, Library of Congress Prints and Photographs Division.

gravel avenues, he also designed the Butler Street gatehouse and lodge—an English Gothic–style complex of sandstone featuring a Gothic arch and twin crenellated polygonal towers. It was completed in 1848. Then between 1870 and 1873, a two-story building featuring an eighty-foot tower was added to the complex by architect Henry Moser (1821–1908). Later, the Penn Avenue Gatehouse was added to the site. The complex, which featured a chapel and caretaker's house, was designed by the architectural firm of Macomb and Dull in the Richardsonian Romanesque style in 1887.

In addition to the development of the circuitous circulation system and the design of the Butler Street gatehouse, Chislett also oversaw the extensive planting of trees, shrubs, and ornamental flowers throughout the site with his son and assistant John Chislett Jr. (1831–1878). By 1857, over twenty thousand trees and shrubs had been added to the cemetery in addition to those planted by private lot-holders. According to the cemetery president's Report of 1857, the cultivation of flowers and flowering shrubs had been "so skillfully disposed in the various parts of the grounds, as to make the Allegheny Cemetery, in the season of their bloom, wear more the appearance of a garden of flowers than that of a somber repository of ashes of the dead."[139] Sometime prior to 1873, a small nursery "of well selected trees and shrubs suitable for ornamenting the lots"[140] was established on the grounds. The 1873 *Historical Account* of the cemetery explained, "By rendering these facilities to those who may not wish to take the trouble of procuring shrubbery elsewhere, a much greater amount is planted out than would otherwise be."[141]

Originally, Allegheny Cemetery—like most rural cemeteries—granted private lot-holders the right to erect monuments and choose lot enclosures without restriction. The eventual result was a jumble of diverse monuments and fences that began to mar the rural landscape. By 1857, eighty-five fences of stone and forty-five enclosures of stone posts with iron bars or chains had been erected. In addition, hedges enclosed thirty-five lots. In 1873, the cemetery company imposed regulations to attempt to preserve the calm, consoling environment originally envisioned. The rules restricted the height of enclosures to eighteen inches and required the manager's approval of all fences. In addition, no "offensive or improper" monuments were allowed.

In 1903, Allegheny's new superintendent William Falconer (1850–1928) took steps to further "modernize" the cemetery and create a more cohesive, graceful environment. In his first ten years at the cemetery, he removed nearly eight miles of stone and iron fences and about three-quarters of a mile of hedges. He also leveled thousands of graves and removed over a mile of cobblestone and gravel paths, seeding them into lawns. Falconer had found his inspiration in the landscape lawn plan that rose to popularity in the late nineteenth century.

Hollywood Cemetery, Richmond, Virginia, 1847

Originally named Mount Vernon Cemetery, Hollywood Cemetery was first conceived after two of Richmond's most prominent business leaders, Joshua Jefferson Fry and William Henry Haxall (1808–1888), visited Mount Auburn outside of Boston. The men returned home determined to develop a similar landscaped cemetery outside of Richmond. Richmond had experienced rapid population growth in the early nineteenth century and had suffered crowded and unsanitary burial grounds within the confines of the city. Richmond's first burial ground, the churchyard of Saint John's Episcopal Church, had reached its capacity by 1821. To alleviate these conditions, the city had established Shockoe Hill Cemetery in 1820 in the northwestern section of the city. Within thirty years it too became overcrowded with approximately 4,500 graves surrounded by increased urban development. A patchwork of other private graveyards could simply not accommodate the growing number of dead in this prosperous city. The rural cemetery model was a timely solution for Richmond's dilemma.

In 1847, Fry and Haxall, along with other investors, purchased about forty-two acres of land known as Harvie's Woods, located about a quarter mile from the western edge of the city. The selected tract possessed all of the prerequisite features necessary to create a Picturesque rural cemetery. Positioned on a steep bluff overlooking the falls of the James River, the site featured gently rolling hills, a main valley running north and south along the property's eastern edge, and stands of holly, poplar, elm, and other hardwood trees. Just prior to the cemetery's dedication in 1848, the *Richmond Enquirer* proclaimed: "Few Cemeteries possess so charming a variety as Holly-Wood—noble trees, bold rocks, dashing streams, dark and wild glens, deep vistas—such are some of the natural

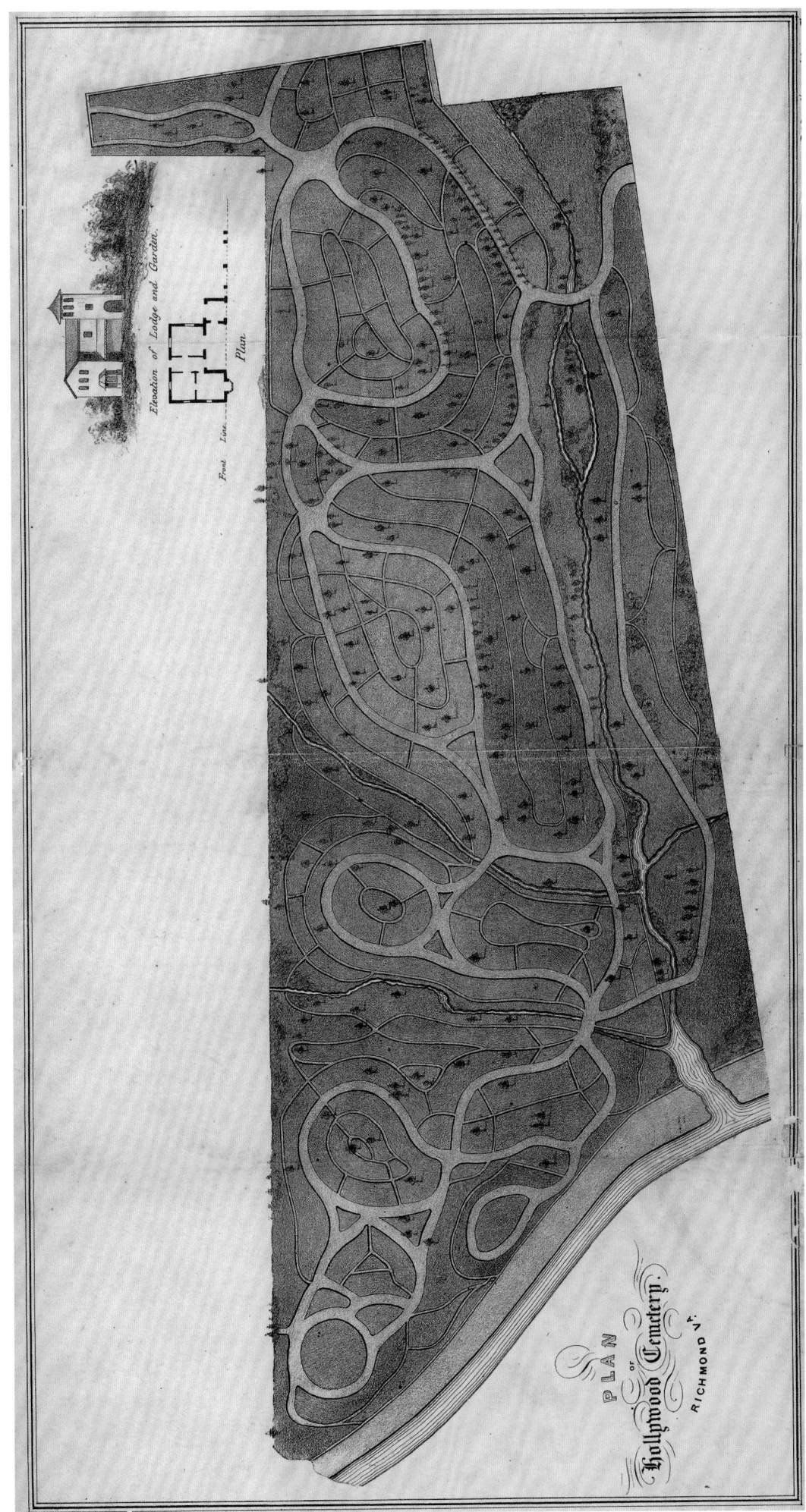

Elevation of Lodge and Garden.

Front Line. ⋯⋯⋯⋯⋯⋯⋯⋯⋯

Plan.

PLAN
OF
Hollywood Cemetery.
RICHMOND Vᵃ.

60. Plan of Hollywood Cemetery. From *Elliot & Nye's Virginia Directory*, 1852, Hibbs Collection, Valentine Richmond History Center.

characteristics, which point it out as a hallowed ground for the dead."[142] A later account heralded the striking views and vistas the site offered of the city and river below and painted the following poetic picture:

> The scene from President's Hill, in Hollywood, is one that never tires the eye, because it embraces a picture which somewhere among its lights and shadows presents features that constantly appeal to imagination and refined taste. In the great perspective which bounds the horizon the distant hills and forests take new color from the changing clouds; while nearer—almost at your feet— the James River, brawling over the rocks, and chanting its perpetual requiem to the dead who lie around, catches from the sunshine playing on its ruffled breast kaleidoscopic hues.... That, however, which attracts the attention of the visitor above all other objects as he views the broad prospect, is the city itself, with its bold yet broken outline of roofs and spires.[143]

In 1848, Hollywood's Board of Trustees chose well-known architect John Notman to design the cemetery's layout. Notman had previously won the design competition for Laurel Hill Cemetery in Philadelphia. As Laurel Hill's prestige grew, Notman was sought after to design other rural cemeteries. These commissions ultimately comprised almost half of his work as a landscape gardener.[144] For Hollywood Cemetery, Notman created a plan that enhanced the inherent picturesque qualities of the site and simultaneously provided practical solutions for issues of access, cost, and functionality. For example, Notman sited the entrance to the cemetery at the northeast corner of the property, because it provided an easy access point from the city and, according to Notman, was "the most desirable point to get the first glance of the beautiful variety of hill and valley."[145] Notman also laid out countless winding roads that created numerous burial lots fronting the thoroughfares. The design followed the contours of the existing topography and eluded the site's steepest terrain. The numerous lots fronting roadways provided opportunities to maximize profits from the sale of choice burial lots and allowed carriages easy access to most lots during funerals, which Notman felt was imperative. Meanwhile, the position of the roads greatly eliminated the cost of grading and cutting the road beds. Notman's curvilinear circulation system also revealed "charming views" at choice turns in the roadways. In addition, Notman proposed that the site's main valley, which was traversed by a wide stream and two creeks, be the chief ornamental feature of the cemetery since burials were not possible there. A report that accompanied his plan for the cemetery called for the creation of an island, in the midst of the stream, judiciously planted with magnolias and other flowering shrubs and for the embellishment of the valley with indigenous trees secured from the surrounding woods. For Notman, the valley had the potential to be "of the most beautiful description, varied and pleasing."[146] Furthermore, it was Notman who suggested that the cemetery's name be Holly-Wood because of the prevalence of holly trees on the site.

By the mid-1850s, Hollywood Cemetery was becoming a popular attraction for the public. As a result, the City of Richmond began operating an omnibus line, a precursor of the American trolley, to the cemetery every afternoon to make the grounds accessible to visitors. By the late 1860s, access was made even easier by the extension of a streetcar to the cemetery's northern gate. In 1871, the *Richmond Whig*, a local newspaper, reported that Hollywood had "become of late the favorite and almost the only resort of our people, as well as for the pleasures of pure air and refreshing scenery, as for the love that is felt for the spot where the lost ones of the family are laid."[147] The following year, Hollywood was featured in *Picturesque America*, a two-volume set of books edited by William Cullen Bryant, which described America's scenery and propelled Americans to explore the natural beauty the country offered. It provided romantic descriptions of America's most celebrated rural cemeteries including Mount Auburn, Laurel Hill, Green-Wood, and Hollywood. In regards to Hollywood Cemetery, it noted: "Far away from the noises of city-life, curtained by Nature with the luxuriant foliage of tree and flower, and presenting at every turn of hill and dell patches of beauty which art cannot improve, there is perhaps no spot in America more suggestive of the solemn associations that attach to the sacred circle of the dead ... and all around the spacious grounds shafts and cenotaphs are reared to pay the tribute of the living to those who have 'gone before.'"[148]

Monuments to the famous drew large crowds to Hollywood. In 1858, former president James Monroe was removed from a cemetery in Manhattan and reinterred in Hollywood on the hundredth anniversary of his birth, after the Virginia General Assembly

61. The dramatic, ninety-foot-high Soldiers' Monument at Hollywood Cemetery. Photograph by James R. Cothran, undated.

Confederate soldiers were buried in the Soldiers' Section of Hollywood Cemetery, and by the end of the war more than eleven thousand soldiers were interred within the cemetery's grounds.

Overwhelmed by the maintenance responsibility for so many graves, the Hollywood Cemetery Company reached out to the community for help. Within a month of the end of hostilities, Thomas Harding Ellis (1814–1898), the president of the cemetery company, encouraged Richmond's women to organize a society to preserve the graves of the Confederate dead. On May 3, 1865, two hundred women convened at a local church and formed the Hollywood Memorial Association of the Ladies of Richmond to raise money to maintain the graves of the South's fallen soldiers. In 1867, the association decided to fund the construction of a fitting memorial in the Soldiers' Section and chose a design by local engineer Charles H. Dimmock (1831–1873)—a dramatic, ninety-foot pyramid made of large granite blocks. Completed in 1869, the monument bares Latin inscriptions that translate: "In eternal memory of those who stood for God and Country." In the early 1870s, the association undertook another mission—to have the remains of all of the Confederate dead that remained at the battlefields around Gettysburg brought to Hollywood for proper burial. Ultimately, 2,935 soldiers from Gettysburg were reinterred at Hollywood Cemetery. Even as decades passed, the Civil War continued to impact Hollywood as confederate veterans were buried within the grounds well into the twentieth century. Visitors also came to find the graves of ancestors who died in the conflict and pay tribute to the dead. And to this day, "the sound of cannon and rifle salutes reverberate frequently throughout the grounds."[151]

At Hollywood, two particularly noteworthy examples of monumental sculpture relate to the Civil War. They stand over the graves of Jefferson Davis (1808–1889), former president of the Confederacy, and his daughter Varina Anne (1864–1898). In 1893, Davis was buried in Hollywood after briefly resting in Metairie Cemetery in New Orleans. Before the end of the century, the Hollywood Cemetery Company erected a bronze statue designed by sculptor George Julian Zolnay (1863–1949) that depicted a dignified Davis dressed as he was when captured by Union troops at the end of the Civil War. Zolnay, a Hungarian native who had recently immigrated to the United States, quickly gained recognition as a superior sculptor and

had convinced Monroe's descendants that he should rest in his native state. Monroe's interment "gave the cemetery lasting prestige" and persuaded Richmond's citizens to "take greater pride in" the new cemetery endeavor.[149] Monroe's gravesite also became a significant tourist attraction. In 1862, former president John Tyler was buried in Hollywood within view of Monroe's plot. Hollywood has the unusual distinction of being the only cemetery, other than Arlington, that has two U. S. presidents buried there.[150]

From June 1861 to April 1865, Richmond served as the capital of the Confederacy during the Civil War. Not only did this greatly expand the city's population but it also placed tremendous demands on the city's physical and economic resources. While Hollywood Cemetery was originally conceived as a burial ground for residents of the city, it soon had to accommodate Confederate casualties resulting from battles and skirmishes in the region. By April 30, 1862, 739

62. "Hollywood Cemetery, Richmond, Virginia—Decorating the Graves of the Rebel Soldiers, May 31, 1867." Engraving drawn by W. L. Sheppard, *Harper's Weekly*, August 17, 1867, Danylchak collection.

63. Monument of Jefferson Davis at Hollywood Cemetery with the monument to the "Daughter of the Confederacy" in the background. Photograph ca. 1905, Detroit Publishing Company Photograph Collection, Library of Congress Prints and Photographs Division.

subsequently won commissions to design busts of many famous Americans. For the cemetery company, Zolnay also completed a seven-foot Carrara marble statue of a seated angel of grief honoring Davis's daughter who was born in 1864 at the height of the Civil War and was known as the "Daughter of the Confederacy." Since its founding, Hollywood Cemetery has served the city of Richmond both as a pastoral "sleeping place" for its dead and as an important cultural institution for its citizens.

Cave Hill Cemetery, Louisville, Kentucky, 1848

In 1832, the civic leaders of Louisville purchased William Johnston's Cave Hill Farm with the expectation of building a railroad through it as well as allocating a portion of the land for a burial ground. The railroad was built elsewhere, however, and the city fathers leased part of the land to local farmers. It was not until 1846 that the city began earnestly considering the development of a cemetery on the site. Edmund Frances Lee (1811–1857), a local civil engineer, examined the tract and declared it particularly well-suited for a Picturesque rural cemetery, calling the natural scenery "bold and panoramic."[152] From the highest knoll in the cemetery, the city of Louisville could be seen in the valley of the Ohio River to the west. To the east, the view was "rewarded by towering forests of beech" and to the south by "fields fruitful with the art and industry of husbandmen."[153] The grounds themselves encompassed rolling hills and valleys as well as the eponymous cave of Cave Hill, which protected a vigorous spring that fed a branch of Beargrass Creek. The creek ran through a ravine on the site and later provided a demarcation between the older, western

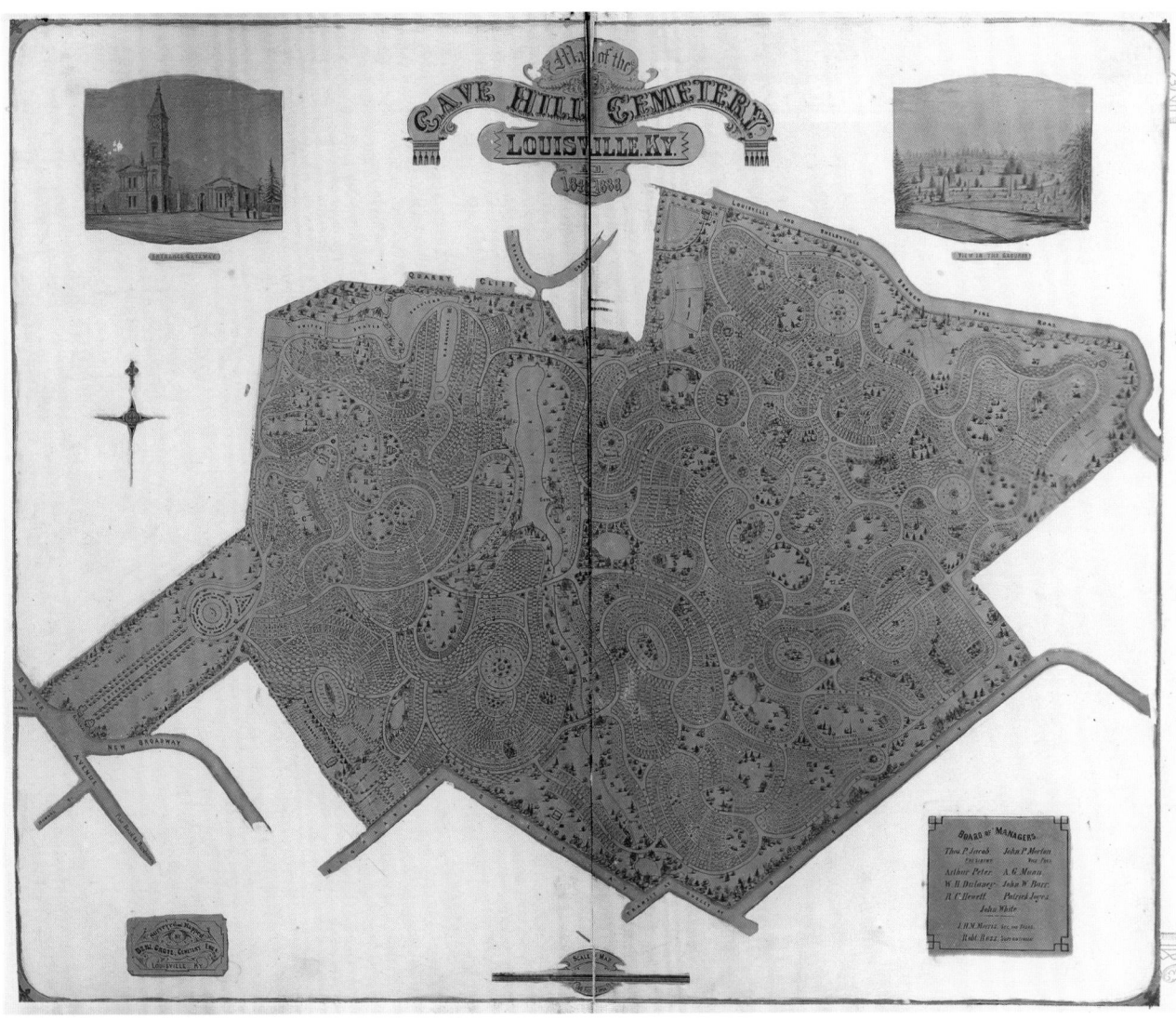

64. 1888 Map of Cave Hill Cemetery. Note the Ross-designed entrance avenue lined with trees at left.
Benjamin Grove Album, the Filson Historical Society, Louisville, Kentucky.

sections of the cemetery and the newer, eastern ones. By the late 1840s, Louisville badly needed a large-scale repository for its dead, and the City consequently deeded nearly forty-eight acres of the tract of land to the newly formed Cave Hill Cemetery Company. The company quickly purchased another twelve acres that would allow for an "imposing entrance" to the cemetery grounds.[154] Lee was commissioned to create a plan for the site, which ultimately served as the "basic pattern" for the superintendents and civil engineers who would work there throughout its history.[155]

After Cave Hill Cemetery was officially chartered in 1848, its trustees appointed David Ross as its first superintendent to oversee landscape gardening and general maintenance. Ross was a Scotsman who had studied under influential garden designer and commentator John Claudius Loudon. One of his first projects for the site was laying out an eight-hundred-foot-long avenue extending from the Louisville and Bardstown Turnpike Road (now Baxter Avenue) into the cemetery grounds. The forty-foot-wide road branched into two avenues as it advanced toward the burial sections, forming semicircular routes. A July 11, 1849 edition of the *Louisville Daily Courier* described the prominent entryway and noted that each side of the entrance road "is ornamented with evergreen shrubbery of various kinds, among which are 20 Hemlock Spruce, 20 Balsam Firs, 20 Norway Spruce, 20 upright Junipers, 20 White Pine, 20 Cedars, in all 120, planted on each side of the avenue. Intermediate between these evergreens, are 160 Dahlias of every variety, and other flowering plants." After Ross died in 1856, his brother Robert, who had been trained in the techniques of landscape gardening at the Duke of Devonshire's Chatsworth estate, was appointed to the superintendent position.

65. The impressive Renaissance Revival Baxter Avenue entrance to Cave Hill Cemetery, featuring a looming clock tower. Photograph ca. 1906, Detroit Publishing Company Photograph Collection, Library of Congress Prints and Photographs Division.

66. A picturesque lake at Cave Hill Cemetery. Postcard 1909, Danyl-chak collection.

By the close of the century, the cemetery had reached a mature stage and had grown to its present size of nearly three hundred acres. By then an impressive gateway, with a gatehouse and flanking waiting room, greeted visitors at the Baxter Avenue gate. A looming clock tower with a copy of Thorvaldsen's *Angel of the Resurrection* at its pinnacle topped the Renaissance Revival-style gatehouse, which was designed by local architect W. H. Redin.

Meanwhile, more than eight miles of stone and gravel-covered avenues and driveways twisted strategically through the grounds to offer views of stunning natural and man-made scenery and advantageously placed architectural elements. Within the confines of the cemetery, over 174,801 square feet of man-made bodies of water pleased the eye, including an old quarry site that had been added to the grounds, enlarged, and filled with water to create a picturesque lake. A series of lakes had also been produced from the creek that ran north-south through the ravine, which had been partially filled in and graded. In addition, the cemetery continued David Ross's initial practice of adding diverse trees and shrubs to the site and in time developed into an impressive arboretum. By 1895, the cemetery included twelve varieties of magnolia, three varieties of Japanese maple, a Japanese Gingko tree as well as cypress, willow, and cedar trees. Meanwhile, twelve miles of bluegrass-sodded walkways invited visitors closer to the gravesites. Over time the hillsides adjacent to the main roads filled with monuments, first of marble then of more durable granite. The *American*

Stone Trade later provided a vivid description of the monuments' layout: "Along the grassy slopes of the cemetery an effort has been made to arrange the hillside lots in symmetrical spoke-like array. Monuments on these side plots invariably face the road and rear their heights one above the other in terrace form, so that the observer sees a tier of beautiful pieces ranging to a cluster of shafts of strikingly massive monuments at the top."[156]

Forest Hills Cemetery, Boston, Massachusetts, 1848

Founded in 1848 as a municipal cemetery, Forest Hills deviated from the model of most earlier rural cemeteries, which were privately spearheaded and funded. In 1845, in the midst of experiencing an influx of immigrants from nearby Boston, the community of Roxbury incorporated as a city. The following year, its Eustis Street Burying Ground, which had operated for over two hundred years, stopped accepting burials because of its overcrowded, dilapidated condition. The city's first mayor called for the creation of a new cemetery in 1846, but the idea of establishing a rural cemetery did not advance until Henry A. S. Dearborn assumed the office of mayor the following year. Dearborn, of course, had been largely responsible for the design of Mount Auburn Cemetery just several miles away. With him leading the charge, the Roxbury City Council approved the purchase of the fifty-six acre farm of Joel Seaverns for $19,944. The rural cemetery was officially established in March of 1848 and consecrated just three months later.

67. Monuments stand in front of a rock outcropping at Forest Hills Cemetery. Photograph by James R. Cothran, 2004.

Topographically diverse, the Seaverns tract included open, cultivated acreage, stands of pine trees, small bodies of water, and glacially formed drumlins with areas of exposed Roxbury puddingstone. In his dedicatory address, Rev. George Putnam, D.D., delivered a dynamic description of the unusual characteristic: "These jagged piles of uptossed rocks record a fearful history of old convulsions and a wild war of the elements; and the mosses on their sides and the gnarled trees in their crevices are the emblems of present stability and peace."[157]

Dearborn worked with the cemetery's new superintendent Daniel Brims, a Scottish gardener, to lay out the site in the Picturesque style, creating a "piece of rural art."[158] Brims built a network of dry laid puddingstone retaining walls to create terraces for burials. Meanwhile, serpentine carriageways and footpaths were designed to highlight the most remarkable natural attractions of the landscape. At the entrance, the broad, gently curving Forest Hills Avenue provided a distinctive and dramatic transition from the secular world to the sacred space of the cemetery as it ascended from the adjacent highway to the main gate. Within the cemetery, the main avenues were named for trees—white oak, walnut, willow, and linden, for example—while the pathways were named for flowers and flowering plants—azalea, myrtle, woodbine, and violet, just to name a few. The designers also deliberately diversified the tree selection throughout the grounds. In his first year, the superintendent transplanted 10,700 seedlings to the site, including ash, oak, elm, chestnut, and walnut, and imported another twenty thousand trees from Europe, including exotic and ornamental varieties.

The cemetery continued to evolve physically in subsequent decades and made a shift operationally twenty years after its founding. During the 1850s, one of the original spring-fed ponds was enlarged to create a four-acre lake, christened Lake Hibiscus for the plants flourishing along its banks. During the same decade, the cemetery's first greenhouses were built. Then in 1865, an impressive Gothic Revival–style, tri-partite entrance gate, flanked by square gatehouses, was built at the end of Forest Hills Avenue to replace an earlier wooden gate. Designed by Brookline architect Charles W. Panter and built with rough Roxbury puddingstone and sandstone trim, the permanent gateway was topped by two conical spires and a central stone pediment. A two-story Gothic Revival gatehouse, designed by Gridley James Fox Bryant (1816–1899) and Louis P. Rogers (1838–1905), was built nearby in 1868 as the gatekeeper's residence. A Gothic Revival receiving tomb followed in 1871; the one-hundred-foot-high Gothic Revival bell tower in 1876; and the Gothic Revival Forsyth Chapel and office building in 1884. In 1868, Roxbury was annexed by the City of Boston and the cemetery afterward became a private, nonprofit corporation when the City deeded the cemetery to the Proprietors of Forest Hills for $1.00.

Over time, distinguished American sculptors including Daniel Chester French (1850–1931), Martin Milmore (1844–1883), Thomas Ball (1819–1911), and Harriet Hosmer (1830–1908) contributed to the cemetery's open air gallery. In fact, Forest Hills exhibits six original works by French—more than any other rural cemetery—including his acclaimed *Death and the Sculptor*.[159] This high relief bronze memorial to sculptor Martin Milmore and his stone-carver brother Joseph is "widely acknowledged to be one of the finest pieces of outdoor art in the nation."[160] Dedicated in 1893, it depicts an artist chiseling a sphinx in low relief, an allusion to one of Milmore's most famous works—the *American Sphinx* (1872) at Mount Auburn Cemetery. Milmore gained widespread recognition, too, for a sculpture he created at Forest Hills Cemetery—

a bronze, seven-foot *Citizen Soldier* in the Roxbury Soldiers' lot, which was completed in 1868. Featuring the common soldier, it was one of the largest bronzes cast in the United States at the time and subsequently inspired imitators throughout the country.[161] With such an impressive collection of funerary sculpture, as well as architect-designed buildings and mausoleums, Forest Hills soon became "a widely acclaimed outdoor museum of art and architecture."[162]

Bellefontaine Cemetery, St. Louis, Missouri, 1849

The founding of Bellefontaine Cemetery in St. Louis, Missouri, was motivated by similar circumstances to those that precipitated the establishment of rural cemeteries in other cities. In the 1840s, St. Louis was experiencing rapid population growth and its existing burial grounds along Jefferson Avenue could not accommodate the need for additional burial space.

68. Daniel Chester French's acclaimed memorial to fellow sculptor Martin Milmore, *Death and the Sculptor*, at Forest Hills Cemetery. Photograph taken between 1893 and 1901, Detroit Publishing Company Photograph Collection, Library of Congress Prints and Photographs Division.

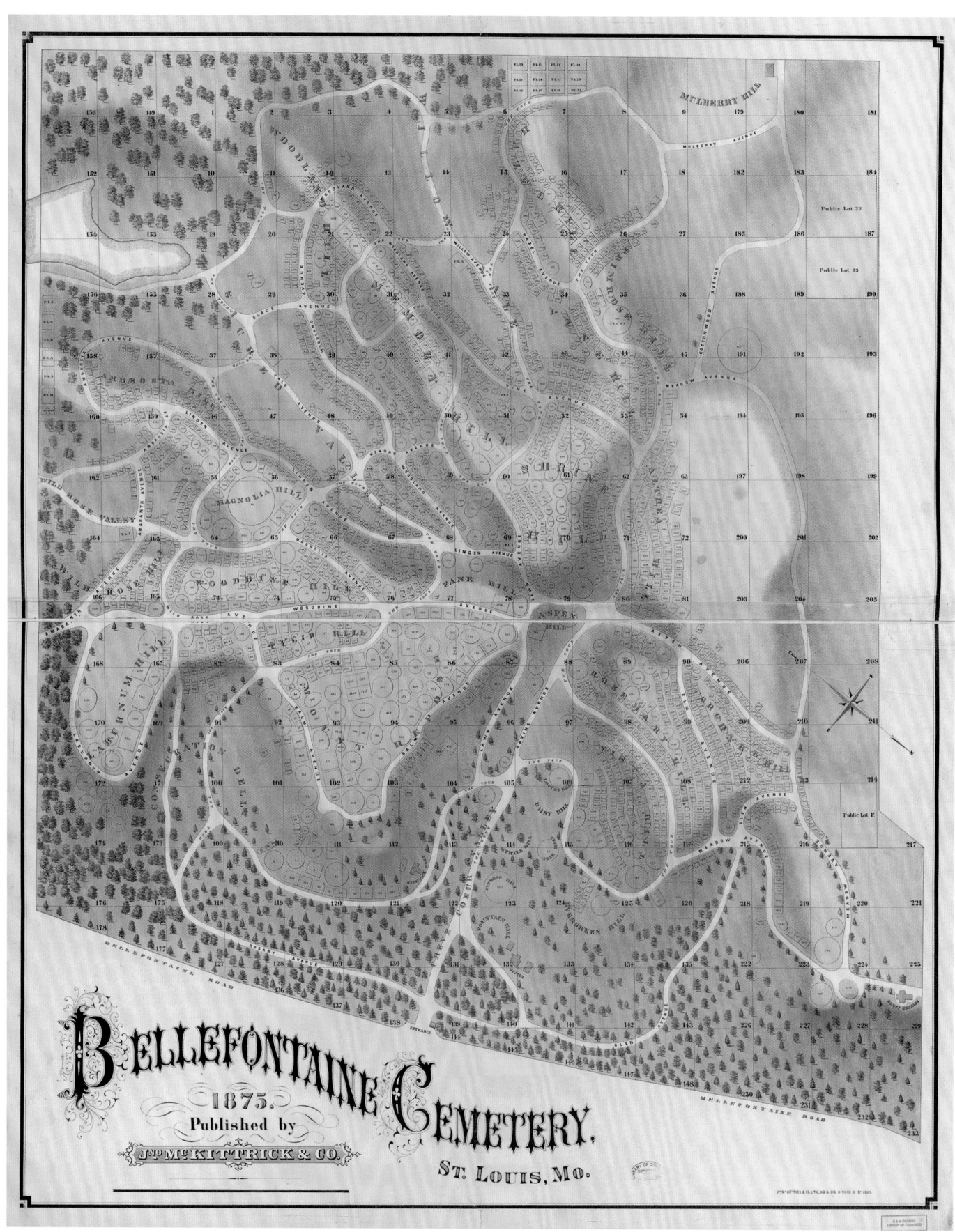

69. Map of Bellefontaine Cemetery showing its curvilinear circulation pattern and numbered burial lots. Published by Jno. McKittrick & Co., 1875, Library of Congress Geography and Map Division.

These sites were also directly in the path of the city's westward expansion and pressure mounted to remove the burial grounds entirely. The establishment of Bellefontaine was inspired by factors beyond these practical considerations, however. Classical scholar Rev. Truman Marcellus Post (1810–1886) later articulated the moral imperative that had influenced the cemetery's founding during its dedication ceremony on May 15, 1850:

> All of us have been pained, and some of us deeply afflicted, at the condition of some of our burial places. With graves crowded, and sometimes packed with double or treble occupancy, as though we grudged the dead room for their rest; with little embellishment, even of the simplest and rudest kind attempted, and little practicable, for want of space, lying in the midst of the dust and din of the city, if not within its corporate limits, they have seemed most unseemly, not to say repulsive places for interring or revisiting our dead. Our tastes and moral sentiments and affections are outraged in committing our loved

forms to such localities, and the whole tone of our civilization suffers also.[163]

The *Daily Missouri Republican* printed Post's address in its entirety the following day.

In 1849, William McPherson, a prominent banker, and John F. Darby (1803–1882), an attorney and former mayor of St. Louis, had organized a group of leading citizens of various religious backgrounds to secure land and establish a rural cemetery outside of the city. The group purchased 138 acres of undulating land ten miles north of downtown St. Louis. Most of the tract, which overlooked the Mississippi River, had been part of the old Hempstead family farm. It also included the family graveyard. In March, the group adopted a constitution and incorporated under the name Rural Cemetery Association. The cemetery was named Bellefontaine because it was located along an old military road that led to Fort Bellefontaine.

Only a few months after the new cemetery site was purchased, a cholera epidemic overwhelmed the city by killing more than 10 percent of its population. As a result, Bellefontaine had to accommodate the dead

70. Driveway in Bellefontaine Cemetery. Postcard postmarked 1913, Danylchak collection.

before it was formally laid out. After the outbreak finally waned, James Yeatman, a trustee of the recently formed cemetery association, traveled to New York to find a qualified landscape designer to work at Bellefontaine. He ultimately convinced Almerin Hotchkiss (1816–1903), who was working on the design and construction of Green-Wood Cemetery in Brooklyn, to come to St. Louis and serve as the first superintendent of the city's new rural cemetery. It was a position Hotchkiss would keep for the next forty-six years. During his tenure, he oversaw the construction of the entrance gate, the superintendent's cottage, the office building, a receiving tomb, and fourteen miles of roadways.

The curving avenues Hotchkiss laid out offered beautiful views of the Mississippi River and surrounding countryside. He was also mindful of the mature trees on the site and sited the roadways to save them. And he gave the avenues botanical names like Cypress, Myrtle, Red Bud, Wildwood, Wild Rose, and Woodbine. Over time, the roadways of the highest section of the cemetery became lined with mausoleums in the Egyptian, Greek, and Classical Revival styles.

The most famous mausoleum in the cemetery belongs to Charlotte Dickson Wainwright (1857–1891), who was the young wife of St. Louis millionaire brewer Ellis Wainwright (1850–1924). In 1892, Wainwright commissioned renowned architect Louis Sullivan (1856–1924) to design the tomb for his late wife. Sullivan had just completed the Wainwright Building, one of the first skyscrapers in the world. For his small-scale cemetery masterpiece, Sullivan designed a smooth, gray limestone cube topped by a simple dome and ornamented by carefully incised tulip and leaf motifs around the edges of each side of the monument and around the door frames. The Wainwright mausoleum was individually listed on the National Register of Historic Places in 1970.

71. General view from the east of the Wainwright Tomb, designed by Louis Sullivan, at Bellefontaine Cemetery. Photograph undated, Historic American Building Survey, Mo.,96-SALU,84A-7, Library of Congress Prints and Photographs Division.

Bonaventure Cemetery, Savannah, Georgia, 1849

By the mid-nineteenth century, over nine thousand graves crowded Savannah's six-acre Colonial Park burial ground. The offensive conditions of the century-old site inspired Captain Peter Wiltberger (1791–1853) to purchase Bonaventure Plantation from Josiah Tatnall III in 1846 for the establishment of a new cemetery. The *Macon Weekly Telegraph* later reported on March 28, 1876, that Wiltberger had "long associated the quiet and peace of the place, its patriarch trees, and their deep, solemn shade, its calm and seclusion, as a fit receptacle for the departed of this earth, as a resting place for the weary pilgrims of life."

In the 1750s, this land—located three miles from the city of Savannah—had been acquired by Col. John Mulryne who left a lasting impression on the landscape. He called his estate Bonaventure, from *buona ventura* meaning "good fortune," and enhanced it with the addition of a sturdy brick home and terraced gardens leading down to the Wilmington River. He also had live oaks planted every fifteen feet along the avenues throughout the estate. In 1761, Mulryne's only daughter married Josiah Tatnall I, and the Tatnall family subsequently left its own legacy on the land. A formal family cemetery was first established at Bonaventure in 1802 when the wife of Josiah Tatnall II passed away.

When Wiltberger purchased six hundred acres from the third generation Tatnall, he intended to use seventy acres adjacent to the river bluff for a public cemetery. (Although the Tatnall family plot was not part of the sale, Wiltberger agreed to maintain it.) In 1850, Wiltberger engaged James Henry Rion (1828–1886), an engineering student, to formally lay out the site, which had accepted its first burial the previous year. A copy of Rion's plan has not been found; however, he did describe the cemetery in a letter to the *Savannah Daily Republican* printed on July 25, 1849. It provided the earliest written account of the new cemetery:

> Long rows of venerable oaks meet the eye on every side, running in single lines in some places, again forming extensive avenues, beautifully arched, *a la Gothique* by the interlacing branches of the lofty trees on either side. These rows cross, not in stiff right angles, but in angles varying from the quite acute to the very obtuse. The hand of man has done this much in planting these living colonnades, and Dame Nature has not been sparing in her favours, but besides having kindly assisted in the growth of these "sturdy sons of the forest," she has richly festooned them with a magnificent drapery of moss which hangs in all possible forms, and conceals the blending of the branches of the trees that form the avenue, thus completing the arch and giving it at once a strange and enchanting appearance.

Rion not only retained these existing avenues of live oaks but he also respected the established family plot and likely hinted at the location of the Tatnall family home site in the pattern of the burial sections.

In 1853, Peter Wiltberger died and the cemetery venture was taken over by his son, William H. Wiltberger (1825–1872). Four years later the cemetery was formally established as the Evergreen Cemetery of Bonaventure. It was not until 1868, however, that the Evergreen Cemetery Company was formed as a public enterprise. In 1869, by-laws and cemetery regulations were adopted. Engineer John Postell was also engaged to design a plan for the site, which presumably built upon the layout Rion had previously created. Postell's plan indicates both linear, tree-lined allées and curved drives; a prominent roundabout; and a focal ellipse that serves as an axis for the design.

In the late nineteenth century, Bonaventure became a destination not only for locals but also for pilgrims from across the country. Again and again, travelers to Bonaventure tried to capture the mood the live oaks created. After camping in the cemetery, famous naturalist John Muir wrote, "Never since I was allowed to walk the woods have I found so impressive a company of trees as the tillandsia-draped oaks of Bonaventure."[164] On March 9, 1880, the *Worcester Daily Spy* printed "A Southern Journey" in which a travel writer painted one of the most evocative pictures of the then-famous live oaks: "The trees are magnificent, their huge arms stretch far across the wide avenues, and support the cloudy, filmy drapery that covers them like a voluminous garment, and yet seems like fog wreaths that a wind will blow away; when the breeze does come, and the millions of delicate tendrils yield to it, and wave back and forth, as if the whole forest were rocking with grief, you can't help imagining that you hear a mighty stifled moan."

72. Oak-lined avenues at Bonaventure Cemetery. Photograph ca. 1901, Detroit Publishing Company Photograph Collection, Library of Congress Prints and Photographs Division.

73. Avenue and visitors at Bonaventure Cemetery. Stereograph published by E. & H. T. Anthony & Co., ca. 1890, Danylchak collection.

In 1907, the City of Savannah purchased the Evergreen Cemetery of Bonaventure and changed its name simply to Bonaventure Cemetery. The following year, Savannah's Park and Tree Commission adopted a new plan for the site. The older sections of the grounds, from the entrance gate to the ellipse and the ellipse to the bluff, remained largely the same. However, the layout for the northernmost part of the site was revised to eliminate curving drives and to adopt a grid system of paths and burial sections. The newer southern portion mimicked this arrangement. The picturesque quality of the site, however, persisted with its variety of monumental art set amidst striking vegetation.

In the late twentieth century, the publication and immense popularity of John Berendt's *Midnight in the Garden of Good and Evil* revived fascination with the cemetery and provoked a renewed surge in visitation. In one of the book's culminating scenes the narrator accompanies voodoo priestess Minerva to Bonaventure where she converses with the dead Danny Hansford, whose murder set the novel's story in motion. In the darkness of night, the narrator describes Bonaventure as a "vast and somber place" with its "ghostly drapery of Spanish moss" echoing visitor accounts from a century before. Fans of the novel and subsequent motion picture flocked to the cemetery, many to see the statue of a young, contemplative girl depicted in a haunting photograph on the novel's cover. So many visitors came to see "Bird Girl" that the family plot it graced and those surrounding it suffered severe damage. The iconic monument was eventually removed to the Telfair Museums' Jepson Center for the Arts to protect it and Bonaventure from the throngs of visitors once again drawn to the cemetery's alluring landscape.

The Evergreens Cemetery, Brooklyn, New York, 1849

New York experienced an extraordinary influx of people in the second and third quarters of the nineteenth century, including refugees fleeing famine in Ireland and political upheaval in Central Europe. The population within the boundaries of today's New York City surged from 242,000 in 1830 to 696,000 in 1850. Twenty years later, the population totaled about 1,478,000, six times larger than it had been just forty years before. Old churchyards became distressingly overcrowded as the population swelled and the city was seized by epidemics of yellow fever, cholera, or small pox every few years. Between 1810 and 1857,

New York's death rate rose by nearly 30 percent, in large part because of these outbreaks of disease. While churchyards struggled to accept all the dead, they were often cited as the cause of the contagion. Numerous laws were enacted to attempt to solve the burial crisis including the seminal 1847 New York Rural Cemetery Act that authorized the incorporation of rural cemetery associations in the state and an 1849 Brooklyn law that banned burials in its most heavily populated wards.

In 1849, the founders of the Cemetery of the Evergreens acquired about 183 acres of age-old farmland in the Green Hills of Brooklyn straddling the boundary line between Kings and Queens Counties. History had already embedded itself in the land, which was once traversed by the Rockaway Indians and later British forces that followed the Rockaway Footpath in a maneuver to outflank George Washington's army on the eve of the Battle of Brooklyn during the American Revolution. The heavily wooded site rose over two hundred feet above the flat land between it and the ocean and offered breathtaking views of Jamaica Bay

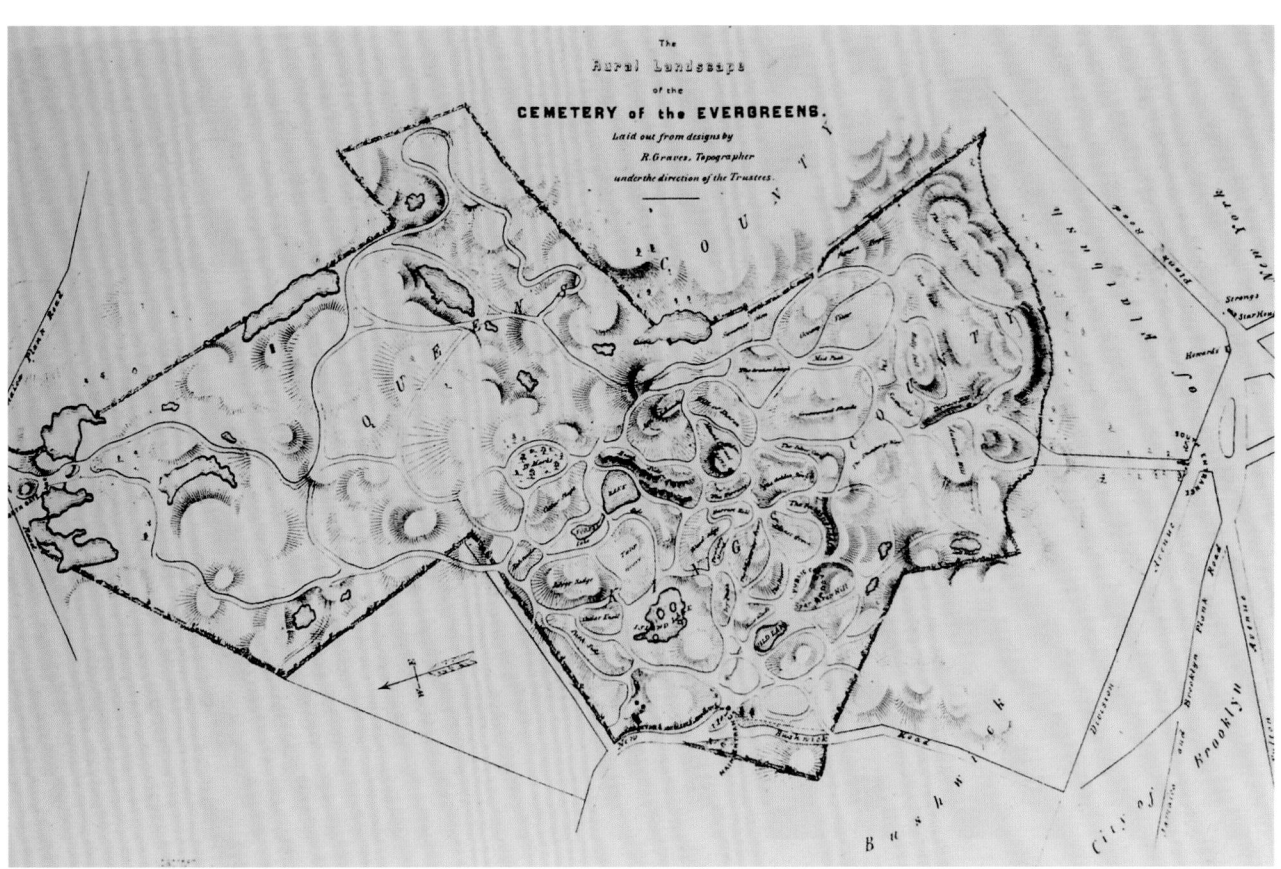

74. *The Rural Landscape of the Cemetery of the Evergreens,* 1852. The southernmost hilly section was developed first, while the northern sections were developed in the twentieth century. Courtesy of the Evergreens Cemetery.

and the Atlantic Ocean to the south and Manhattan and the East River to the north. Its richly varied terrain (particularly in the southern section that was laid out first) served as a perfect canvas for a Picturesque cemetery. Some of the diverse natural features of the site, including its variety of indigenous trees, were formally highlighted by the names assigned certain sections— Sylvan Dell, Tulip Grove, Hickory Knoll, and Greenwood Shade to cite just a few. Ironically, the Cemetery of the Evergreens initially had few evergreens within its borders. After the cemetery's establishment, one of its trustees, along with a local pastor, went to the Catskill Mountains and brought back numerous varieties of evergreen trees, including pines, furs, and spruces, to plant within the grounds. In addition to enhancing the assortment of trees throughout the landscape, the evergreens stood as symbols of eternal life.

The original board of trustees of the cemetery included Pres. Luther Bradish (1783–1863), a former lieutenant governor of New York and then-president of the New York Historical Society; Vice Pres. William Bedloe Crosby (1786–1865), one of the richest men in New York; and Vice Pres. Edward Copeland, the mayor of Brooklyn. These influential founders appointed Andrew Jackson Downing, a highly esteemed landscape commentator and gardener, as the cemetery's own "rural architect and landscape gardener." Although it is unclear whether Downing was directly responsible for the layout of the site, it was designed according to the principles he preached, including the enhancement of the natural character of the landscape with the addition of picturesque architecture and plantings. In its May 25, 1852, edition, the *Brooklyn Eagle* provided readers with a vivid portrayal of the grounds:

> At this season its hills and dells are whitened with the blossoms of the dogwood, and are colored with the thousand varieties of wild flowers now in bloom. The deep recesses of the forest

75. General view of the grounds and curvilinear drive at the Evergreens Cemetery. Photograph by Erica Danylchak, 2013.

studded with evergreens—the open glades—the numerous small sheets of water reflecting the sky, the trees, and the grass, like a mirror—the broad ocean, the bays on the one side; on the other, the sister cities of New York, Williamsburgh, and Brooklyn—beneath, the quiet plain, studded with villages—all conduce to render this the most interesting quiet resort in this vicinity.... The beauty with which the two hundred acres, of which the cemetery consists, is traversed by its many miles of broad, graveled, carriage drives, is perceptible at first glance.

The cemetery founders also commissioned well-known architect Alexander Jackson Davis (1803–1892) to design the cemetery's stone chapel, which was built in 1852. The Norman-style, cross-gabled building features a pyramidal-roofed tower with distinctive polychromatic slate shingles. The chapel was later converted into the cemetery's administration building. Davis also designed the Norman-style gatehouse, which was later torn down during the Great Depression.

Over time, the cemetery's rolling hills were adorned with Gothic, Egyptian, and Greek Revival-style monuments, many reflecting the romanticized view of death embraced during the years of the rural cemetery movement. Family plots in the cemetery also became increasingly encircled by fences and low stone walls that provided a sense of privacy and distinction from the encircling memorials. In response to the increasingly haphazard appearance of the grounds, however, the cemetery's trustees adopted regulations to try to control the proliferation of what they perceived as obstructive fences and railings. Surviving family members continued to favor such enclosures, however, until scrap metal drives encouraged the donation of fences and railings during World War II.

One of the most distinctive features of the Evergreens is the profusion of group plots dedicated to indigents, victims, and social outcasts. The first large group plot in the cemetery was dedicated by the Seamen's Cemetery Association of the Port of New York to destitute seaman who died in New York aboard ship or on shore. The Seaman's Grounds accepted sailors of diverse nationalities and was the first plot for foreign seaman in America.[165] Plots were also later dedicated for victims of the 1911 Triangle Shirtwaist fire and casualties of the 1923 Ward's Island asylum fire.

76. "Dedication of the Actors' Monument in the Cemetery of the Evergreens." Drawn by Graham and Rogers, From *Harper's Weekly*, June 18, 1887, Danylchak collection.

In 1887, the Actors' Fund of America purchased a large plot for the burial of its membership—a disrespected demographic in the nineteenth century. The dedication of the plot, however, drew over eight thousand spectators—likely the largest crowd in the history of the cemetery.[166] Chinese and African American burials were also accepted at the cemetery. In 1880, the *New York Herald* dispatched a reporter to investigate claims that Chinese men and women were buried among Christians at the Evergreens. The reporter spoke to the cemetery's foreman who replied, "It's all the same to me. I am Irish, thank God; the chief clerk, Mr. Pfeiffer, is German, and we bury any man who comes along."[167] Over time, the Evergreens's population became as diverse as the crowded city that spurred its creation.

Forest Home Cemetery, Milwaukee, Wisconsin, 1850

Milwaukee was a frontier town of ten thousand people experiencing extraordinary growth—and a burial crisis—when it received its city charter in 1846. Six urban burial grounds were created during the 1840s to accommodate the city's dying settlers, but by the end of the decade, most of them had already been removed or were threatened by encroaching development. When the German Protestant burying ground was endangered by the extension of Thirteenth Street, lot-owners were given thirty days to remove the bodies of their family members. Those buried in the East Side graveyard, on the other hand, had been largely forgotten and were dug up by road crews and "unceremoniously heaped by the wayside."[168]

In 1847, the influential leadership of St. Paul's Episcopal Church appointed a committee to identify a site for its congregation's new burying ground. However, in a letter published in the August 10, 1850, *Milwaukee Sentinel*, St. Paul's rector explained that, "The Vestry felt the urgent necessity of having a cemetery for the city, in which the dead might repose undisturbed. ... They freely invite all to unite with them in making this cemetery a monument of the taste and liberality

77. General view of the undulating landscape with monuments at Forest Home Cemetery. Photograph by James R. Cothran, undated.

THE RURAL CEMETERY MOVEMENT

of the citizens of Milwaukee."[169] Although touted as the city's cemetery, the forthcoming institution became mainly a Protestant one.

The location chosen for what became known as Forest Home Cemetery was a seventy-two acre site at the junction of the highly traveled Janesville Plank Road and Kilbourn Road, now W. Forest Home Avenue and S. Twenty-Seventh Street, respectively, about four miles south of downtown Milwaukee. St. Paul's rector noted that the land encompassed "valleys and hills, deep ravines and gently sloping lawns, . . . secluded nooks and quiet groves."[170] The "well wooded" grounds were thereafter "forever appropriated" for the interment of the dead.[171]

The grounds of the new cemetery were part of a larger area known as the Indian Fields, the largest Native American agricultural site in the Milwaukee vicinity. The site had been studied by Increase Allen Lanham (1811–1875), a pioneer scientist, naturalist, and surveyor who identified fifty Indian mounds in the area, including a significant number within the current boundaries of the cemetery. Not all, but many, included burials. In 1850, Lanham was charged with laying out a system of curvilinear drives, which ultimately divided different-sized sections of land into

irregular shapes. He created a map of roadways that respected the topography of the land but then left the development oversight to the Cemetery Committee. Unfortunately, several Indian mounds were demolished during grading and road building. By 1876, five miles of carriage roadways and twelve miles of footpaths had been completed throughout the cemetery, which doubled in size through a series of land acquisitions through 1880.

Forest Home focused considerable attention on the ornamental from a very early date. The earliest pictorial evidence of the cemetery in 1871 illustrates greenhouses on the grounds as well as a sexton's house, horse barns, and possibly a small chapel. The greenhouses supplied flowers for sale to lot-owners who were permitted to improve their plots with trees, plants, and shrubs. The cemetery also actively improved common areas; in 1877, work crews set out almost forty thousand potted plants.[172]

The appointment of James Currie (1853–1922) as superintendent in 1880 fostered the cemetery's floral fascination as well as its continued consideration of the site's tree canopy. In 1875, Currie had established the Currie Brothers Company, a flower and seed business in Milwaukee; it was an enterprise he continued

78. Rockwork fountain built in the early 1880s at Forest Home Cemetery. Photograph by James R. Cothran, undated.

to be involved with until his death in 1922. Currie's expertise in horticulture, arboriculture, and design had garnered the recommendation of Forest Home's treasurer—who patronized Currie's business—for his appointment to the position of cemetery superintendent, a post Currie would hold for forty-two years. Under Currie's direction, crews planted "bright flower beds from the extensive greenhouses, adopting the style of the French parterre."[173] The beds, laid out with mathematical precision, appeared along roadsides and other attention-grabbing areas throughout the cemetery, including around the elaborate rockwork fountain built in the early 1880s near the cemetery's original entrance. Under Currie's tenure, the cemetery also imported numerous trees to both replace those at the end of their lifespan and extend the forest canopy to newly annexed land. In 1895, the cemetery added two hundred elm, two hundred sugar maple, two hundred silver maple, two hundred ash-leaf maple, and two hundred basswood trees to the grounds.

Flowers and plants also decorated another one of the visual highlights of the cemetery—the Forest Home Cemetery Chapel—currently the oldest extant building on the site. Designed by the Milwaukee architectural firm of Ferry and Clas, the Gothic Revival–style building was constructed between 1890 and 1892 of Lake Superior sandstone, which has a dark red hue. The main rectangular, side-gabled sanctuary is flanked by a tower on the main façade and leaded-glass conservatories on either side. One cemetery official noted that the conservatories were always filled with palms, ferns, and other decorative tropical plants, which were "especially effective and pleasing in the winter season."[174]

Magnolia Cemetery, Charleston, South Carolina, 1850

In 1839, Charleston mayor Henry L. Pinckney extolled the virtues of rural cemeteries over urban burial grounds in a public address to the citizens of his city. Pinckney contended that Charleston's graveyards

79. Rendering of the Chapel in Forest Home Cemetery. From *American Architect and Buildings News*, November 23, 1891, Danylchak collection.

THE RURAL CEMETERY MOVEMENT

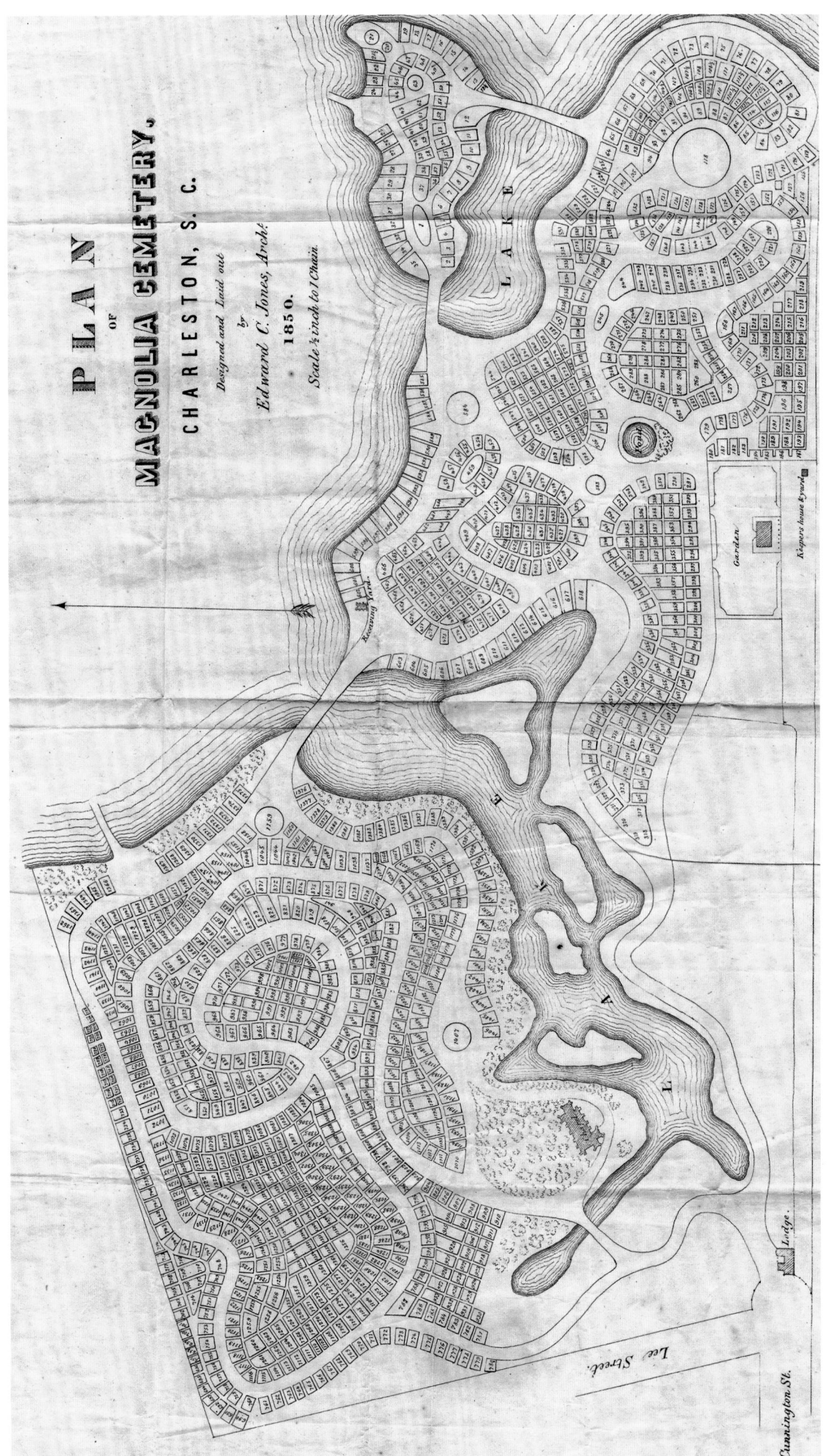

80. Plan of Magnolia Cemetery, designed and laid out by Edward C. Jones, architect, 1850. South Carolina Historical Society, call no. 33-74-17.

would soon become so overcrowded that they would be injurious to the public health. It had been proven, he told them, that "putrid miasmata" emanated from graveyards to spread disease to the population. Charleston, he said, should follow the example of Northern cities like Boston and Philadelphia, which had already established cemeteries located a distance from town. Pinckney went beyond these practical considerations, however, to convince Charlestonians of the need for their own rural cemetery. He declared, "Our city grave yards excite little or no reverence for the dead.... A public cemetery, on the contrary, is eminently adapted to ensure the quiet of the dead, and to excite religious meditation in the living."[175]

More than a decade passed, however, before plans began in earnest for the establishment of a rural cemetery outside the city. In 1850, the nonprofit Magnolia Cemetery Company was incorporated by Edward Sebring, William C. Dukes, George N. Reynolds Jr., William S. Walker, Frederick Richards, and William D. Porter. The founders copied the rules for governing the cemetery from Mount Auburn and Green-Wood.

For the cemetery site, they selected the low, broken ground of the old Magnolia Umbra rice plantation, about three miles north of City Hall. The site, adjacent to the Cooper River, offered magnificent views of Charleston and the harbor in the distance. It also included a two-story, Federal-style house, which had been part of the original plantation and built around 1805. It later became the superintendent's office. It still houses administrative offices today.

In 1850, the cemetery's founders hired prominent Charleston architect Edward C. Jones (1822–1902) to survey and design the site. Jones, along with his junior partner Francis D. Lee (1826–1885), created a plan in which curvilinear drives snaked around burial plots, a pond, and two lakes, which added variety to the landscape. The original plan also incorporated a chapel, lodge, formal garden, keeper's house, and receiving

81. Live oak tree in Magnolia Cemetery. Photograph by William Henry Jackson (1843–1942), ca. 1900, Detroit Publishing Company Photograph Collection, Library of Congress Prints and Photographs Division.

82. Confederate Monument and burial section at Magnolia Cemetery. Photograph ca. 1880 to 1901, Detroit Publishing Company Photograph Collection, Library of Congress Prints and Photographs Division.

yard into the site. The original receiving tomb—a small, Gothic Revival-style, stuccoed brick building—was likely designed by Jones. It still stands today.

Ironically, the cemetery's most famous feature, recounted time and again, was not its magnolia trees but its majestic live oaks draped in Spanish moss. Some, according to *Picturesque America,* were "exceptionally fantastic and queer in form."[176] An 1893 Baedeker's guide informed potential visitors that "the boughs of one of the live oaks have a spread of 100 ft., and the trunk of another is 17–18 ft. in girth."[177] It was Charles Fraser, in his dedicatory address of November 19, 1850, however, who created perhaps the most memorable portrayal of these live oaks. "These venerable trees," he said, "whose spreading branches have been so long tuneful with the harmonies of Spring, are now destined to re-echo the wail of sorrow and mourning."[178]

Another mournful feature, which Magnolia shared with other rural cemeteries in both the North and South, was a burial section devoted to those soldiers who died during the Civil War. More than seventeen

hundred Confederate troops and a few Federal combatants, both known and unknown, were buried in Magnolia Cemetery. An account in an 1875 *Guide to Charleston Illustrated* painted a haunting picture of the scene just beyond the massive gate of the cemetery's front entrance: "Passing in, and keeping on the right, you soon see an array of a score or more of white wooden head-boards, that look like ghostly sentinels at the gates of death. These mark the resting place of the Federal soldiers who have died in Charleston. Just beyond these is the Confederate burying ground. Side by side and rank on rank, as when they charged the bristling breastworks of the enemy, now lie these patriot soldiers of a vanquished country, in sweet oblivion of the stupendous ruin that has crushed the land of their nativity and love. Of that crowd of hillocks, there are some that have no mark to tell who lies beneath."[179]

Magnolia Cemetery has endured as a setting for Confederate remembrance. It held its first Memorial Day observance on June 16, 1866. Subsequent years saw increasingly elaborate ceremonies where prayers, hymns, instrumental music, and original poetry stirred sentimental feelings for the Lost Cause. Memorial Day events often drew crowds of two to three thousand people. An even larger crowd participated in the funeral for the final crew of the illustrious Confederate submarine, the *H. L. Hunley*. In 1864, the *Hunley* sank after torpedoing the USS *Housatonic*—the first successful attack by a submersible vessel on record. Enormous fanfare accompanied the eight man crew's final interment after the submarine was recovered more than a century later. In 2004, approximately twenty thousand spectators and three hundred reporters looked on as nearly nine thousand people in nineteenth-century period costumes followed horse-drawn caissons in a four-and-a-half mile procession that ended at Magnolia Cemetery. The event has often been called the last Confederate funeral.

Evergreen Cemetery, Portland, Maine, 1854

By the mid–nineteenth century, Portland was in need of a new burial ground as it had "outgrown the two narrow graveyards within its limits, and the modern taste for ornament, beauty, and refinement in the last resting-place of the dead demanded a larger and more secluded cemetery."[180] Sylvester B. Beckett (1812–1882), a local newspaper reporter, attorney, and politician, successfully advanced the cause. After investigating potential sites, he wrote in an October 1850 diary entry, "I have been examining the woods of Mr. Buckley, at Stevens' Plains, with a view of endeavoring to prevail upon the city authorities to purchase the place for a burying-ground."[181] In early 1852, the city did, indeed, acquire three adjoining parcels totaling fifty-five acres about two-and-a-half miles from Portland, near the village of Stevens' Plains. As reported in the June 18, 1853, edition of the *Portland Transcript*, the land was sufficiently diverse for the purpose of creating a Picturesque cemetery with some areas "open and elevated, from which may be caught glimpses of the mountains upon the one hand and the city upon the other."[182] It was, however, largely covered in evergreens, a fact that inspired its name; Evergreen Cemetery was consecrated in 1854.

In 1855, Charles H. Howe, a local civil engineer,

83. Map of Evergreen Cemetery. By C. R. Goodell, published by John Russell, 1869, Collections of the Maine Historical Society, courtesy of www.VintageMaineImages.com.

drew the first plan for the cemetery, which included both formal and informal features. Originally, the site stood behind residential development along Stevens Avenue. Howe's plan illustrated a long, straight entrance drive that ran between two houses fronting the street and distanced the contemplative space of the cemetery from the hustle and bustle of everyday life. The cemetery's original circulation pattern included both curvilinear and rectilinear main drives and narrower footpaths between burial plots. It also included circular intersections—similar to those seen at Mount Hope Cemetery in Bangor—that served as focal points.[183] Although Howe's system of avenues took into account the existing topography, "it was an engineer's plan with regular curves."[184] It was also a conceptual plan that did not address grading or planting. The only planting recommendation Howe made was for a formal allée of trees along the entrance drive. Howe also identified sites for an office, a receiving tomb, a chapel, and a keeper's lodge.

Howe's original vision for the cemetery was implemented and further improved over several decades.

By the mid-1860s, a receiving tomb, "a turf-covered mound, with granite front" built by J. T. Emery, stood just within the entrance, which was reached by "an avenue bordered by shade trees and arbor vitae hedges."[185] By 1869, the southern part of the original cemetery acreage featured two formal circular intersections that had been indicated on Howe's original plan. As illustrated on a map of the cemetery published by John Russell, one of the circular intersections was ringed with burial lots, while the other encompassed a water feature. Water was an integral part of the early design of the cemetery, particularly the ponds at the northwestern portion of the site, which were indicated on the Howe plan with organic silhouettes. An 1881 travel guide described the ponds as being "bordered with seats, spanned with rustic bridges, the shore adorned with rustic arches and arbors."[186] The travel book continued, "On the surface of the ponds float swans and ducks, the feeding of which is a delight to children."[187] This picturesque scene was no accident; expenditures made in the 1870s for the cemetery included swans and geese.[188]

84. A pond at Evergreen Cemetery. Postcard ca. 1910, Danylchak collection.

As improvements were being made, additional land was also being acquired for the cemetery. The City of Portland purchased sixty-seven acres for the cemetery in 1869 and made major land purchases again in 1871, 1876, 1880, and 1883. Much of this land ultimately featured sections with more consistent grid-like patterns for their avenues thus helping to distinguish the earliest development from later additions. Also, the earlier burial lots tended to be raised slightly above the grade of the adjacent avenues. The lots were often enclosed by granite curbing, reached by a short flight of granite steps. In the later sections, the pattern noticeably changed to emulate the design principals adopted by Adolph Strauch at Spring Grove Cemetery—the lawn was generally level, peppered with fewer and smaller trees, and undivided by lot enclosures. In addition, by 1929, all but two of the houses between the cemetery and Stevens Avenue were purchased, demolished, and the land converted to open lawn. By the end of the twentieth century, Evergreen Cemetery encompassed 239 acres making it the largest open space—as well as the largest urban forest—in the city of Portland.[189]

Oakwood Cemetery, Syracuse, New York, 1859

The civic leaders of Syracuse began discussing the need for a rural cemetery just four years after the city incorporated in 1848. However, lack of leadership and economic challenges delayed the prospect. An 1857 editorial in the *Standard* reported, "Mortified are we that our city cannot boast of a Rural Cemetery."[190] The following year, Elias Leavenworth (1803–1887), a former and future mayor of Syracuse, and Hamilton White (1807–1865), a prominent businessman, reenergized the effort and the "Association of Oakwood" was established in August of 1859.

For the creation of its cemetery, the association chose a ninety-two acre site about one-and-a-half miles from the Syracuse city center. It was remarkably diverse and included drumlins, complex hills, and rounded knolls as well as complementary low-lying land. The northern part of the site featured a series of ridges running north-south as well as a narrow, yet striking, ravine. To the south, subtler hills and valleys graced the landscape. The natural elevations within the site provided sweeping panoramic vistas of both

85. The chapel in Oakwood Cemetery. Note too the monuments on the hillside in the background. Postcard ca. 1909, Danylchak collection.

the tranquil Onondaga Valley to the southwest and the burgeoning city to the north. The old Comstock farm stood between the cemetery and the city, providing a pastoral foreground, while Onondaga Lake provided a glimpse of serenity beyond the northwest limits of the city. Oakwood was so named because the original site was covered by sixty acres of almost uninterrupted oak forest, including the Northern red oak, white oak, and black oak.

The Oakwood Cemetery site was designed by landscape gardener Howard Daniels (1815–1864) and laid out with a workforce of sixty men beginning in 1859. Daniels was able to create diverse interior views and vistas by carefully laying out a hierarchy of roads and pathways through the diverse landforms of the site. He also selectively removed existing trees, in part to open up views where desired, and added native and exotic species, in part to carefully frame a selected scene. Noteworthy species introduced at Oakwood over time included bald cypress, chestnut, cucumber magnolia, gingko, Kentucky coffee tree, Japanese katsura, Norway spruce, and yellowwood. Daniels also enhanced internal views by altering the existing

terrain, including some rounding of natural landforms to emphasize these interesting features and their silhouettes.[191]

Over time mortuary sculpture was also placed strategically within the landscape to provide picturesque glimpses of distinctive art. Surrounding foliage or the terrain itself was often used to reveal or frame individual monuments. "A beautiful clump of oaks," for instance, served as "an elegant background" for the symmetrically proportioned obelisk honoring Horace Candee.[192] Meanwhile, large monuments were often located on high ground. The Loyal C. Taber monument, described as being "unique in design, symmetrical in outline, elegant and imposing in its general appearance from any point of view," was positioned on one of the most "prominent and sightly knolls" in the cemetery.[193] In addition, it was surrounded by striking shrubbery and a variety of magnificent trees upon and near the knoll, thereby rendering "the scene extremely picturesque" and eliciting "expressions of the deepest admiration from all who view it."[194] The Longstreet tomb, an "elegant pyramidal mausoleum," was also positioned to crown "one of the loveliest

86. Office building framed by trees in Oakwood Cemetery. Postcard postmarked 1911, Danylchak collection.

knolls in Oakwood."[195] Careful attention was always paid, however, to preventing the monuments from overwhelming the natural beauty of the grounds. In addition, fences were prohibited from being more than three-and-a-half feet high in order to preserve "the sylvan effect so essential in rural cemeteries."[196]

From the beginning, the cemetery's trustees cautioned against monotony in its monuments. In fact, the cemetery's 1860 Rules and Regulations declared that "the *character* and *variety* of the structures [are] essential to a permanently pleasing effect on the mind."[197] Oakwood referenced a publication of the Laurel Hill Cemetery Association that cited criticism from its visitors for a monotony in the "style and form of the improvements" where "obelisk succeeds obelisk, etc., with only slight variations."[198] Oakwood paid particular attention to Laurel Hill's warning that its visitors would see, in time, "too dull a uniformity to strike the mind with agreeable sentiments."[199] Oakwood had received an early gift, however, that helped its lot holders avoid being tediously repetitious in their monument selections. The 1894 publication *Picturesque Oakwood* recalled that the Honorable Andrew D. White, "while absent on one of his many visits to Europe . . . made it his pleasure to look for and obtain elegant books of engravings containing views of celebrated tombs and suggestions as to the erection of monuments considered in the best taste in great foreign cities."[200] White, who had long been associated with the cemetery, bequeathed the books to Oakwood—"a most unusual possession in the way of reference to be found in the archives of any American cemetery."[201]

The monuments and mausoleums throughout the cemetery indeed exhibit a variety of form and architectural styles. The first monument erected at Oakwood in 1860 belongs to James Crouse and is a simple pedestal and obelisk exhibiting classical details and soaring twenty-eight feet high. The White family plot, meanwhile, features a Gothic Revival–style chest tomb embellished with tracery erected around 1865. The Romanesque Revival style is showcased in the William Sabey monument (ca. 1880), a rough-faced limestone and granite vault recessed into a hillside. Meanwhile, the ornate, free-standing mausoleum of Burr Burton (ca. 1866) is an $8,000 baroque-inspired work of Syracuse architect Horatio N. White (1814–1892). An ever-increasing collection of varied sculptures and structures enhanced the site throughout its

history and, in effect, made Oakwood an outdoor museum open to the citizens of Syracuse.

Mountain View Cemetery, Oakland, California, 1863

At the end of 1863, a few civic-minded citizens of Oakland met to discuss the establishment of a rural cemetery under the California Rural Cemetery Act of 1859. The following year, a tract of land of nearly two hundred acres was purchased by the newly formed Mountain View Cemetery Association, and its board commissioned Frederick Law Olmsted (1822–1903), one of the principal designers of New York's Central Park, to create a plan for the grounds. Mountain View is the only cemetery that Olmsted played a significant role in designing.[202] Olmsted began what he called his "very elaborate & complicated pattern"[203] for the cemetery in 1864, and its initial implementation began in February of the following year under the direction of Edward C. Miller, a Central Park surveyor and civil engineer whom Olmsted brought to California. Although the cemetery was dedicated in May 1865, the plan for the entire site was not completed by Olmsted and his partner Calvert Vaux (1824–1895) until July of 1866.

Oakland's semiarid climate was quite different from that of Olmsted's native East Coast, and it forced him to deviate from the English-inspired design aesthetic that he had used in previous projects such as Central Park. Since large pastoral areas of grass would be difficult to maintain at Mountain View, he recommended instead creating a series of more formal spaces enclosed by vegetation that would limit views of the middle ground.[204] The vegetation would also act as a screen to the strong winds the site had to endure. In addition, it would provide a sense of seclusion for the graves within plots, which would foster an appropriately deferential atmosphere for mourners.

Olmsted's planting proposal considered the site's semiarid climate as well as the physical form and "poetic suggestion" of certain species.[205] He chose primarily Mediterranean and native plants that were drought tolerant and known to withstand punishing winds. He proposed using tree species with simple yet distinctive forms that complemented each other. He also recommended evergreen trees that possessed meanings related to grief and immortality. He specifically recommended importing Italian cypress—a narrow evergreen that seemed "more than any other tree to point toward heaven."[206] He advocated introducing

87. Contemporary view of the winding circulation system on the elevated ground in Mountain View Cemetery. Photograph by James R. Cothran, 2007.

the distinctly horizontal masses of the cedar of Lebanon and Italian stone pine, trees indigenous to "very dry and exposed situations," to provide "relief and contrast" to the cypress.[207] He also explained in his preface to the Plan for Mountain View Cemetery that "the brooding forms of the coppices and the canopy of the cedars would unite in the expression of a sheltering care extended over the place of the dead, the heaven-pointing spires of the immortal cypress would prompt the consolations of faith."[208] Olmsted also proposed using the native, flat-headed Monterey cypress, a species that branches out horizontally "as if to present the least possible surface to the direct action of the wind."[209] In addition, he recommended the Canyon live oak, which features horizontal branches and a rounded crown of evergreen foliage.

Olmsted examined the existing surface of the grounds to select the appropriate design treatment, which ultimately combined a formal approach with a dose of the Picturesque. Olmsted argued that the plain, level ground that ran through the heart of the site was "as far as possible . . . from being suggestive of picturesque treatment."[210] In fact, he contended that cemeteries, in general, were not conducive to the

Picturesque aesthetic because of how the land had to be broken up into small divisions for family plots and how man-made monuments marred a cemetery's natural beauty. On the level part of the ground, at the entrance, Olmsted proposed an oval court as a place of "waiting and assemblage." It served as the head of three straight avenues lined with trees. The central avenue, which still exists, extends nearly the length of the site, terminating at a receiving tomb. Three rounded carrefours along the avenue are punctuated by public monuments. From the focal points along the avenue, Olmsted then planned winding pathways emanating outward to the irregular, elevated ground on each side. These curved lanes, flanked and protected by what Olmsted called in his explanation of the cemetery plan "more picturesque belts of shrubs and coppice-wood," gradually ascended the adjacent hillsides. By 1889, four miles of macadamized avenues and six miles of pathways had been installed throughout the site.

In 1891, pioneering environmental journalist Charles Howard Shinn (1852–1923) visited the cemetery and provided a vivid description of its planting progress for *Garden and Forest*. He noted that flowers

88. Mountain View Cemetery, 1885. Frank B. Rodolph (1843–1923) Photographic Collection. Courtesy of the Bancroft Library, University of California, Berkeley.

and shrubs graced the site's rounded hills, while most of the trees rose from the richer soil of the valleys. On the hillside, he observed about thirty kinds of roses, "immense clumps" of irises, and white and rose-colored peonies, along with English laurel, Japanese quince, and spirea. "French Marigolds mingled with wild Poppies and early Lupines," he reported, while "in many a nook the native flowers of the coast range still hold their own."[211] Meanwhile, along the western and southern sides of the site, an "almost continuous belt" of Monterey cypress, Eucalypti (a tree, incidentally, that Olmsted cautioned against using at the site), and pines screened out views of the urbanization beyond.[212] All of the trees, vines, flowers, and running water, he noted, "unite to make a quiet loveliness."[213]

The Influence of the Landscape Lawn Plan

The Cemetery of Spring Grove, Cincinnati, Ohio, 1844, Modified 1856

The establishment and early history of the Cemetery of Spring Grove mimics that of earlier rural cemeteries; however, the site spurred an evolution in the rural cemetery design aesthetic after Adolph Strauch's appointment as Landscape Gardener in 1854. In the 1840s, Cincinnati—the nation's sixth-largest city at the time—faced epidemics and concerns about proper burial practices for the multiplying casualties of disease. In 1844, members of the Cincinnati Horticultural

Society formed a cemetery association to establish a large-scale burying ground, and members of the Society traveled east to visit cemeteries they wished to imitate, including Mount Auburn, Laurel Hill, and Green-Wood. The following year, the Proprietors of the Cemetery of Spring Grove were granted a charter by the State of Ohio. The charter required that after paying for the land for the cemetery, all future receipts of the association "be applied exclusively, under the direction of the Board, to laying out, preserving, and embellishing the Cemetery, and the avenues leading thereto."

The original 166 acres of former farmland chosen for the cemetery contained "numerous springs" and "ancient groves of trees" inspiring the name Spring Grove.[214] One of the features that motivated the site selection was, in fact, the "number and variety" of native forest trees on the tract.[215] Located in a valley four miles from the city, the land was also "surrounded on all sides by forest clad hills."[216] Topographically diverse, the tract encompassed elevated plateaus, picturesque ravines, and areas of wetlands ideal for converting into scenic ponds.

The cemetery's founders commissioned John Notman, the designer of Laurel Hill Cemetery, to create a plan for the site. However, Notman's layout was deemed impractical and too geometric for the undulating grounds. For the cemetery directors, the plan failed to capture the "woodsy naturalism they admired at Mount Auburn."[217] The board then turned to architect and landscape gardener Howard Daniels to create a more appropriate design and sent him on a four-month tour of the celebrated rural cemeteries of the East to gain inspiration. When he returned, he was hired as the "cemetery architect and superintendent."

Daniels laid out Spring Grove in the Picturesque style revered at the time with the aid of Thomas Earnshaw, a local surveyor and civil engineer. Together they created a labyrinth of winding roads and paths, a layout motivated by both practical and aesthetic considerations. The roadways respected the topography of the grounds by following "natural drainage swales, deliberately running through ravines or depressions between the gentle slopes, using land undesirable for burials."[218] Meanwhile, higher, dryer ground was reserved for interments. The proliferation of roadways encircling burial lots allowed easy access for burials. The sinuous drives also provided continually changing rural views for the visitor. Daniels did not have

the time or money, however, to improve the swampy ground near the cemetery entrance, so instead, the cemetery association leased the land to local farmers for pasturing their cows during the cemetery's first decade of existence.

During the first decade, other cemetery improvements multiplied as individual lot proprietors and members of the board made additions to the grounds. Lot owners were allowed to enhance their small parcels and often added fences or hedges to demarcate their property. By 1854, more than 75 percent of the site's family plots were encompassed by privet hedges or cast iron, wrought iron, or post-and-chain fences. In the early years, cemetery rules allowed railings and fences to reach a maximum height of two feet, eight inches, while hedges were permitted to grow up to three feet. The directors were fairly lax in enforcing the regulation, however, and many enclosures were even taller. Meanwhile, lot owners were encouraged by the president of the board to plant grasses, vines, shrubs, flowers, and weeping trees within their own lots. In the meantime, members of the board and "other horticulturists" added plantings to public areas. By 1850, forty-three hundred ornamental plant varieties populated Spring Grove.

89. Spring Grove Cemetery, with large open lawn areas, widely interspersed family monuments, and relatively few curving roadways within the cemetery, ca. 1858. By Middleton, Strobridge & Co., Library of Congress Prints and Photographs Division.

In 1854, Adolph Strauch, a Prussian landscape gardener, was hired by the board of directors to improve the cemetery. Strauch had arrived in Cincinnati in 1852 and had provided his services to wealthy residents of the nearby Village of Clifton who wanted to create rural "showplaces" there. H. A. Rattermann, a German American historian and acquaintance of Adolph Strauch, later wrote that Strauch had discussed his thoughts on improving Spring Grove with his friends in Clifton, including men involved in the Cemetery Association.

During his subsequent tenure at Spring Grove, Strauch markedly changed the cemetery's appearance, management structure, and maintenance practices. In a report to the board of directors in 1856, Strauch delivered his cogent and unique views on how a rural cemetery should be laid out. First and foremost, he said, "Good taste would seem to suggest that a rural Cemetery should partake more of the character of a cheerful park or garden, than of a common grave yard, where everything has a gloomy and dismal appearance, and every inch of ground is used for graves."[219] His use of the word "cheerful" signaled a decidedly different way of looking at the funerary landscape—which during the rural cemetery movement had been deliberately infused with an indulgent melancholy. Moreover, Strauch advocated "dispensing with unsightly fences, hedges, head and foot stones, and other useless appendages."[220] By this time, the proliferation of monuments and markers at Spring Grove had begun to tip the balance toward artificiality over nature. In order to tilt the scales back in favor of rural simplicity, Strauch promoted a number of fundamental changes to family lots. Four low-lying, unobtrusive cornerstones, he said, engraved with the family name and lot number was more than sufficient to delineate a lot boundary. He also advocated the installation of a single family monument at the center of the lot as opposed to having too many memorials within its boundary. The latter approach, he said, produced "the appearance of a marble yard, where they are for sale."[221] In contrast, one stately monument within the confines of a lot would help unify it visually as "a family burial place."[222]

In his report, Strauch also laid out his views on appropriate planting schemes for the site to promote its park-like appearance. He endorsed, for example, the preservation of corner lots at the junction of avenues for the planting of forest trees but cautioned against planting too many varieties together. He also derided the overabundance of trees on family lots, because the crowded conditions caused the trees and shrubs to destroy each other, obstruct the monuments, and leave insufficient space for burials. Instead, he said that trees and shrubs should be carefully arranged to "form a background to the monument."[223] They should also be carefully selected based on aesthetic, symbolic, and practical considerations, like the spread of their root systems.

Strauch was also quite practical in his approach to laying out rural cemetery grounds by considering maintenance and cost concerns. As part of his argument against unsightly lot enclosures, for example, he posed the pointed question, "How much will it ultimately cost to keep the grounds in proper order, supposing all the lots to be enclosed?"[224] His answer to the board was compelling: "Certainly more than four times the amount requisite to the keeping a Cemetery without enclosures."[225] In his report, he also ridiculed gravel walkways within burial lots, in part because of the expense and hassle of keeping them weed-free. Meanwhile, part of his reasoning for limiting the number of monuments within each lot was to spare the family unnecessary expense.

Strauch also emphasized the need to consolidate control by the cemetery association and limit "private fancy or caprice" that could "deform the harmonious beauty of the grounds."[226] As such, he expressed in his 1856 report that all the grading for cemetery sections should be done prior to the sale of lots "to produce a natural and pleasing surface."[227] Over just a few years, Strauch acquired increasing authority over decisions related to the cemetery's landscape design. In 1859, the board named Strauch "superintendent of the grounds and landscape gardener" and rewrote his job description to give him control over "all improvements in the Cemetery, such as grading, planting, pruning the plants and trees, laying out avenues, and keeping the grounds, lots, and avenues in proper order."[228] Strauch served in this powerful role until his death in 1883.

New rules regulating the improvement of lots codified Strauch's vision for the cemetery. Significantly, the rules pronounced: "Enclosures around burial lots, wooden trellises and head-boards of any description whatsoever, are considered useless incumbrances, and are therefore prohibited."[229] A later 1869 publication by the cemetery association evaluated the regulation's

90. Mirror Lake and Chapel at Spring Grove Cemetery. Postcard ca. 1910, Cothran collection.

effect and asserted, "In abandoning useless enclosures which obstructed cultivation, and occasionally disfigured the grounds, a truer art has ascertained the superiority of nearer conformity to Nature."[230] A contemporaneous account in *Appletons' Hand-book of American Travel* (1869) commented on the difference between Spring Grove and other large rural cemeteries: "The great feature of Spring Grove is the open-lot system, which has been adopted. Unsightly fences and railings nowhere offend the eye, and the entire absence of all superfluous ornamentation affords a marked and pleasing contrast to not a few of our largest and most frequented burying-grounds."[231]

In order to create a more harmonious landscape with fewer obstructions, Strauch also planned fewer avenues and eliminated existing pathways. Believing that the cemetery's six- to ten-foot-wide pedestrian pathways that traversed burial sections created unattractive fragmentation and needless work to keep them in good condition, he had them removed. In general, he felt that avenues "should have an easy grade, graceful curves, and be so located as to give to each section

a natural outline."[232] Strauch's vision differed from the more densely arranged maze of avenues Daniels had planned. Strauch did not believe that every burial lot needed avenue frontage. Instead, he asserted that "seclusion is more in unison with the feelings of many friends of the dead than publicity, glare and notoriety."[233]

During his tenure, Strauch also transformed the entrance to the cemetery. He replaced the unattractive swampy ground along Hamilton Road with five acres of ornamental lakes by 1869. Dirt removed during the excavation was used to create irregularly shaped peninsulas and islands in the lakes that became woodland areas. Later in 1876, Strauch installed fountain jets in the lakes to help ensure water circulation. The fountains also "added dynamic elements of visual interest to the landscape."[234]

Under Strauch's management, the cemetery continued to grow its horticultural collection. An 1857 cemetery report proudly provided a catalogue of two hundred species of trees and shrubs cultivated at Spring Grove and asserted that the cemetery was

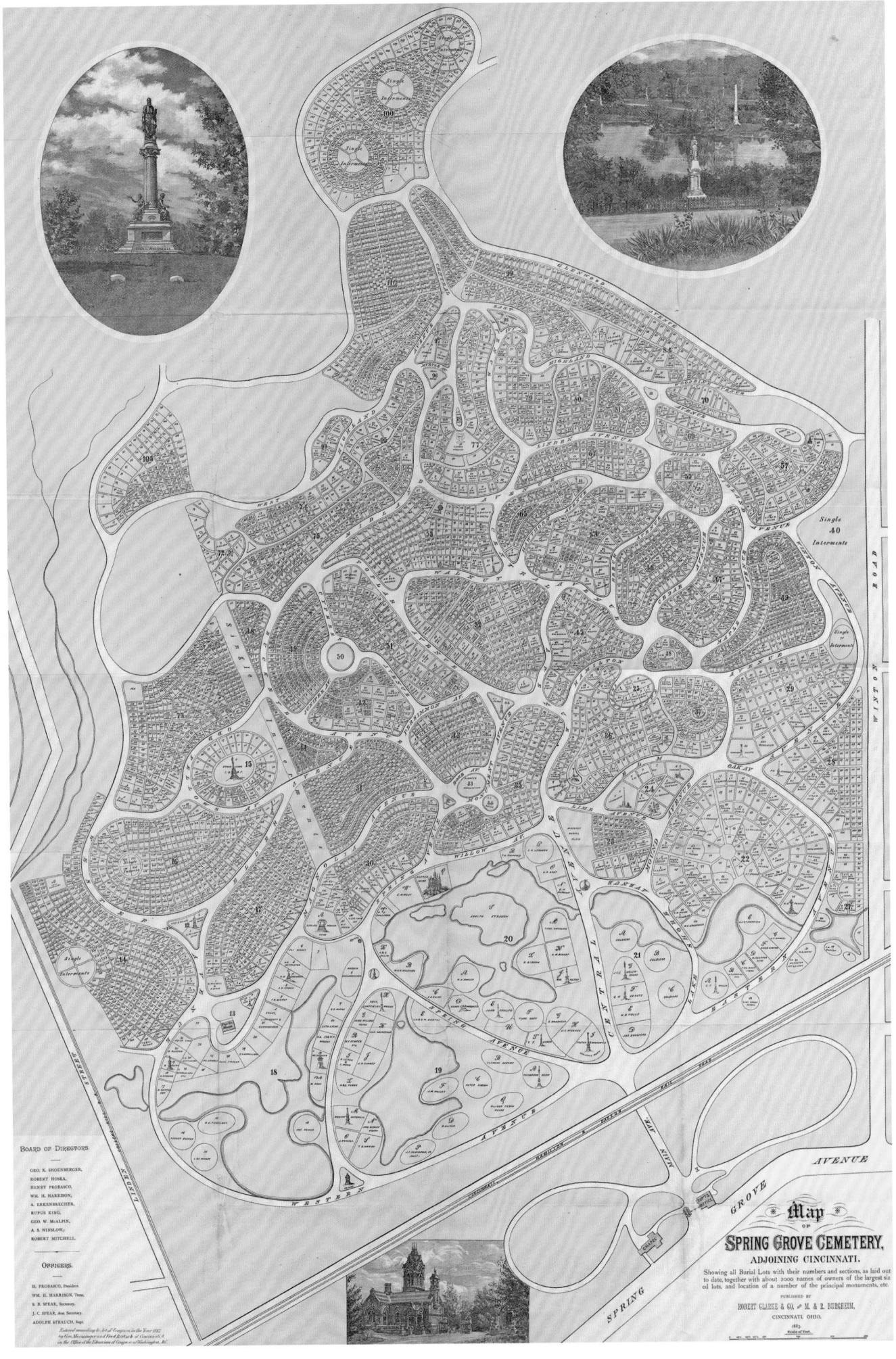

BOARD OF DIRECTORS

GEO. K. SHOENBERGER,
ROBERT HOSEA,
HENRY PROBASCO,
WM. H. HARRISON,
A. ERKENBRECHER,
RUFUS KING,
GEO. W. McALPIN,
A. S. WINSLOW,
ROBERT MITCHELL.

OFFICERS.

H. PROBASCO, President.
WM. H. HARRISON, Treas.
S. B. SPEAR, Secretary.
J. C. SPEAR, Asst. Secretary.
ADOLPH STRAUCH, Supt.

Entered according to Act of Congress in the Year 1883
by Geo. Messenger and Fred Burkart & Cincinnati O.
in the Office of the Librarian of Congress at Washington, DC.

Map
OF
SPRING GROVE CEMETERY,
ADJOINING CINCINNATI.

Showing all Burial Lots with their numbers and sections, as laid out
to date, together with about 2000 names of owners of the largest sized
lots, and location of a number of the principal monuments, etc.

PUBLISHED BY
ROBERT CLARKE & CO. and M. & R. BURGHEIM,
CINCINNATI, OHIO.
1883

Scale of Feet.

determined to add to its collection until it included "all those which can be made to flourish in this climate."[235] The cemetery asserted that a "valuable arboretum will thus be established, in a favorable situation, as well for the study of their peculiarities, as the enjoyment of their attractions."[236] Between 1855 and 1865 alone, Strauch planted over two hundred tree varieties. During his tenure, he introduced azaleas and laurel to the site. In 1865, he ordered four hundred holly trees

91. (left) *Map of Spring Grove Cemetery, adjoining Cincinnati : showing all burial lots with their numbers and sections, as laid out to date, together with about 2000 names of owners of the largest sized lots, and location of a number of the principal monuments, etc.* Note, too, the ornamental foreground at the entrance to the cemetery. Robert Clarke & Co. and M. & R. Burgheim, Cincinnati, Ohio, 1883, Library of Congress Geography and Map Division.

from Paris, Kentucky. In 1876, he brought in magnolias from Memphis, Tennessee. In 1870, he ordered vines, shrubs, and trees from England. He imported evergreens from the Himalayan, Caucasian, and Rocky Mountains. He also imported the Canadian poplar, Chinese ailanthus, European alder, Norway spruce, and Persian lilac as well as Corsican and Scotch pines and French and German tamarisk. By the 1860s the cemetery had "a more diverse collection of trees than any other landscape in the nation, except New York's Central Park."[237]

It was not only the sheer number of new trees and shrubs that Strauch added to the landscape that was noteworthy but also the thoughtfulness in his arrangement of the collection that won Spring Grove admirers. He carefully constructed "foliage frames" for monuments, contrasting an evergreen backdrop with luminous white, gray, and rose colored granite

92. The Lake at Spring Grove Cemetery. Photograph ca. 1906, Detroit Publishing Company Photograph Collection, Library of Congress Prints and Photographs Division.

sculpture. He created groupings of trees juxtaposed with open lawns, thus perceptibly alternating areas of light and dark. Meanwhile, in corner lots, he played with the "delightful distribution of varied coloring, the magical interchange of tints, and the delicate transition from light to shade."[238] He felt particularly strongly that the "monotonous appearance" of evergreens should be relieved by trees that showcased "brilliant colors in autumn; such as the Scarlet Oak, the Scarlet Maple, the Sour Gum, the Tulip Tree, and the Sugar Maple."[239]

In order to create this attractively arranged and evenly manicured property, the cemetery association, under Strauch's direction, assumed greater maintenance responsibilities, including care of individual lots. To pay for such services, Spring Grove offered lots at a higher price to establish a perpetual care fund. As an alternative, the association also offered prospective purchasers the option of a slightly lower initial lot price and annual-care payments. Spring Grove was thus able to hire a large crew of gardeners to care for the entire property. Meanwhile, the relatively new mechanical lawn mower, which had been invented in England in 1830, made maintenance easier. With the elimination of most vertical obstructions in the cemetery, large expanses of grass could be maintained fairly efficiently throughout the year. In these ways, Strauch's new approach married "aesthetic ideals to the gospel of efficiency," thus setting it apart from the rural cemetery model from which it had evolved.[240]

The board of directors of the cemetery continued to add land to its holdings to guarantee room for burials far into the future and to ensure that the site's visual balance remained in favor of nature over the "hand of man." In 1857, the cemetery association emphasized that its recent land acquisitions had been "a judicious investment" that would allow the cemetery to avoid the "crowded appearance which a superabundance of monuments already gives to Mount Auburn and Laurel Hill."[241] In 1866, the cemetery added the 133-acre Hill Farm to its holdings, bringing its total acreage to 412 and making it the largest cemetery in the world at the time.[242] In 1867, the cemetery acquired another thirty acres southeast of Spring Grove Avenue as a buffer between the cemetery's main entrance and the Cincinnati and Marietta Railroad as well as potential industrial operations. In the local newspaper, the cemetery's director explained that the board intended "to prevent the establishment of hog-pens,

distilleries, starch factories, slaughter-houses, bone-boiling establishments, or stink factories of any kind, or dram-shops in disagreeable proximity to the Cemetery proper."[243] Land purchases continued; by 1875, the cemetery encompassed 594 acres; by 1904, six hundred. Today, it includes 733 acres, only 450 of which are developed.

Strauch's new aesthetic approach at Spring Grove was termed the landscape lawn plan. His reforms quickly won praise, and Spring Grove eventually became the new standard for large-scale designed cemeteries. In 1870, the *Cincinnati Commercial Tribune* reported that Spring Grove had been visited by directors and superintendents from "various principal cemeteries throughout the country—from New York, Chicago, Cleveland, Detroit, Rochester, and other cities, in search of information regarding the laying out and management of rural cemeteries."[244] In 1880, the same paper asserted that Spring Grove had become the "acknowledged model for all popular modern rural cemeteries."[245] Twenty years later, the cemetery won the gold medal at the Paris International Exposition as the best designed landscape in the United States. In 2007, Spring Grove was designated a National Historic Landmark.

Graceland Cemetery, Chicago, Illinois, 1860

In Chicago during the mid-nineteenth century, development pressures and mounting health concerns spurred the relocation of graves from urban graveyards to burial grounds outside the city. Chicago's earliest municipal burial grounds were closed in 1843, and their burials were relocated to the newly established City Cemetery, which had been created on land adjacent to Lake Michigan well north of the city limits the previous year. In 1859, however, Chicago's Common Council prohibited the sale of burial plots within the City Cemetery in large part because of rising fears regarding the contamination of the city's major water supply. Then in 1865, the Common Council voted to remove and relocate all the burials from City Cemetery. They allowed lot owners to exchange their lots for ones of equal size in Chicago's new rural cemeteries. The city's three largest rural cemeteries—Graceland, Rosehill, and Oak Woods—had all been recently created to receive the swelling city's dead—both new and relocated burials.

In 1860, Thomas Barbour Bryan (1828–1906), a successful attorney and civic booster, had purchased

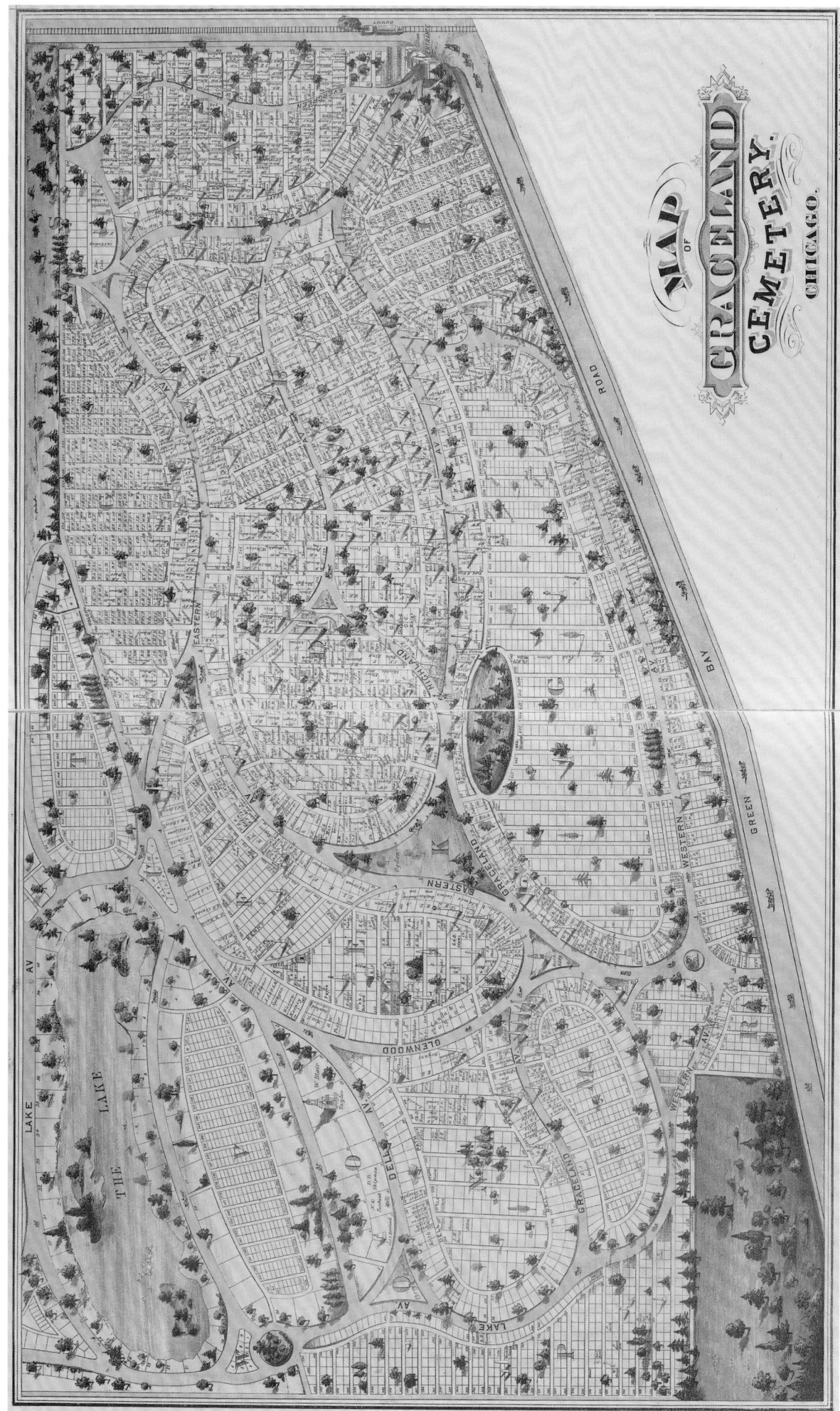

93. 1878 Bird's-eye view of Graceland Cemetery. The southern part of the site is pictured at right. Green Bay Road runs along the western boundary of the cemetery. Published by Charles Rascher, Chicago History Museum, ICHi-27725.

eighty-six acres of land two miles north of the city limits and about one mile west of Lake Michigan for the establishment of Graceland Cemetery. (The land was located on the Graceland spit, a sandy shoal extending into the great lake, inspiring the burial ground's name.) Not incidentally, Thomas Bryan's infant son had died in 1855, and Bryan had subsequently purchased a plot in City Cemetery for his burial. Bryan later remarked, "The neglected and actually repulsive condition of the cemetery induced my search of land for a rural burying ground, more remote from and more worthy of the city."[246] Bryan's son was exhumed from City Cemetery and became the first interment at Graceland.

Swain Nelson (1828–1917), a local landscape gardener and nurseryman, and William Saunders (1822–1900), a well-known landscape gardener from Philadelphia, laid out about fifty acres of the original section of the cemetery, now the southwest portion of the site. (Saunders had also been retained to design Chicago's Rosehill Cemetery in 1859.) Graceland's southwestern portion is a quintessential example of the early rural cemetery movement with masses of elevated monuments interspersed with trees and plants in sections

skirted by narrow carriageways and traversed by grassy footpaths. Lot owners used stone curbing and hedges to enclose family plots and were allowed to use ornamental plantings at their discretion.

About ten years later landscape gardener H. W. S. Cleveland (1814–1900) was commissioned to create a plan of improvement for the cemetery, which marked Graceland's transition to the landscape lawn plan. Cleveland utilized plantings to create a harmonious landscape composition that alternated areas of light and shadow. The cemetery's secretary described Cleveland's work where "each section resembles a beautiful lawn, covered with green turf, and dotted with graceful trees."[247]

The site's eastern portion of low-lying land was laid out beginning in 1878. Architect and engineer William LeBaron Jenney (1832–1907) is credited with draining the marshy area to create burial sections, laying out the road system and network of earthworks, and creating Lake Willowmere in the northeast portion of the site. The artificial lake, complete with sinuous banks and a striking wooded island, not only enhanced the beauty of the grounds but also acted as a needed drainage reservoir.

94. View of Lake Willowmere in Graceland Cemetery. Photograph by James R. Cothran, undated.

THE RURAL CEMETERY MOVEMENT

95. East and north façades of the Louis Sullivan–designed Getty Tomb at Graceland Cemetery. Photograph by Harold Allen, 1964, Historic American Building Survey, ILL,16-CHIG,47–1, Library of Congress Prints and Photographs Division.

Much of the eastern land, however, was enhanced by Jenney's assistant Ossian Cole Simonds (1855–1931) after he was appointed the cemetery's "superintendent, landscape gardener, engineer, and surveyor" in 1881. He remained in the position officially until 1900 but continued to work on the landscape until his death in 1931. Simonds worked closely with Graceland's president Bryan Lathrop (1844–1916). Under Lathrop's leadership, the height restrictions on markers were continually reduced and the number of monuments per lot was ultimately restricted to just one. As a result, the southeast portion of the site, in particular, offers the uncluttered views commonly sought by the landscape lawn model. It was Simonds, however, who carefully controlled plantings at the site to shape internal views. Under his direction, the addition of dense plantings as well as walls around the perimeter of the site served to shield the cemetery from views of urban encroachment beyond the cemetery's gates. Unlike most rural cemeteries that showcased external

views of adjacent bodies of water or cityscapes in the distance, Graceland concentrated views internally. Simonds also adeptly used plantings to meet the challenges posed by the "vast dome of the prairie sky and the omnipresent horizon, together with the openness and immense lateral spread of Graceland's setting."[248] As Christopher Vernon conveys expertly in his design history of the cemetery, Simonds "employed an internal axis—defined and accentuated by foreground plantings of native trees and shrubs—as a design device to establish and visually control a sense of infinite space within the cemetery. Simonds's axial constructions reduced the boundless prairie to a series of controllable, comprehensible pictures, enabling the viewer to establish his psychological place on the land through the carefully determined foreground."[249] Meanwhile, Simonds's planting compositions relied heavily—although not exclusively—upon indigenous species, which helped foster a sense of pride in American landscape design.

The nationally renowned firm Holabird & Roche (which had formerly included O. C. Simonds until 1883) designed the cemetery's major buildings in the Richardsonian Romanesque style, using thoughtful color palettes and horizontal lines to integrate them into the landscape. In the interior of the site, Holabird & Roche designed the chapel (1886–1888) with underground vaults built into a hillside and façades of rusticated red granite blocks that set a stylistic precedent for the firm's later commissions at the cemetery's southwest entrance. The chapel complements the site's landscape chromatically "with the earthy red, brown, and green tonalities of its granite walls and reddish-brown Spanish tile-roof."[250] Completed in 1896 of similar coursed ashlar blocks of granite, a one-story, L-shaped waiting room building features porticos at grade on the north and east façades and a low-pitched roof that helps the structure blend into the landscape. To the south of this building, the firm created a contemporaneous and complementary one-story administration building, thereby fashioning an entry ensemble that is "visually absorbed" into the landscape.[251]

The most noteworthy structure at Graceland, however, was designed by famed Chicago architect Louis Sullivan, a former employee of William LeBaron Jenney. Sullivan's 1890 Getty Tomb, which stands prominently on the bank of Lake Willowmere, is cited by the Commission on Chicago Historical and Architectural Landmarks as marking "the maturity of Sullivan's architectural style and the beginning of modern architecture in America." The commanding geometry and solidity of Sullivan's limestone cube is balanced with delicate, structured ornament, including the interlaced geometric and floral patterns of the bronze gates that stand prominently in a punctuated opening in the structure. The organic patterns he used also served to integrate the monument into the broader landscape, a reoccurring theme at Graceland.[252]

Crown Hill Cemetery, Indianapolis, Indiana, 1863

Indianapolis's public cemetery had served the city since its founding in 1821. By 1863, it was in a state of "public disgrace" as it faced an intensifying burden caused by local population explosion and Civil War fatalities, including prisoners who perished at Camp Morton and soldiers who died at City Hospital. Beginning in 1862, one wagon after another brought dead soldiers to the burial ground, where the graves were marked expediently with makeshift wooden headboards with painted epitaphs.[253] In the midst of the mounting crisis, James M. Ray, an Indianapolis pioneer who had helped establish the city cemetery, and other civic leaders began to explore the idea of establishing a large-scale rural cemetery for Indiana's capital city.

To begin formulating their plan, Ray and others traveled to Cincinnati to meet with Spring Grove Cemetery's superintendent Adolph Strauch about his cemetery's design and management. Afterward, twelve of the city's leading citizens met with John Chislett Sr., the superintendent of Pittsburgh's Allegheny Cemetery and the designer of Fort Wayne's Lindenwood Cemetery. Subsequently, Chislett was appointed to lead a committee to scout possible cemetery sites and plan for incorporation. When the landscape gardener glimpsed the elevation known as Crown Hill, part of Martin Williams's farm nearly three miles north of downtown, he reportedly said, "That is the spot. Buy those grounds at whatever price you have to pay."[254] Encompassing the "most conspicuous" and "most attractive" elevation around the city and standing between the White River and Fall Creek, the location was already a popular picnic retreat.[255] Ultimately, five tracts of land in the area, totaling about 274 acres, were purchased within six months of the cemetery's incorporation as a nonprofit organization on September 25, 1863. The cemetery was officially dedicated nine months later.

John Chislett declined the job of superintendent, but recommended instead his son, Frederick W. Chislett (1827–1899), who accepted the position and directed the layout and development of the cemetery until his death in 1899. By the time of the dedication ceremony, Chislett had, according to the *Sentinel*, "already conformed his plans to the topography of the ground, and the winding walks, drives and plats harmonize[d] delightfully with the configuration of the surface."[256] Chislett adopted the landscape lawn plan for the cemetery from the start of the site's development. In 1870, journalist W. R. Holloway keenly observed, "To the natural beauties of the grounds, in their picturesque undulations and abundance of forest trees, individual taste and affection have been added (under the judicious regulations by the managers), the ornaments of evergreens and flowering plants. Enclosures of lots have been forbidden, as marring the appearance of a cemetery, and tending, with the rust and decay of time, to disfigure rather than beautify."[257] In an 1896 published history, the cemetery association contended that the decision to adopt and carry out the lawn plan from the beginning put their site "in the front rank of modern rural cemeteries."[258]

Over time, Crown Hill Cemetery accepted the remains of Civil War soldiers from the very cemetery that had inspired its establishment. In 1866, the Federal government purchased Section 10 of Crown Hill for the interment of Union dead. Over seven hundred soldiers were disinterred from the city cemetery and other dishonorable burial locations in the area and reburied in orderly rows within the 1.4-acre section. These graves, too, were marked by temporary headboards at first, but were later replaced with the upright marble headstones generally associated with National Cemeteries. Eighty-five veterans were also laid to rest

in the section, until its last space was filled in 1898. About thirty years later, 1,616 soldiers—mostly fatalities from Camp Morton—were exhumed from a mass grave at the old city cemetery and reinterred in the Confederate Mound at Crown Hill.

The three most significant structures in the cemetery were constructed within twenty-five years of its founding. A High Victorian Gothic chapel was built of gray limestone between 1875 and 1877. Designed by Indianapolis architect Diedrich A. Bohlen (1827–1890), it was prominently positioned at the center of cemetery. In 1884, considering the trends in the movement of the city's population, the board of corporators elected to move the cemetery's main entrance from its western side on Michigan Road to the eastern side on Boulevard Place. Architect Adolph Scherrer (1847–1925), who completed the design for the Indiana State Capitol Building, was selected to design an

96. Monument to Benjamin Harrison, the 23rd President of the United States, on one of the rolling lawns at Crown Hill Cemetery. Photograph 1904, Detroit Publishing Company Photograph Collection, Library of Congress Prints and Photographs Division.

97. Front façade and setting of the Chapel and Vault, Crown Hill Cemetery. Photograph by Jack E. Boucher, 1970, Historic American Building Survey, IND,49-IND,13B-1, Library of Congress Prints and Photographs Division.

98. Adolph Scherrer's waiting station and High Victorian Gothic gateway, Crown Hill Cemetery. Postcard ca. 1910, Danylchak collection.

administration building and a new, impressive gateway at the 34th Street and Boulevard Place entrance. Scherrer's plan called for a "gate keeper's residence and office" that included a sitting room, dining room, kitchen and three bedrooms for the residence as well as a general waiting room, a ladies' waiting room, two offices, lavatories, and a bell tower. The stone-trimmed, brick building—a place where people rendezvoused —became known as the Waiting Station. Scherrer's companion High Victorian Gothic gateway of Indiana limestone featured three prominent Gothic arches. It was completed just in time for the funeral procession of the vice president of the United States Thomas A. Hendricks on November 30, 1885.

Although critics initially decried Crown Hill's distance from the city, the cemetery became increasingly accessible through improved public transportation options and soon became a popular retreat for the citizens of Indianapolis. Omnibuses began servicing the cemetery in 1864. However, the eight-hour, fifty-cent roundtrip was burdensome for those traveling to the site. The cemetery leaders consequently donated $10,000 for the creation of a streetcar line from today's 16th Street and Martin Luther King Jr. Boulevard to the cemetery's Michigan Road entrance. Cars operated on demand for funerals, special occasions, and memorial days. However, by 1875 the Indianapolis Street Railway Company was regularly operating streetcars to the cemetery, "where perambulating citizens disembarked for relaxation and contemplation, joining others traversing the winding lanes in their carriages."[259]

Woodlawn Cemetery, Bronx, New York, 1863

In 1863, a group of prominent New Yorkers led by Rev. Absolom Peters (1793–1869) purchased 313 acres north of New York City in the Bronx River Valley for the establishment of a new cemetery. The property was far enough removed from the congestion of the city to satisfy contemporary sensibilities regarding cemetery sites. However, the parcel sat along the New York and Harlem Railroad (now the Metro-North Railroad Harlem Line) and thus found favor for its accessibility. In its March 29, 1876 edition, the *Evening Post* highlighted this virtue in comparison to the city's earlier rural cemeteries: "The seeming necessity that compelled the establishment of our older cemeteries at points remote from the thickly-peopled districts of the metropolis has certainly entailed upon families

some extra expense and inconvenience.... While the newer cemetery is sufficiently secluded, it is reached in thirty minutes by rail from the Grand Central Depot, and the Harlem Railroad Company has made a station for express trains at its very gates." The railroad also eventually offered private funeral cars that could respectfully transport coffins and mourners to the grounds.

About a quarter of the chosen cemetery site was covered with deciduous trees; the rest was farmland fed by three brooks, which had been cultivated by the Bussing family for generations. After a visit in 1865, the secretary of the Laurel Hill Cemetery in Philadelphia praised the site for its "beautiful range of woodland hills" and its "extensive and picturesque views in every direction, including the Sound on one side and the Palisades on the other."[260] The founders chose architect James C. Sidney to lay out and enhance the inherent beauty of the landscape on the rural cemetery model.

In 1871, the *Evening Post* painted a vivid portrait of the first fifty-five acres developed in the northeast part of the grounds adjacent to the railroad station.

> The scene at the entrance here is charming. On one side is a deep ravine, left in its natural state of wild loveliness, through the midst of which a tumbling brook finds its way to a little lake. In the centre of the latter is a fountain which throws its jet to the height of thirty-four feet. To the border of the lake, beyond the ravine, a grassy slope descends from a belt of trees which skirts the entrance driveway. Just within the gateway the office of the cemetery forms an additional attraction to the eye, it being a picturesque stone cottage, overrun with English ivy. Judicious groupings of trees, with beds of flowers at spots where their bright colors appear most favorably, are other elements of a view which is certain to charm the spectator.[261]

From the start, a variety of natural and man-made elements were carefully organized to create a vividly picturesque setting. The Woodlawn trustees, however, soon questioned the practicality of Sidney's design scheme, and in 1867 Woodlawn representatives made three visits to Spring Grove Cemetery to study the new landscape lawn plan being implemented there. The Woodlawn trustees subsequently adopted the modified landscape style, a decision that was reported in the

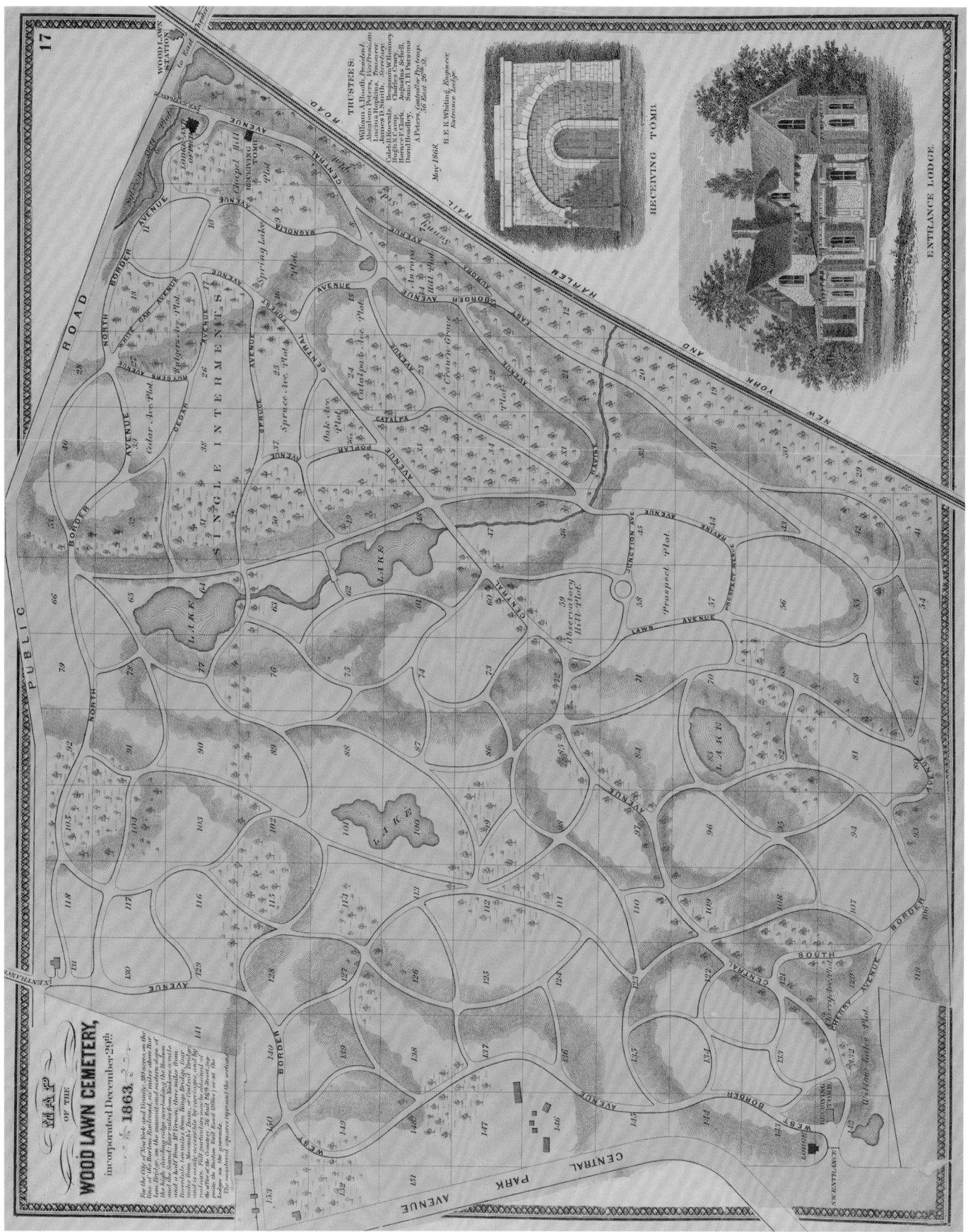

MAP
OF THE
WOOD LAWN CEMETERY,
incorporated December 29th
1863.

TRUSTEES:

William A. Booth, President.
Absalom Peters, Vice President.
Lucius Hopkins, Treasurer.
James B. Smith, Secretary.

Caleb Barstow,   Benjamin Wheeney,
Hugh N. Camp,   Charles Crary,
Horace F. Clark,   Augustus Schell,
Isaac Hoadley,   Sam. B. H. Parsons,
                    A Peters, Cashier by Temp.
                    56 East 25th St.

May 1868.   H. E. K. Whiting, Engineer.
              Entrance Lodge.

RECEIVING TOMB.

ENTRANCE LODGE.

NEW YORK AND HARLEM RAIL ROAD

Evening Post. The newspaper explained that excessive ornamentation of undivided lots would be eliminated to achieve "a pleasant harmony throughout."[262] The natural topography would be retained wherever possible. Visible lot boundaries would be prohibited. And graves, for the most part, would be marked with small slabs laid flush with the lawn. The *Evening Post* later observed that art was made "subservient to nature" with these most recent cemetery improvements.[263]

The cemetery's staff and the Trustees' Committee on Taste retained a strict level of control in the implementation of the landscape lawn plan, which ensured that the overall design concept was achieved. The cemetery strictly monitored the construction and

99. (left) Map of the Woodlawn Cemetery, 1868. From the *Atlas of New York and Vicinity: From Actual Surveys*, From the Lionel Pincus & Princess Firyal Map Division, the New York Public Library.

siting of the site's private monuments, which ensured they would not detract from their natural setting or create cluttered views. Woodlawn also encouraged creative designs for individual lots with plantings judiciously used to frame monuments and screen out other memorials from carefully constructed scenes. In addition, the cemetery adopted a circulation system where avenues and pedestrian pathways encircled lots and created clearly delineated boundaries without the intrusion of vertical elements like fences. Circular lots—one of the most distinctive features of the cemetery—were seen as ideal settings for single mausoleums or large monuments into the 1930s. In 1884, Hamilin Q. French designed a Classical Revival–style mausoleum for financier Jay Gould (1836–1892) that was modeled after the Maison Carrée temple in Nîmes, France. The mausoleum was carefully sited atop a rise at the center of the cemetery's largest circular lot allowing unrivaled views of all four imposing façades.

100. Woodlawn Cemetery, with its distinctive circular drives. From *The New Metropolis*, 1899, Danylchak collection.

Woodlawn welcomed the addition of grand mausoleums and memorials commemorating New York's well-to-do, who selected the cemetery more and more frequently because of its accessibility. Moreover, mausoleums had become increasingly popular among the city's elite after the body of department store mogul A. T. Stewart (1803–1876) was stolen from a Manhattan churchyard in 1878 and held for a $200,000 ransom. The robbers eventually surrendered the body at a secret meeting for a mere $20,000. Many moneyed New Yorkers commissioned influential architects or firms, including Carrère and Hastings; McKim, Mead & White; John Russell Pope; James Renwick; James Gamble Rogers; and Hunt and Hunt to create funerary fortresses that would display their status after death and keep them safe at the same time. Woodlawn Cemetery boasts 1,271 freestanding private family mausoleums—"likely the largest and most distinctive collection in the nation."[264]

Cedar Hill Cemetery, Hartford, Connecticut, 1864

In 1863, a group of prominent Hartford citizens assembled at the home of James C. Jackson (1818–1882) to discuss solutions to the overcrowded burial grounds of the city—the Ancient Burying Ground in the town center and the North and South Cemeteries, which had all reached capacity. The group appointed a committee, which included Jackson along with Hiram Bissell, a masonry contractor, and Jacob Weidenmann (1829–1893), the superintendent of construction of Hartford's Bushnell Park, to identify an appropriate site for the establishment of a rural cemetery—"one sufficiently removed from the city, possessing suitable soil and the largest number of other desirable characteristics, such as a variety of surface, beauty of landscape and running water."[265]

The committee investigated several different sites before locating the one that was ultimately chosen

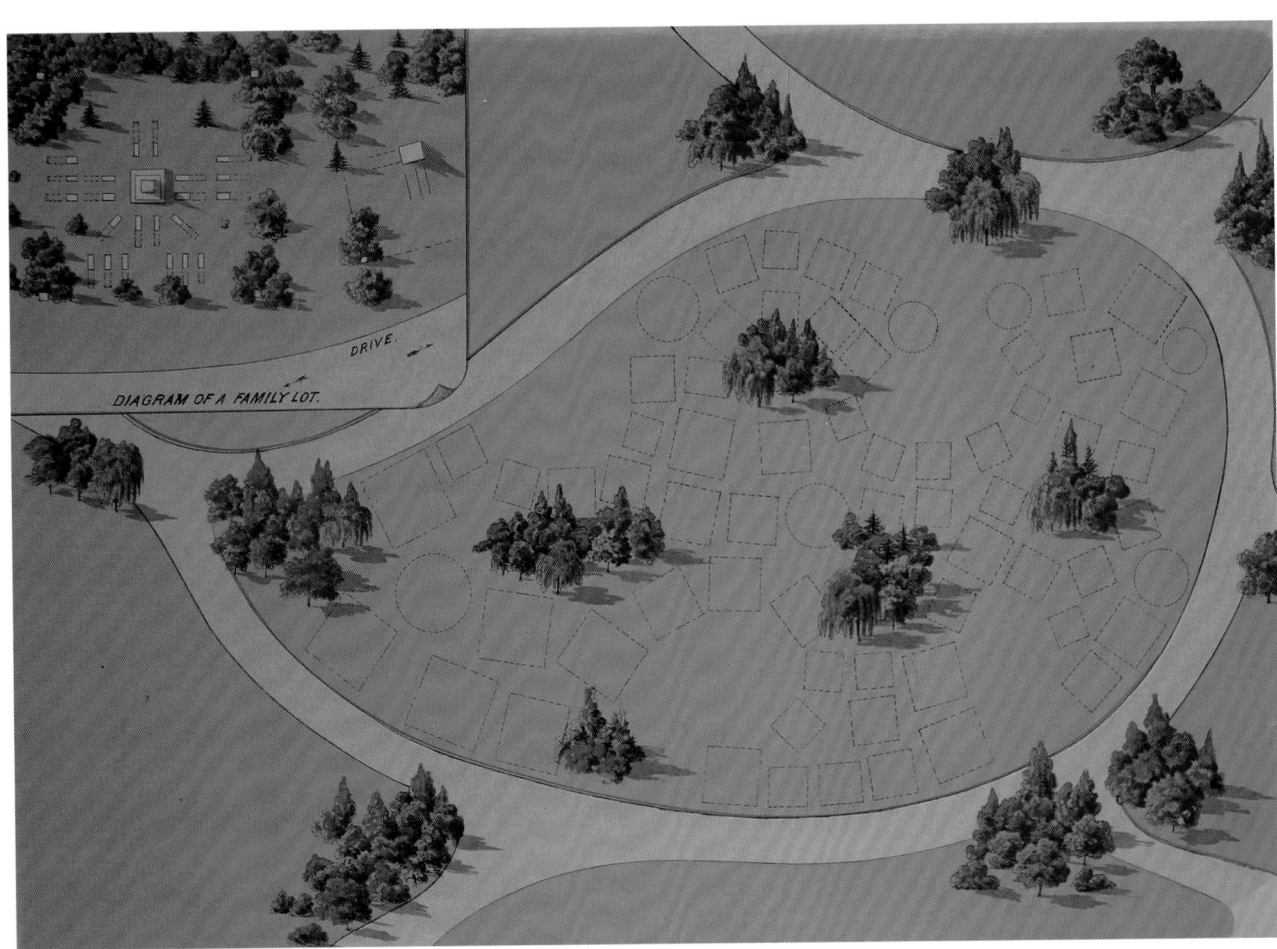

DRIVE.

DIAGRAM OF A FAMILY LOT.

101. Section XV of Cedar Hill Cemetery. Note the one central monument in the family lot. Plate XXIV from Weidenmann's *Beautifying Country Homes*, 1870. Courtesy of the Cherokee Garden Library at the Kenan Research Center at the Atlanta History Center.

for the cemetery—a 270-acre tract of land three miles from the center of the city. The undulating site possessed several desirable features including dry, gravelly loam soil suitable for interments, existing water features, and "a natural arboretum of all evergreen trees."[266] One of its greatest advantages, however, was the vast panorama of beautiful views offered by the site. A 1903 history of Cedar Hill described the scenery in detail:

> To the northward the gilded dome of the capitol building is seen, towering aloft in the midst of Hartford's church spires. Beyond and forty miles away is the Holyoke mountain range, with the familiar summits of Mount Tom and Mount Holyoke. The broad and fertile valley of the Connecticut river sweeps away eastward. Here and there, amid its rolling sea of meadow and forest, the clustered homes of many towns are distinctly visible; Rocky Hill, Wethersfield, Glastonbury, East Hartford, Manchester, South Windsor, and Rockville nestling between the eastern hills. Farther away and forming the background of a panorama, gorgeous in the colors of spring or autumn, there is the rugged range of hills extending from Eastbury northward to Bolton and beyond, with the Somers Mountains in view.[267]

The Hartford group accepted the site recommendation despite the challenge that it consisted of nine separate parcels, with some of the property owners not wishing to sell. In May of 1864, a Special Act of the General Assembly incorporated the Cedar Hill Cemetery Association, named for the grove of red cedar trees growing along the western ridge of the chosen site. The act also allowed the incorporators to purchase four contested parcels by eminent domain, and by June of 1866, all nine parcels had been assembled.

102. Gallup Memorial Gateway to Cedar Hill Cemetery. Photograph ca. 1900, Detroit Publishing Company Photograph Collection, Library of Congress Prints and Photographs Division.

103. The legacy of Weidenmann's open lawn concept at Cedar Hill Cemetery. Photograph by James R. Cothran, undated.

Jacob Weidenmann, who had come to Hartford a few years earlier to design Bushnell Park, was appointed the cemetery's first superintendent and given the responsibility of designing the site. Following the example of earlier cemetery prototypes, Weidenmann laid out a curvilinear circulation system that followed the undulating topography of the site. However, the landscape designer found inspiration in Adolph Strauch's work at Spring Grove and incorporated elements of the lawn plan into his overall design for Cedar Hill. Weidenmann incorporated a striking ornamental foreground, an unusual landscape element for a cemetery, into the design for the site. Sixty-five landscaped acres separated the burial sections of the cemetery from the roadway. Llyn Mawr, a man-made lake along the entrance avenue, covered nearly eight acres. In succeeding years, the foreground saw the addition of the Superintendent's Cottage (1875), the Northram Chapel (1882), and the Gallup Memorial Gateway (1889).

Weidenmann also created smaller burial lots than in other rural cemeteries and laid them out so they were not contiguous. This allowed the land between the lots to be reserved for plantings by the superintendent. Weidenmann also banned fences, hedges, and copings around lots, which helped create beautiful open vistas, a unified aesthetic, and a harmonious feeling throughout the cemetery. Overall, his open-lawn concept emphasized a balance between the natural and man-made features of the landscape. In 1889, Weidenmann codified the principles of his design scheme at Cedar Hill Cemetery in his book *Modern Cemeteries*.

Mount Auburn Revisited

In the latter part of the nineteenth century, Mount Auburn's landscape evolved dramatically to reflect more closely the design principles of Adolph Strauch at Spring Grove as well as the mid-century vogue for the "gardenesque"—a style that favored ornamental plant displays.

In its first twenty-five years of existence, Mount Auburn was a heavily forested landscape. However, as early as 1855, the cemetery corporation began removing superfluous trees and trimming others so that, according to its 1856 Annual Report, "the whole ground has a more finished and ornamental appearance than it before possessed."[268] The forest, which had become quite dense over time, was by then seen as "detrimental and inconvenient." Views were obstructed, leaves and debris accumulated quickly, and the sun was blocked out in many areas inhibiting the cultivation of healthy lawns and flowers. In 1860, Jacob Bigelow, the president of the corporation, made the radical recommendation to remove one-half of the trees on the site in order to leave "broad vistas and open spaces, through which the works of art could be seen; and the light of the sun might be admitted to the grass and cultivated flowers."[269] With this approach, he said, the "perfection of Mount Auburn, as far as its natural features are concerned, would be attained."[270] Throughout the 1860s Mount Auburn removed numerous trees, particularly evergreens, from the site. As trees were removed, the cemetery corporation replaced them with more burial space and unimpeded lawns that could be easily maintained with the lawn mower, which had become widely manufactured by the 1860s. Meanwhile, Bigelow instituted a program of ornamental shrub planting, which continued through the 1870s. He favored native rhododendron, mountain laurel,

and roses as well as newly available varieties of deciduous shrubs like spirea.

Mount Auburn's Picturesque landscape was also subdued in the latter part of the nineteenth century with the trimming of some of its steepest hills. The regrading program commenced, in part, so that the soil and gravel could be used to fill in bogs, creating more burial space. Some of the soil was also used to smooth the shorelines of other water features. The cemetery's extensive regrading program eliminated much of the site's uneven terrain. Cedar Hill, for instance, was trimmed into a symmetrical, oval mound and planted with grass.

During its first several decades, Mount Auburn saw increasingly dense accumulations of fences and stone curbing around family plots. Fencing had remained fashionable into the 1850s. Meanwhile, granite curbing reached its peak popularity in the 1860s. In 1861, Mount Auburn commentator Wilson Flagg echoed Adolph Strauch and others who recognized the unfavorable effect that incessant man-made additions had on the naturalistic funerary landscape. At Mount Auburn, he found fault with the multiplicity of small, individual ornaments, many of which had been added by those "very defective in judgment." All the "ridiculous" and "meretricious embellishments," he said,

104. Mount Auburn Cemetery with a more ornamental landscape than it had possessed in its earliest decades of existence. Stereograph ca. 1914, Underwood & Underwood, publishers, Library of Congress Prints and Photographs Division.

prevented the solemnity and grandeur of the place to be experienced. Instead, he promoted the exclusion of fences, excessive monumental stones, and useless adornments. "By avoiding this defect," he said, "we should promote both that unity and harmony which are so necessary to produce a deep influence on the mind."[271] By the 1870s, the cemetery's management encouraged the removal of curbing and fencing by lot owners to remedy the negative visual impacts on the naturalistic landscape. The first documented fence removal was in 1871, and by the late 1870s "they were being swept away in large numbers."[272] Meanwhile, the 1870s and 1880s witnessed the removal of stone curbing as the "reaction against it intensified."[273]

Notably, when the cemetery corporation developed its "Stone Farm" section south of Washington tower in the 1870s, it utilized the landscape lawn plan. The cemetery prohibited lot enclosures in the new section and only allowed low headstones. The result was described in the cemetery's 1875 Annual Report: "lawns ornamented with flowers and shade trees; where the monuments are not obtrusive, the boundaries of the lots only marked by sunken posts; and where, from the absence of stonework and iron fences, a general aspect of rural beauty, and quiet is the characteristic feature."[274]

Although the Mount Auburn landscape continued to be reshaped over time in response to changing tastes, the original rural cemetery landscape can still be seen at Consecration Dell, where Joseph Story shared the founders' vision for a new type of burial place. And, although the American cemetery landscape style evolved in the latter part of the nineteenth century, Mount Auburn's original model of a large-scale, designed, public cemetery away from the confines of the city continued to endure. In 2003, Mount Auburn Cemetery was designated a National Historic Landmark by the Secretary of the Interior recognizing it as one of the country's most significant designed landscapes.

CHAPTER 4

Physical and Design Characteristics of Rural Cemeteries ❧

Rural cemetery landscapes featured a specific set of physical and design characteristics that markedly differentiated these spaces from past urban burial grounds. Mount Auburn Cemetery set influential precedents that were adopted repeatedly by rural cemeteries of the mid-nineteenth century. Rural cemetery corporations chose extramural sites large in scale. They sought sites with existing collections of diverse trees and shrubs and varied, broken terrain that lent themselves to Picturesque treatment. The layout of these burial grounds generally respected the topography of the site and showcased various and changing views. Perimeter walls or fences and defined, often monumental, gateways announced the safety of the grave. Distinctive and stylized monuments marked gravesites and impressive mausoleums publicized the wealth of their inhabitants. With their defined boundaries, family and group plots checkered the landscape declaring the increasing importance of familial and group connections. Eventually, the accumulation of man-made elements unfavorably tipped the balance between nature and art, prompting a reevaluation of the appropriateness of plot enclosures and so many monuments. A quarter century after the rural cemetery movement began, Adolph Strauch made significant modifications to the prevailing collection of design characteristics with the development of his landscape lawn plan.

Size

Rural cemeteries were established on large tracts of land because they were, in part, a reaction against the overcrowded conditions associated with church or meetinghouse graveyards in the urban core. The economic and political value of land in the center of cities necessarily limited the size of urban graveyards. As American cities grew and the number of citizen burials increased over time, limitations on space created increasingly objectionable graveyard practices. Burials were often stacked atop one another or the remains of decomposed bodies were removed from the landscape to accommodate new burials. Leaders in America's largest cities were eventually compelled to establish new burial grounds with an eye to the future—having enough space to accommodate perpetual burials for years to come. Pastoral tracts on the outskirts were less expensive than city real estate; therefore, larger landscapes could conceivably be acquired and dedicated to the permanent burial of the dead.

America's largest cities were served by extensive rural cemeteries anywhere between about fifty and three hundred acres in size. Boston, Massachusetts, with a population of 61,392 people, was the fourth-largest city in the United States in 1830. The following year, Mount Auburn Cemetery was established on seventy-two acres of land outside the city. By comparison, the Granary Burying Ground, one of the city's principal graveyards up until that time, encompassed less than two acres. Mount Auburn's original acreage was actually one of the smaller rural cemetery land acquisitions among the country's largest cities. In 1840, Pittsburgh, Pennsylvania, ranked as the seventeenth-largest city in the United States with 21,115 people. In 1844, Allegheny Cemetery was established on one hundred acres of land outside that city. A year later, Albany Rural was established on 240 acres. In the 1840 census,

Albany, New York, had counted 33,721 people, ranking it as the ninth-largest city in the nation that year.

Small towns established rural cemeteries, too. Although they were on a scale smaller than those of the largest American cities, they were still larger than what had previously been considered necessary for burial grounds. For example, in 1838, Worchester Rural, in Worchester, Massachusetts, was established on twenty-four acres of land. The city—the fifty-fourth largest in the country in 1840—only had 7,497 inhabitants. Established in 1851, Fort Hill Cemetery in Auburn, New York, had twenty-two acres of land even though the town only had a population of 9,548. These rural cemetery examples had significantly more land than the burial ground Richmond, Virginia, established in 1820 as the city of twelve thousand inhabitants was facing a burial crisis. Prior to the establishment of the rural cemetery model, Richmond acquired property in the northwestern portion of its city to accommodate burial for its citizens. Just four acres of land was devoted to what soon became the city's primary municipal burial ground.

105. Aerial view of Laurel Hill Cemetery, which now encompasses seventy-four acres. Photograph by Jack E. Boucher, 2003, Historic American Building Survey, Pa., 51-PHILA,100–99, Library of Congress Prints and Photographs Division.

PHYSICAL AND DESIGN CHARACTERISTICS OF RURAL CEMETERIES

106. Laurel Hill Cemetery, established on the former country estate of Joseph Sims outside of Philadelphia, Pennsylvania. Drawn from nature by Aug. Kölllner; lith. by Deroy; printed by Cattier, ca. 1848, Library of Congress Prints and Photographs Division.

Location

Rural cemeteries were established beyond the dense urban cores of cities to both respect and protect the living and the dead. Rural cemeteries were, in part, established as a reaction against the unsanitary conditions of urban graveyards and the alleged miasmas that emanated from decaying bodies and made people in adjacent areas sick. It was thus assumed that removing burial grounds to remote locations protected city dwellers from disease.

Establishing burial grounds outside the city also protected them from immediate real estate pressures. As cities grew exponentially in the early part of the nineteenth century and urban land became more valuable, greed or negligence sometimes trumped the respect of human remains. Entire graveyards—like the

Hammond Street burial lot in Bangor, Maine—were often removed from the path of development. Meanwhile, in his dedication address for Forest Lawn Cemetery in Buffalo, New York, the Honorable G. W. Clinton (1807–1885) lamented the condition of the city's earlier graveyard: "Long before another generation shall have passed away, it will be a mass of hideous desolation, if it be not unholily uprooted."[1] However, in the minds of the civic leaders who established them, rural (or perhaps more aptly described as exurban) cemeteries were beyond the pressure of commercial improvements. As transportation improvements throughout the nineteenth century enabled cities to grow outward, beyond the "walking city," however, many of these exurban cemeteries eventually did become surrounded by urban sprawl.

Cemeteries outside the city, beyond the din and disorder of everyday urban life, also offered a morally appropriate final resting place for the dead and a consoling retreat for family members and visitors. In his compelling dedicatory address at Forest Hills Cemetery, Rev. George Putnam explained, "It is out of keeping with all our affectionate memories of the departed, and with our ideas of the sacred repose due to their remains, that their tomb-doors should echo the worldly talk and angry disputes, and light laugh and jest of the thronged street and market-place."[2] Meanwhile, *Green-Wood Illustrated* emphasized the refuge the exurban cemetery offered the city's citizens: "A short half-hour ago, he was in the midst of a discordant Babel; he was one of the hurrying, jostling crowd; he was encompassed by the whirl and fever of artificial life. Now he stands alone, in Nature's inner court—in her silent, solemn sanctuary. Her holiest influences are all around him, and his heart whispers, It is good to be here!"[3] In contemplating the site selection for Spring Grove Cemetery, its founders deemed it necessary that the site be close enough to the city to be convenient but far enough away to be an escape: "It should be as near the city as would be consistent with the necessary distance from the annoyances which the smoke, the turbulence and the noises of the city of industry and commerce, might occasion to visitors of the 'city of the silent.'"[4] Ultimately, Spring Grove was established on a site four miles from Cincinnati, Ohio.

While these cemeteries were sited in exurban locations, they were close enough to allow convenient access for family members and visitors by horse and carriage and later by public transportation options like the omnibus. When it was founded, Forest Home Cemetery was located about two miles outside the city limits of Milwaukee, Wisconsin; Mount Hope Cemetery was sited about two-and-one-half miles from the city center of Bangor, Maine; Oakwood Cemetery was one-and-one-half miles from the central business district of Syracuse, New, York; while White Plains Rural Cemetery was established just on the northern boundary of the small town of White Plains, New York.

107. Richmond, Virginia, from Hollywood Cemetery. Engraving from *Picturesque America*, 1874, Danylchak collection.

Grounds

The early rural cemetery aesthetic drew inspiration from the Picturesque English landscape garden tradition. Cemetery organizers chose parcels upon which to build that already possessed striking natural features, especially diversified ground that included a variety of landscape elements such as prominent knolls, deep valleys, and even shadowy grottos. In his consecration address at Albany Rural Cemetery, the Honorable D. D. Barnard testified with enthusiasm: "The grounds where we are now assembled have been selected for a cemetery . . . with a special view to their natural beauty, and their capability of improvement after the manner of landscape gardening. . . . What pleasant hills and knolls—what gentle slopes—what abrupt declivities—what bushy dells—what trees and groves—what silvery, soft-toned, gentle, living waters, are here—and what expressive silence—what religious repose!"[5] The founders of Spring Grove Cemetery also selected a topographically diverse site that was exceedingly suitable for applying the "picturesque aesthetics they knew from reading Bryant, Wordsworth, Sir Uvedale Price, and William Gilpin."[6] At the height of the rural cemetery movement, Andrew Jackson Downing commented on what constituted the Picturesque ideal. The Picturesque, he said, "aims at the production of outlines of a certain spirited irregularity, surfaces comparatively abrupt and broken, and growth of a somewhat wild and bold character. The shape of the ground sought after, has its occasional smoothness varied by sudden variations, and in parts runs into dingles, rocky groups, and broken banks. The trees should in many places be old and irregular, with rough stems and bark; and pines, larches, and other trees of striking, irregular growth, must appear in numbers sufficient to give character to the woody outlines."[7]

Rural cemetery founders particularly valued land that encompassed or overlooked picturesque water features. For instance, the founders of Rose Hill Cemetery in Macon, Georgia, chose an elevated site on the banks of the Ocmulgee River to create a burial place, both soothing and thought-provoking. The cemetery's designer Simri Rose emphasized the importance of the waterway in his description of site: "The river, murmuring over its rocky bed, wheeling around immovable

108. Elmwood Cemetery, Detroit, Michigan. Postcard ca. 1914, Cothran collection.

Scene in Forest Lawn Cemetery, Buffalo, N. Y.

109. Lake and bridge in Forest Lawn Cemetery, Buffalo, New York. Postcard ca. 1913, Danylchak collection.

cliffs of granite and flint, rolling, on and on for ever, like the tide of human life, to mingle in the unfathomed and undefined abyss of eternity, imparts an instructive lesson, while the beauties of the scene disarm death of half its terrors."[8] In addition, sites often encompassed existing water features like springs or streams; in time, some of these were used to create picturesque ponds or waterfalls. For Downing, water—in the Picturesque style—took certain characteristic forms: "the lake or stream with bold shore and rocky, wood-fringed margin, or the cascade in the secluded dell."[9]

Layout

Landscape gardeners and surveyors, in laying out rural cemetery grounds, tried to further enhance the picturesque qualities of the sites. Nature was not only something to be preserved but actually improved upon to make it more dramatic. Using existing and engineered landforms, native and introduced plants, designers created a variety of spatial relationships and framed desirable views and vistas. Most important, they created circulation systems that showcased the

site's striking scenes and conspicuously announced to visitors their return to nature.

Rural cemetery designers laid out informal, curvilinear circulation systems that served to purposely create an aesthetic and psychological distinction from the gridiron pattern of most city streets. Urban planners had realized that a straightforward grid system helped stimulate growth, because it was easier to buy and sell land lots described by a Cartesian grid.[10] This urban desire for efficiency and geographic legibility created a mundane repetitiveness of gridded roadways. In sharp contrast, winding cemetery drives generally respected the uneven topography of their rural sites. Curvilinear drives and walkways fostered satisfying surprise and thus emphasized the cemetery's role as a retreat from the monotony of the urban environment. The names given to the avenues and pathways within the new cemetery sites also had rural connotations. At Mount Auburn, most of its avenues took the names of trees like cedar, cypress, and beech. Meanwhile, its paths often took the names of flowering plants like snowdrop, tulip, and violet. Other cemeteries followed the trend of naming roadways with plant names and occasionally other landscape features.

Curvilinear circulation systems also served to enhance the visitor's interaction with the picturesque environment. The roadways often deliberately had sharp turns, which acted to slow down traffic and encourage visitors to take in the sights in an unhurried fashion. The roadways led their travelers to the most scenic cemetery views and vistas within the site, often creating purposeful sequences of landscape scenes, including carefully framed monuments. The circulation routes also enabled the visitor to experience the alteration of open and closed spaces and shaded and sunny areas, which contemporary aesthetes valued. The layout of drives and walkways also purposely cultivated a sense that the traveler within the cemetery was on a journey, exploring the twists and turns of life.

110. General view of roadway and hillside monuments, with the site's chapel in the background, Oak Hill Cemetery, Washington, D.C. Photograph by Erica Danylchak, 2010.

111. Mulberry Avenue sign at Green-Wood Cemetery, Brooklyn, New York. Photograph by James R. Cothran, undated.

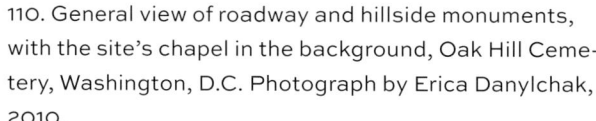

Because the labyrinth of pathways was often so extensive within these rural landscapes, guide-boards were sometimes placed along avenues and guidebooks were often published to help the visitor navigate the system. Albany Rural Cemetery, for instance, produced a "little manual" and recommended it as an "intelligent and agreeable companion" for a journey along "their weirdly wrought network of serpentine avenues and paths, so perfectly bewildering in the intensity of its complication."[11]

112. Road in Sleepy Hollow Cemetery, Concord, Massachusetts. Photograph ca. 1910– 1920, Detroit Publishing Company Photograph Collection, Library of Congress Prints and Photographs Division.

Entrance and Perimeter

Over time, rural cemetery corporations encompassed their sites with fences or hedges, in part, to reassure families that the graves of their loved ones would not be desecrated. Urban burial grounds had generally lacked enclosures, which allowed animals to graze on hallowed ground or even disturb gravesites. More disturbing to descendants, however, were reports of grave looting and robbing. Just prior to the rise of rural cemeteries, the theft of bodies from burial grounds had become prevalent as dissection became a standard part of the anatomical training of medical professionals.[12] In 1847, *Green-Wood Illustrated* emphasized and promoted the fact that the cemetery offered a protected resting place. The cemetery, it said,

113. The secure South Avenue Entrance, Mount Hope Cemetery, Rochester, New York. Postcard postmarked 1909, Cothran collection.

"furnishes, in its well-guarded enclosure, full security against those violations of the grave, by which the zeal of science or of gain has so often shocked public sentiments, and deeply injured the feelings of survivors."[13] Green-Wood's first fence, which was wooden, was completed by 1840. It was common for rural cemetery associations to erect temporary fences quickly. Sturdier, sometimes more decorative fences, however, usually took a lengthier time to install. Green-Wood's current fence was built in segments over a forty-year period beginning in 1860.

Rural cemeteries also offered defined entrances into their enclosed spaces. Early in their existence, rural cemeteries typically had simple cast-iron or stone gateways. Substantial rural cemeteries, however, often replaced those initial enhancements with imposing

114. The Gothic Revival main gate at Forest Hills Cemetery, Boston, Massachusetts. Photograph ca. 1890, Detroit Publishing Company Photograph Collection, Library of Congress Prints and Photographs Division.

structures. The gateway, often flanked by a keeper's lodge or superintendent's gatehouse, reinforced a sense of security. Moreover, the gateway had a symbolic function—it represented the passage from the frenzied everyday world into a sacred, quiet space. The gateway helped set the mood for the transition. Gothic Revival–style architecture was often employed, for example, to conjure a romantic sensibility. This picturesque style of architecture was seen as supremely suitable for rural environments. It offered a visually distinctive break from the city streetscape and reinforced the visitor's transition into a setting where architecture and nature would complement each other.

Chapels and Receiving Tombs

Rural cemeteries incorporated other structures into their sites—including chapels and receiving tombs—that were not only functional but also added to the picturesque character of the landscape. Receiving tombs were necessary structures in the nineteenth century.

During winter months when work crews were unable to dig graves in frozen soil, cemeteries needed a place to temporarily deposit bodies until the spring thaw. If families requested a temporary delay in interment, receiving tombs could also serve as brief waystations. Such requests were often motivated by the fear of having the presumed dead buried alive—a real concern in nineteenth century society. Cemeteries also recognized the need to build chapels for funeral services. Prior to the construction of a chapel at Green-Wood Cemetery, Nehemiah Cleaveland persuasively argued in 1847, "When the great number of interments made in [the cemetery] is considered, it cannot be doubted, that there are many families, summoned by these mournful errands to the grave, to whom such a building would be a great accommodation. Nowhere, certainly, could the last rites of love and religion be more decently paid, than in such a place, set apart for funereal purposes; while, at the same time, the afflicted home might be relieved from what is too

115. The James Renwick–designed Chapel in Oak Hill Cemetery, Washington, D.C. Photograph by Jack E. Boucher, 1969, Historic American Building Survey, D.C.,GEO,41B-1, Library of Congress Prints and Photographs Division.

often the intrusive bustle of a crowded funeral."[14]

Rural cemeteries frequently commissioned accomplished architects to design these structures as eye-catching edifices integrated thoughtfully into the landscape. These structures were often designed in the Gothic Revival style, reflecting in part the influence of American tastemaker Andrew Jackson Downing, who preached that the style was particularly fitting for a landscape exhibiting picturesque irregularity. Downing had himself been influenced by the ideas of earlier English landscape commentators including William Gilpin and Richard Payne Knight (1750–1824) as well as the contemporary English architectural critic John Ruskin (1819–1900). Meanwhile, rural cemetery advocates identified the style as being especially appropriate for sepulchral architecture: "This style, admitting of an endless variety of ornament if required, or of exhibiting beauty in severe simplicity, if necessary, is peculiarly suitable for sacred architecture; and the ancient cathedrals of Europe, by the adoption of this style, have become perpetual models of beauty and grace."[15] The style had, in fact, become increasingly popular for church designs in the United States beginning in the early nineteenth century. In 1850, James Renwick Jr. (1818–1895), the celebrated designer of the Smithsonian Institution Building in Washington, D.C., was commissioned to design the chapel at Oak Hill Cemetery in Georgetown. Perched atop the highest ridge in the cemetery, Renwick's chapel is a small, but exquisite, example of the Gothic Revival style with its steeply pitched roof, buttresses, and stained glass lancet windows accented with tracery. Meanwhile, Richard Upjohn (1802–1878), a British-born American architect, was commissioned to design a new receiving tomb for Green-Wood Cemetery. Upjohn had already garnered acclaim for his Gothic Revival–style churches, including Trinity Church in Manhattan, which had been completed in 1846. Built into a hillside, Upjohn's receiving tomb features an elegant Gothic Revival style façade of red sandstone.

Monuments

The originators of the rural cemetery movement actively sought to create a visual disparity between their new landscapes and earlier urban burial grounds. They embraced new monument materials as one way to create a marked difference. Urban burial grounds had primarily featured markers made of slate or limestone. Rural cemetery supporters, however, embraced marble and granite because of their aesthetic and symbolic qualities. The types of marble and granite used in rural cemeteries were lighter in hue than stones used in earlier burial grounds, and they contrasted sharply with and became more luminous against carefully constructed backgrounds of trees and shrubs. Often starkly white, the marble and granite monuments "provided a newly desirable, optimistic symbolism consonant with new attitudes toward death and the hereafter, more appropriate in the mind of the times than the grim gray slate of old."[16]

Rural cemetery advocates also embraced the use of sculptural memorials over the simplistic markers seen in earlier burial grounds. They aspired to emulate English landscape gardens, which were dramatically punctuated by sculptural monuments and architectural objects. Cemetery management, therefore, encouraged the placement of large, three-dimensional monuments within their grounds, at least early in the movement. Meanwhile, in 1833, Mount Auburn actually prohibited the use of thin, perpendicular slab markers within the cemetery, setting a powerful precedent. The desire for sculptural monuments also necessitated a change in monument materials. The properties of slate made it conducive to creating thin markers with surface engraving but not fashioning three-dimensional figures. Marble and granite, however, could be ornately sculpted. Marble became popular in New England after it was first quarried in Vermont in the 1780s and was the stone of choice in the first decades of the rural cemetery movement. Notably, marble held associations with the art of classical antiquity, a connotation the founders of rural cemeteries wanted to foster. After the Civil War, however, new technology made granite—a much harder stone—easier and cheaper to carve, which facilitated its growing popularity.

As time passed, rural cemeteries became outdoor sculpture museums showcasing work from the first generations of American sculptors as well as renowned sculptors from abroad. Leading American artists like Thomas Crawford, Henry Dexter, Daniel Chester French, and Martin Milmore contributed works to rural cemeteries. Notable European sculptors also garnered commissions for memorials. Italian sculptor Nicola Cantalamessa-Papotti (1833–1910), for instance, contributed two significant marble sculptures to Mount Hope Cemetery in Rochester, New York. The sculptor had previously completed commissions for

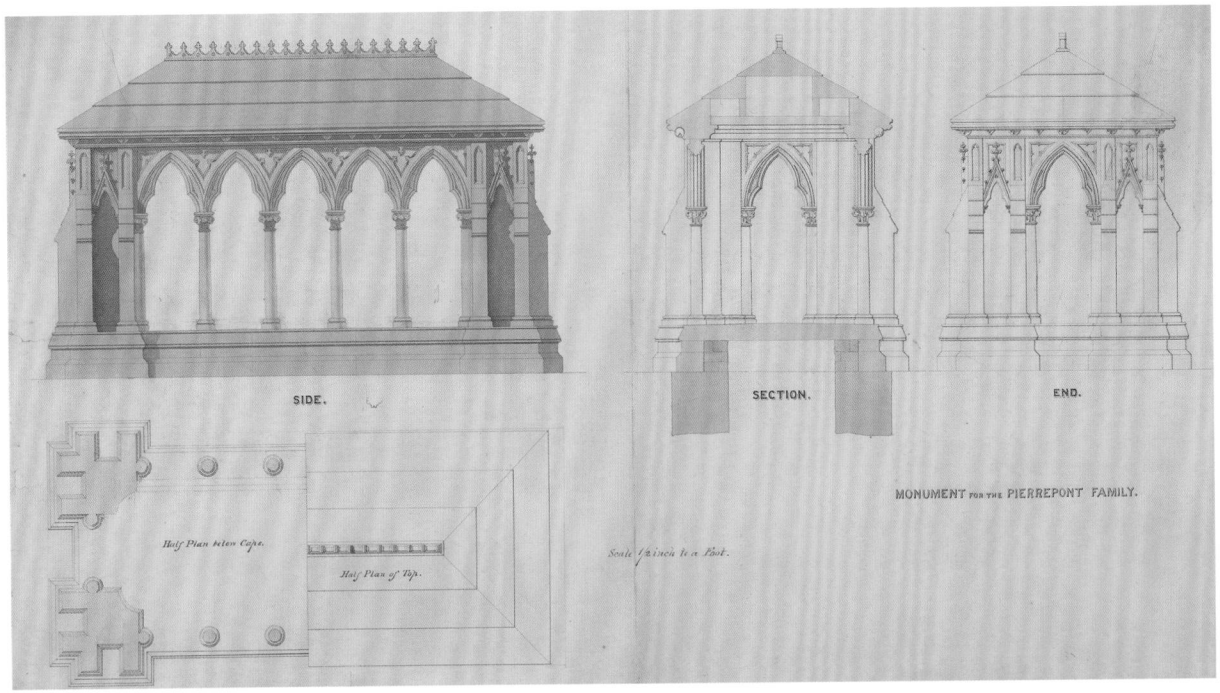

116. Pierrepont family monument, Green-Wood Cemetery, Brooklyn, New York. Elevations, plans, and section, Richard Upjohn, Architect, 1863, Library of Congress Prints and Photographs Division.

King Ferdinand II and Pope Pius IX. At Mount Hope, his *Weary Pilgrim* (1882) marks the Aaron Erickson family plot and depicts a pilgrim during the Crusades taking a rest on his journey to the Holy Land. His *Saint John on the Isle of Patmos* (1874) graces the George Ellwanger family plot and portrays, in the words of an 1885 guidebook to the cemetery, St. John the Divine "in a listening attitude and recording the revelation from Heaven."

Guidebooks often included extensive descriptions of a site's art work for the visitor; in fact, these books helped advanced the goal of cemeteries to act as cultural institutions—"school[s] of instruction . . . in architecture, sculpture, landscape gardening, arboriculture and botany."[17] *Smith's Illustrated Guide to and Through Laurel Hill Cemetery,* for instance, noted that the first objects worthy of seeing inside the gates of the cemetery were English sculptor Thom's celebrated statues of *Old Mortality, His Pony, and Sir Walter Scott,* "being exquisite specimens of art."[18] The guidebook noted that the sculpture of Scott was "superb in design, execution and finish," while the sculptures of Old Mortality and his pony were "rich in expression and pictural effect."[19] The guidebook also included an extensive passage from Scott's novel *Old Mortality* to illustrate for the visitor how faithful the sculptor had been to the inspirational source.

Both rural cemetery corporations and individual families hastened the variety of monumental forms added to these new burial landscapes. Cemetery corporations encouraged diversity to enhance the visual appearance of the grounds. *Green-Wood Illustrated* asserted that variety was essential to having a "pleasing effect" and avoiding "a wearisome sameness." Meanwhile, in the nineteenth century, a growing sense of individualism spurred distinctive memorials to the deceased, which often incorporated symbolism representing their profession, age, social status, or achievements. Pride also helped drive the swelling number of unique individual monuments as families vied to have monuments at least as fashionable, if not more so, as their eternal neighbors. Rural cemeteries, therefore, became visual registers of social status—and stratification—in their communities.

The desire for middle- and upper-class families to mark their cemetery territory with commemorative monuments drove the growth of the monument manufacturing industry. An 1852 guidebook to Laurel Hill Cemetery indicated that it had only been "within the last twelve or fifteen years that monumental architecture has had an existence, as such, in the United States."[20] Prior to that, sepulchral memorials were of a "very primitive character."[21] Concurrent with the rise of rural cemeteries, an ever-increasing network of railroad lines allowed local artisans to obtain large blocks of marble for their sculptural creations. As demand for monuments by cemetery proprietors increased, however, large monument companies replaced smaller shops and vied for business with ads in cemetery guidebooks. The largest cemeteries even saw monument companies set up enterprises conveniently adjacent to their grounds. For instance, in the 1864 Mount Auburn Cemetery *Visitors Reference Book,* the Mount Auburn Marble Works advertised its services. Located "near the cemetery" in Cambridge, the company was a "Dealer and Manufacturer of Monuments, Head-Stones, Tablets, And every description of Plain and Ornamental Marble Work." The guidebook

also included advertisements for eight other area firms that specialized in either granite or marble monuments. Monuments even became available in the latter part of the nineteenth century through mail order catalogs like the *Excelsior Statuary Book* (1895) and the Monumental Bronze Company's *White Bronze Monuments* (ca. 1882).

The rise of large monument companies, often dealing in precut, standardized monumental art, actually hastened the decline of variety in memorial forms. In fact, visitors to rural cemetery sites often found identical monuments within the grounds, sometimes even within the same burial section. Duplicates became more abundant as the century progressed because of mail order catalogs and improved transportation networks. The country's extensive network of railroad lines enabled proprietors at almost any rural cemetery to obtain stock monuments from large manufacturers. In fact, identical monuments could actually be found in distant cemeteries. For example, Cleveland's Lake View Cemetery, Chicago's Graceland, Boston's Mount

117. General view down the avenue of central section J at Laurel Hill Cemetery in Philadelphia, Pennsylvania. Photograph by Jack E. Boucher, 1989, Historic American Building Survey, Pa.,51-PHILA,100–38, Library of Congress Prints and Photographs Division.

Auburn, Baltimore's Green Mount, and Brooklyn's Green-Wood all witnessed the addition of the same circa-1860 male angel pointing upward and downward.[22] As a result of these developments, cemeteries actually advised families to exercise caution when purchasing monuments to avoid tedious monotony in cemetery art. Cemeteries like Green-Wood advised its lot holders to make more probing inquiries when ordering monuments and not always take the suggestion of the stone-mason in order to help ensure variety and quality in the monument collection at the site.

The marker messaging in rural cemeteries was also markedly different from colonial burial grounds. Inscriptions in earlier burial places generally noted basic vital statistics. For example, an inscription in the Ancient Burying Ground in Hartford, Connecticut reads:

> Here lies Interr'd
> The body of Mrs.
> SARAH BURR
> Who departed this life
> Oct. ye 16th
> 1750, Aged 69
> years.

Meanwhile, if verses appeared on colonial markers, they were "meant to provide instruction, not comfort."[23] Many carried the message of *momento mori:*

> Stranger, stop and cast an eye,
> As you are now, so once was I,
> As I am now, so you shall be,
> Prepare for death and follow me.[24]

Monument inscriptions changed, however, with the rise of Romanticism and decline of Puritanism. Nineteenth-century gravestone language emphasized messages of hope and immortality, reflecting significant changes in America's religious climate. At the same time, family and friends of the deceased felt "a rising need to proclaim one's grief, to advertise it on the tomb," which by this time had become something it was not before—"the privileged place of memory and regret."[25] The gravestone or monument became an important device of commemoration; expressive, personal, and sentimental epitaphs became pervasive in rural cemeteries. Reflecting this shift toward commemorative burial, the most basic introductory language used on gravestones changed from "Here lies the body of" to "In memory of."[26]

An 1860 guide to Forest Hills Cemetery highlighted types of epitaphs common throughout its grounds. Some stones were engraved with words "expressive of the fond remembrance in which the lost are held by the mourner":

> She lives in every thought,
> In every dream she smiles again
> And speaks a blessing to the heart.

Other monuments, it said, featured lines "descriptive of a serene and peaceful death":

> The mother gave her infant life and breath,
> Then calmly yielded to a blissful death;
> Soon followed her the babe, as if to share
> A sainted mother's fostering love and care.
> Together here their moldering relics rest,
> Their glorious spirits are together blest.

Most frequent, the guide said, were "words which are the utterances of Faith and Hope, looking beyond the graves to an immortal life":

> In realms of bliss above,
> By guardian angels led,
> Safe in the arms of love
> She lives, whom we call dead.

These examples were not extraordinary, the guide said, but were common examples of epitaphs etched in the cemetery's monuments.

Mausoleums

Inspired by relatively recent archaeological discoveries, rural cemeteries incorporated mausoleums—stately structures constructed to house one or more tombs—into their large-scale landscapes. The beginning of the rural cemetery movement marked the start of a "Golden Age of Mausoleums."[27] The era lasted roughly until the Great Depression.[28] The word mausoleum derives from the name Mausolus, the king of the ancient Greek city of Halicarnassus. His monumental, above-ground burial chamber—one of the seven wonders of the ancient world—was built between 353–350 B.C.E. and inspired the building of mausoleums throughout the ancient Greek civilization and later the ancient Roman one. Archaeological discoveries of ancient ruins in the eighteenth and nineteenth centuries, particularly those investigations at Herculaneum in 1737 and Pompeii in 1748, inspired interest in the architecture of antiquity. One Italian architect-illustrator,

118. Row of mausoleums at the Evergreens Cemetery, Brooklyn, New York. Photograph by Erica Danylchak, 2013.

119. Ornately carved mausoleum at Forest Hills Cemetery, Boston, Massachusetts. Photograph by Erica Danylchak, 2008.

Giovanni Battista Piranesi (1720–1778), published hundreds of illustrations of ancient architecture, including Roman tombs and mausoleums. Mausoleums appeared contemporaneously in the English landscape gardens of the eighteenth century.

When rural cemeteries were established, America's wealthiest were inspired to erect above-ground mausoleums for their eternal interment. The elite knew that these edifices would serve as perpetual reminders to the community of their status. Green-Wood Cemetery, which now boasts 790 freestanding and hillside mausoleums, began its extensive collection in the 1840s. For example, the free-standing Egyptian Revival–style mausoleum dedicated to Peter Schermerhorn was built in 1847. Mausoleums became more popular, however, after the theft of the remains of A. T. Stewart from a Manhattan burial ground in 1878. Toward the end of the century, Green-Wood saw the construction of the Mackay mausoleum, the final resting place of John William Mackay (1831–1902), one of the four Bonanza Kings, a partnership that capitalized on the wealth generated by Nevada's Comstock Lode of silver ore. Guidebooks from the period of the mausoleum's dedication estimated the cost of the structure at $100,000. Mackay spared no expense—the mausoleum was even equipped with heating and electrical systems.

Family plots

Concurrent with the rise of rural cemeteries, the social unit of burial shifted from the congregation to the family, reflecting the secularization of American culture.[29] In earlier urban burial grounds, space had not generally been set aside for family members to be buried in proximity to one another. If it had, the space was rarely demarcated as a family burial plot. In most early burial grounds in America, people had simply been buried with the congregation to which they belonged. The precedents for private family plots, other than those on private family estates, were the New Burying Ground in New Haven, Connecticut, and Père Lachaise in Paris, France. When Mount Auburn was founded, the required real estate investment for the original incorporators was a plot of land fifteen by twenty feet for a total of three hundred square feet, providing room for twelve to twenty or more graves. The family lot-holders were empowered to elect the board of directors who in turn managed the operations of the cemetery association. This governing structure reflected the importance placed on the family unit within these new burial grounds.

Within rural cemeteries, the primacy of the family lot was visible in the landscape. Family lots were often located adjacent to the major avenues to facilitate easy access by visiting family members. This prominent location also reflected the social status of the lot holder. A central commemorative monument generally dominated the family plot and designated it with the family name. Meanwhile, individual upright markers surrounded it. Families also often erected fences, planted hedges, or later installed granite curbing, to conspicuously demarcate their land and create the illusion of privacy.

Fences became a particularly popular device used to define a family or group plot especially in the 1840s and 1850s, because of improvements in metallurgical technology and the rise of the cast iron industry. By the 1840s, cast iron had become more widely used than wrought iron for both decorative and industrial uses. It could be mass produced and shaped into intricate patterns. Pattern books, like Asher Benjamin's 1833 *Practice of Architecture*, showcased cast iron fence designs. Ironwork dealers also advertised in both newspapers and cemetery guidebooks, thus driving demand for the fashionable product. In the 1850s, at Mount Auburn Cemetery, families who encircled their lots with fences generally spent anywhere between $140 and $350 for their enclosures. Other proprietors commissioned custom-made fences by artists or architects. In 1847, the Scots Charitable Society, for example, hired local architect Theodore Voelckers to create a fence to enclose its lot. The architect's creation incorporated figures of Saint Andrew as well as images of the Scotch thistle and battle axes. Its cost was $1,644—a significant sum at the time.[30]

In the latter part of the nineteenth century, many rural cemeteries actually advocated for the removal of fences from their properties, because of the cluttered look an accumulated collection of enclosures created as well as concerns about the cost and work required to maintain them. In fact, the one criticism that Andrew Jackson Downing had of rural cemeteries in 1846 was the "exhibition of *ironmongery*, in the shape of vulgar iron railings, posts and chains, balustrades, etc., all belonging properly to the front-door steps and areas of Broadway or Chestnut-street."[31] He called them mostly "barbarous and cockneyish in their forms" and "totally out of keeping with the aspect of nature, the repose, and seclusion of a rural cemetery."[32] By the mid-1860s, at Green-Wood Cemetery, Nehemiah Cleaveland was able to observe the physical and visual effects of the deterioration of fences over time. Iron was not the durable material most imagined, he said, and once oxidized exhibited a uniform surface discoloration of brown ochre. He continued, "Corrosion, in such cases, as might be expected, goes on most rapidly at the points of junction, and when these are eaten through, the fabric becomes a ruin. . . . An extensive and careful observation of the inclosed lots in Green-Wood, with reference both to the condition and the effect of their metallic fences, has convinced me that the best thing to be done with many of them, would be to sweep them away. As old iron, they are worth something; as they stand, they are worse than useless."[33] Mount Auburn, too, recognized the problems fences created. Its first documented fence removal was in 1871, and by the latter part of the decade, these iron enclosures were being eradicated from the site in large numbers.

The iron fences that did survive in rural cemeteries into the twentieth century generally did not outlive World War II. In September 1942, the United States War Production Board, General Salvage Program addressed a letter "To All Cemeteries": "A great many people have asked us if the metal from their cemetery plots would constitute a valuable contribution to the

120. Iron Fencing. From *Green-Wood Illustrated*, 1847, Danylchak collection.

121. Family plot encompassed by stone curbing, Green-Wood Cemetery, Brooklyn, New York.
Photograph by Erica Danylchak, 2013.

war effort. The answer is, "Yes." Metal of this type is used in making the very highest grade of fighting equipment and is constantly needed for this purpose."[34] Very few of the lot holders who were contacted by Green-Wood Cemetery to help with the war effort in this way refused.[35] Ultimately, very few examples of nineteenth century metal enclosures exist at this quintessential rural cemetery. In fact, this is the case with most of these early romantic burial grounds.

Family (or group) plots were often bordered by stone curbing after fencing fell into disfavor. The area within the curbing was commonly built up with good soil and was, therefore, higher than the surrounding ground, visually elevating the stature of the family plot. One or more steps generally rose up from the adjacent path or avenue. Stone curbing was usually engraved with the associated family name and lot number. At Mount Auburn, the first curbing was installed in 1858. By the 1870s and 1880s, however, even this less obtrusive form of lot enclosure lost favor at Mount Auburn.

Garden furniture and vases also became common adornments in the family plot. The furniture was functional, providing a place for family members to rest during visits to the grave. These personalized embellishments enabled the family to domesticate their cemetery space, exemplifying the dramatic change in

the role of burial grounds for survivors. Early in the rural cemetery movement, cemetery corporations encouraged such additions. An 1852 guide to Laurel Hill Cemetery, for example, recommended the work of a local firm, Woods' Iron Works, which produced garden and arbor chairs and settees. These embellishments, the guide stated, "generally combine lightness, strength and stability. Some of these articles are of superior execution; the decorations, principally foliage and flowers, are designed with great force and spirit, and are reproduced with truthfulness of effect. These chairs and settees form agreeable and appropriate adornments to a family burial lot."[36]

In the early years of the rural cemetery movement, lot holders were responsible for choosing monuments and enclosures, arranging for plantings within the lot, adding decorative embellishments, and maintaining the features installed. Although some cemetery associations did provide guidelines for lot improvements, the family lots of early rural cemeteries were highly individualistic and varied. Over time, problems developed as a result of the autonomy given to lot holders. Cemetery associations observed, for example, that not all lots were being properly maintained. Although reluctant to assume responsibility for the private property of family lots, in the early 1840s, Mount Auburn's board of directors developed the idea for a trust that would provide funds for repairs within these lots. Other cemeteries soon followed Mount Auburn's lead. The freedom given to lot holders had also led to an overpowering multiplicity of ornamentation that marred the naturalistic landscape of the rural cemetery ideal. Gradually, stricter regulations were enacted on lot holders. Eventually, however, the rural cemetery model underwent a significant, and perhaps inevitable, change under the direction of the visionary superintendent at Spring Grove Cemetery in Cincinnati.

Individual Graves

The new cemetery enterprises were praised as being egalitarian. Family lots were generally available to members of any religious or ethnic group. In the North, burial space was often open to African American citizens as well. However, the cost of family lots was prohibitive for many American families. In 1846, the smallest family lot at Green-Wood Cemetery, measuring three hundred square feet, cost eighty dollars. However, some cemetery associations made provisions for the sale of single graves, making burial within these landscapes more attainable for the lower classes. In 1860, a single grave at Oakwood Cemetery in Syracuse, New York, cost eight dollars for an adult and five dollars for a child. Some cemeteries even allowed people to barter for single lots in exchange for services provided to the association.[37]

However, stark differences between middle- and upper-class family lots and single graves purchased by poorer individuals raised questions about the true democratic nature of these ideal institutions. Single graves were generally separated physically and visibly from the more fashionable family sections. They were typically relegated to the least charming portions of the grounds, generally in areas along the boundaries of the site. In addition, cemetery associations made few improvements, such as additional plantings or pathways, to these sections. The associations also generally restricted family members from adding ornamental plantings or even monuments to individual gravesites. Moreover, families purchasing single graves were not allowed to reserve side-by-side plots, which meant poor families were largely separated in death.

Group Plots and Monuments

Fraternal and charitable associations sometimes purchased group plots in rural cemeteries that became options for the burial of their brethren. During the nineteenth century, fraternal associations became increasingly prevalent in the United States. These

122. The Seaman's Grounds with Seaman's Monument at the Evergreens Cemetery, Brooklyn, New York, Photograph by Erica Danylchak, 2013.

groups, as well as many fellowship, artisan, and labor organizations, often provided death benefits to their members, including granting space for burial in a group plot in a rural cemetery if one had been purchased. Benefactors of marginalized groups like orphans and homeless people also occasionally purchased group plots for their use. Some rural cemeteries actually encouraged the establishment of group plots. For example, the founders of Cypress Hills in Brooklyn, New York, asserted: "It is our ambition and our hope to see all religious denominations, orders of benevolence, and national and industrial societies meet together on this common ground."[38] The cemetery even offered such groups discounts. As a result, Cypress Hills became the site of burial plots for numerous groups over time including the local chapters of the Odd Fellows, St. Andrew Society, and Masons as well as the Metropolitan Police Benevolent Burial Association and the American Dramatist Fund. Marked by a stately, four-tiered granite obelisk placed atop a knoll, the plot belonging to the St. Andrew Society is particularly prominent. Small footstones around the central monument indicate individual graves. This pattern of a centralized memorial surrounded by small individual markers was common to group plots in rural cemeteries.

The magnitude and meaning of the American Civil War in the midst of the rural cemetery movement prompted many cemetery associations to establish separate burial sections for the conflict's dead and erect substantial commemorative memorials in their honor. The Trustees of Elmwood Cemetery in Memphis, Tennessee, for example, donated eight acres within the cemetery grounds for the burial of both Confederate and Union soldiers. (After the war had concluded, the Union soldiers who had been buried there were removed to National Cemetery by Federal authority.) In 1878, a grand monument was unveiled in the cemetery section called Confederate Rest to stand guard over more than one thousand Confederate graves there. On the base of the monument, the words "CONFEDERATE DEAD" are boldly written. Meanwhile, the back of the base features the inscription: *Illis Victoriam Non Immortalitatem Fata Negaverunt,* which translates as "The Fates Which Refused Them Victory Did Not Deny Them Immortality."[39] The monument's striking shaft features a trophy of flags and arms in high relief. It is topped by an ornate capital with a finial composed of cannon balls. The monument cost $5,000. Civil War burial sections and similar monumental memorials were established in both northern and southern cemeteries. In these sections, individual burial markers are generally simple and placed in compact, stately rows, creating a sharp visual contrast between the Civil War section and others in the cemetery. In many cemeteries, the sheer number of markers that stretch across the landscape creates a haunting visual reminder of the human cost of conflict.

Nature versus Art

At Mount Auburn Cemetery and its imitators, the works of nature were intended to dominate the scene with man-made memorials secondarily scattered throughout the Picturesque landscape. At Mount Auburn, the monuments were originally isolated in a wooded environment, which visually elevated nature above the "hand of man" and fostered secluded contemplation. Landforms or vegetation or both were often used as backdrops or enclosures for monumental art. At Mount Auburn, the original one hundred family plots were spread throughout the grounds. Although the need to lay out lots more efficiently soon precluded this scattered approach, the distance between lots was regulated in the mid-1830s to preserve six feet of space between them. Nature continued to reign as the primary design element of the site until after mid-century.

In 1867, naturalist John Muir camped among the tombs of Bonaventure Cemetery beyond the city of Savannah, Georgia, and experienced the original intent of the rural cemetery movement—to allow nature the power to heal and to instruct. He noted immediately that the visitor was *with* nature "in the grand old forest graveyard, so beautiful that almost any sensible person would choose to dwell here with the dead rather than with the lazy, disorderly living."[40] Obviously inspired by his surroundings, he advised, "Let children walk with Nature, let them see the beautiful blending and communions of death and life, their joyous unity as taught in woods and meadows, plains and mountains and streams of our blessed star, and they will learn that death is stingless indeed, and as beautiful as life, and that the grave has no victory, for it never fights. All in divine harmony."[41] For Muir, the most "conspicuous glory" of the cemetery was its "noble avenue of live-oaks."[42] He noted that these awe-inspiring trees were joined by thousands

123. Live oaks dominate the landscape at Bonaventure Cemetery, Savannah, Georgia. Wood engraving with hand coloring, 1872, Cothran collection.

of smaller trees and bushes as well as the "rippling of living waters, the song of birds, the joyous confidence of flowers."[43] For Muir, art—the gravestones and fences—brought disorder to the landscape. But nature, for the time being, was still predominant at Bonaventure.

Eventually, however, the noticeable "hand of man" tipped the balance away from the predominance of nature within America's rural cemeteries. At Mount Auburn, by the 1850s, the continual accumulation of monuments and fencing had significantly transformed the original appearance and intent of the site. Families had also zealously added garden furniture like settees and arched arbors popular during the period. In addition, the need for more burial lots had necessitated the conversion of natural terrain into grounds for interment. Monuments were no longer isolated in the woods. Instead, a dense and overwhelming network of variously ornamented family lots tarnished the naturalistic landscape. Mount Auburn and its successors

124. Green-Wood Cemetery, Brooklyn, New York. Stereograph ca. 1885, Danylchak collection.

had begun to look more and more like the congested cemetery of Père Lachaise. The ascendancy of art and embellishments over nature in these cemeteries actually initiated a new lexicon to describe them. By the 1860s, Mount Auburn and its brethren were referred to less often as "rural" cemeteries; instead the terms "ornamental," "sculptured," and "garden" were employed with increasing frequency.[44]

Evolution into the Landscape Lawn Plan

The ideal of the Picturesque rural cemetery was ultimately unsustainable in its aim to create a largely naturalistic and contemplative environment. As time progressed, unfettered additions of monuments and ornamentation became visually and psychologically oppressive. Adolph Strauch, the superintendent of Spring Grove Cemetery, was the first to suggest and implement an intentional set of landscape principles to remedy the excesses created by the earlier rural cemetery model. The 1900 *Cyclopedia of American Horticulture* gave Strauch credit for creating "the modern art of garden cemetery making—in which, as in the park, the continuous expanse of greensward is the fundamental conception of the fabric."[45] The *Cyclopedia* called this style of burial ground "the landscape-garden cemetery." Strauch himself referred to the design style as "the landscape lawn plan" or "the scientific plan." Strauch began instituting his modified design style in the late 1850s. It became widely popular after the Civil War.

The landscape lawn plan was based on the landscape aesthetics of the Beautiful. These cemeteries were not wildly romantic; instead, they were more pastoral and scientific in their conception. Strauch and his followers emphasized expanses of open, well-manicured lawns carefully framed by masses of trees and shrubs. The greenswards generally stretched over gently rolling hills. The avenues were more gently curved, with easier grades, than the twisting roadways of earlier rural cemeteries. Fewer avenues overall meandered through the grounds creating a less divided landscape. Moreover, pathways to gravesites were eliminated; visitors instead walked across green sod to reach their destinations. Lake shores were smoother and more rounded.

As the "superintendent of the grounds and landscape gardener" at Spring Grove, Strauch promoted the adoption of new, stricter regulations on family lots to help prevent the grounds from obtaining a disparate, patchwork quilt–like appearance. Instead, he promoted a less cluttered, less individualistic landscape—one that was a visually integrated whole. The family unit remained the primary division of burial, but the unit was not permitted to be as visibly delineated and distinctive as in earlier rural cemeteries. Rules published in 1869 concerning improvements on lots at Spring Grove prohibited "enclosures around burial lots, wooden trellises and head-boards of any description." Garden furniture was also outlawed. Meanwhile, individual markers were required to lay flat and even with the ground, while the family marker remained a dominant, sculptural memorial.

The landscape lawn cemetery, with its large sun-lit greenswards and softer, more fluid design characteristics ultimately "suggested the pleasures of a park more than the meditative mysteries of a cemetery."[46]

CHAPTER 5

Plants in Rural Cemeteries

Cemetery reformers of the nineteenth century drew inspiration for their burial landscapes from historical precedents that used trees, shrubs, and flowering plants to create reverential spaces. Mount Auburn Cemetery's principal designer, Gen. Henry A. S. Dearborn, was among many of the rural cemetery movement's originators who cited numerous examples within ancient and foreign cultures where plants embellished burial grounds. During the "age of the patriarchs" the ancient Hebrews, for example, selected groves as their places of sepulture. The Greeks and Romans, he said, often "selected recesses of wooded

125. Oaken Bluff, Green-Wood Cemetery, Brooklyn, New York. Engraving by J. Smillie, from *Green-Wood Illustrated*, 1847, Danylchak collection.

heights and vales, as favorable places of interment, or the borders of the great public highways, where elegant monuments were erected, and surrounded with cypress and other ever-verdant trees."[1] The Turks, too, used evergreens to enhance their burial landscapes. Within their culture it was a "religious duty to plant trees around the graves of their kindred."[2]

During the nineteenth century, influential commentators on cemetery design expressed the indispensable role that trees played in creating evocative, picturesque landscapes appropriate for burial and commemoration. Adolph Strauch, Spring Grove Cemetery's landscape gardener, remarked rather poetically on the sentimental influence of trees: "A rural Cemetery without trees, would be like a sandy desert without water, affording as little nourishment to the heart, as the latter can give to the body. The first impression of each, would be a desire to turn from it our steps, and our thoughts."[3] Dearborn, too, noted the comforting effect of trees upon those visiting a cemetery to mourn: "what a consolation to visit the bower-sequestered monument of a much-loved friend."[4] Meanwhile, Mount Auburn Cemetery commentator Wilson Flagg noted that there was "no object more solemn and impressive than a venerable wood, full of majestic trees. Poets have always delighted to celebrate their stillness, their seclusion, their grandeur, and their deep and benevolent shade; and we may ultimately secure all these effects by judicious planting and selection."[5]

An emerging appetite for horticultural studies among cemetery promoters also influenced the appearance of the new burial grounds. Early cemetery associations were sometimes directly linked to area horticultural societies—which were forming contemporaneously with the new rural burial grounds. The Massachusetts Horticultural Society, founded in 1829, was the earliest formally organized horticultural society in the country and played an instrumental role in the founding of Mount Auburn Cemetery. Meanwhile, members of the Cincinnati Horticultural Society, including its founder Robert Buchanan, established Spring Grove Cemetery. Laurel Hill Cemetery's founder John Jay Smith, Oakwood Cemetery's

organizer Elias W. Leavenworth, and Forest Lawn's key trustee Lewis F. Allen were all involved in their local horticultural societies as well. These men also read and contributed to horticultural journals like Andrew Jackson Downing's *Horticulturist and Journal of Rural Art and Rural Taste*. Historian David Charles Sloane has observed, "Horticulture was an important part of their lives. They planted orchards and exotic trees on their estates, argued about the best varieties of fruits and flowers, shared seeds, and exchanged information about a wide assortment of plants."[6] Most important, they believed that horticulture could positively impact society. In fact, Andrew Jackson Downing wrote in the July 1847 volume of the *Horticulturist* that "horticulture and its kindred arts, tend strongly to fix the habits, and elevate the character, of our whole rural population." In the same publication in 1856, John Jay Smith, Laurel Hill Cemetery's founder and president, commented on the horticultural value of rural cemeteries: "The next generation will expect to find examples of well-grown trees from which they can form some ideas of what they should plant themselves, in grounds of their own; the time taken to attain certain heights will here be studied. It is, in fact, as leaders of *public taste* that we look upon public cemeteries as of much importance."[7] Furthermore, Smith emphatically argued, "In a large rural cemetery, trees offer the first means of improvement, and afford the greatest beauty; they are, if there were but one essential beauty to be studied, *the* essential."[8]

Creating Cemetery "Arboretums"

Given the importance assigned to trees and shrubs within the new type of burial landscape, rural cemetery founders often sought sites already imbued with botanical riches. The existing abundance and variety of trees was often one of the most desirable qualities of potential rural cemetery locations. The founders of Mount Auburn Cemetery set a precedent by choosing a tract of land formerly known as Stone's Woods—a name derived from its original proprietor and the "abundance and variety of its beautiful trees."[9] Meanwhile, in 1869, *Appletons' Hand-book of American Travel* observed that one of the greatest attractions of Spring Grove Cemetery was "undoubtedly its fine trees and shrubs" and remarked that the number and variety of trees contained within the Garrard farm formed "one of the strongest inducements operating in its selection

126. Bird's-eye view of Green-Wood Cemetery. By John Bachmann (1814–1896), Library of Congress Prints and Photographs Division.

for the purposes of a cemetery."[10] In Brooklyn, New York, those who chose the land on the Gowanus Heights for the establishment of a new cemetery admired the diversity of trees on the grounds, including oaks, chestnuts, walnuts, gum trees, tulip trees, and dogwoods, which were in abundance. Many specimens of beech, maple, cedar, pine, and plane trees were also interspersed throughout the grounds. Butternut, ironwood, pepperidge, and persimmon trees were not uncommon. A later history of the institution offered a descriptive glimpse into the virgin state of the land: "Many of these trees were old and large, and handsome, and all of them in their natural, but not ungraceful grouping, presented fine masses of variegated foliage."[11]

The significance of trees to these rural burial places is apparent by the number of cemeteries that drew inspiration from the landscape feature for their monikers. For example, the name chosen by the founders of Brooklyn's first rural cemetery—Green-Wood—was "an indication of the importance which they attached to this remarkable feature of the place, and of their purpose to keep that feature unimpaired."[12] Meanwhile, the name of Oakwood Cemetery in Syracuse, New York, was inspired by the oak forest that originally covered its elevated acreage. In Mystic, Connecticut, magnificent elm trees not only inspired the name Elm Grove Cemetery but also motivated the landscape designer to lay out the grounds in the shape of this native tree.

Although the existing assortment of trees as well as shrubs within rural cemetery sites was often remarkable in and of itself, early rural cemetery advocates urged the addition of exotics to further enhance the horticultural collections of the sites. In the *Horticulturist*, John Jay Smith persuasively argued for the use of a diversity of trees and shrubs, including nonnative species in rural cemeteries.

It is an error, in planting a large cemetery, to employ only the trees that succeed in the immediate neighborhood; even in a well-wooded site, where, to the eye of the citizen, there is shade in abundance, and perhaps to spare, a judicious addition of hardy trees and shrubs, with a foreign air, are of great importance. Thousands of persons who visit Laurel Hill do not *define* this source of gratification though they are sensible of something novel and pleasing. Had they been accustomed to the study of foliage, they would at once ascertain that they were surrounded, not only by the beautiful in form, but by the rare; they, perhaps, carry away with them an impression that it is the monuments, and the river, and the general views, that have so struck their minds; but the element of variety in the trees was still one of the charms.[13]

In fact, the *Guide to Laurel Hill Cemetery* reported that the cemetery's managers "desire that one specimen at least of every valuable tree and shrub which will bear the climate of this latitude, shall be found in these grounds, to form a species of Arboretum."[14] And the *Guide* proudly provided a catalogue of the most "remarkable and interesting varieties" which grew within the confines of the grounds. In 1849, Andrew Jackson Downing noted that Laurel Hill had nearly "every procurable species of hardy tree and shrub growing there,—among others, the Cedar of Lebanon, the Deodar Cedar, the Paulownia, the Araucaria, etc. Rhododendrons and Azaleas were in full bloom; and the purple Beeches, the weeping Ash, rare Junipers, Pines, and deciduous trees were abundant in many parts of the grounds.... It is a better *arboretum* than can easily be found elsewhere in the country."[15] The first official public arboretum in the United States—the Arnold Arboretum in Boston, Massachusetts—was not established until 1872.

TABLE 1. PRINCIPAL TREES, SHRUBS, AND OTHER PLANTS AT LAUREL HILL

Clematis Flammula, *L.*	The Inflammatory-Juiced Clematis, or Sweet-Scented Virgin's Bower
Clematis Vitalba, *L.*	The White-Vine Clematis, or Traveller's Joy
Clematis Virginiana, *L.*	The Virginian Clematis
Clematis Cærulea, *Lindl.*	The Blue, or Violet-Flowered Clematis
Magnolia Grandiflora, *L.*	The Large-Flowered Magnolia
Magnolia Glauca, *L.*	The Glaucous-Leaved Magnolia
Magnolia Tripetala, *L.*	The Three-Petaled Magnolia

TABLE 1. (*cont.*)

Magnolia Macrophylla, *Mx.*	The Long-Leaved Magnolia
Magnolia Acuminata.	The Pointed-Leaved Magnolia, or Cucumber, Tree
Magnolia Cordata, *Mx.*	The Heart-Leaved, or Yellow, Magnolia
Magnolia Auriculata, *Lam.*	The Auricled-Leaved Magnolia
Magnolia Conspicua, *Salisb.*	The Yulan, or Conspicuous-Flowered Magnolia, called sometimes the Chandelier Tree
Magnolia Purpurea, *Sims.*	The Purple-Flowered Magnolia
Liriodendron Tulipifera, *L.*	The Tulip-Bearing Liriodendron, or Tulip Tree
Berberis Vulgaris, *L.*	The Common Berberry
Berberis Aristata, *Dec.*	The Bristled Tooth-Leaved Berberry
Mahonia Aquifolium, *Nutt.*	The Holly-Leaved Mahonia, or Ash Berberry
Tilia Europæ, *L.*	The European Lime Tree
Tilia Americana, *L.*	The American Lime Tree
Stuartia Virginica, *Cav.*	The Virginian Stuartia
Gordonia Pubescens, *L'Her.*	The Pubescent Gordonia, or Loblolly Bay, formerly the Franklinia Americana, *Marsh.*
Hypericum, *L.*	The St. John's Wort, a number of species
Acer, *L.*	The Maple, many species, among which may be noted,
Acer Striatum, *L.*	The Striped-Barked Maple
Acer Platanoides, *L.*	The Platanus-Like, or Norway, Maple
Acer Saccharinum, *L.*	The Sugar Maple
Acer Pseudo-Platanus, *L.*	The Mock Plane Tree, the Sycamore, or Great Maple
Acer Opalus, *Ait.*	The Opal, or Italian Maple
Acer Rubrum, *L.*	The Red-Flowering, or Scarlet, Maple
Aesculus Hippocastanum, *L.*	The Common Horse Chestnut
Aesculus Ohioensis, *Michx.*	The Ohio Horse Chestnut, or the Ohio Buckeye
Aesculus Rubicunda, *Lois.*	The Reddish-Flowered Horse Chestnut
Pavia Rubra, *Lam.*	The Red-Flowered Pavia, or Small Buckeye
Pavia Macrostachya, *Mx.*	The Long-Racemed Pavia
Kolreuteria Paniculata, *Laxm.*	The Panicled Flowering Kolreuteria
Vitis Riparia, *Michx.*	The River-Side, or Sweet-Scented Vine
Ampelopsis Hederacae, *Michx.*	The Ivy-Like Ampelopsis, or Five-Leaved Ivy
Xanthoxylum Fraxineum, *Willd.*	The Ash-Leaved Xanthoxylum, or Common Toothache Tree
Ptelea Trifoliata, *L.*	The Three-Leafleted Ptelea, or Shrubbery Trefoil, or Hop Tree
Ailantus Glandulosa, *Desf.*	The Glandulous-Leaved Ailanto
Staphylea Trifoliata, *L.*	The Three-Leafleted Staphylea, or Bladder-Nut Tree
Staphylea Pinnata, *L.*	The Pinnated-Leaved Staphylea, or Bladder-Nut Tree
Euonymus Europæus, *L.*	The European Euonymus, or Spindle Tree
Euonymus Americana, *L.*	The American Euonymus, or Spindle Tree
Celastrus Scandens, *L.*	The Climbing-Stemmed Celastrus, or Staff Tree
Ilex Aquifolium, *L.*	The Prickly-Leaved Holly
Ilex Opaca, *Ait.*	The Opaque-Leaved, or American Holly
Rhus Cotinus, *L.*	The Cotinus Rhus, or Venetian Sumac, or Mist Tree
Sophora Pendula, *L.*	The Weeping Sophora
Virgilia Lutea, *Mich.*	The Yellow-Wooded Virgilia, or Yellow Wood
Spartium Junceum, *L.*	The Spanish Broom

Cytisus Laburnum, *L.*	The Common Laburnum
Cytisus Laburnum Pendulum, *L.*	The Weeping Laburnum
Cytisus Laburnum Purpureum, *L.*	The Purple Laburnum
Amorpha Nana, *Nutt.*	The Dwarf Amorpha, or False Indigo
Robinia Pseud-Acacia, *L.*	The Common Robinia, or False Acacia
Robinia Viscosa, *Vent.*	The Clammy-Barked Robinia
Robinia Hispida, *L.*	The Rose Acacia
Colutea Arborescens, *L.*	The Bladder Senna
Wistaria Frutescens, *Dec.*	The Shrubby Wistaria, or Glycina
Wistaria Chinensis, *Dec.*	The Chinese Wistaria
Glenditschia Triacanthos, *L.*	The Three-Thorned Gleditschia, or Horny Locust
Glymnocladus Canadensis, *Lam.*	The Kentucky Coffee Tree
Cercis Canadensis, *L.*	The Common Judas Tree
Amygdalus Communis, *L.*	The Common Almond Tree
Cerasus Padus, *Dec.*	The Bird-Cherry Tree
Cerasus Avium Flore Pleno, *Mœnch.*	The Flowering Cherry Tree
Rosa.	A great variety of hardy roses will be found on the grounds, including the best varieties
Cratægus, or Thorn.	A great variety of the most ornamental
Cotoneaster Microphylla, *Wall.*	The Small-Leaved Cotoneaster
Cydonia Japonica, *Pers.*	Pyrus Japonica, or the Japan Quince Tree, three varieties
Calycanthus Fragrans, *Lindl.*	The Fragrant-Flowered Calycanthus
Philadelphus Coronarius, *L.*	The Garland Philadelphus, or Mock Orange
Philadelphus Inodorus, *L.*	The Scentless-Flowered Mock Orange
Hydrangea Hortensia, *Sieb.*	The Common Hydrangea
Hydrangea Quercifolia, *Bartram.*	The Oak-Leaved Hydrangea
Hedera Helix, *L.*	The Common Ivy
Hedera Poetica, *Bauh.*	The Poet's Ivy, &c.
Cornus Florida, *L.*	The Florida Dogwood
Aucuba Japonica, *Thunb.*	The Japan Aucuba. Hardy at Laurel Hill
Lonicera.	Honeysuckle. All the varieties known to be hardy in America
Cephalanthus Occidentalis, *L.*	The Western Buttonwood
Rhododendron Ponticum, *L.*	The Pontic Rhododendron, or Rose Bay
Rhododendron Maximum, *L.*	The largest Rhododendron, or American Rose Bay
Rhododendron Catawbiense, *Michx.*	The Catawba Rhododendron
Kalmia Latifolia, *L.*	The Common Laurel
Halesia Tetraptera, *L.*	The Four-Winged-Fruited Halesia, or Common Snowdrop Tree
Halesia Diptera, *L.*	The Two-Winged-Fruited Halesia, or Snowdrop Tree
Chionanthus Virginica, *L.*	The Virginian Snow-Flower, or Fringe Tree
Syringa, *L.*	The Lilac, Several varieties
Fraxinus Americana, *Willd.*	The American Ash
Fraxinus Exelsior Pendula, *Ait.*	The Weeping Ash and other varieties
Sorbus Americana, *Willd.*	The Mountain Ash
Jasminum Officinale, *L.*	The Officinal, or Common Jasmine
Vinca Major, *L.*	The Great Periwinkle
Vinca Minor, *L.*	The Less Periwinkle

TABLE 1. (*cont.*)

Periploca Græca, *L.*	The Greek Periploca, or Virginia Silk-Vine
Bignonia Capreolata, *L.*	The Tendrilled Bignonia, or Trumpet-Flower
Bignonia Radicans, *L.*	The Rooting Bignonia, or Trumpet-Flower
Catalpa Syringæfolia, *Sims.*	The Lilac-Like-Leaved Catalpa
Laurus Sassafras, *L.*	The Sassafras Laurel, or Sassafras Tree
Shepherdia Argentea, *Nutt.*	The Silver-Leaved Shepherdia, or Buffalo Berry
Aristolochia Sipho, *L'Herit.*	The Siphon-Like Birthwort
Aristolochia Tomentosa, *Sims.*	The Tomentose Birthwort
Buxus Sempervirens, *L.*	The Evergreen, or Common Box Tree
Buxus Argentea.	The Silver Box
Buxus Aurea.	The Golden Box
Buxus Variegata.	The Variegated Box
Macluria Aurantiaca, *Nutt.*	The Osage Orange
Ulmus Campestris, *L.*	The English, or Common Elm
Ulmus Glabra, *Mill.*	The Wych Elm
Ulmus Americana, *L.*	The American Elm
Juglans Nigra, *L.*	The Black-Wooded Walnut Tree
Juglans Cinerea, *L.*	The Gray-Branched Walnut Tree, or Butternut
Carya Alba, *Nutt.*	The Shellbark Hickory of several varieties
Salix Babylonica.	The Babylonian, or Weeping Willow
Salix Annularis.	The Curled Willow
Populus Alba, *L.*	The White Poplar, or Abele Tree
Populus Canenscens, *Smith.*	The Gray, or Common White Poplar
Populus Tremula, *L.*	The Trembling-Leaved Poplar, or Aspen
Populus Trepida, *Willd.*	The American Aspen
Populus Græca, *Ait.*	The Grecian, or Athenian Poplar
Populus Nigra, *L.*	The Black-Barked, or Common Black Poplar
Populus Fastigiata, *Desf.*	The Lombardy Poplar
Betula Alba, *L.*	The White, or Common Birch
Betula Pendula.	The Weeping Birch
Betula Papyracea, *Ait.*	The Paper Birch
Betula Nigra, *L.*	The Black Birch
Quercus Lucombeana, *Swt.*	The Lucombe Oak
Quercus Macrocarpa, *Willd.*	The Large-Fruited American Oak
Quercus Alba, *L.*	The White Oak
Quercus Prinos, *L.*	The Chestnut-Leaved Oak
Quercus Rubra, *L.*	The Red, or Champion Oak
Quercus Coccinea, *Willd.*	The Scarlet Oak
Quercus Tinctoria, *Willd.*	The Quercitron, or Dyer's Oak
Quercus Palustris, *Willd.*	The Pin Oak
Quercus Nigra, *Willd.*	The Black Jack Oak
Quercus Phellos, *L.*	The Willow Oak
Quercus Cerris, *L.*	The Turkey Oak
Fagus Sylvatica, *L.*	The Wood, or Common Beech
Castanea Vesca, *G.*	The Eatable Spanish Chestnut
Castanea Americana, *Michx.*	The American Chestnut

Carpinus Betulus, *L.*	The Birch, or Common Hornbeam
Carpinus Americana, *L.*	The American Hornbeam
Corylus Avellana, *L.*	The Hazelnut, several varieties
Platanus Orientalis, *L.*	The Oriental Plane
Platanus Occidentalis, *L.*	The Western Plane, or Buttonwood
Liquidambar Styraciflua, *L.*	The Sweet-Gum Liquidambar
Taxus Baccata, *L.*	The Berried, or Common Yew
Taxus Canadensis, *Willd.*	The North American Yew
Taxus Hibernica, *Hook.*	The Irish Yew
Salisburis Adiantifolia, *Smith.*	The Gingko Tree
Pinus Sylvestris, *L.*	The Scotch Fir
Pinus Pinaster, *Ait.*	The Pinaster, or Cluster Pine
Pinus Pinea, *L.*	The Stone Pine
Pinus Inops, *Ait.*	The Jersey Pine
Pinus Resinosa, *Ait.*	The Resinous, or Red Pin
Pinus Mitis, *Michx.*	The Yellow Pine
Pinus Australis, *Michx.*	The Southern Pine
Pinus Strobus, *Lindl.*	The Weymouth Pine
Abies Canadensis, *Michx.*	The Hemlock Spruce Fir
Abies Excelsa, *Dec.*	The Norway Spruce Fir
Abies Alba, *Michx.*	The White Spruce Fir
Abies Nigra, *Poir.*	The Black Spruce Fir
Abies Balsamea.	The Balm of Gilead, or American Silver Fir
Larix Europæa, *Dec.*	The European Larch
Larix Americana, *Michx.*	The American Larch
Cedrus Libani, *Barr.*	The Cedar of Lebannon
Thuja Occidentalis, *L.*	The American Arbor Vitae
Thuja Orientalis, *L.*	The Chinese Arbor Vitae
Taxodium Distichum, *Rich.*	The Deciduous Cypress
Juniperus Virginiana, *L.*	The Virginian Juniper, or Red Cedar
Juniperus Communis, *L.*	The Common Juniper
Juniperus Suecica, *L.*	The Swedish Juniper
Yucca Gloriosa, *L.*	The Glorious Yucca, or Adam's Needle
Yucca Filamentosa.	The Thready, or Filamentose Yucca
Bulbs, &c.	Lily of the Valley, Christmas Rose, Monkshood, Sweet Violets, White Violets, Lilies, Phlox, &c., &c.

Source: Laurel Hill Cemetery, *Guide to Laurel Hill Cemetery*, 54-60.

At Spring Grove Cemetery, Adolph Strauch also sought to create a valuable arboretum for study and for the enjoyment and emotional satisfaction of the visitor. It was widely recognized, according to Strauch, that a deep forest, with its endless variety of trees, affected "solemn thoughts and feelings, without terror or repulsive gloom."[16] Rural cemeteries aimed to inspire similar emotional responses with appropriate and varied selections of trees and shrubs. *The Cincinnati Cemetery of Spring Grove: Report for 1857* provided an extensive catalogue of trees and shrubs cultivated at the site thus emphasizing the importance of diverse vegetation to its landscape aesthetic.

TABLE 2. TREES AND SHRUBS CULTIVATED AT SPRING GROVE CEMETERY

Acer dasycarpum	Silver Leaved Maple
Acer platanoides	Norway Maple
Acer rubrum	Red Maple
Acer saccharinum	Sugar Maple
Acer saccharinum nigrum	Black Sugar Maple
Acer striatum	Striped Barked Maple
Aesculus hippocastanum	Common Horse Chestnut
Aesculus ohioensis	Ohio Buckeye
Ailanthus glandulosa	Chinese Ailanthus
Alnus glutinosa	European Alder
Aralia spinosa	Hercules Club
Betula alba	White Birch
Castanea americana	American Chestnut
Carpinus americana	American Hornbeam
Carya alba	Shell Bark Hickory
Carya amara	Bitter Nut
Catalpa syringifolia	Catalpa
Celtis occidentalis	Nettle Berry
Cercis canadensis	American Red Bud
Chionanthus virginiana	White Fringe Tree
Cornus florida	White Flowering Dogwood
Cratægrus Crus-galli	Cockspur Thorn
Cytisus laburnum	Laburnaum, or Golden Chain
Diospyros virginiana	American Persimmon
Fagus sylvestris	American Beach
Fagus purpurea	Purple Leaved Beach
Fagus purpurea pendula	Purple Weeping Beach
Fraxinus americana	White American Ash
Fraxinus americana sambucifolia	Elder Leaved Ash
Fraxinus aurea	Gold Barked Ash
Fraxinus aurea pendula	Gold Weeping Ash
Fraxinus excelsior	English Ash
Fraxinus excelsior pendula	English Weeping Ash
Fraxinus lentiscifolia	Lentis Leaved Ash
Fraxinus integrifolia	Entire-Leaved Ash
Fraxinus quadrangularis	Blue Ash
Fraxinus salicifolia	Willow-Leaved Ash
Gymnocladus canadensis	Kentucky Coffee-Tree
Juglans nigra	Black Walnut
Kœlreuteria paniculata	Chinese Kœlreuteria
Laurus Sassafras	Sassafras
Larix europæa	European Larch
Larix microcarpa	American Larch
Liquidambar styraciflua	Sweet Gum
Liriodendron tulipifera	Tulip Tree
Maclura aurantiaca	Osage Orange
Magnolia acuminata	Cucumber Tree
Magnolia glauca	Fragrant Magnolia
Magnolia macrophylla	Large Leaved Magnolia
Magnolia tripetala	Umbrella Magnolia
Magnolia purpurea	Purple Magnolia
Mimosa jullibrissin	Sensitive Tree
Negundo fraxinifolia	Ash Leaved Maple
Nyssa aquatica	Sour Gum
Ornus europæa	Flowering Ash
Ostrya virginica	Virginia Hop-Hornbeam
Platanus occidentalis	American Sycamore
Platanus orientalis	European Sycamore
Populus alba	White or Silver Poplar
Populus alba acerifolia	White Maple Leaved Poplar
Populus balsamæa	Balsam Poplar
Populus hudsonica	Hudson Poplar
Populus canadensis	Canadian Poplar
Populus fastigiata	Italian Poplar
Populus trepida	American Aspen
Ptelia trifoliata	Shrubbery Trefoil
Quercus alba	White Oak
Quercus coccinea	Scarlett Oak
Quercus ambigua	Gray Oak
Quercus ferruginea	Black Jack Oak
Quercus macrocarpa	Burr Oak
Quercus rubra	Red Oak
Quercus imbricaria	Laurel Oak
Quercus lyrata	Over-Cup Oak
Quercus prinus acuminata	Yellow Oak
Quercus prinus discolor	Swamp-White Oak
Quercus cerris	Turkey Oak
Rhus cotinus	Venetian Sumach
Rhus typhina	American Sumach
Robinia pseudacacia	Common Locust
Robinia viscosa	Pink Flowering Locust
Salisburia adiantifolia	Maiden-Hair Tree
Salix vitellina	Yellow Willow
Salix babylonica	Weeping Willow
Salix fragilis	Brittle Willow
Salix forbyana	Basket Willow
Salix purpurea	Purple Willow
Salix rosmarinifolia	Rosmarin Leaved Willow
Salix americana pendula	American Weeping Willow
Salix crispa	Crisp-Leaved Weeping Willow
Sorbus aucuparia	Mountain Ash

TABLE 2. TREES AND SHRUBS CULTIVATED AT SPRING GROVE CEMETERY (*cont.*)

Sorbus aucuparia pendula	Weeping Mountain Ash
Sorbus aria dentata	White Beam Tree
Sophora japonica	Japan Sophora
Sophora japonica pendula	Weeping Japan Sophora
Taxodium distichum	Deciduous Cypress
Tilia americana	American Linden
Tilia platyphylla	European Linden
Ulmus americana alba	American White Elm
Ulmus americana rubra	American Red Elm
Ulmus campestris	European Elm
Ulmus suberosa	Cork Elm
Amorpha fruticosa	Indigo Shrub
Amygdalus pumila	Dwarf Almond
Berberis atropurpurea	Purple-Leaved Berberry
Berberis vulgaris	Common Berberry
Calycanthus floridus	Sweet-Scented Shrub
Corchoros japonica	Japan Globe Flower
Cornus alba	White-Fruited Dogwood
Cornus variegata	Variegated-Leaved Dogwood
Daphne mezereum	
Deutzia scabra	White Flowering Deutzia
Deutzia gracilis	Graceful
Elæagnus argentea	Silvery Oleaster or Wild Olive
Elæagnus hortensis	Garden Oleaster
Euonymus americanus	American Burning Bush
Euonymus europæus	European Burning Bush
Forsythia veridissima	Green Forsythia
Hibiscus syriacus	Althæa
Hydrangea hortensis	Garden Hydrangea
Hydrangea quercifolia	Oak-Leaved Hydrangea
Hippophæa rhamnoides	Sea Buckthorn
Laurus benzoin	Spice-Wood
Ligustrum vulgare	Common Privet
Lonicera tartarica	Tartarian Honeysuckle
Mohonia aquifolia	Holly-Leaved Berberry
Pavia macrostachia	Dwarf Horse Chestnut
Philadelphus coronarius	Fragrant Syringo
Philadelphus grandiflorus	Large Flowering Syringo
Philadelphus gordoniana	Gordons Syringo
Philadelphus nana	Dwarf Syringo
Philadelphus speciosa	Scarlet Syringo
Pyrus japonica	Japan Quince
Rhamnus catharticus	Purging Buckthorn
Robinia hispida	Rose Acacia
Sambucus nigra	Black Alder
Shepherida argentea	Buffalo-Berry

Spartium junceum	Spanish Broom
Spiræa chamædrifolia	Germander-Leaved Spiraa
Spiræa salicifolia	Willow-Leaved Spiraa
Spiræa sorbifolia	Mountain Ash-Leaved Spriaa
Spiræa opulifolia	Snowball-Leaved Spriaa
Spiræa prunifolia	Plum-Leaved Spriaa
Spiræa ulmifolia	Elm-Leaved Spriaa
Spiræa leavigata	Smooth-Leaved Spriaa
Spiræa Reevesii	Pure White Spriaa
Spiræa Niconderti	Nicondert's Spriaa
Spiræa japonica	Japan Spriaa
Spiræa species du Nepaul	Species from Nepaul Spriaa
Spiræa rotundifolia	Round-Leaved Spriaa
Symphoria racemosa	Snowberry
Syringa vulgaris	Common Lilac
Syringa vulgaris alba	Common White Lilac
Syringa sinensis	Chinese Lilac
Syringa persica	Persian Lilac
Syringa josikea	Chionanthus-Leaved Lilac
Syringa laciniata	Cut-Leaved Lilac
Tamarix gallica	French Tamarisk
Tamarix germanica	German Tamarisk
Tamarix africana	African Tamarisk
Viburnum lantana	Wayfaring Tree
Viburnum oxycoccus	Cranberry Tree
Viburnum opulus	Snowball
Vitex Agnus castus	Chaste Tree
Weigelia rosea	Chinese Weigelia
Abies alba	North American White Spruce
Abies excelsa	Norway Spruce
Abies canadensis	Hemlock Spruce
Abies morinda	Hymalaya
Cupressus thyoides	White Cedar
Juniperus communis	Common Juniper
Juniperus suecia	Swedish Juniper
Juniperus sabina	Savin
Juniperus virginiana	Red Cedar
Juniperus pendula	Weeping Juniper
Picea balsamæa	Balsam Fir
Picea pectinata	English Silver Fir
Picea nobilis	Noble Silver Fir
Picea religiosa	Mexican Silver Fir
Pinus austriaca	Austrian Pine
Pinus excelsa	Bhotan Pine
Pinus laricio	Corsican Pine
Pinus rigida	Pitch Pine
Pinus strobus	White Pine

TABLE 2. *(cont.)*

Pinus cembra	Cembran Pine
Pinus sylvestris	Scotch Pine
Pinus pumila	Dwarf Pine
Pinus inops	Jersey Pine
Pinus rubra	Red Pine
Taxus baccata	Canadian Yew
Thuja occidentalis	American Arbor Vitæ
Thuja orientalis	Chinese Arbor Vitæ
Thuja tartarica	Tartarian Arbor Vitæ
Thuja filiformis	Thready-Leaved Arbor Vitæ
Buxus suffruticosa	Dwarf Box
Buxus arborescens	Tree Box
Cotoneaster microphylla	Small-Leaved Cotoneaster
Cratægus pyracantha	Pyracanthus Thorn
Euonymus japonica	Japan Euonymus
Yucca filamentosa	Thready Adamsneedle

Source: Notman and Strauch, *The Cincinnati Cemetery of Spring Grove*, 24–29.

In 1987, the cemetery officially changed its name to Spring Grove Cemetery & Arboretum accentuating its function as a botanical garden in addition to being a burial landscape.

Planting Burial Landscapes with Meaning

The plants chosen to grace rural cemetery landscapes were frequently imbued with particular meaning based on their historical associations or physical appearance. In 1854, the *Horticulturist* emphatically stated that trees are "the most appropriate ornaments for the tomb; the shade and shelter which they impart are soothing and agreeable, and there are ideas suggested by their outward forms and moral and historical associations, which address themselves to the reflecting, intelligent mind, quite as forcibly and distinctly as do lettered inscriptions on marble."[17] Scottish garden designer and prominent tastemaker John Claudius Loudon also asserted that the botanical riches found within cemeteries served to "cultivate the intellect."[18] The symbolic language spoken by living trees, as well as flowering plants, motivated reflection and summoned appropriate sentiments in Victorian-era visitors to these memorial spaces. Plants frequently represented death and mourning, hope and immortality.

The cypress is perhaps more closely associated with mourning than any other tree because of its physical character, its historical association with burial landscapes, and the myth that gave it its name. In his *Metamorphoses*, the Roman poet Ovid (43 B.C.E.–C.E. 17/18) relayed the tragic story of the boy Cyparissus, a special friend of the God Apollo, who accidently killed his beloved stag and in his overwhelming grief pleaded to die and mourn forever.

> Tears drained the manhood from his slender
> thighs,
> His fair white body took a greenish tint;
> The waving hair that used to hide his forehead
> Grew upward like a green and thorny tower.
> He was a tree whose shapely topmost branches
> Stared at the stars across the circling night.
> Apollo sighed, his own eyes filled with sadness,
> "You whom I weep for, shall share grief with
> others,
> And you shall stand wherever mourners are."[19]

And, in fact, the cypress was historically planted in places where mourners grieved. In ancient Greece and Rome, the cypress was often planted within burial landscapes. In his influential *On the Laying Out, Planting, and Managing of Cemeteries*, Loudon pointed out that "noble cypresses" frequently inhabited Turkish burial grounds. In the same work, Loudon called Italian cypress (*Cupressus sempervirens*) the best of all trees for a cemetery landscape. Meanwhile, in *The Language of Flowers*, Frederic Shoberl lyrically described the connotation the cypress visually conveyed: "Wherever these trees meet our view, their doleful look excites melancholy ideas. Their tall pyramids, pointing to the sky, moan when shaken by the wind. The sun's rays cannot penetrate through their gloom, and when his last beams throw their long shadows upon the ground, you would almost take them for dark phantoms."[20]

The yew, too, has a long-standing association with burial landscapes and is emblematic of sorrow. Wilson Flagg noted that the yew had long been planted by the English in their burial grounds. The use of this tree, he said, "must have originated in the sombre shades of its foliage, and in its adaptedness to the topiary art."[21] The *Horticulturist* noted that yews were regarded as particularly appropriate for American rural cemeteries, because their "wonderful longevity" and "dark, unchanging verdue" conferred a "sombre and solemn expression which belongs to no other tree."[22]

The influential journal recommended several varieties of the yews for rural cemeteries including the English yew (*Taxus baccata*), the Irish yew (*Taxus baccata* 'Hibernica'), and the American or Canadian yew (*Taxus canadensis*).

Cemetery designers also commonly used weeping varieties of trees and shrubs for dramatic emotional and visual effect. Patrick Barry of the Mount Hope Garden and Nurseries in Rochester, New York, wrote in 1850 that drooping trees were "peculiarly appropriate for planting rural cemeteries."[23] Of all the drooping trees, the weeping willow (*Salix babylonica*) was the most familiar type and was esteemed by "all civilized nations . . . as one of the most fitting ornaments for cemeteries."[24] With its "long slender flowing branches, falling in profusion perpendicularly from the summit of the tree to the ground," it formed a graceful contour and embodied melancholic associations.[25] For small cemetery lots, the *Horticulturist* recommended the American weeping willow (*Salix Americana* 'Pendula'), with its "light and comparatively sparse foliage" forming an "airy and pleasing"

weeper.[26] The common or European weeping ash (*Fraxinus exelsior* 'Pendula'), meanwhile, offered a different form—stiff, horizontally spreading branches that bent gradually as they increased in length, forming an almost umbrella-like shape. The weeping ash was commonly cultivated during the Victorian era. Meanwhile, Barry reported that the weeping golden ash (*Fraxinus excelsior* 'Aurea Pendula') "was a new and interesting variety, with golden yellow bark, which is brightest and shows to the best advantage in winter."[27] The weeping birch (*Betula pendula*), also known as the European white birch, provided an impressive and distinctive expanse of gracefully drooping shoots. Finally, Barry called the weeping Japanese Pagoda tree (*Sophora japonica* 'Pendula') "one of the most beautiful weeping trees" with its rounded canopy of thin, green branches and dark green, dense pinnate foliage. For large trees, the *Horticulturist* recommended the hemlock spruce (*Abies Canadensis*), an elegant tree with dark green foliage and "gracefully drooping" branches. It also recommended the weeping common Juniper (*Juniperus communis* 'Pendula'), which offered

127. Weeping willow tree (*Salix babylonica*), Forest Home Cemetery, Milwaukee, Wisconsin. Photograph by James R. Cothran, undated.

a distinctive drooping form. To showcase their elegant drama, the *Horticulturist* recommended planting weeping trees singly or in well-spaced groupings where sufficient distance would allow them to "exhibit their peculiar habits and develop freely their forms."[28] Such trees were particularly valuable and striking in cemetery landscapes when planted along the edge of ponds or other water features.

The *Horticulturist* largely recommended the use of evergreens within rural cemetery grounds. Evergreens, it said, were particularly appropriate, because "in summer they have a quiet and somber hue; and in winter they impart a certain degree of warmth and cheerfulness, which relieves the gloomy and desolate aspect of nature at that season."[29] However, cemetery designers and advocates recognized attractive visual qualities in deciduous trees as well. Adolph Strauch argued that they relieved the "monotonous appearance of a plantation of evergreens" and recommended trees that exhibited brilliant colors in autumn, like the scarlet oak, tulip tree, and sugar maple.[30] Lady Emmeline Stuart Wortley provided one of the most charming accounts

of the visual effect of deciduous trees within a rural cemetery landscape. On her travels to the United States at mid-century, she noted that the perfectly extraordinary autumn colors at Green-Wood Cemetery "all cast their sumptuous shadowings over the quiet graves, like the reflections from richly-painted windows, 'blushing with the blood of kings and queens,' in some mighty old cathedral."[31]

Deciduous trees also held symbolic meaning and spurred the contemplation among visitors of the life cycles of nature. At the dedication of Oakwood Cemetery, the Honorable William J. Bacon provided the oration in which he commented on the symbolic nature of deciduous trees.

> We stand here today, surrounded by the emblems and memorials of the fading year, and legibly written around us is the inscription "Passing away." The sighing wind and the deciduous leaf of autumn are the harbingers and witnesses of that temporary death that falls upon the natural world. Bud and leaf and flower and fruit

128. Entrance to Hollywood Cemetery, Richmond, Virginia. Postcard postmarked 1908, Danylchak collection.

129. Azaleas (*Azalea indica*) drape a monument and fencing. Photograph by James R. Cothran, undated.

have alike yielded to the inevitable law by which death follows life, and suspended animation the freshness and glory as well of nature as of sentient existence. These emblems are not unfitting accompaniments of this day and this occasion, reminding us, as they do, of our own mortality, and of the change that will come to us as it has to the millions that have gone before and will succeed us,—"for we all do fade as a leaf."[32]

But spring, he reminded his listeners, would bring the resurrection of the denuded trees. With their reawakening, they represented the promise and hope that mourners could also associate with their loved ones' ascent to heaven.

The *Guide to Laurel Hill Cemetery* noted that one of the "most simple, yet beautiful and affecting customs of antiquity" was the adornment of graves with flowers.[33] Wilson Flagg also referenced the powerful

sentiment flowers connoted on gravesites. He remarked that flowers "have been regarded in all ages as the most appropriate ornaments of a burial place, and have always been strewed upon the bier and grave of a friend, as the most significant offerings of affection. So many tender recollections of flowers are linked with the memory of a beloved friend who has departed from us, that when we see them springing up from a new-made grave, the image of the dead is brought vividly before the mind, and while our sorrows are revived, they are soothed and tranquilized."[34] Flowers, in general, held comforting connotations, too, because they acted as symbols of hope and the immortality of the soul with "their return to life after their death in winter."[35]

Mount Auburn Illustrated highlighted comments made by the editor of the Edinburgh-based *Chambers' Journal* regarding the superiority of ornamented burial grounds to those previous barren churchyard landscapes. The sentimental effect of flowers particularly helped alleviate the horror of death.

> How different it is with such cemeteries as Père la Chaise! When we lay down a loved one there, we can still hold sweet communion with him. We can show our affection by planting the loveliest flowers of summer above his head, and please ourselves with the belief that the tribute is not unbeheld or unappreciated. We can pull a flower from the place of his repose, and carry it about with us, gratified with the thought, that if we cannot have our friend again, we have something, at least, that has sprung up from his dust. The place of death is no longer, in our eyes, a place of gloom, desertion, and sorrow, at the bare idea of which we shudder with horror and dismay. It is an agreeable resting-spot, to which we retire at the close of life, still to be visited, and gazed on, and cared for, by those we hold dear.[36]

Rural cemetery advocates particularly embraced the use of flowers that held symbolic meanings or connotations fitting for their funerary gardens. In his dedicatory address at Cave Hill Cemetery, Rev. E. P. Humphrey, D.D., stated that the rose was "first in beauty and appropriateness" for cemetery grounds. The rose generally symbolized beauty, hope, love, and condolence. When John Muir camped among the tombs in Bonaventure Cemetery in Savannah in 1867, he reported that rose bushes were frequently planted near the foot of the gravesites. Humphrey also recommended the use of violets, periwinkle, and forget-me-nots to adorn graves. For family lots, the *Horticulturist* recommended white roses, violets, or daisies, which all had associations "in harmony with the place."[37]

Choosing the Right Plant for the Right Place

Those commenting on appropriate plants for cemeteries often differentiated their lists based upon whether the plantings were for individual lots or for general cemetery purposes along borders or pathways or on land unsuitable for burials. Site managers and landscape gardeners at rural cemeteries widely accepted the idea that the appropriate form of tree or shrub, rightly sited, visually enhanced memorial art. In 1854, the *Horticulturist* observed that the "finest tombstones or monuments strike us as bare and unfinished, without the accompaniment of trees, and especially such trees as in their form and character harmonize with their style."[38] Monuments and trees together created a vignette.

The *Horticulturist* emphasized the importance of assessing the suitability of each tree's growth patterns when deciding whether to plant it in cemetery lots adjacent to monuments. The journal particularly recommended low, round-headed trees like the Norway maple (*Acer platanoides*) to ornament individual lots and provide shade. In fact, it stated that there was "no more suitable large tree for a single lot" than the Norway maple, because no tree would "produce a better head, or a more impenetrable shade" nor did it "attain a great height."[39] In its September 1856 issue, the *Horticulturist* provided a list of trees and shrubs suitable for individual lots, including the hop tree (*Ptelea Trifoliata*, L.), the bladdernut tree (*Staphylea trifolia*), and several species of magnolias like the southern magnolia (*Magnolia grandiflora*) and the Umbrella-tree (*Magnolia tripetela*).

The journal also recommended trees and shrubs with extremely compact forms for individual lots. Although not hardy in all parts of the country, the journal recommended the Irish Juniper (*Juniperus communis* 'Hibernica') for its "tapering cylindrical habit" making it "one of the best of all the Junipers for planting

130. Trees frame a family plot and Bigelow Chapel at Mount Auburn Cemetery.
From *Gleason's Pictorial Drawing-Room Companion*, Boston, 1853, Danylchak collection.

on small cemetery lots."[40] In fact, the *Horticulturist* recommended using a variety of species of junipers in rural cemeteries. The Red Cedar (*Juniperus virginiana*), it said, could be shorn into a compact, formal pyramidal shape suitable for narrow spaces. Meanwhile, it called the Chinese Juniper (*Juniperus chinensis*) a "handsome, compact, little tree."

The *Horticulturist*, however, cautioned against certain trees for cemetery lots because of their potential to interfere visually or physically with the monuments. For example, trees with low-spreading limbs, like the Norway spruce (*Picea abies*), would overwhelm a small lot. (The journal did recommend the tree for other areas of rural cemeteries.) Very tall, narrow trees like the Lombardy poplar (*Populas nigra* 'Italica') would also be "in bad keeping with a monument or a tombstone, by overtopping them, reducing their apparent height, and yielding little or no shade below."[41] Wide trees or those with large root systems would also be inappropriate in these spaces. In 1861, Green-Wood Cemetery's trustees required lot owners to obtain permission from the officers of the cemetery company

before any planting of trees or shrubs to insure the suitability of the vegetation.

During the middle part of the nineteenth century, the *Horticulturist* also recommended the use of plants to physically define rural cemetery plots. As early as 1847, the journal expressed disdain toward the use of iron railings to enclose family lots. These devices, it said, too closely resembled those used to encircle the front stoops of urban dwellings and destroyed "the feeling of repose and rural beauty which should pervade a cemetery."[42] If railings could not be removed, the prominent journal suggested mitigating their offensive nature by wreathing them with beautiful vines or twining shrubs. It endorsed the fast growing Chinese twining honeysuckle (identified as *Lonicera flexuosa*) because of its dark, subevergreen foliage and fragrant, abundant flowers. It also suggested Chinese wisteria (*Wisteria sinensis*), "a luxuriant vine, with long clusters of pale lilac blossoms," as well as the silk vine (*Periploca graeca*) with its "rich green leaves and curious brownish flowers" that would "soon make a rich drapery over a piece of iron railing."[43] It also

131. Red cedar (*Juniperus virginiana* L.) at Rose Hill Cemetery, Macon, Georgia. Photograph by James R. Cothran, undated.

recommended mingling one or two sweet-scented clematis (*Clematis flammula*) to these vines for pleasing effect when its "delicate showers of pale star-like blossoms" bloomed.

The most appropriate enclosure at the time, however, according to the *Horticulturist*, was an evergreen hedge, especially American arborvitae (*Thuja occidentalis*). The journal noted that in its tapering conical shape and general effect, it looked similar to cypress trees often seen in the cemeteries of southern Europe. However, the arborvitae offered a color of a "rather more cheerful hue of green" and was, therefore, more agreeable in the opinion of the journal. And it could be sheared annually to maintain a three-foot hedge. Wilson Flagg also noted the appropriateness of the

different species of arbor vitae for burial grounds, "on account of their slender, pyramidal growth, which agrees with the general forms of the monuments. The shape of the arbor vitae is not unlike that of an obelisk" and the various species "charm every beholder while gracefully pointing to heaven with their slender, evergreen spire."[44]

Another acceptable hedge, offering both easy maintenance and beauty, was the Double White Scotch Rose (*Rosa pimpinellifolia* 'Double White'), which would grow to three or four feet in height. Delicate roses would stud its thick, compact mass of foliage in May and June. The Japanese Euonymus (*Euonymus japonica*) was another excellent low hedge. The *Horticulturist* noted that it was a relatively recent arrival to the United States but was already commonly founded in Philadelphia's nurseries. Its compact, upright form and dark, shiny evergreen leaves made it ideal for forming a beautiful hedge around cemetery lots. The journal also suggested the European holly

132. Live oak at Magnolia Cemetery, Charleston, South Carolina. Photograph ca. 1900, Detroit Publishing Company Photograph Collection, Library of Congress Prints and Photographs Division.

(*Ilex aquifolium*), particularly in more temperate climates. "It is," the journal stated, "perhaps, the most beautiful evergreen hedge in the world and we cannot too strongly recommend it to those farther south."[45]

Meanwhile, trees of different forms often added picturesque variety along borders and roadways and upon land not suited for burials. Along thoroughfares Loudon advocated the use of evergreen trees with narrow, conical heads or those that could be easily pruned into such silhouettes for they were "classically and popularly associated with places of sepulture."[46] He recommended, for example, the eastern red cedar (*Juniperus virginiana*) and the Italian cypress (*Cupressus sempervirens*). However, Wilson Flagg noted that pine trees were probably the most common ornament used in New England cemeteries. He deemed the white pine (*Pinus strobus*), which was the most predominant native tree of the region, one of the most "appropriate and magnificent accompaniments of the gardens of the dead" because of the "solemnity and grandeur of its appearance."[47] The *Horticulturist* also recommended that cemetery companies plant the western white pine (*Pinus monticola*), which has an unmistakable long, straight trunk free of branches for about two-thirds of its substantial height; the Scots pine (*Pinus sylvestris* L.), which also has a long, bare trunk but is topped by a rounded mass of foliage; the Swiss pine (*Pinus cembra*), an irregularly shaped, medium-sized tree; and even the sugar pine (*Pinus Lambertiana*), which is the largest species of pine tree in the world. Numerous varieties of oak trees were also

commonly used in rural cemeteries. In his influential *Remarks on Forest Scenery*, William Gilpin had argued that the oak was the most picturesque tree because of its twisting branches that grow in various contortions, "sometimes in long reaches, sometimes in short elbows."[48] The *Horticulturist* recommended "all the varieties" of oaks for general planting purposes by cemetery companies. It particularly endorsed the white oak (*Quercus alba*), a broad-crowned tree that can stretch to twenty feet wide and reach heights of one hundred to one hundred and fifty feet. The journal also advised the use of the overcup oak (*Quercus lyrata*), a medium-sized, rounded-crown tree that can grow to sixty-five feet tall.

Establishing Cemetery Nurseries

Some rural cemetery companies prudently established nurseries not only to facilitate the work of their cemetery superintendents but also to provide plants to proprietors that were appropriate for funereal use and hardy for the climate. In 1860, Forest Hills Cemetery reported that nurseries had been established within its grounds to provide a "constant and ready supply of the most desirable trees and shrubs" to fill in open space and to replace those that needed to be removed.[49] Meanwhile, Laurel Hill Cemetery had eight acres devoted to a nursery on the road leading to the entrance to the burial ground. *Smith's Illustrated Guide* reported that a florist tended a hothouse in which a great variety of flowering plants and shrubs

133. Entrance to Oakwood Cemetery in Syracuse, New York, with greenhouses in the background. Postcard 1913, Danylchak collection.

were grown. This helped ensure that lot owners could obtain plants from a "proper person." Without good guidance, lot owners could easily plant unsuitable trees and shrubs in a family plot, particularly those that would grow to be quite large, overwhelm the size of the lot, and become entangled with each other.

Allegheny Cemetery also kept a small nursery of suitable trees and shrubs for its grounds. In addition to ensuring that the proper trees and shrubs were made available to proprietors, Allegheny Cemetery's management understood that a convenient nursery would make lot owners much more likely to ornament their parcels. The grounds would thus be more heavily adorned with vegetation, still a paramount goal for the cemetery in the early 1870s. The following trees and shrubs were for sale at the cemetery at the time.[50]

TABLE 3. TREES AND SHRUBS FOR SALE AT ALLEGHENY CEMETARY

Coniferous Trees and Plants

BOTANICAL	COMMON
Abies alba	Spruce, White
Abies canadensis	Spruce, Hemlock
Abies excelsa	Spruce, Norway
Abies nigra	Spruce, Black
Buxus arborescens	Spruce, Box Tree
Buxus latifolia	Spruce, Upright
Buxus aurea	Spruce, Golden
Juniperus communis	Juniper, Upright
Juniperus sabina	Juniper, Savin
Juniperus chinensis	Juniper, Chinese
Juniperus suecica	Swedish Juniper
Juniperus virginica	Red Cedar
Picea balsamea	Fir, Balm of Gilead
Pinus austriaca	Austrian Pine
Pinus cembra	Siberian Pine
Pinus laricio	Larch
Taxus baccata	Yew, English
Taxus hibernica	Yew, Irish
Taxus stricta	Yew, Upright
Thuja aurea	Arborvitae, Golden
Thuja occidentalis	Arborvitae, American
Thuja orientalis	Arborvitae, Chinese
Thuja plicata	Arborvitae, Fan-Leaved

Deciduous Trees and Plants

BOTANICAL	COMMON
Acacia julibrissin	Silk Tree
Acer dasycarpum	Silver-Leaved Maple
Acer negundo	Ash-Leaved Maple
Acer pseudoplatanus	English Sycamore
Acer saccharinum	Sugar Maple
Æsculus hippocastianum	Horse Chestnut
Æsculus ohiensis	Buckeye

BOTANICAL	COMMON
Amygdalus persica, fl. pl.	Double-Flowering Peach
Azalea nudaflora	Wood Honeysuckle

BOTANICAL	COMMON
Azalea pontica	Yellow Azalea
Calycanthus floridus	Sweet Scented Shrub
Catalpa syringæfolia	Common Catalpa
Cerasus mahaleb	Austrian Cherry
Cerasus multiplex	Double-Flowering Cherry
Cerasus pendula	Weeping Cherry
Cercis canadensis	Judas Tree
Chionanthus virginica	Fringe Tree
Cydonia japonica	Japan Quince
Cytisus laburnum	Golden Chain
Deutzia gracilis	
Deutzia scabra	Ornamental Shrubs
Deutzia crenata	
Euonymus americanus	Burning Bush
Forsythia viridissima	Golden Bell
Halesia tetraptera	Snowdrop Tree
Hibiscus syriacus, fl. pl.	Double-Flowering Althæa
Larix americana	American Larch
Larix europea	European Larch
Ligustrum vulgare	Common Privet
Liriodendron tulipifera	Tulip Tree
Lonicera	Honeysuckle
Magnolia acuminata	
Magnolia conspicua	
Magnolia cordata	
Magnolia glauca	
Magnolia purpurea	
Magnolia macrophylla	
Magnolia tripetala	
Philadelphus coronarius	Mock Orange
Philadelphus japonicus	Japan Orange
Populus balsamifera	Black Poplar
Populus dilatata	Lombardy Poplar

134. Forest Hills Cemetery receiving tomb with gardenesque plantings. Photograph ca. 1900, Detroit Publishing Company Photograph Collection, Library of Congress Prints and Photographs Division.

Changing Attitudes and Practices

Time and experience motivated changes in planting practices in rural cemeteries. Over time, cemetery superintendents discovered the drawbacks of having certain tree species in cemetery grounds, even those that had been wholeheartedly embraced just a couple decades before. For example, Green-Wood Cemetery's managers found that the dust from flowering chestnut trees stained and spoiled monuments. Meanwhile, the weeping willow, long popular for its mournful connotations, had a short life-span and was highly vulnerable to decay near the root system. The cemetery spent many man-hours removing the species. The Norway spruce was also a maintenance

nuisance because its branches grew rapidly outward.

By the 1860s, as Adolph Strauch's influence spread, attitudes changed dramatically regarding the appropriate density of trees and shrubs in cemetery grounds. In an 1866 publication, Green-Wood Cemetery condemned its overabundance of trees as "offensive by obstructing the light and the air, and shutting out the view of everything beyond them."[51] In fact, the cemetery railed that the "inconsiderate and reckless planting of trees and bushes in and around the spots where our dead repose, is one of the absurdities of fashion."[52] After three decades in cemetery management, Jacob Bigelow also asserted that the "multiplication of trees has already become in Mount Auburn a serious evil." Densely planted trees obstructed views of monuments. And those planted too closely together destroyed each other. Instead, most cemeteries promoted thinned, highly controlled groupings of trees that interspersed a rolling lawn.

Meanwhile, at mid-century, the use of flowering plants, particularly exotics, became more profuse in rural cemeteries. While proprietors placed flowering plants over graves, many cemetery associations cultivated flowering plants along borders and in the triangles formed where avenues and paths intersected. In the 1850s, Mount Auburn Cemetery's trustees authorized funds for the introduction of ornamental shrubs to the grounds. Jacob Bigelow imported rhododendrons from England and about a hundred mountain laurel shrubs (*Kalmia latifolia*) from the White Mountains for use around the entrance gateway and Meadow Pond. By the 1860s, Wilson Flagg observed "dazzling horticultural exhibitions" of flowering plants reared abundantly in borders and parterres in many rural cemeteries.[53] Meanwhile, Green-Wood Cemetery commentator Nehemiah Cleaveland observed artificial beds, graveled walks, and trim parterres, filled quite often with flaunting exotics.[54] By the mid-nineteenth century, some rural cemetery landscapes were becoming more "gardenesque" in appearance. John Claudius Loudon had first introduced the term *Gardenesque* in 1832. He felt the Gardenesque was a more enlightened approach to rural art than the Picturesque and encouraged the use of exotics and the creation of geometric plant displays. In 1855, Forest Hills Cemetery called itself a true "garden cemetery" because of its profusion of flowering plants.[55] The term garden cemetery began replacing the term rural cemetery more widely by the 1860s reflecting a retreat from the Picturesque aesthetic that had dominated cemetery design since the founding of Mount Auburn.

CHAPTER 6

Symbolism in Rural Cemeteries 🌿

Rural cemeteries are landscapes infused with symbolism, most apparent to the visitor in the individual markers that populate the grounds. In 1847, *Green-Wood Illustrated* contended that within "the whole range of mortuary memorials, there is probably nothing which gives so complete satisfaction, as this embodiment of thought in marble speech, when it is felicitously conceived, and properly executed."[1]

Interpreting gravestone symbolism is not as straightforward as it may seem at first. Gravestone carvers rarely left behind written documentation explaining their artistic expressions or a purchaser's request for meaning in stone. So, those interpreting gravestones today are often left to examine other writings from the era (or contemporary studies that have done so) to try to understand the intended implication of a historic motif. One such source is Edward Fitzgerald's *A Hand Book for the Albany Rural Cemetery* (1871), which provided—as a tool for convenience—a list of emblems and their meanings most often misapplied. A palm branch was an emblem of victory and rejoicing. A weeping willow, an emblem of sorrow. An urn with blaze, an emblem of undying friendship. A dove, an emblem of innocence, gentleness, affection, and the Holy Ghost.

Symbols used during a certain era may also have suggested several traits or emotions, making interpretation even more complicated.[2] Symbols often had multiple meanings attached to them over time. For instance, a pagan religion may have attached one meaning to a symbol, while the Christian faith may have later appropriated the symbol and assigned another

meaning to it. Which did the purchaser or carver intend? Perhaps neither. They may have chosen a specific flower, for instance, because of its innate beauty or because it was a favorite of the deceased. Or, they may have seen a particularly well-crafted or poignant headstone in a cemetery and wanted to copy it even if the symbolism was not quite appropriate for the deceased.

Although reading intended meaning in gravestones can be an enigmatic exercise, it can also be a fascinating pursuit. When armed with the knowledge of the origins and evolution of certain symbols, sleuthing among cemetery monuments can be a thought-provoking experience about cultural identity, immersing the visitor in traditions and attitudes of a particular period. Visual symbols on gravestones have been used for as long as markers have indicated a burial place, but they have changed over time and ultimately reflect a culture's attitude toward death at the time they were carved. In the seventeenth and eighteen centuries, for example, symbols prompting thoughts of memento mori (remember death) dominated American graveyards. By the nineteenth century, however, the death's head motif of Puritan New England had been cast aside in favor of symbols that drew inspiration from numerous sources—classical antiquity, Egyptian mythology, Christian precedents, and floriography. The use of such a diverse palette of symbols represented a shift away from the strict religious orientation of gravestone art of the eighteenth century "to a more ecumenical, individualistic atmosphere, imbued with nature and hope."[3]

Investigating symbolism in rural cemeteries can also foster a more personal connection to the people buried there—real people with distinctive personalities and experiences. How did the deceased live his life? How did his loved ones cope with his death? In the nineteenth century, burial became a more commemorative exercise and monuments assumed variety to honor the individualistic traits of the dead. The number of gravestone symbols seen in rural cemeteries multiplied and implied distinctive characteristics about the deceased such as profession, religious affiliation, organizational associations, age, social status or achievements, or even personal attitudes toward mortality. In an 1876 volume, a minister noted the contemporary prevalence of visiting rural cemeteries and connecting with the dead through gravestone art:

> Reader, have you ever walked slowly and thoughtfully through a cemetery? I know you have. It was, perchance, on a pleasant Summer evening, before the twilight shadows had fallen, when all was still hushed, that you wended your way amid the tombstones, and thought of the dead.... There, on one tombstone, was a finger pointing upward, which told of the hope cherished by some stricken heart. And again, on the head-stone of a little grave was carved a lamb or dove, symbol of innocence. Here, too, were choice flowers, expressions of love, emblems of the soul's immortality. As you strolled about beneath the weeping willows, and read the epitaphs, and saw the emblems of hope and love, you felt a strange drawing toward the better life which lies just beyond the boundary of our present vision.[4]

Willow-and-Urn and Classical Antiquity

The weeping willow (*Salix babylonica*) had long been used in burial grounds in its native China, such as at the Vale of Tombs, near the Lake See Hoo. But it was a relatively new species to the burial landscapes of Europe and America in the eighteenth and nineteenth centuries. The weeping willow was introduced from China to England in 1692 and subsequently gained increasing popularity there, especially within the newly designed elegiac landscape gardens of the country's elite. Alexander Pope, for example, planted the weeping willow within his grounds at Twickenham. It was not until 1790 that the weeping willow

made its first appearance in an American nursery catalog. At about the same time, the weeping willow motif began appearing on American gravestones. The image gained widespread popularity in the early nineteenth century and was commonly used in rural cemeteries until the middle of the century.

The weeping willow motif was an early example of gravestone symbolism that reflected a growing sentimentalism about death in the eighteenth century. The willow commonly expressed the sentiment of sorrow or mourning. As historian James A. Hijiya strikingly describes, "The willow, with its slumping posture, intimates the spiritual weariness of someone bereaved; and when the wind blows, there is something melancholy in the soft clatter of a thousand leaves."[5] It could also, however, represent immortality. The tree is easily regenerated from cuttings and as one of the first trees to turn green in spring and the last to lose its leaves in autumn, it represents "the persistence of life."[6]

135. Willow-and-urn motif on a headstone at Magnolia Cemetery, Charleston, South Carolina. Photograph by James R. Cothran, undated.

The urn motif, often used in conjunction with the willow, also appeared in America in the late eighteenth century. An urn, draped with a cloth or shroud, was likely the most common funerary symbol used in American cemeteries in the nineteenth century.[7] Urns had been used to hold the cremated remains of the dead in the ancient civilizations of Greece and Rome. After the American Revolution, the United States embraced Greek and Roman architectural forms and symbols to associate the new nation with the democratic and republican ideals of those ancient civilizations. Publications illustrated archaeological findings, including those at Herculaneum and Pompeii in the mid-eighteenth century, and informed architects and designers interested in appropriating classical motifs. The proliferation of the cinerary urn as a cemetery symbol in the United States unquestionably reflected the influence of Greek and Roman culture. Cinerary urns were not commonly used funerary devices in the United States, because cremation was not a widely accepted practice in the nineteenth century. In conjunction with the urn, the veil was "seen as either a reverential accessory or as a symbol of the veil between earth and the heavens."[8]

Other classical forms began to fill rural cemeteries toward mid-century as interest in the architecture of antiquity grew. The inverted torch, with its flame snuffed out, often represented the extinction of life or of the family line. The fragmentary column symbolized sorrow or a life cut short; it became widely popular because of its visual impact. The use of these classical symbols was not always wholeheartedly embraced by a Christian culture where, by the nineteenth century, hope for eternal life tempered the sadness surrounding death. As *Green-Wood Illustrated* noted, "To the mourners of pagan antiquity, death was extinction. To them, no voice from heaven had spoken. For them, no page of revelation shone. No seer divine had taught them those lessons of faith, which alone can give to the bereaved and sorrowing, assurance of immortality and reunion; when the broken pillar will be more than restored, and the extinguished blaze shall be re-lumined, never to fade again."[9] Despite such protestations, however, classical symbols burgeoned in an increasingly secular society.

Egyptian

Since at least the third millennium B.C.E., the pyramidal form has simultaneously evoked the thought of death and eternity. The famous pyramids at Giza, which date to about 2620–2500 B.C.E., and others throughout ancient Egypt served as tombs for Egyptian pharaohs as well as repositories for the belongings they would need in the afterlife. The embalmed body of a pharaoh was entombed within or underneath a pyramid to protect it, thus allowing the pharaoh to inhabit the afterworld.

American rural cemeteries appropriated the pyramidal form of ancient Egypt and its powerful connotation. *Smith's Illustrated Guide to and Through Laurel Hill Cemetery* contended that "Egypt surpasses all other nations, either ancient or modern, in the magnificence and grandeur of her monuments and tombs. Among these the Pyramids are particularly worthy of

136. Monuments topped by draped urns, with classical columns framing the inscriptions, at Laurel Hill Cemetery, Philadelphia, Pennsylvania. Photograph by James R. Cothran, undated.

137. (right) William B. Smith pyramidal mausoleum at Magnolia Cemetery, Charleston, South Carolina. Photograph by James R. Cothran, undated.

SYMBOLISM IN RURAL CEMETERIES

remark, for their magnitude and solidity."[10] Mirroring the functionality of the Egyptian pyramid, many American cemeteries appropriated the form for their mausoleums. Charleston's Magnolia Cemetery features one particularly noteworthy example—the imposing pyramidal mausoleum of banker William B. Smith. Similar to those erected in ancient times, pyramids in rural cemeteries signified spiritual attainment, resurrection, and eternal life.

Obelisks, first used in Egypt during the era of the Old Kingdom between 2650–2134 B.C.E., symbolized the sun god Ra who was believed to be the source of all life. In ancient Egypt, obelisks were typically seen in pairs flanking temple entrances. The Romans appropriated the architectural form and even transplanted some Egyptian obelisks to the city of Rome. By the sixteenth century, the obelisk was used as a funerary monument throughout Western and Northern Europe, and in the eighteenth century, small obelisks became favored garden ornaments in English elegiac landscape gardens. The form soon migrated to colonial America.

The obelisk was a popular addition to rural cemeteries from the beginning of the movement to the American Civil War. In its heaven-bound, needle-like form, it conferred the idea of ascension. It also symbolized the creator. On a practical level, obelisks were less expensive than elaborately carved monuments and fit gracefully within small cemetery plots. Obelisks became one of the most common types of cemetery monuments in rural cemeteries in the 1840s and 1850s.

Common Egyptian symbols were also adopted for American gravestones and cemetery gateways. For Egyptians, the winged globe, like the obelisk, symbolized the sun god Ra and, therefore, implied both the power to create and divine protection. In American usage, the winged globe lost its pagan attachment and

138. Central section peppered with obelisks at Laurel Hill Cemetery in Philadelphia, Pennsylvania. Photograph by Jack E. Boucher, 1989, Historic American Building Survey, Pa.,51-PHILA,100–42, Library of Congress Prints and Photographs Division.

just meant God. In ancient Egypt, the ouroboros (a serpent devouring its own tail) represented the daily cycle of the sun thus connoting rejuvenation, eternity, and immortality. Meanwhile, the sphinx was a protector of those who had entered the afterlife and symbolized strength. Those meanings translated to rural cemeteries.

Just as some contemporaries raised objections to using the pagan symbols of ancient Greece and Rome in rural cemeteries, some commentators also questioned the appropriateness of Egyptian symbols in Christian places of burial. The October 1836 edition of the *North American Review* noted caustically that "Egyptian architecture reminds us of the religion which called it into being, the most degraded and revolting paganism which ever existed. It is the architecture of embalmed cats and deified crocodiles; solid, stupendous, and time-defying, we allow; but associated in our minds with all that is disgusting and absurd in superstition." An 1855 volume on Forest Hills Cemetery, however, countered:

> There is a difference of opinion as to the propriety of using, as is much the custom, the Egyptian architecture about our burial places. A relic of paganism, it is by some esteemed out of place in a Christian cemetery. But is it essentially the architecture of the grave. Its original examples are the monuments of remote ages, of buried cities, of nations passed away; marking the burial places of kings, of dynasties and of peoples. Imposing and somber in its form and mysterious in its remote origin, it seems peculiarly adapted to the abode of the dead, and its enduring character contrasts strongly and strangely with the brief life of mortals. Nor is it without the symbols of immortality, which the purer faith of the Christian can well appropriate and associate with the more sacred and divine promises of the gospel.[11]

Christian

Although pagan-inspired symbols did adorn cemetery landscapes of the nineteenth century, Christian symbols certainly persisted from earlier times. The Christian emblems that graced these new landscapes of hope, however, were ones charged with faith instead of the gloomy motifs that had been used in churchyards.

Angels inhabit most religions but have become closely associated with the Christian faith. Angels populate both the Old and New Testaments of the Bible, appearing over 270 times.[12] As the 1847 volume *Green-Wood Illustrated* explained, "Our earliest and most cherished associations have accustomed us to blend some image of cherub or seraph, with every thought of the spiritual world. Sacred verse, from the nursery rhyme to the lofty epic, has made these winged messengers of heaven seem almost familiar to our senses. The Bible itself, through its whole course . . . is one continuous record of angelic visitations."[13]

139. Winnie Davis memorial with seated angel dropping flowers on the grave at Hollywood Cemetery, Richmond, Virginia. Photograph 1908, Detroit Publishing Company Photograph Collection, Library of Congress Prints and Photographs Division.

Belief in angels among Protestants was widespread in the nineteenth century and angels frequented the consolation literature written by Protestant clergy of the period.

The angel was one of the most ubiquitous Christian symbols used in rural cemeteries and became decidedly more prolific after 1850. Angels were seen as solid Christian symbols indicating the "maintenance, even the strengthening, of traditional beliefs."[14] A spike in the use of the decidedly Christian motif around mid-century likely reflected "a reaction against the dominance of neoclassicism" and "a reaction against the introduction of neo-Egyptian monuments like obelisks and pyramids into cemeteries."[15] Angels were particularly appropriate additions to the rural cemetery landscape, too, because they "fascinated the Romantics for their compassionate nature and beauty that spoke directly to the sentimental heart."[16]

140. The William J. Mullen monument featuring an angel brandishing a trumpet, Laurel Hill Cemetery, Philadelphia, Pennsylvania. Photograph by Jack E. Boucher, 1989, Historic American Building Survey, Pa.,51-PHILA,100–59, Library of Congress Prints and Photographs Division.

Angels in rural cemeteries assumed many poses to carry different messages. In its solitary form, the angel signified a messenger between God and man: a trumpeting angel, a call to resurrection; a weeping angel or one dropping flowers on a grave, mourning; an angel pointing toward heaven, an indication the soul had departed the earth; a flying angel, either a guardian or rebirth. Of the angels on the famous Charlotte Canda monument, *Green-Wood Illustrated* noted, "These we may regard as guardian angels, waiting, with half-expanded wings, to convey the liberated soul to the abodes of the blessed."[17]

Other female figures in the cemetery, especially those seen in groupings, often represented the seven Christian virtues: faith, hope, charity, temperance, prudence, fortitude, and justice. Often the name of the virtue was part of the sculpture. Even if it was not named, however, the virtue could be identified by specific associated symbols. Faith was typically represented as a woman with a cross, a chalice, or candle. She was sometimes depicted at a baptismal font or with an oil-burning lamp. Hope was almost always represented with an anchor, a long-standing symbol for hope. Charity was often seen in the process of revealing one of her breasts to nurse a child. She also may have been represented with a flame or candle, or clothing or food for the needy. Temperance, sometimes seen on the tomb of a prohibitionist, was generally depicted with a water pitcher or a torch. Prudence, rarely seen in cemeteries, often had two heads and carried a snake or dragon and a mirror. Fortitude was represented as a female warrior often brandishing a club or sword at her side. Justice, also rare in cemeteries, gripped the scales of justice and was generally blindfolded.[18]

The cross motif has been used by many cultures. It is one of the oldest symbols in the world. Christians adopted a cross as their primary symbol after the Roman Emperor Constantine converted to Christianity in 312. At the Battle of Milvian Bridge, Constantine reportedly saw a vision of a cross of light in the sky accompanied by the Greek words *"Ἐν Τούτῳ Νίκα"* ("in this sign you shall conquer"). Afterward, Constantine ordered his troops to adorn their shields with the Chi-Rho cross, which took the form of the intersection of the letters X and P. It was already popular among Christians for it represented the first two letters of the word Christ in the Greek language. When Constantine's army was subsequently victorious, he ordered

the symbol to adorn banners and grace alters in the church.

The cross motif has many iterations and associated meanings. It is the Latin Cross, which looks like the letter "t," that has become most closely associated with Christianity. This was the form of the cross upon which Jesus was crucified. In its basic form, the cross adorning a grave represents the deceased's religious faith. When set atop a three-tiered pedestal base, it is known as the Calvary cross. In this form, the base structure represents the Trinity or the three Christian virtues of faith, hope, and charity. Meanwhile, St. Andrew's cross, which takes the form of an X, symbolizes suffering and humility. When he was sentenced to be crucified, St. Andrew requested to be nailed to a cross unlike the one used to crucify Jesus for he felt unworthy of the symbol that had become associated with him.

Biblical verses have given rise to numerous other Christian symbols that were widely used in rural cemeteries. With symbolic accessories, a lamb signified Christ, the Lamb of God, as referenced in the Gospel of John: "The next day he saw Jesus coming toward him, and said, 'Behold, the Lamb of God, who takes away the sin of the world.'" (John 1:29) In mortuary sculpture, the lamb's attachments may have included a cross, banner, halo, shepherds' crooks, or alpha/omega symbols. If the lamb was simply depicted singularly, however, it generally represented innocence. Meanwhile, a large stone next to a tomb generally represented Resurrection because of verses in the New Testament, such as: "But on the first day of the week, at early dawn, they went to the tomb, taking the spices which they had prepared. And they found the stone rolled away from the tomb, but when they went in they did not find the body" (Luke 24:1–3).

In an 1856 volume entitled *The Loved and the Lost,* an American writer noted that the anchor had long been used in funerary symbolism and that it was still commonly used in Christian nations. It often symbolized "steadfastness and Christian resignation amid the howling tempests of life."[19] Its meaning as hope came from the Bible: "We have this as a sure and steadfast anchor of the soul, a hope that enters into the inner shrine behind the curtain, where Jesus has gone as a forerunner on our behalf, having become a high priest forever after the order of Mel·chiz´-e·dek" (Hebrews 6:19–20). An anchor may also have signified the deceased's seafaring profession.

Plants

Meaning has been attributed to flowers for millennia. As one nineteenth-century author observed, "The language of flowers was known to the ancients."[20] Curiosity in and awareness of the language of flowers rose markedly in Victorian England as well as Continental Europe and the United States during the nineteenth century. This interest in the symbolic meaning of flowers, also known as floriography, coincided with a growing interest in botany at the time. Flowers, whether in bouquets or on gravestones, communicated specific, coded messages.

In the nineteenth century, those curious about floral symbolism had ample resources to consult. The first floriography dictionary was likely *La langage des Fleurs* (1819) written by Louise Cortambert under the pen name Madame Charlotte de la Tour. This edition sparked a multiplicity of imitators; ultimately, the nineteenth century saw the publication of hundreds of editions of books exploring the language of flowers. In the United States, the first printed accounts of floriography appeared in 1827, on the brink of the founding of the first rural cemetery. French American naturalist Constantine Samuel Rafinesque contributed features to the *Saturday Evening Post* under the title "The School of Flora," which provided both plant descriptions and symbolic meanings.

These floriography sources can help decipher meanings suggested by floral symbols on mortuary art in cemeteries. Floral motifs were often used in rural cemeteries to convey messages of sorrow and melancholy or hope and immortality. Frederic Shoberl's 1848 edition of *The Language of Flowers* noted floriography's particular suitability for assuaging grief. "Flowers have their language," he said, and "the softest impressions may be thus conveyed without offence, and even profound grief alleviated, at a moment when the most tuneful voice would grate harshly on the ear, and when the stricken soul can be soothed only by unbroken silence."[21] (Although nineteenth-century floriography dictionaries can aid in interpreting floral symbolism in cemeteries, not all entries or flowers listed in such volumes are applicable. After all, plants, blooms, or bouquets were often used during the Victorian era to send coded messages to a recipient—particularly during courtship—that were too forthright to be spoken openly.)

The language of flowers has drawn upon many traditions—Greek, Egyptian, Christian and others. Flowers, therefore, often have more than one meaning. (This helps account for the fact that not all floral dictionaries suggest the same meaning for every flower.) For example, the Narcissus or daffodil can sometimes suggest vanity because of the legend of Narcissus, a Greek youth who perished because of his own narcissism. One day, he became entranced by his reflection in a pool of water, accidentally fell in, and drowned. A daffodil purportedly emerged upon the spot of Narcissus's demise. Christians later changed the meaning of the beautiful flower. Since the perennial blooms each spring around the time of the Easter

141. Monument depicting a tree with limbs cut short at Allegheny Cemetery, Pittsburgh, Pennsylvania. Photograph by James R. Cothran, undated.

holiday, Christians associated it with the resurrection and the ultimate triumph of divine love.

The oak was a sacred tree to the Greek, Roman, and Teutonic cultures, all of which attached meanings to the tree. In ancient Greece, a sacred grove of oaks at Dodona served as an oracle, relaying messages from Zeus to the local priests and priestesses through the rustling of the tree's leaves. Zeus, the father of the Greek Gods, was himself symbolized by the oak tree. The Romans conferred a wreath of green oak, known as a civic crown, upon those who had saved the life of a Roman citizen in battle. As the second-highest military decoration a Roman citizen could attain, the civic crown visually signaled honor and strength. In

Germanic folklore, the oak had the power to protect against evil. It also represented the patriarch of the family, and, as such, masculine vitality. The oak cut short with branches severed, therefore, "symbolized the end of a family line."[22] It could also stand for an individual cut down in the prime of life, like a tree suddenly felled by a storm.

Egyptian mythology also attached meanings to flowers that were later referenced in nineteenth-century mortuary sculpture. The blue Egyptian lotus (*Nymphaea caerulea*) was frequently used in ancient Egyptian art. It was enshrined by Egyptian mythology as one of the instrumental elements of creation. It was recounted that the lotus arose through the primordial

142. Monuments at Forest Hills Cemetery, Boston, Massachusetts. Mother's with a bouquet of varied flowers, Henry's with oak leaves and a sheath of wheat. Photograph by James R. Cothran, 2004.

ooze, opened its petals, and revealed the Sun God—the source of all life—at its golden heart. It derives meaning, too, from its cycle of closing its flowers at night and opening them back up with the rising sun. It has thus become linked with "the sun god, creation, intelligence, rebirth, immortality and royal power."[23] The lotus flower was a ubiquitous symbol used on Egyptian funerary architecture.

The innate characteristics of other plants also gave rise to symbolic associations. In rural cemeteries, the lily of the valley, one of spring's early bloomers, generally connoted resurrection and renewal. Meanwhile, the morning glory, which blooms in the morning but wilts in the afternoon, invited contemplation about "two of life's grand themes: reproduction and death."[24] Moreover, its ephemeral nature provoked reflection upon the brevity of life.[25] Ivy was used as a symbolic device for numerous characteristics tied to its properties. Because it stays green yearlong, it was often associated with fertility and immortality. Because it holds steadfastly to support, it was linked to friendship or attachment. Frederic Shoberl offered a vivid explanation of the trait in *The Language of Flowers* by quoting Bernardin de Saint-Pierre, "Nothing…can separate it from the tree which it has once embraced: it clothes it with its own leaves in that inclement season when its dark boughs are covered with hoar-frost. The faithful companion of its destiny, it falls when the tree is cut down: death itself does not relax its grasp, and it continues to adorn with its verdure the dry trunk which once supported it."[26] Basis for this meaning of attachment was also rooted in Greek mythology where the altar of Hymen, a god of marriage ceremonies, "was encircled with Ivy, and a branch of it was presented to the new-married couple, as a symbol of the indissoluble knot."[27] Because of its three-pointed leaves, ivy was also representative of the Trinity.

143. Monument to "our darling Lizzie," with child and Latin Cross, Magnolia Cemetery, Charleston, South Carolina. Photograph by James R. Cothran, undated.

Children

In the nineteenth century, new attitudes toward children emerged. They were viewed as foils to adults who were exposed to the immoral, corrupt, impersonal environment of emerging industrial cities. Children, still swaddled by the nurturing atmosphere of the Christian home, were regarded as innocent, sincere, untainted. They were also portrayed as being close to nature—a connection many adults had lost with their immersion in the city sphere. In their deaths, children were assured everlasting purity and protection from the corrupting influences of the time.[28] Such attitudes affected the symbolism that infused the gravesites of children in rural cemeteries.

The lamb was the most common symbol associated with nineteenth-century children's grave markers. For centuries, the representation of a lamb had been equated with Christ. In rural cemeteries, the lamb also represented childhood innocence. When paired with the figure of a child, a common combination, the lamb portrayed the innocent child's closeness to nature, a pure force permeated by God in the eyes of American Romantics.

Children's graves also sometimes featured empty furniture which represented a life unfulfilled. Small vacant beds or chairs were common and became sentimentally charged symbols reminding the mourner of the nurturing home from which the child departed. These small domestic objects also reminded the grieving mother that it was "this very same smallness—this inability to ever achieve the full size of adulthood— which kept her children pure and unsullied, separate and distant from the outside world."[29] Other domestic props, those distinctly associated with children, were often incorporated into the grave marker as well. A rattle or a doll, for instance, reinforced the representation of childhood simplicity.

Fraternal Organizations

During the nineteenth century, fraternal societies proliferated in the United States. Along with social benefits, most provided life, accident, sickness, or other welfare benefits to members and their dependents. Since the mid-1800s, about two thousand fraternal societies have likely existed in North America.[30] Gravestones often incorporated the symbol of one (or more) of these groups to recognize the deceased's affiliations. Many acronyms, or emblems with acronyms, that appear on headstones indicate the deceased's association with a fraternal order, benevolent society, club, or secret society.[31]

Freemasonry, the largest fraternal order in the world and the oldest in the United States, has adopted numerous symbols over time that represent moral lessons or virtues and that are strongly associated with the organization. One is the all-seeing eye, which was an ancient symbol for God. It is immediately recognizable to Americans because it appears on the dollar bill. Many of the founding fathers, including George Washington and Benjamin Franklin, were Masons. Meanwhile, the square and compasses—two architect's tools—form the Freemason's most recognizable symbol standing for reason and faith. In the English-speaking world, a "G" is often depicted in the middle of the two instruments. The letter is often interpreted to stand for God, reminding Masons that God is at the epicenter of Freemasonry. Others interpret the "G" to stand for geometry, a reference to Freemasonry's belief in sacred geometry.

The Independent Order of the Odd Fellows (IOOF), an American fraternal order founded in Baltimore in 1819, spun off from the eighteenth-century English Odd Fellows organization, a working-class social and charitable association. By the Civil War, membership in the IOOF had soared to over two hundred thousand members. One of the major benefits of membership was death care, including payments for funerals or grave markers or the allotment of space in the organization's plot in a rural cemetery. One of the most common symbols of the IOOF is three joined links of a chain. This symbol and the Freemason's square and compasses are the most common fraternal emblems found in cemeteries.[32] The letters FLT— for friendship, love, and truth—also often appear on IOOF member headstones, along with a shepherd's crook, clasped hands, a tent, or a bow and arrow.

The Improved Order of the Red Men, which traces its origins to certain pre-Revolutionary secret patriotic societies, was founded in Baltimore in 1834. Although Native Americans were not accepted into the group until the second half of the twentieth century, the fraternal organization modeled its rituals and regalia on nineteenth-century views of Native American culture. Members were part of a "tribe" and meetings were held at lodges known in the organization's parlance as wigwams. Members' gravestones often incorporated either a Native American profile or an eagle accompanied by a hatchet, an arrow and quiver, a shield, and a peace pipe. The letters TOTE, standing for "totem of the eagle," also often appear.

The Knights of Pythias, founded in Washington, D.C., in 1864, became one of the most popular post–Civil War fraternal organizations. The organization's insignia often appears on the gravestones of deceased members. The insignia includes a medieval knight in armor with a sword, battle ax, and shield emblazoned with the letters FCB., standing for the central tenets of the order—friendship, charity, and benevolence. As part of the insignia, a bird sits atop the knight's helmet.

Contemporary historians have compiled lists of common symbols found in cemeteries and their meanings to help instruct contemporary visitors. The following list has been adapted from several such sources along with Fitzgerald's 1871 *A Hand Book for the Albany Rural Cemetery.*[33]

Acanthus leaves: heavenly wisdom

Acorn: prosperity; strength

All-seeing eye: watchfulness; the Supreme Being (a common Masonic symbol)

Alpha and Omega: The first and last letters of the Classical Greek alphabet, thus symbolizing the beginning and the end. It was an appellation assigned Jesus Christ in the book of Revelation, which was originally written in Greek.

American eagle, with stars and stripes: eternal vigilance; universal liberty

Anchor: hope; steadfastness; faith

Angel: messenger between God and man

Archways: passageway to the next realm; entry; triumph

Bed, empty: loss, usually of a child; anguish

Beehive: industriousness; domesticity

Bellflowers: constancy; faithfulness; gratitude

Bird, flying: rebirth; winged soul

Book: wisdom

Book, open: the Bible; faith; perfect knowledge

Book with crown: God and the Bible

Bouquet: condolence; grief

Butterfly: resurrection; natural cycle of birth and death; short-lived

Calla lily: beauty; marriage

Chair, empty: loss of a loved one

Chain, with three links: Independent Order of Odd Fellows; Trinity; faith

Chalice: Christ

Chi-Rho (XP): Christ (derived from the first two letters of the Greek word for Christ, XPICTOC); also the abbreviation of the Greek word *chreston,* meaning "good omen"

Chrysanthemum: longevity

Circle: no beginning and no end; eternity; completeness; resurrection

Circle, broken: end of life

Closed book: completed life; the Bible; secrecy

Clouds: transition to heaven

Column, unbroken: a completed life; steadfastness

Column, paired: passageway to the next realm

Clover: Trinity; vitality

Corn: ripe old age

Cross: faith

Cross, Celtic: faith, eternity

Cross with crown: sovereignty of the Lord; triumph over death

Crown: victory; triumph over death; resurrection; faith

Cypress: mourning; hope

Daffodil (Narcissus): rebirth; resurrection; vanity

Daisy: the Virgin Mary; innocence; purity of thought; gentleness

Dog: loyalty; vigilance

Dogwood: eternal life; symbolic of the Crucifixion and Resurrection

Dove: purity; innocence; gentleness; affection; peace; the Holy Ghost

Drapery/pall: mourning; sorrow; death

Eagle: resurrection; St. John the Evangelist; national emblem of the US

Egg and dart: life (egg) and death (dart); resurrection; rebirth

Eye: all-seeing God

Fern: humility; sincerity; immortality

Fish: faith; Christ; Christ's followers; plentifulness

Flame: eternal life; religious fervor

Fleur-de-lis: Trinity; purity

Flower, broken stem: life cut short

Flower bud: died young

Garland: victory over death; tribute

Gate: passage to the kingdom of heaven

Grape clusters: the Eucharistic; body and blood of Christ

Grape vine: Christ

Griffin (body of a lion and head and wings of an eagle): power; guardian

Handshake: a farewell to mortal life; God's welcome to heaven; fraternal bond (if the sleeves are gender neutral); matrimony (if one sleeve is masculine and one is feminine-looking)

Hand coming down from a cloud: the presence of God

Half carved/half unfinished stone: transition from life to death

Harp/lyre: heavenly music; hope; the arts; praise of God; Irish heritage

Heart: love; life

Heart pierced or broken: grieving mother; Virgin Mary

Horseshoe: protection from evil

Hourglass: time; time runs out; death and resurrection, which is implied when the hourglass is turned over

Hourglass, with wings: swift passage of earthly time

IHC: Jesus (the first three letters of Jesus's name using the Roman alphabet)

IHS: Jesus (the first three letters of Jesus's name using in the Greek alphabet)

INRI: Jesus of Nazareth, the King of the Jews (in Latin: *Iesus Nazarenus Rex Iudaeorum*)

Iris: faith; hope; wisdom; admiration

Ivy: undying affection; friendship; faithfulness; bonding; remembrance; immortality; the Trinity

Knot: love; marriage

Lamb: innocence; purity; Christ

Lamb, lying down: Christ's suffering

Lamb, standing up: risen, triumphant Christ

Lamp: wisdom; piety; immortality of the soul

Laurel: distinction; triumph; success

Lily: resurrection; innocence; purity; marriage

Lily of the valley: purity; humility; reawakening

Lion: bravery; strength; resurrection

Lion, winged: St. Mark the Evangelist

Lotus: creation, rebirth, immortality; sleep; intelligence; royal power

Morning glory: resurrection; brevity of life; beginning of life—associated with the death of a child

Oak tree, leaves: strength; eternity; longevity; faith; honor; hospitality; virtue. The number of branches on a tree trunk traditionally symbolizes the number of children born to the deceased.

Olive tree, branch: peace; forgiveness; humanity; purification

Open bible: devotion; religious faith

Open book with scrolled pages: wisdom

Quatrefoil: an ornament with four foils or lobes commonly used in Gothic architecture; it is symbolic of the four evangelist saints: Matthew, Mark, Luke and John.

Palm leaves: resurrection; spiritual victory; eternal peace

Pansy: remembrance

Passion flower: Christ; sacrifice; suffering and redemption

Pax: peace (in Latin; it may also be abbreviated as PX)

Phoenix: resurrection

Pine cone: immortality; regeneration; incorruptibility; spiritual fertility

Poppy: eternal sleep; consolation

Pyramid: eternal life; stability; spiritual attainment

Ring, broken: family circle broken

Rising sun: resurrection

Rock: God; permanence; strength; reliability

Rose: motherhood; beauty; hope; love (roses were

144. Reverend Walter Munford Monument with an open book atop a tree stump at Laurel Hill Cemetery, Philadelphia, Pennsylvania. Photograph by Jack E. Boucher, 1989, Historic American Building Survey, Pa., 51-PHILA,100–61, Library of Congress Prints and Photographs Division.

frequently used on women's graves during the nineteenth century)

Scallop shell: pilgrim's journey; resurrection

Snake: sin; fall of man; Satan

Snake biting its tail (ouroboros): eternity

Sphinx: spiritual triumph; strength; guardian of the tomb

Square and compasses: reason and faith (associated with Freemasonry)

Stag: solitude; contemplation

Stag with crucifix: piety; devotion

Star: divine guidance

Star, five-pointed: the Virgin Mary

Star, six-pointed: the Star of David, a Jewish symbol of divine protection

Star, seven-pointed: the Holy Spirit

Tree: tree of Life; family; creation

Triangle: Holy Trinity

Upright torch: eternal life

Upward pointing forefinger: departed; gone home; with Jesus

Urn: death

Urn, draped: sorrow, mourning

Urn, with blaze: undying friendship; soul departing; remembrance

Vine: Christ; fidelity; friendship; love

Weeping willow: sorrow, mourning

Wheat: divine harvest; aged deceased—ripe for harvest

Winged globe: disk symbolizes the Creator; the wings represent "God over all"; divine protection

Wings: flight of soul to heaven

Wreath: tribute; honor; circle of eternal life

Wreath, laurel: victory tribute

Impact of Rural Cemeteries on the American Landscape and the Profession of Landscape Architecture ❧

The rural cemetery movement had a profound and far-reaching impact on the American landscape. The popularity of rural cemeteries propelled the movement for public parks in the United States. Moreover, the layout and features of rural cemeteries—the first large-scale, designed landscapes in America open to the public—significantly shaped the design of the parks themselves. Before long, large-scale planned suburbs developed using similar design elements that marked an embrace of nature. These new forms of designed landscapes required men experienced in the art of landscape gardening to arrange them. And, in fact, many of the men responsible for early park and suburb designs had tested and refined their talents in arranging rural cemeteries. It was the development of rural cemeteries that initially spurred the professionalization of landscape gardening in America. The ensuing creation of public parks and garden suburbs and the continued proliferation of large-scale cemeteries ultimately demanded the recognition and cultivation of the specialized field known as landscape architecture.

The Impetus for Parks

By the middle of the nineteenth century, the popularity of rural cemeteries as leisurely retreats was unmistakable. They served local populations escaping the confines of the city to commune with nature and became fashionable tourist attractions marketed to out-of-town visitors. In 1849, Theodore D. Woolsey (1801–1889), the president of Yale University, observed: "Already not only the larger towns, as Boston, New York, and Philadelphia, but smaller ones, as Springfield and Worcester, and we know not how many others, have large areas in their neighborhood laid out for the mansions of the dead, where beauty of scenery, taste in landscape gardening, elegance and costliness of monuments awaken wide curiosity, so that the stranger who should not visit them would be regarded as having only half finished his sightseeing."[1]

In 1848, Laurel Hill Cemetery hosted an estimated thirty thousand visitors, while Mount Auburn and Green-Wood, in Andrew Jackson Downing's estimation, likely accommodated twice that number. By 1860, the visitor statistics had grown considerably. An estimated 140,000 people visited Laurel Hill. Meanwhile, the number of Green-Wood sight-seers ranged from four hundred thousand to five hundred thousand annually.[2]

As the number of visitors enjoying rural cemeteries ballooned, critics became increasingly vocal about the inappropriateness of cemeteries serving as pleasure grounds. Even as early as 1838, native Bostonian and author Caroline Gilman (1794–1888) wrote of her beloved Mount Auburn: "Probably few persons, of contemplative minds, now visit this sacred spot, without feeling that there is too much *life*, too much of the world collected there. Idle questions of childhood, flippant jests of the gay who have none to mourn for, criticisms over the model of monuments where affection longs to come and lie down and weep alone, press on the ear with painful dissonance to the still harmonies of nature."[3] Andrew Jackson Downing, too,

145. Men recreating by a lake at Green-Wood Cemetery, Brooklyn, New York.
Stereograph ca. 1870s, Danylchak collection.

derided the "gala-day air of *recreation*" within rural cemeteries, noting that people seemed to visit them to "enjoy themselves, and not indulge in any serious recollections or regrets."[4] Cemetery corporations had enacted rules of conduct over time to try to curtail the most offensive visitor behavior, but even frivolous chatter among friends invading the quietude of nature diminished the appeal of these cemeteries for those who had ardently supported their establishment.

However, the widespread embrace of these naturalistic landscapes as restorative and entertaining retreats ultimately prompted the consideration of an alternative urban oasis—dedicated public parks. In 1848, Downing stated emphatically in the *Horticulturist*, "Judging from the crowds of people in carriages, and on foot, which I find constantly thronging Green-Wood and Mount Auburn, I think it is plain enough how much our citizens, of all classes, would enjoy public parks."[5] In fact, he estimated that public gardens, full of the most varied amusements, would attract ten times the number of visitors as Mount Auburn.[6] He demanded, "Can you doubt that if our large towns had suburban pleasure grounds, like Greenwood, (excepting the monuments,) where the best music could be heard daily, they would become the constant resort of the citizens."[7] Although a few examples of park-like grounds already existed, such as Boston Common and the grounds around the water works in

Philadelphia, which later became Fairmount Park, at the time of Downing's editorializing, "no American city had begun to make provision for public parks."[8]

Although the America rural cemetery was a strong and immediate influence on the public parks movement in the United States, it was certainly not a solitary one. There were, in fact, public park precedents in Europe. In October of 1848, Downing contrasted American cities devoid of parks with Paris, Frankfort, and other European cities that boasted large public parks and gardens. Two years later, Downing took his readers on a tour of London's great Royal Parks— Hyde Park, Regent's Park, St. James's Park, and Green Park, which became public parks as a result of the Crown Lands Act of 1851. In the interim, Frederick Law Olmsted—the future codesigner of New York's Central Park—visited England and was escorted to Birkenhead outside of Liverpool to view Birkenhead Park, which is often cited as the first publicly funded civic park in Britain.

In his advocacy efforts for public parks in America, Downing echoed arguments similar to those articulated by rural cemetery supporters regarding the benefits of increased contact with nature. Downing asked if anyone could doubt that public pleasure grounds "would tend to soften and allay some of the feverish unrest of business which seems to have possession of most Americans, body and soul?"[9] Downing argued that public pleasure grounds would offer Americans an escape from the "stifling atmosphere" of cities. Downing anticipated loftier results, too. He contended that public park projects, carefully planned, would "largely civilize and refine the national character, foster the love of rural beauty, and increase the knowledge of and taste for rare and beautiful trees and plants."[10] Unlike cemeteries, however, public pleasure grounds would fittingly foster good spirits and social enjoyment for the benefit of a weary urbanized population.

To achieve these curative effects, Downing advocated that public parks or gardens emulate the rural design of the country's celebrated cemeteries. Cemetery companies had demonstrated good judgment in their site selections, he said, and those establishing public parks should follow suit. He maintained that park sites should "have a varied surface, a good position, sufficient natural wood, with open space and good soil enough for the arrangement of all those portions which require to be newly planted."[11] He envisioned large-scale grounds laid out with carriage drives through wooded terrain. And, he imagined these landscaped spaces, like rural cemeteries, exhibiting botanical collections of all the hardy trees and shrubs that would thrive in their particular climate.

Downing's rhetoric struck a national cord and drove interest in establishing naturalistic parks within America's cities. Although the acceptance of public parks as important urban institutions is widespread today, in the middle of the nineteenth century, Downing's arguments in the *Horticulturist* were "unique, fresh, and original."[12] Downing strategically mounted a campaign for the creation of parks with a series of persuasive, forceful essays, which were often copied by the press and printed in local newspapers. In *A History of Horticulture in America*, the esteemed botanist and horticulturist U. P. Hedrick asserted, "It is not too much to say that as a result of the inspiration created by Downing's *Landscape Gardening*, his *Rural Essays*, and his editorials in the *Horticulturist*, the movement for parks in all American cities was begun."[13]

New York's Central Park

New York City saw mounting public desire for the realization of Downing's vision, culminating in the creation of the first-major-designed public park in the United States—Central Park. As early as 1844, the editor-in-chief of the *New York Evening Post*, William Cullen Bryant, who had penned the influential poem "Thanatopsis" earlier in his career, began calling for the creation of a city park in editorials in his newspaper. Then in 1850, Ambrose C. Kingsland made the formation of a park an issue in his winning bid for New York City mayor. In 1851, Downing praised the mayor for his overall vision of establishing a park but forcefully declared that Kingsland's call for one hundred and sixty acres was far too small for the ever-growing metropolis. Instead, Downing insisted: "Five hundred acres may be selected between 39th-street and the Harlem river, including a varied surface of land, a good deal of which is yet waste area, so that the whole may be purchased at something like a million of dollars. In that area there would be space enough to have broad reaches of park and pleasure-grounds, with a real feeling of the breadth and beauty of green fields, the perfume and freshness of nature. In its midst would be located the great distributing reservoirs of the Croton aqueduct, formed into lovely lakes of limpid water, covering many acres, and heightening the charm of the sylvan accessories by the finest natural contrast."[14]

The agitation of these influential citizens and others finally resulted in the City of New York's acquisition of over 750 acres of land in the middle of Manhattan, encompassing the reservoirs of the Croton aqueduct, for a "green oasis for the refreshment of the city's soul and body."[15] The state legislature had authorized the City to use the power of eminent domain to do so. The land acquisition for the park began in 1853 and took three years to complete. The land procured embraced a long rectangular area lying between Fifth and Eighth Avenues and 59th Street and 106th Street. An extension of the park in 1863 to 110th Street brought the total acreage to eight hundred and forty-three. The acquired land was irregular and punctuated by swamps, meandering waterways, and rocky outcroppings.

In 1857, the Park Commissioner announced a design competition for what would become known as Central Park. In response, Frederick Law Olmsted, who had recently been appointed as the park's superintendent, approached architect and Downing disciple Calvert Vaux about partnering to create a design for the competition. Thirty-three proposals were submitted; in April of 1858, Vaux and Olmsted's Greensward Plan was selected. Olmsted was subsequently named "architect-in-chief" and Vaux "assistant to the architect-in-chief."

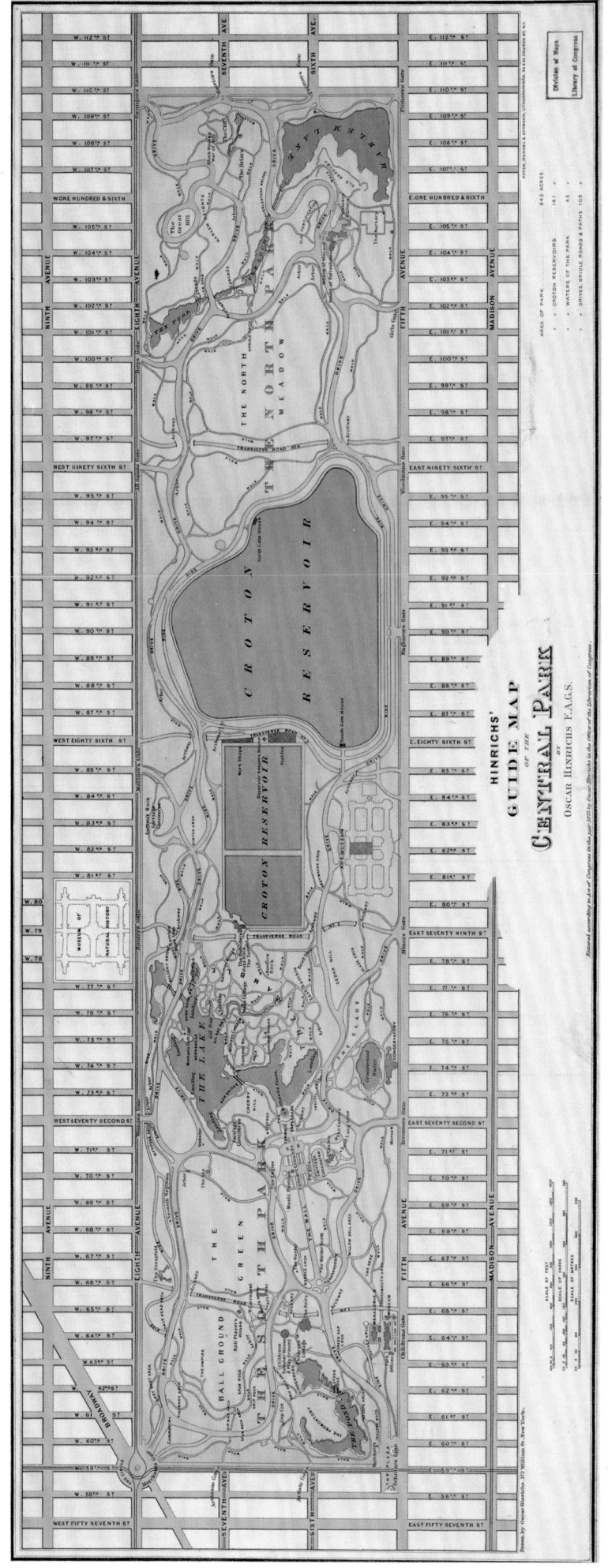

146. *Hinrichs' guide map of the Central Park*, 1875. Library of Congress Geography and Map Division.

The Greensward Plan incorporated numerous Picturesque landscape elements, imitating in many ways the design precedent set by the nation's rural cemeteries, which had themselves been shaped by earlier English landscape gardens. The Ramble, an area in the southern portion of the Central Park site, exemplified the Picturesque. The area was naturally composed of barren rock, a feature originally viewed as a shortcoming of the selected site. In an 1859 description of the park, however, Olmsted explained the actual advantage the rocky site conferred. He noted that once soil and foliage was added to the lower park, "that peculiar picturesqueness of effect, which can only be obtained in a high degree where rocky masses exist as a basis of operations, will become strikingly obvious. Grass and shrubbery can be formed anywhere, but great rocks, and those salient forms of earth-surface which are only found in nature where rock exists, can never be imitated on a large scale with perfect success. Although, therefore, it will require a

147. Scenes in Central Park. From *Picturesque America*, 1873, Danylchak collection.

heavy expenditure to make the Park complete, the final artistic effect will be much finer than could possibly be obtained upon a tract of the richest and most easily worked soil, the natural outlines of which were tame and prosaic."[16] To create their desired effect, Olmsted and Vaux covered much of the Ramble's surface with soil and planted it thickly with vines such as honeysuckle, wild grape, trumpet-creeper, and wisteria as well as flowering shrubs. In their choice of plantings, the designers intended to give the Ramble "the delicate flavor of wilderness."[17] They then judiciously used the site's rock formations to create interspersed picturesque elements. To provide visual variety, the design team allowed rock outcroppings to peek out at irregular intervals. Over one outcropping, the designers engineered the course of a brook to create a charming cascade. They also carved a cave out of one of the great rock formations from which visitors could see a striking view of a lake below.

One of the most heralded design features of the park was its overall circulation system, which Olmsted and Vaux designed to provide visitors with uplifting experiences, while also being optimally functional. Their hierarchical system included footpaths, bridle paths, carriage drives, waterways, and sunken transverse roadways. Curvilinear carriage drives generally ran north-south with bridges creating connectivity over the sunken east-west roadways. Similar to the carriage drives in rural cemeteries, these drives curved through the park to allow the visitor to "make a leisurely tour, taking in each scene successively."[18] Meanwhile, the east-west roadways were an urban necessity allowing traffic to cross the geographically extended park. The designers skillfully depressed these pragmatic roadways, however, to avoid disrupting rustic views. Meanwhile, footpaths and bridle paths interlaced parts of the landscape without any discernable pattern. Brick, stone, and iron arches allowed

148. An afternoon procession on one of the driveways, Central Park, New York. Photograph ca. 1905, Detroit Publishing Company Photograph Collection, Library of Congress Prints and Photographs Division.

pedestrians on the footpaths to pass under the drives and over the bridle paths unobstructed. Meanwhile, arched pedestrian bridges spanned the waterways allowing pedestrians to cross over and rowboats to traverse under unimpeded.

Olmsted and Vaux not only held the Picturesque in high esteem but also revered the Beautiful, an aesthetic that Adolph Strauch was encouraging and implementing at Spring Grove Cemetery at about the same time. Instead of choosing one landscape aesthetic over the other, however, Olmsted and Vaux skillfully incorporated elements of the Beautiful to strikingly contrast both the Picturesque style within the park and the constrained, straight lines of the external city. In an 1859 description of the park, Olmsted argued that "breadth and expanse" in the landscape was necessary to provide visual and psychological balance to the Picturesque. If the landscape exemplified by the Ramble was repeated throughout the entire park, Olmsted

explained, the landscape would be "monotonous in its irregularity, the eye soon wearying of the ceaseless repetition of rocks and hillocks with meagre depressions of surface between them."[19] So, on the Central Plateau, for instance, the designers ordered the removal of rock and the addition of fill to fashion thirty acres of "level or but slightly undulating ground."[20] Measuring about a quarter mile across, the stretch of lawn was unbroken by trees or roadways thus forming an open common perfect for play. In his description of the park, author and art critic Clarence Chatham Cook (1828–1900) observed the contrast of approaches in the landscape's southern section, noting that a visitor could look "across the broad Play-Ground with its delightful sweeps of verdant lawn unbroken by the smallest shrub or tree, to where, on the opposite side there rises above the thick enclosing wall of foliage, the rocky knoll."[21] The northern section of the park was even more conducive to the pastoral treatment.

149. Sheep in an expansive, open lawn in Central Park, New York. Photograph ca. 1900, Detroit Publishing Company Photograph Collection, Library of Congress Prints and Photographs Division

In the Greensward submission, the designers noted that "horizontal lines of the upper park are bold and sweeping and the slopes have great breadth in almost every aspect in which they may be contemplated." They expressed their desire to preserve the unity of character in this section and avoid as much as possible the addition of crossroads. The designers contended that the character of this section was "in most decided contrast to the confined and formal lines of the city" and was therefore "the highest ideal that can be aimed at for a park under any circumstances."[22]

Like its rural cemetery predecessors, Central Park became a richly varied botanical garden. Only forty-two species of trees originally inhabited the park site. However, by 1873 the park contained "402 species of deciduous trees and shrubs, 149 non-coniferous evergreens and American plants in open ground, 81 conifers, and 815 hardy perennials and alpines."[23] By that time, a total of four to five million trees, shrubs, and vines had been planted in the park. In 1869, Clarence Cook commented that the deliberate cultivation of a wide variety of plants native to the United States was "one of the chief advantages of the Park."[24] As a de facto botanical garden, the park served an important educational function. Cook noted that some of the species introduced were rare, and without their display within the park, the public would remain ignorant of their beauty and advantages. He argued, "This is in some respects, for practical purposes, the best sort of botanical garden. Of course it is not the sort that a scientific man will desire, but it probably teaches the general public more than a more formal scientific arrangement would, perhaps for the very reason that it makes no pretense of teaching us at all. We make the acquaintance of many trees, shrubs, vines, and flowers here in a familiar, easy way, as we would of people in their homes."[25]

Central Park exhibited additional features in common with the design of rural cemeteries including numerous and varied water features and picturesque views of the retreat's environs. In his description of the park, Cook took note of the "abundant provision of water for man and beast" in every part of the park. Although the water for the lakes, pools, brooks, and fountains was a "natural product" of the park's own ground, the water features visitors viewed were not indigenous to the site. As Cook explained, "The water that used to stagnate in these marshes, or to creep lazily along in slender streams, half choked with duckweed

and cress, has been thus transformed by the skill of the engineers and landscape gardeners, and made to minister both to use and beauty."[26] Meanwhile, although the site was located within the confines of the city, it still offered opportunities for striking outward-facing views. Visitors who surmounted a rocky summit on the northern edge of the park were rewarded with beautiful views, east, west, north and south, including the Hudson and East rivers, the Harlem flats, and farther afield, the uplands of Westchester.

Olmsted and Vaux fervently felt that any buildings in the park should be subordinate to the landscape. In the text they submitted for their winning Greensward Plan, they stated, "We conceive that all such architectural structures should be confessedly subservient to the main idea, and that nothing artificial should be obtruded in view as an ultimatum of interest. The idea of the park itself should always be uppermost in the mind of the beholder." Calvert Vaux, who had been trained as an architect in England before immigrating to the United States, designed most of the original structures in the park. Most of the buildings were designed in the Victorian Gothic style and blended harmoniously into the rural landscape. The idea that the architecture as well as the engineering in the park should be subordinated to rural nature became a central tenet of design in the urban parks movement in the United States.[27]

Although most of Central Park exemplified the naturalistic style, the designers did include one significant formal feature—the Mall and Terrace, also called the Esplanade, at the southern end of the park. Looking northward, the Mall terminates with a vista of the picturesque, Vaux-designed, Victorian Gothic Belvedere in the distance. The physical termination point of the Mall, however, is the two-tiered Terrace at the edge of the Lake. The lower level of the Terrace prominently showcases the Bethesda Fountain with a sculpture, *The Angel of the Waters*, designed by Emma Stebbins (1815–1882). Stebbins, one of the first notable female sculptors in the United States, became the first woman to receive a sculptural commission in New York City with this Central Park work.

The Terrace was the only place within the park that Olmsted and Vaux's Greensward Plan proposed a sculptural program. However, over time, the park—like its cemetery predecessors—became an open air museum showcasing the works of major sculptors, many

150. The formal terrace with its Bethesda Fountain, Central Park, New York. Photograph ca. 1901, Detroit Publishing Company Photograph Collection, Library of Congress Prints and Photographs Division.

of whom had previously added works to the nation's rural cemeteries. In 1851, in his call for the establishment of a park in New York City, Downing had argued: "Where would be found so fitting a position for noble works of art, the statues, monuments, and buildings commemorative at once of the great men of the nation, of the history of the age and country, and the genius of our highest artists?"[28] In Central Park, a memorial to American inventor Samuel Finley Breese Morse (1791–1872), sculpted by Byron M. Pickett (ca. 1834–1907), was dedicated in 1871. The following year saw the dedication of a sculpture of English poet and playwright William Shakespeare (ca. 1564–1616), created by American John Quincy Adams Ward (1830–1910), and a monument to Scottish poet and novelist Sir Walter Scott (1771–1832), sculpted by his countryman Sir John Steell (1804–1891). In 1873, the editor of *Harper's New Monthly Magazine* wrote

151. Statue commemorating American inventor Samuel Finley Breese Morse, Central Park, New York. Stereograph ca. 1871–1890, Marian S. Carson Collection, Library of Congress Prints and Photographs Division.

that the raising and unveiling of statues to the dead including those of Shakespeare and Scott was "a moderating and refining influence which cannot easily be exaggerated."[29]

Central Park was largely completed by 1866 and attracted, according to Clarence Cook's contemporary account of the park, 3,412,892 pedestrians, 86,757 equestrians, and 1,519,808 carriages in that year alone. The main features of the original design prepared by Olmsted and Vaux are still largely intact today.

The Impact of Central Park

Central Park's popularity had immediate impact. The park quickly captured the public's imagination, "much as Mount Auburn had a generation before."[30] Its success further fueled the parks movement and inspired the creation of urban oases in Philadelphia, Baltimore, Brooklyn, Hartford, and Detroit within a decade. The Commissioners of Central Park, according

152. The Island House set within a Picturesque landscape at Druid Hill Park, Baltimore, Maryland. Photograph ca. 1906, Detroit Publishing Company, Library of Congress Prints and Photographs Division.

IMPACT OF RURAL CEMETERIES ON THE AMERICAN LANDSCAPE

to an authority on urban planning, "must have been proud and not a little astonished at how eagerly other communities busied themselves in similar projects."[31] In an 1868 report, only ten years after the Greensward Plan was adopted and initiated, the commissioners observed: "There is scarcely a city of magnitude in this country that has not provided, or taken measures to provide a Park for the pleasure of its citizens."[32]

Central Park set the standard for the first generation of urban park design in America, combining elements of the Picturesque and the Beautiful.[33] Druid Hill Park in Baltimore, Maryland (1860), was one of its earliest imitators. The park's design contrasted a rolling landscape of broad lawns, graceful shade trees, and scenic lakes with the picturesque qualities of the Wilderness—"a mature forest that provided rugged topography, abundant, green forest growth and such elements as the dramatic, rustic stone Garrett Bridge."[34] Howard Daniels designed and oversaw the initial development of the park until his tragic death in 1863. Daniels had previously honed his landscape gardening skills with commissions for at least twelve rural cemeteries including Oakwood in Syracuse, New York. His compelling vision for Druid Hill Park, which juxtaposed open vistas with the wildness of the woodland, continued to shape the park's development during the latter part of the nineteenth century. Meanwhile, Olmsted and Vaux joined forces again to plan Prospect Park in Brooklyn, New York (1866). Their creation featured the gracefully undulating Long Meadow—a seventy-five acre expanse stretching over a mile in length—that was "artfully planned to give the viewer an impression of infinite space."[35]

153. The Long Meadow at Prospect Park, Brooklyn, New York. Photograph ca. 1900, Detroit Publishing Company Photograph Collection, Library of Congress Prints and Photographs Division.

They contrasted this pastoral feature with a deep, secluded ravine traversed by a meandering stream. These park designs arose at a time when rural cemeteries were having their own aesthetic debate on the merits of the Picturesque versus the Beautiful. As the century progressed, large-scale cemeteries embraced the landscape lawn approach while public parks similarly employed more completely the aesthetic of the Beautiful.

In 1873, as the parks movement was accelerating, Allegheny Cemetery's James R. Speer cautioned against creating cemeteries with too much of a park-like appearance and noted that each landscape type had its own distinctive sphere. If the landscape park ideal was fully applied to cemeteries, he said, "it would be found that parties of pleasure, and pic-nics, and all sorts of objectionable amusements would be the order of the day, and that a cohort of policemen would not be sufficient to restrain within the bounds of order and decorum the crowds of disorderly people that would flock every returning Sunday to the Cemetery, to participate in scenes of amusements and dissipation."[36] Instead, he said, the cemetery should revere the "personality of grief, affection and veneration" connected with the distinctive family plot and maintain the sacredness of the site. Noting the success of Central Park in New York City and Fairmount Park in Philadelphia, Speer noted that each city in the United States should and would, in fact, have both its rural cemetery and its public park: "Hundreds of thousands will visit these parks, and will carry back to their respective communities the enthusiastic admiration they will inspire, and through the influence thus diffused, we doubt not, that at no distant day, every city of respectable population in the country will have not only its spacious and well arranged rural Cemetery, but its rural park also, each adapted in its own separate and appropriate sphere, to meet the wants and necessities of the public."[37]

In fact, as urban parks proliferated, rural cemeteries returned to a quieter state. Cemetery visitation decreased, but certainly did not cease, as the public chose to recreate in public parks. Parks were often located just beyond the developed areas of cities and were, therefore, more accessible than rural cemeteries, generally located farther afield. Parks had fewer restrictions on admission and behavior, which allowed visitors to have a more relaxing experience. With boating, ice skating, music, food, and other entertainments, parks cultivated cheerful experiences that appealed to urban dwellers more readily than the moralizing, somber atmosphere intended for the cemetery.

The Creation of Garden Suburbs

Early suburbs in the United States drew inspiration from some of the same cultural forces that motivated the founding of rural cemeteries. The Romantic literary and artistic movements of the period shaped the founders of both landscape types who sought to create "counterbalances"to the city. The writings of transcendentalists like Emerson who revered nature and those of Downing who promoted the use of the naturalistic landscape style created a powerful milieu for the development of both.

However, America's rural cemeteries preceded the development of the country's romantic suburbs and certainly influenced their design with a well-defined and popular landscape model. By mid-century, rural cemeteries had been widely established and embraced. As Downing noted in 1849, there was hardly a city in the country without its rural cemetery. These large-scale sites had adopted and refined a romantically Picturesque landscape style, with a distinctive recurring set of design characteristics. Design elements seen repeatedly in these early rural cemeteries, including curvilinear carriage drives, attractive water features, and diverse plant material, became prominent features within forthcoming suburbs as well.

Llewellyn Park, New Jersey, was the first Picturesque suburb in the United States. In 1853, New York businessman Llewellyn S. Haskell (1815–1872) established the suburb in the eastern foothills of the Orange Mountains. By 1856, Haskell and his business partners owned four hundred acres for the community. The expansive site was reminiscent of those chosen for rural cemeteries. On April 23, 1865, an *Independent* article eloquently described the location: "This tract of land consisted of a series of natural terraces, ascending by easy gradations, from the level of the village roads below, up to a summit seven hundred feet high—affording from every terrace a beautiful and unobstructed view of a wide and varied landscape reaching into the distance—while, for a near view, the tract itself was threaded by mountain streams, pierced with picturesque ravines, rimmed and ribbed

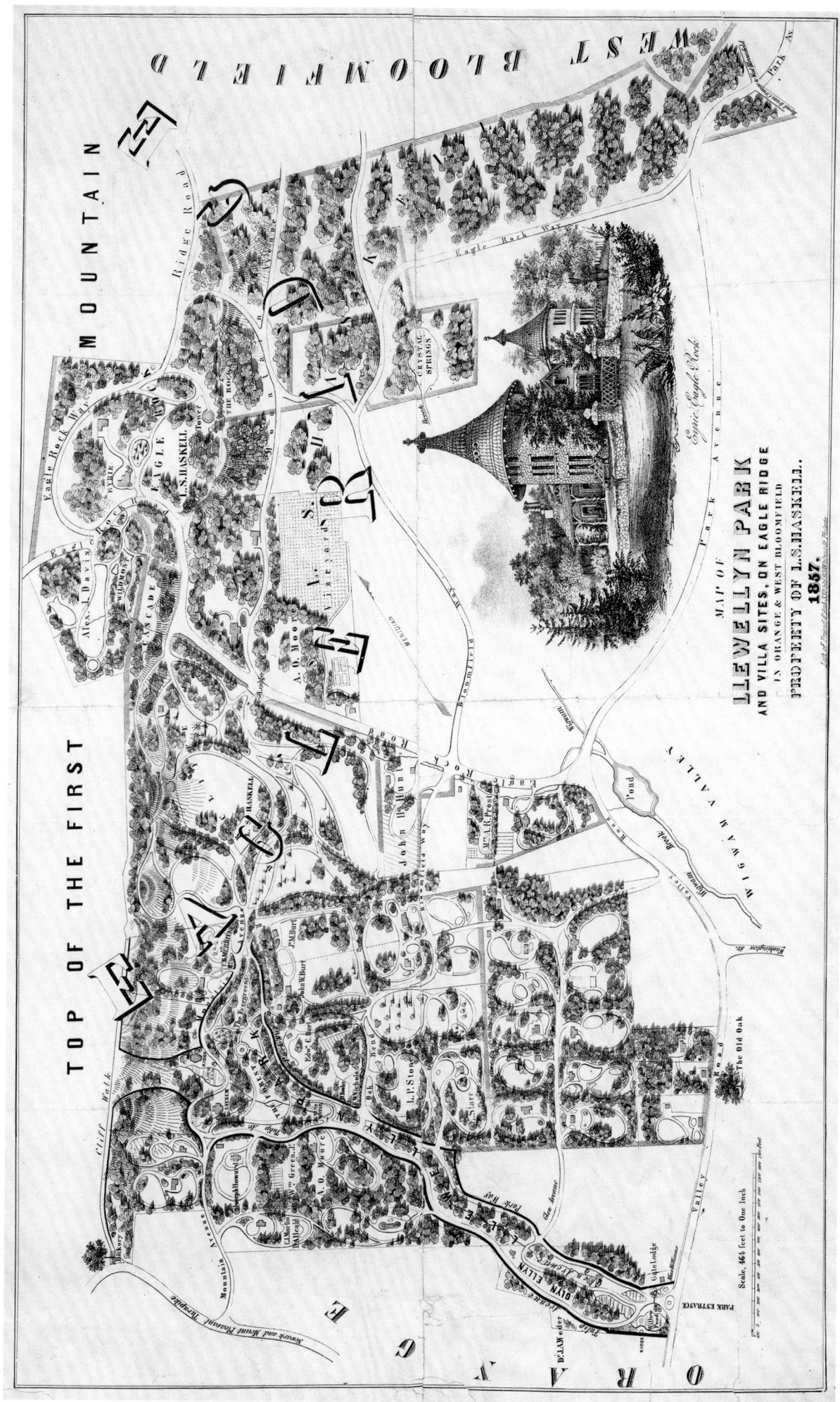

154. *Map of Llewellyn Park and Villa Sites, on Eagle Ridge in Orange & West Bloomfield*, After Alexander Jackson Davis. Published by Friend & Aub, 1857, the Metropolitan Museum of Art, www.metmuseum.org.

with rocks, monumented with venerable trees as old as the Pilgrim Fathers, and altogether diversified with a beautiful brokenness of scenery such as defies an adequate description." Following the pattern of rural cemeteries, the chosen tract was geographically removed from the city; it was thirteen miles by rail from Manhattan. Other early American suburbs followed suit. (Historian Thomas Bender has observed that the next generation of suburbs—those of the late nineteenth and early twentieth centuries—deviated from this pattern as they were adjacent to and actually extensions of the dense metropolis.)

Haskell likely collaborated with Alexander Jackson Davis, one of the most important architects of his generation and a close friend of Andrew Jackson Downing, to develop the site plan for the community. It is worth noting that the earliest map of Llewellyn Park's layout predates the Greensward Plan. Davis and Haskell's design for Llewellyn Park placed the development in harmony with nature. Significantly, the suburb incorporated a serpentine circulation system instead of the unnatural gridded system of typical city streets. As the physician and writer Daniel Drake (1785–1852) noted at the time, "Curved lines, you know, symbolize the country, straight lines the city." At Llewellyn Park, seven miles of gracefully curving lanes followed the contours of the terrain. Road names reflected the natural features of the site, such as Valley Way, Ridge Road, and Oak Bend. The curving roadway pattern subsequently became part of the suburban ideal.

Other picturesque elements were incorporated into the site plan making the descriptions of Llewellyn Park remarkably similar to those of previously established rural cemeteries. Of the suburb, the *Independent* noted the inclusion of "unexpected ponds, artful waterfalls, rustic bridges, seats, kiosks, and the like; offering, at every turn, some comfort or beauty to make the place lovable and memorable." Its entrance showcased a picturesque, stone gate lodge designed by Davis in 1857. Davis had previously worked within a rural cemetery setting, having been engaged to design the cemetery gatehouse and sepulchral chapel at the Evergreens Cemetery in Brooklyn in 1849. Meanwhile, to the thickly forested Llewellyn Park site, "unfamiliar trees" were added, which represented "every quarter of the globe, as, for instance, the pipe from the Himalayan Mountains, and the more wondrous evergreen

155. Davis-designed cylindrical gatehouse to Llewellyn Park. Postcard postmarked 1913, Danylchak collection.

of California."[38] With the addition of ornamentals and exotics by both Haskell and individual property owners to the already diverse collection of native species, the community became a de facto arboretum.

Lake Forest, Illinois—another early important example of the application of the romantic, Picturesque landscape style to community planning—was shaped by a respected rural cemetery designer. In 1855, a group of Chicago Presbyterians set out to locate a suitable site for a Presbyterian college. The following year, five trustees of the newly formed Lake Forest Association purchased the site the scouts had found—nearly 1,400 acres of land on the shore of Lake Michigan about twenty-seven miles north of the city. About half of the land was reserved for the college, while the other half was retained by the association for a commercial-residential development. The association subsequently hired Almerin Hotchkiss to design the community, which he platted in 1857. Hotchkiss had begun his career at Green-Wood Cemetery as the site's superintendent where he played an important role in the cemetery's initial layout. He later took the lead on designing a two-hundred-acre expansion of the cemetery in the 1840s. In 1850, Hotchkiss was commissioned to design Bellefontaine Cemetery in St. Louis, the first large-scale rural cemetery developed west of the Mississippi River. Hotchkiss brought his experience designing these large-scale Picturesque landscapes to the Lake Forest site. Taking advantage of the existing topographic and scenic features there, he planned curvilinear drives that conformed to the topography of the land and responded thoughtfully to existing natural features including lake bluffs and ravines. A later visitor to the community noted in 1869: "The design here, everywhere manifest, is to aid Nature by Art and not to bully her, which a great many men in Western towns seem to have aimed to do and succeeded in accomplishing. . . . Winding graveled walks, smooth green lawns, rustic bridges—spanning ravines . . . and grand old trees present a scene the eye is never weary of."[39]

By the post–Civil War years, the romantic landscape style, exemplified by Llewellyn Park and Lake Forest, had become the accepted form for new suburban developments.[40] And by the late nineteenth century, "most large cities could boast of one or more suburban communities or outlying subdivisions planned in curvilinear fashion."[41]

The Development of the Profession of Landscape Architecture

During the period when rural cemeteries were first established, the field of landscape architecture, as we know it, did not yet exist. The first documented use of the professional title *landscape architect* was on May 12, 1863, by Olmsted and Vaux in a letter of resignation to the New York Park Commission.[42] (The resignation stemmed from their exasperation with political interference in the implementation of the Greensward Plan.) In the letter, the duo identified themselves by the title. It was in the second half of the nineteenth century, particularly through the design of public parks and the impact of Frederick Law Olmsted—who created more parks than any other landscape architect—that an "American profession of landscape architecture began to be fully defined."[43]

However, the field was foundationally shaped earlier in the century by the creation of America's rural cemeteries and the men who designed them. Most of the early rural cemetery designers were not trained as landscape gardeners, the contemporaneous term for designers of landscapes. Instead, the designs were the work of architects, surveyors, engineers, and gentlemen horticulturists. In the early nineteenth century, no educational or apprenticeship programs in the field of landscape gardening existed in the United States and very few individuals with refined experience designing large-scale landscapes practiced in America. After all, at the beginning of the nineteenth century in the United States, "landscape art existed if at all only in private estates."[44] H. W. S. Cleveland later noted "that the demand for the services of an educated landscape gardener was too limited to warrant the adoption of the profession as a means of support."[45] So, surveyors, architects, and amateurs filled a professional void and simultaneously helped mold a profession as they created the first large-scale designed landscapes open to the public in the country—rural cemeteries.

Jacob Bigelow and Henry A. S. Dearborn, the two seminal figures in the creation of Mount Auburn Cemetery, were not trained landscape gardeners. In a preprofessional era, however, these well-connected Renaissance men assumed the responsibility for fashioning an unprecedented type of landscape. Jacob Bigelow, who initiated the idea of a designed, natural-

156. Portrait of Frederick Law Olmsted Sr. From in the *Century Illustrated Monthly Magazine*, October 1893, Danylchak collection.

istic burial ground outside of the city, was trained as a medical doctor at the University of Pennsylvania. He also studied under the university's noted botanist Benjamin Smith Barton (1766–1815). In 1811, Bigelow settled in Boston and established a medical practice. He continued to practice medicine for the next sixty years. He also began teaching botany at Harvard College and subsequently published *Florula Bostoniensis: a collection of plants of Boston and its vicinity: with their generic and specific characters, principal synonyms, descriptions, places of growth, and time of flowering, and occasional remarks* (1814 and 1824). He also became a cultural leader, engaging in the elite intellectual societies of the state—the Anthology Club, the Athenaeum, the American Association of Arts and Sciences, and the Massachusetts Historical Society. In addition, he became an instrumental member of the newly formed Massachusetts Horticultural Society (1829). Bigelow's training as a botanist and his involvement in these societies no doubt shaped his conception of a romantic, moralizing burial ground where family plots would be "separated and interspersed with trees, shrubs, and flowers, in a wood or landscape garden." In the early molding of Mount Auburn's grounds, however, Bigelow's contributions were primarily architectural. Although not trained as an architect, he designed the site's three major architectural embellishments—the Egyptian Revival–style main gate, the Gothic Revival–style chapel, and the Gothic Revival–style Washington Tower. As the distinguished historian Walter Muir Whitehill once observed, "At the beginning of the nineteenth century the practice of architecture was considered to be within the grasp of any literate gentleman who had a mind to try his hand at it."[46]

Meanwhile, Dearborn was the man chiefly responsible for laying out the cemetery's grounds. Dearborn had begun his career as a lawyer but later dedicated himself to public service through politics. He also engaged in other activities that helped prepare him for his work at Mount Auburn. During the War of 1812, he was appointed to the position of general in the Massachusetts Militia and was charged with building forts in Portland's harbor, which gave him applied engineering experience. In addition, he engaged in architecture as an avocation; he completed a two-volume "Treatise on Grecian Architecture" in 1828. He also experimented extensively with plants at his private estate and became the founder and first president of the Massachusetts Horticultural Society. With these pursuits to his credit, Dearborn became a quintessential example of the "gentleman architect" and "gentleman horticulturist." To assist with the design of Mount Auburn, Dearborn ordered books and maps from Europe illustrating the principles of the English landscape garden. Notably, he also consulted John Evelyn's *Silva; or, A Discourse of Forest-Trees* (1664) and illustrated descriptions of Père Lachaise. In addition, Dearborn was aided by Alexander Wadsworth, a civil engineer and surveyor, as well as a committee of gentlemen horticulturists established by the cemetery association. It was not unusual for early rural cemeteries to be laid out by gentlemen like Dearborn, and many of these men elevated the art of landscape gardening. An 1856 *New York Times* article on the establishment and planning of Central Park noted, "Landscape gardening has been but little cultivated among us as a profession, and it may not be an easy matter to secure the services of a competent person at first. But there is no lack of amateurs in this noble art among us, and the attention recently paid to the laying out of rural cemeteries in various parts of the country has greatly improved the public taste."[47]

In the early years of rural cemetery management, most sites simply had a caretaker while the cemetery board of directors retained decision-making authority for both financial and maintenance issues. These boards generally included businessmen and civic leaders, a few of whom were often gentlemen horticulturists or gardeners. After Dearborn's relationship with Mount Auburn ended in 1835, most decisions regarding landscape development were made by volunteer committees and later primarily by Bigelow while he served as president of Mount Auburn Cemetery from 1845 to 1871. In time, however, it became clear that these large-scale landscapes demanded more expertise and time than the volunteer boards could offer.

With his ground plan for Laurel Hill Cemetery, John Notman became one of the first trained architects in America to apply his skills to the design of large-scale landscapes. A native of Edinburgh, Scotland, Notman had apprenticed with eminent Scottish architect William Henry Playfair (1790–1857). In 1831, Notman immigrated to the United States, settling in Philadelphia. There he met John Jay Smith, a gentleman horticulturist and the librarian of the Library Company of Philadelphia. Smith would become Notman's most influential patron and advocate. Smith spearheaded the creation of Laurel Hill Cemetery, and in 1836 the cemetery's organizing committee held an informal design competition for the layout of the site and for its gatehouse. When Notman won the competition, Laurel Hill became one of his first commissions in the New World.

The design competition for Laurel Hill Cemetery also drew submissions from notable architects William Strickland (1787–1854) and Thomas U. Walter (1804–1887), illustrating that "architects were moving naturally into the realm of landscape design."[48] Or, at least, they were attempting to do so. The plans that Strickland and Walter submitted for the cemetery grounds were "haphazard and awkward," demonstrating their lack of understanding in designing romantic landscapes that utilized the existing natural features of a site like those created in England.[49] However, Notman's training in Scotland exposed him to the Picturesque landscaping ideal that had been embraced across Europe. This experience likely gave him an advantage.

Notman's work at Laurel Hill Cemetery advanced his reputation and helped him earn commissions for private estates and other rural cemeteries. He was recruited to design Hollywood Cemetery (1848) in Richmond, Virginia, and Spring Hill Cemetery (1850) in

Lynchburg, Virginia. Over time, with these additional commissions, he developed a "greater facility in landscape gardening," as shown by a comparison of his plans for Laurel Hill and Hollywood.[50] In addition to features that respected the natural qualities of the site, Laurel Hill still included strict, geometric forms imposed on the landscape.[51] Notman's later plan for Hollywood Cemetery, however, showcased his ability to "design in relation to the topography and 'genius of the place.' In Richmond, Notman achieved a successful integration of the natural demands of the landscape with the aesthetic and practical purposes of the rural cemetery."[52]

Notman's skills as an architect were important to his success designing large-scale landscapes. His architectural education "meant that he came to landscape gardening with a knowledge of design, unlike the horticultural bias of his landscape contemporaries."[53] His education had exposed him to engineering and construction techniques. As an architect, he created detailed plans and specifications for his projects. He did the same for his landscape commissions. With his success, Notman paved the way for architects to practice within the expanding field of landscape design. These architects, including Calvert Vaux, increasingly instilled the emerging field of landscape gardening with greater professionalism with their use of design drawings and specifications and the pursuit of uniform standards.[54]

While amateur horticulturists and trained architects were making significant contributions to American landscape design, few individuals trained in the specific art of landscape gardening practiced in the United States even into the 1850s. The *Horticulturist* noted in an 1853 article entitled "Rural Cemeteries" that large cities often had "competent artists and workman" who could tastefully lay out one of these burial grounds. However, interior cities often had to rely on mere land surveyors to plan their burial sites. The journal noted passionately that in these cases, "where every improvement has been made under the direction of persons not having the shadow of a qualification, one finds, as might well be expected, scarcely anything but a repetition of blunders—violations of taste the most aggravated, and a worse than waste of both labor and material."[55] The journal persisted by making a powerful analogy that highlighted the need to recognize landscape gardening as a profession requiring special training and skill and to employ such

specialists in the work of improving landscapes to obtain the best results.

It seems very singular that people should not act in these [rural cemeteries] as in their ordinary business affairs. If a company of capitalists unite in constructing a steamship they will not be likely to employ a blacksmith, or a shoemaker, or a gardener, to build it. If they would do so foolish a thing, they certainly would be placed in an insane asylum directly. Now the building of a ship is just as possible to the gardener, or the blacksmith, or the shoemaker, as the laying out of a cemetery would be to any of these craftsmen. Acting like wise men, they will employ the most competent shipbuilder that can be found—one who has mastered the theory and practice of his profession by long years of study and practice. So in everything that people wish to be well done, they employ competent and skillful workmen. It happens, however, that in certain communities the landscape gardener is not a recognized individual. People who would not deny the necessity of employing a good artist to paint a landscape on canvass, do not understand the necessity of employing a skillful and well-trained artist to work a beautiful landscape out of nature's raw material. Here is a piece of ground for a rural cemetery—it is to be laid out—intersected with walks and avenues—improved and embellished—and the surveyor is called in to do it. He, with an eye merely to certain conveniences in getting from one point to another, carves it up into patches as though he were mapping out the site of a new city; and the ground is ruined.... Let a competent person be at once employed who will carefully study the features of the ground and draw up a complete general plan, upon which, and conformable to which, all future improvements shall be made; and let this plan be rigidly adhered to, and tastefully and skillfully carried out, from year to year, as the improvements progress.[56]

The subsequent appointment of Adolph Strauch —a trained landscape gardener—as the "superintendent of the grounds and landscape gardener" at Spring Grove Cemetery was an "important step . . . in the development of the profession of landscape architecture."[57] Strauch acquired his education and valuable training in Europe before immigrating to the

157. Portrait of Adolph Strauch. Steel engraving from *Cincinnati Sonst und Jetzt*, published in 1878, Danylchak collection.

United States. By the early nineteenth century, Europe had well-established training and apprenticeship programs in landscape gardening. In high school, Strauch majored in botany. He subsequently received an appointment at the Imperial Gardens in Vienna where he worked under respected landscape gardeners, including Prince Hermann von Pückler-Muskau (1785–1871), for six years. He later worked at the Royal Botanical Gardens at Regent's Park in London until his departure to explore America in 1851. When Spring Grove Cemetery hired him in 1854 to improve its grounds, Strauch initially envisioned a short-term arrangement with the cemetery. However, in 1859, the board of directors offered him a permanent position.

He accepted on the condition that he be given greater authority and broader responsibilities. The board responded by granting him unprecedented control over design and maintenance—all issues that affected the appearance of the site. He was charged with directing "all improvements in the Cemetery, such as grading, planting, pruning the plants and trees, laying out avenues, and keeping the grounds, lots, and avenues in proper order." He was also tasked with employing and managing the "hands and subordinate officers" and keeping a record of the number of employees engaged and the work they performed. In addition, Strauch was empowered to set guidelines for monuments and grant approval for plantings in family lots, thereby further consolidating his control over the aesthetics of the site. He reported to and was accountable only to the board of directors. (The board still retained control over the financial affairs of the organization including selling lots.) This arrangement elevated the role of the cemetery superintendent. And by installing Strauch, a trained landscape gardener who had studied under renowned professionals in Europe, the board of directors of Spring Grove Cemetery spurred the professionalization of the position.[58]

The importance of the superintendent position and the need to have a trained professional in the role further grew as cemetery corporations took on more responsibility for maintaining the overall landscape.[59] In order to ensure the consistent appearance of the grounds and guarantee that all lots were properly maintained, Spring Grove Cemetery took on responsibility for not only the common areas of the site but for private lots as well. The cemetery created perpetual care payments and annual-care fees to cover the cost of such services as "cleaning monuments, when necessary, resodding lots, and taking some extra care in general."[60] By the end of the 1870s, the use of annual-care fees and perpetual care payments became widespread, signaling a corresponding expansion of the maintenance responsibilities of cemetery corporations. Large cemeteries often employed hundreds of laborers to care for the grounds from spring to fall. Management of such a large physical plant required a superintendent with the combined skills of "a horticulturist, manager, civil engineer, and mechanic."[61]

In 1887, representatives from the largest and most prestigious cemeteries in the East and Midwest, including delegates from Mount Auburn, Green-Wood, and Graceland, gathered in Cincinnati and formed a professional organization—the Association of American Cemetery Superintendents (AACS). (In 1996, it was renamed the International Cemetery, Cremation and Funeral Association.) The purpose of the organization was to disseminate information on best practices in the field, strengthen the profession's claims to authority over volunteer boards, and elevate the public perception of the profession. The organization held annual conventions at which participants discussed approaches for improving both administration and landscape maintenance. Presentations were given on such diverse topics as "record keeping, employee relations, permanent-maintenance funds, and equipment maintenance" as well as "tearing out enclosures, lowering grave mounds, and planting shrubs to fit with the landscape."[62] In addition, the group advocated for the adoption of model rules and regulations for cemetery improvements that would be overseen directly by the superintendent—not the board of directors—which reflected Strauch's enduring influence. The organization also promoted the creation of minimum professional standards for the superintendent position. In 1908, in the *AACS-Proceedings of the 22nd Annual Convention,* the organization proudly noted that it held the distinction of being the "oldest society conserving the landscape gardening and rural art of the country." It had predated the founding of the American Society of Landscape Architects (ASLA) by twelve years.

The landscape ideology Adolph Strauch implemented at Spring Grove Cemetery influenced the design of other sites in the latter part of the nineteenth century. By the 1860s, Strauch had won far-reaching admiration for the landscape he created at Spring Grove and he actively spread his ideas by consulting on projects in other cities. He was often asked for advice or assistance on plans for cemeteries as well as parks. Before the 1890 convention of the AACS, Frank Eurich—one of the association's cofounders—declared, "Many cities in the union have called the services of this genius to their aid in planning and laying out of parks and cemeteries, notable among which are Nashville, Hartford, Chicago, Buffalo, Indianapolis, Detroit, Cleveland, and even New York, as well as many others too numerous to mention."[63] Strauch is credited with designs for Oak Woods Cemetery in Chicago, Illinois (1864), Woodmere Cemetery in Detroit, Michigan (1867), and Lake View Cemetery in Cleveland, Ohio (1869). Meanwhile, James R. Ray, the president of Crown Hill Cemetery in Indianapolis, Indiana (1863), recognized Strauch's influential impact on that site: "Before we determined upon a plan for our cemetery we visited beautiful Spring Grove and received from its gifted superintendent many ideas and much useful knowledge which were of vital importance in the final consummation of our plans."[64] The AACS helped to disseminate Strauch's ideas even further by promoting the design principals and standards he implemented at Spring Grove in its early publications.

Strauch's work at Spring Grove also influenced other landscape gardeners and architects, thus broadening his reach. O. C. Simonds, who was one of eleven founding members of the ASLA in 1899, for instance, "learned a great deal from Strauch's masterpiece, Cincinnati's Spring Grove Cemetery, before gaining recognition for his own work at Graceland Cemetery, in Chicago."[65] Frederick Law Olmsted also esteemed Strauch's work at Spring Grove. It was Simonds who later related in an article on Strauch in *The Standard Cyclopedia of Horticulture* that "Olmsted used to say that when he needed inspiration he visited Spring Grove."[66] Further stressing Strauch's impact, Simonds wrote, "Perhaps no man in the United States since A. J. Downing's time has done more for the correction and cultivation of public taste in landscape gardening than Adolph Strauch."[67]

Ultimately, the design and management of large-scale cemeteries trained many men who went on to design public parks and suburbs and continued to shape the emerging field of landscape architecture. H. W. S. Cleveland, who began his career as a scientific farmer, established a landscape gardening practice in 1854 in partnership with Robert Morris Copeland (1830–1874). In the early years of their practice they designed two rural cemeteries—Sleepy Hollow in Concord, Massachusetts (1855), and Oak Grove in Gloucester, Massachusetts (1855). During this period, Cleveland was personally introduced to Ralph Waldo Emerson who had a profound impact on his design philosophy, which drew inspiration from the existing landscape and excluded artificial adornments. The design for Sleepy Hollow Cemetery skillfully demonstrated this aesthetic by respecting the natural amphitheater of the site and employing native plants to picturesque effect. After he moved to Chicago in 1869, Cleveland established a landscape architectural partnership with civil engineer William Merchant Richardson French (1843–1914). In 1870, Cleveland was engaged to create an addition to Graceland Cemetery. He and his partner also began designing public parks and suburbs, including the community of Highland Park, Illinois (1869–1874), which was advertised as "one vast natural park." At the end of his career, Cleveland moved to Minneapolis, where he created the Minneapolis Parks, which landscape historian Robin Karson deems "one of the most significant open-space systems in the United States."[68]

Cleveland's influence spread with his *Landscape Architecture, as Applied to the Wants of the West* (1873). In his treatise, he defined the term landscape architecture as "the art of arranging land so as to adapt it most conveniently, economically and gracefully to any of the varied wants of civilization."[69] His book was, in fact, the first to use the term "landscape architecture" in the professional sense.[70] For Cleveland, the distinct province of the landscape architect was to harmoniously blend the "grandest features of natural scenery" and the "noblest specimens of architectural skill" to achieve the best effects.[71] Prof. Norman T. Newton explains the significance of the volume: "The remarkable fact is that in so early a treatise the aims and techniques of a new profession could be in such large part analyzed and clearly enunciated."[72]

The proliferation of large-scale designed cemeteries, followed by the establishment of public parks and garden suburbs in America, offered expanding opportunities for professionals practicing the art of what became known as landscape architecture. At century's end, the ASLA was created by eleven charter members. The organization sought to "establish landscape architecture as a recognized profession in North America, develop educational studies in landscape architecture, [and] provide a voice of authority in the 'New Profession.'" None of the founding members of ASLA had university training in the field of landscape architecture. Although a handful of apprenticeship opportunities were available in the United States in the second half of the nineteenth century, no formal training programs existed. The nation's first university curriculum of professional training in landscape architecture was established in 1900 at Harvard University in Cambridge, Massachusetts—the same community that witnessed the establishment of the nation's first rural cemetery.

Biographical Sketches

Jacob Bigelow (ca. 1787–1879) was born in Sudbury, Massachusetts, to a minister of modest means. Bigelow graduated from Harvard College in 1806 and later received his doctor of medicine from the University of Pennsylvania in 1810. He moved to Boston the following year and set up his medical practice with James Jackson. Bigelow continued to practice medicine for the next sixty years. He also became a member of the Athenaeum, the Massachusetts Historical Society, the American Philosophical Society, and the American Association of Arts and Sciences—an organization in which he served as president from 1847 to 1863. In 1812, Bigelow began teaching botany at Harvard College and subsequently published *Florula Bostoniensis* in 1814. The second edition of this influential work became the primary manual for New England plants for the next thirty years. In 1815, Bigelow was appointed professor of material medica at Harvard Medical School; he retained this position teaching courses on the medicinal use of plants until 1855. In 1825, Bigelow gathered influential Bostonians together and proposed that the group form a voluntary association to create a sprawling burial ground outside the confines of the city. The plan to create the new burying place, however, stalled for several years. In the interim, the Massachusetts Horticultural Society was established in 1829 and Bigelow became its corresponding secretary. Then in 1830, Bigelow joined with Henry A. S. Dearborn and John C. Gray to call together leading Bostonians to consider establishing the cemetery under the auspices of the new society. Mount Auburn Cemetery, America's first rural cemetery, was founded in 1831.

H. W. S. Cleveland (1814–1900) was born in Lancaster, Massachusetts, in 1814. In the 1830s, Cleveland began his professional career as a railroad surveyor in Illinois and studied civil engineering there. After only a few years in the West, however, he returned to New England where he married Maryann Dwinel of Maine. Shortly thereafter, in 1841, he established a scientific farm known as Oatlands in Burlington, New Jersey. In 1854, he returned to New England once again and formed a landscape gardening partnership with Robert Morris Copeland. Together, Cleveland and Copeland designed Sleepy Hollow Cemetery in Concord, Massachusetts, and Oak Grove Cemetery in Gloucester, Massachusetts. During this period in his career, Cleveland was influenced by the transcendentalist philosophy and aesthetic concepts of Ralph Waldo Emerson. Consequently, Cleveland cultivated an organic approach to design, which he applied not only to cemeteries but also to residences and later to parks and suburbs. In 1869, Cleveland moved to Chicago and established a landscape architecture practice with civil engineer William Merchant Richardson French. While in Chicago, Cleveland designed an addition to Graceland Cemetery. He also began writing about the importance of thoughtful planning in the *Atlantic Monthly* and other publications. In 1873, Cleveland authored *Landscape Architecture, as Applied to the Wants of the West,* in which he explained the broader role that the emerging field of landscape architecture could play in arranging the land to adapt it to the various wants of civilization.

Howard Daniels (1815–1864) was an architect and landscape gardener who, by 1855, was advertising his services in the *Horticulturist* for "Plans for Parks, Cemeteries, Country Seats, Villas, Farms, Orchards, Gardens &c., also designs in all styles for Mansions, Villas, Cottages, Conservatories, Green-houses, Rustic Statuary, &c." His most well-known commission as an architect was the Greek Revival–style Montgomery County Courthouse in Dayton, Ohio, which was built between 1848 and 1850. Meanwhile, his first documented commission as a landscape gardener was the design and development of Spring Grove Cemetery in Cincinnati, Ohio, in 1846. In that year, the cemetery's board of directors sent Daniels on a four-month tour of the celebrated rural cemeteries on the East Coast to study their layouts and organization. Upon his return to Cincinnati, Daniels was hired by the board as Spring Grove's "cemetery architect" and the site's first superintendent—a post he held until 1848. During his tenure at Spring Grove, Daniels enhanced the picturesque grounds with a sinuous system of roads and diverse trees and shrubs. His work at Spring Grove prepared him for additional cemetery commissions including Green Lawn Cemetery in Columbus, Ohio (1848); Erie Cemetery in Erie, Pennsylvania (1851); Dale Cemetery in Ossining, New York (1851); Poughkeepsie Rural Cemetery in Poughkeepsie, New York (1853); Riverside Cemetery in Waterbury, Connecticut (1853); Woodland Cemetery in Cleveland, Ohio (1853); Brookside Cemetery in Watertown, New York (1854); Laurel Grove Cemetery in Jervis, New York (1856); and Oakwood Cemetery in Syracuse, New York (1859). In addition to his cemetery work, Daniels designed the plan for Druid Hill Park in Baltimore, Maryland, in 1860. It was just the third large municipal park built in the United States.

Henry A. S. Dearborn (1783–1851) began his career as a lawyer, practicing in Salem, Massachusetts, and Portland, Maine (which was part of Massachusetts at the time). He later oversaw the construction of Fort Preble and Fort Scammel in Boston Harbor in 1808 and served as a brigadier general during the War of 1812. From 1812 to 1829, Dearborn served as the collector of customs in Boston—a post that had been recently vacated by his father. In 1829, Dearborn served as a member of the Massachusetts House of Representatives, and in 1830, he served as a member of the Massachusetts Senate. From 1831 to 1833, he represented the Massachusetts 10th Congressional District in the US House of Representatives. From 1847 to 1851, he served as the second mayor of Roxbury, Massachusetts. In addition to his military and political career, Dearborn also studied architecture and horticulture. In 1828, he completed a "Treatise on Grecian Architecture," a two-volume work in which he also provided the illustrations. When the Massachusetts Horticultural Society was founded in 1829, Dearborn served as its first president. It was Dearborn who was primarily responsible for laying out the grounds of America's first rural cemetery, Mount Auburn Cemetery, beginning in 1831. Later, while serving as the mayor of Roxbury, Dearborn founded and designed that city's Forest Hills Cemetery.

David Bates Douglass (1790–1849) was born in Pompton, New Jersey, in 1790. He graduated from Yale University with a degree in civil engineering in 1813 and subsequently served in the Engineering Corps of the United States Army during the War of 1812. From 1815 to 1831, he taught mathematics and civil engineering at West Point. During this time, he also surveyed uncharted land in the Michigan Territory and worked on several canal construction projects. In 1831, he moved to Brooklyn, where he was appointed a professor of mathematics at the University of the City of New York. He also acted as the engineer of the Croton Aqueduct and the surveyor for a railroad route between Brooklyn and Jamaica, New York. These projects intimately acquainted Douglass with the topographic qualities of the land around the city. He is credited with assisting Henry Pierrepont in choosing the site for Brooklyn's Green-Wood Cemetery, one of the country's earliest and largest rural cemeteries. In 1839, Douglass began laying out the roads, paths, and plots of Green-Wood. He simultaneously served as the cemetery's president through the initial construction phases. In 1840, he left his position at Green-Wood to become president of Kenyon College, where he is credited with improving the grounds of the institution. In 1844, he left his post at the college to once again pursue his career in civil engineering. He subsequently designed Albany Rural Cemetery in Albany, New York, beginning in 1845.

Andrew Jackson Downing (1815–1852) was born in Newburgh, New York, as the son of a nurseryman. After he completed his studies at Montgomery Academy, Downing joined his brother in the management of the nursery, which his father had left behind upon his death. Downing later assumed full responsibility for the operation. He found inspiration in the work of J. C. Loudon, a renowned garden designer, writer, inventor, and social reformer from Scotland, and began publishing articles on botany and landscape improvement as early as age seventeen. In 1841, he authored the seminal volume *A Treatise on the Theory and Practice of Landscape Gardening, adapted to North America.* This widely popular book inspired ordinary Americans to embellish the landscapes around them and gave them practical instructions on how to do so. A year later, Downing collaborated with Andrew Jackson Davis to produce *Cottage Residences.* In 1850, Downing authored *The Architecture of Country Houses,* in which he showcased his architectural interests, but always within the context of the landscape. In 1846, he became the editor of a new publication, the *Horticulturist and Journal of Rural Art and Rural Taste.* He served in that capacity until his death. Throughout the 1840s, Downing worked as a landscape gardener designing the grounds of private residences as well as the grounds of rural cemeteries. He is generally credited for the design of the Evergreens Cemetery in Brooklyn, New York (1849). Evidence also points to his involvement in the layout of Oak Hill Cemetery in Washington, D.C. (1849). In addition, Downing designed numerous country houses in New England in the latter part of his career including the Matthew Vassar Estate in Poughkeepsie, New York, which is the only known Downing cottage still in existence. In 1852, Downing died tragically in a steamboat accident.

Almerin Hotchkiss (1816–1903) began his career as the superintendent at Green-Wood Cemetery in Brooklyn, New York, and was instrumental in laying out the cemetery's expansion after David Bates Douglass left his role as cemetery designer and president in 1840. In 1849, Hotchkiss was chosen to design Bellefontaine Cemetery in St. Louis, Missouri, after one of Bellefontaine's board members traveled to Brooklyn to examine Green-Wood Cemetery—one of the country's first of its type. Hotchkiss remained at Bellefontaine as its superintendent for forty-six years, during which time he oversaw the cemetery's expansion from 138 to 332 acres. In 1855, Hotchkiss also laid out Chippiannock Cemetery in Rock Island, Illinois. In 1857, he platted the land for a suburb outside of Chicago called Lake Forest, which was one of the earliest large-scale, suburban residential developments in the country. The suburb featured a curvilinear street pattern and was touted as a city within a park. Because of the Panic of 1857, however, Hotchkiss was never paid the fee for his plan by the Lake Forest Association. After this foray into real estate development, Hotchkiss returned exclusively to his work at Bellefontaine, where he remained until his death in 1903.

John Notman (1810–1865) was born in Edinburgh, Scotland, and attended the Royal Scottish Academy. He began his career as an architect in the office of William Henry Playfair, one of the most highly regarded Scottish architects of the nineteenth century. In 1831, Notman immigrated to Philadelphia. There he met John Jay Smith, the librarian of the Library Company of Philadelphia, who became an influential supporter of Notman's work. In 1835, Smith hired Notman to design a building for the Library Company. The following year, Notman won the design competition for Laurel Hill Cemetery, a project spearheaded by Smith. For his landscape design for the cemetery, Notman drew inspiration from Henry E. Kendall's proposed plan for Kensal Green Cemetery outside of London. Notman also designed the gatehouse, chapel, and superintendent's house on the grounds. Notman was subsequently hired by two of the cemetery's investors, Nathan Dunn and Bishop George Washington Doane, for private commissions in 1837 and 1839, respectively. Both of these projects were published in Andrew Jackson Downing's *A Treatise on the Theory and Practice of Landscape Gardening* in 1841. In several instances, Notman worked with Downing in Princeton, New Jersey, to design buildings within Downing's Picturesque landscapes. In 1845, Notman designed the Athenaeum of Philadelphia, the first Italianate building in the city. Notman was also well-known for designing churches including Philadelphia's St. Mark's Church in 1849 and the Church of the Holy Trinity from 1856 to 1859. He also designed two more rural cemeteries—Hollywood Cemetery in Richmond, Virginia, in 1848 and Spring Hill Cemetery in Lynchburg, Virginia, in the early 1850s. In 1857, Notman was one of the founding members of the American Institute of Architects.

Frederick Law Olmsted Sr. (1822–1903) was born in Hartford, Connecticut. Just prior to matriculating at Yale University in 1837, Olmsted suffered from severe sumac poisoning that affected his eyesight and kept him from attending the school. Instead, he spent the next twenty years engaging in various activities and occupations that later informed his work as a landscape architect. He studied surveying and engineering, chemistry, and scientific farming. From 1848 to 1855, he ran a farm on Staten Island. During this same period, he made a six-month trip to Europe, where he saw numerous parks and private estates. During the late 1850s, he served as a reporter for the *New York Times* and managing editor of *Putnam's Monthly Magazine*. His literary connections in New York enabled him to secure the position of superintendent of Central Park in 1857. In April of the following year, Olmsted and Calvert Vaux won the design competition for the site—the first-major-designed public park in the United States. From 1859 to 1861, Olmsted served as "architect-in-chief" of the park. Then from 1861 to 1863, he served as the director of the US Sanitary Commission. From 1863 to 1865, he managed the Mariposa Estate, a gold-mining site in central California. During this time, Olmsted also designed Mountain View Cemetery in Oakland, California, in collaboration with his partner Calvert Vaux. In 1865, he returned to New York to work with Vaux to finish their work at Central Park and to design Prospect Park in Brooklyn. Over the next thirty years, Olmsted was engaged in countless landscape architecture projects that aimed to enhance quality of life and civic virtue in the communities in which he worked. Just a few of his most well-known works include the Emerald Necklace in Boston, Massachusetts; the grounds of the US Capitol in Washington, D.C.; and the residential suburb of Riverside, Illinois. Olmsted retired in 1895 when he began to suffer from senility. He died in 1903.

James Henry Rion (1828–1887) was born in Montreal, Canada, to Henry and Margaret Hunter Rion. Rion's father died before he was born, and his mother moved the family to Savannah, Georgia, where she worked as a housekeeper at the Pulaski Inn. Rion and his mother moved to Pendleton, South Carolina, when he was a teenager. He later graduated from South Carolina College in 1850. Prior to his graduation, he returned briefly to Savannah and was asked to create a plan for what became known as Bonaventure Cemetery by an acquaintance associated with the property. This is the only known landscape plan that Rion completed. In 1851, Rion married Mary Catherine Weir (1829–1901), who later penned *Ladies' Southern Florist*—the first garden book published by a woman in the South. James Rion also accepted a position teaching math, history, and military science at the Mount Zion Institute in

Winnsboro, South Carolina. In 1854, he passed the bar and started his law practice in South Carolina. In addition, Rion served as president of the Planter's Bank of Fairfield, served on the boards of Mount Zion Institute and South Carolina College, and owned a granite quarry.

William B. Saunders (1822–1900) was born in Scotland. He studied horticulture and landscape gardening at Madras College in St. Andrews and at the University of Edinburgh. He subsequently received training at London's Kew Gardens. In 1848, he immigrated to the United States and became the superintendent at Clifton Park—the Baltimore estate of Johns Hopkins. From 1854 to 1862, he and partner Thomas Meehan (1826–1901) ran a nursery and landscape gardening business in Pennsylvania. During this period, Saunders was commissioned to design Rosehill Cemetery in Chicago (1859) and Oak Ridge Cemetery in Springfield, Illinois (1855). He also provided guidance to Chicago landscape gardener Swain Nelson for Graceland Cemetery's original plan. In 1862, Saunders was appointed the Superintendent of Horticulture and Botanist for the US Bureau of Agriculture (later the Department of Agriculture), which he led until 1900. During his tenure, he designed the grounds for the Bureau in Washington, D.C., and designed its agricultural exhibits at the Philadelphia Centennial Exhibition of 1876, 1884 New Orleans Exposition, and 1889 Paris Exhibition. In 1863, Saunders designed the nation's first military cemetery—the Civil War Soldier's National Cemetery at Gettysburg (now Gettysburg National Cemetery). President Lincoln gave his famous Gettysburg Address at the dedication ceremony for the new cemetery on November 19, 1863. Saunders later designed the grounds for President Lincoln's tomb at Oak Ridge Cemetery. Throughout his career, Saunders wrote for *Gardener's Monthly, Hovey's Magazine*, and the *Horticulturist.*

Niles Bierragaard Schubarth (1818–1889) was born in a small town outside of Oslo, Norway, in 1818. He immigrated to the United States when he was just twenty-two years old and settled in western New York. In 1840, he began working for a civil engineering firm that was involved with the expansion of the Erie Canal. Although not formally trained, Schubarth exhibited a natural aptitude for drawing and was quickly promoted to a draftsman within the firm. In 1842, seeing a need for civil engineers in Providence, Rhode Island, he moved to the city where he began collaborating with Stephen Atwater in Providence's only established engineering firm. In 1845, the firm was engaged to lay out a new section of the old North Burial Ground. The firm was subsequently chosen to design the city's new Swan Point Cemetery in 1846 and River Bend Cemetery in Westerly, Rhode Island, in 1849. Schubarth also designed

Elm Grove Cemetery in Mystic, Connecticut, in 1853; Oak Hill Cemetery in Woonsocket, Rhode Island, in 1856; and Juniper Hill Cemetery in Bristol, Rhode Island, in 1857. From the mid-1840s to the mid-1880s, Schubarth was also involved in surveying and platting housing lots. In the 1850s, he began to speculate in real estate. In addition to all of these activities, he was awarded several architectural commissions in Providence including the Arnold Block in 1854 and the Oriental Mill in 1860.

James Charles Sidney (1819–1881) was an English-born architect, engineer, and landscape gardener who immigrated to the United States and worked in Philadelphia and New York. His earliest documented work was as a cartographer for John Jay Smith, librarian of the Library Company, in Philadelphia. He also worked for Smith's son, Robert Pearsall Smith, a well-known map publisher during the mid-nineteenth century. Smith produced *Sidney's Map of Ten Miles Around—Map of the Circuit of Ten Miles around the City of Philadelphia* in 1847 and *Sidney's Map of the Township of Germantown with the Names of the Property Holders* around 1848. By the mid- to late-1840s, Sidney had embarked on his career as a civil engineer and architect. In 1849, he was retained by the founders of Easton Cemetery in Easton, Pennsylvania, to help select an appropriately picturesque site for the town's new burial ground. He subsequently designed the cemetery's layout. In 1850, he designed the plan for Oakwood Cemetery in Troy, New York. The same year, Sidney formed an architectural and engineering firm with James P. W. Neff; the partnership lasted until 1854 or 1855. In 1854, the partners designed the Oaklands Cemetery in West Chester, Pennsylvania. Sidney then moved to New York City for a couple of years where he worked for Robert Pearsall Smith's firm, which was charged with mapping New York State. He later returned to Philadelphia and formed a partnership with Andrew Adams; the partners created the master plan for Fairmount Park in 1859. With yet another partner, Frederick C. Merry, Sidney designed houses in the suburban community of Chestnut Hill outside of Philadelphia in the early 1860s. In 1863, Sidney designed the original plan for Woodlawn Cemetery in the Bronx. He then spent most of his later career designing schools in Philadelphia. Sidney died prematurely in 1881, at the age of sixty-three, after he fell from the roof of his home.

Ossian Cole Simonds (1855–1932) was born in Grand Rapids, Michigan, and grew up on his family's farm, which inspired his love and respect for nature. In 1874, he began attending the University of Michigan, where he studied civil engineering and architecture under the tutelage of William Le Baron Jenney. In 1878, Simonds graduated from the university and moved to Chicago to work in

Jenney's firm. At the firm, Simonds was responsible for implementing Jenney's plan for a new section of Graceland Cemetery. The work was his introduction to landscape gardening. It profoundly impacted his career. Simonds was later appointed the superintendent of Graceland Cemetery and served in that capacity from 1883 to 1888. During his tenure, he transformed the site by emphasizing the use of indigenous plants, replacing paved walks with grass, and advocating the removal of fences and railings to accentuate the natural attributes of the site. After leaving his post at Graceland, Simonds designed parks, private estates, grounds for government institutions, and university campuses. In 1888, Simonds created a site plan for Fort Sheridan outside of Chicago. He was later commissioned to design Frick Park in Pittsburgh, Pennsylvania; Washington Park in Springfield, Illinois; and Palmer Park and Subdivision in Detroit, Michigan. From 1895 to 1912, he also designed at least eight parks in Quincy, Illinois. In addition, he designed residential work for many prominent Chicagoans including Gov. Frank Orren Lowden's estate, Sinnissippi Farm in Oregon, Illinois. Along with Jens Jensen, Simonds is credited with the development of the Prairie style of landscape architecture, which emphasizes native plants of the Midwest, horizontal lines, expansive views, and open space. In addition, Simonds was one of eleven founding members of the ASLA and served as the organization's president in 1913.

Adolph Strauch (1822–1883) was born in the Prussian province of Silesia and grew up on the estate of Count Magnis in Eckersdorf, where his father served as the estate's manager. In high school, Strauch studied botany, and in 1838, Count Magnis obtained an appointment for him at the Imperial Gardens in Vienna, where Strauch studied under renowned landscape gardeners, including Prince Hermann von Pückler-Muskau, for six years. In 1844, Strauch began traveling throughout Europe to study some of its most famous gardens. In the late 1840s, Strauch visited London and was employed by the Royal Botanical Gardens at Regent's Park. It was at Regent's Park where Strauch first met Robert B. Bowler, a wealthy Cincinnati merchant, who was visiting the gardens and became impressed with Strauch's horticultural knowledge. In 1851, Strauch visited the United States determined to see the dramatic landscape of the American West. While traveling in the States, however, Strauch missed a connecting train in Cincinnati and decided to contact Bowler, whom he had met just a few years before. Bowler immediately offered Strauch a commission to complete his estate, Mt. Storm, in Clifton, Ohio. Upon seeing Strauch's transformation of the Bowler estate, other wealthy landowners around Cincinnati subsequently employed Strauch to enhance their estates in the English landscape tradition. In 1855, Strauch

was then hired by the founders of Spring Grove Cemetery to serve as the cemetery's superintendent. It was at Spring Grove where Strauch made alterations to the rural cemetery model and established what became known as the landscape lawn plan. Strauch remained at Spring Grove until his death in 1883.

Burton A. Thomas (1809–1880) was born in rural Rensselaer County, New York, the son of Peleg Rowland and Freelove (Arnold) Thomas. He grew up on his parents' farm in West Sand Lake, just east of Troy, New York. He had marked interests in landscape gardening and surveying but also studied law and was admitted to the bar in 1842. He subsequently practiced probate law, served as a town clerk, and became a justice of the peace. In addition to his legal career, Thomas reportedly surveyed a large portion of Rensselaer County and its adjoining territory, laid out twenty-five public cemeteries, and later designed numerous parks in the state of New York. His cemetery designs included Green Hill Cemetery in Amsterdam, New York (1858); Vale Cemetery in Schenectady, New York (1857); Riverside Cemetery is Oswego, New York (1855); and Dellwood Cemetery in Manchester, Vermont. He also served as the superintendent of Albany Rural Cemetery from 1848 to 1879, during which time he directed the construction of most of the dams, bridges, roads, and ponds in the cemetery.

Calvert Vaux (1824–1895) was born in London, England, and trained as an apprentice under Lewis Nockalls Cottingham, a renowned London architect on the forefront of the Gothic Revival movement. Vaux trained with Cottingham until the age of twenty-six. In 1850, Vaux was introduced to Andrew Jackson Downing, who offered Vaux a job in the United States. Vaux and Downing subsequently worked together for two years, during which time they designed the grounds of the White House and the Smithsonian Institution in Washington, D.C. In 1851, Vaux became a partner in the firm, and when Downing died in 1852, Vaux took control of the operation. In 1858, he collaborated with Frederick Law Olmsted in a design competition for a park in New York City. Their plan, called "Greensward," was ultimately chosen the winner, and the two worked together on the construction of what became known as Central Park for the next twenty years. In 1865, the two created an official partnership—Olmsted, Vaux and Company—and subsequently designed Prospect Park and Fort Greene Park in Brooklyn, and Morningside Park in Manhattan. They also collaborated on the plan for Riverside outside of Chicago, one of the first suburbs in the United States. In 1872, Vaux dissolved the partnership with Olmsted and formed an architectural firm with George Kent Radford. Over the course of his career, in partnership with others and on his own, Vaux designed dozens of parks as well as numerous buildings including private residences, apartment complexes, public housing, and public institutions like the American Museum of Natural History and the Metropolitan Museum of Art. Vaux collaborated with Olmsted on the design of Mountain View Cemetery in Oakland, California (1863), and also designed Hillside Cemetery in Middletown, New York (1861). He later designed Riverside Cemetery in Macon, Georgia, in 1887; its plan was based on the landscape lawn model.

Alexander Wadsworth (1806–1898) was born in Hiram, Maine, and grew up on his family's farm there. He attended the Gardiner Lyceum in Gardener, Maine, where he took courses to prepare himself for a career as a civil engineer and surveyor. In 1825, at the age of nineteen, he moved to Boston to find work. In the early 1830s, Wadsworth assisted Henry A. S. Dearborn in laying out Mount Auburn Cemetery, the first rural cemetery in the United States. Wadsworth later laid out Harmony Grove Cemetery in Salem, Massachusetts (1839–40). In the interim, Wadsworth had won a design competition for the layout of Pemberton Square at the base of Pemberton and Beacon Hills in Boston. Over the course of his long career, he also surveyed large portions of the city and its suburbs. In addition to his work as an engineer and surveyor, Wadsworth served as a Common Councilman in Boston for six or seven years and as a Massachusetts legislator for two years.

Jacob Weidenmann (1829–1893) was born in Winterthur, Switzerland, and studied architecture and engineering at the Akadomie der Bildenden Kunste. He began his professional career working in Paris and London before traveling to New York City, where he was hired as an assistant engineer on the Panama Canal. He did not work long in Panama, however, and traveled to Lima, Perú, where he worked as an engineer and architect for several years. In 1856, he returned to New York, where he began to pursue a career in landscape gardening. He worked with landscape gardener Eugene A. Baumann and studied the works of John Claudius Loudon and Andrew Jackson Downing. He later moved to Hartford, Connecticut, and in 1861 was commissioned to design Bushnell Park. He subsequently served as the superintendent of the Hartford park system for eight years. In 1863, Weidenmann was chosen to design the city's new Cedar Hill Cemetery, which he laid out using the landscape lawn plan. In 1871, he settled again in New York City and formed a close working relationship with Frederick Law Olmsted. The two collaborated on numerous projects including Congress Park in Saratoga Springs, New York; the New York State Asylum in Buffalo, New York; Mount Royal Park in Montreal, Canada; and the US Capitol grounds in Washington, D.C. In 1884, Weidenmann was commissioned to design the grounds of the Iowa State Capitol and he subsequently received several commissions in the Midwest. In 1886, he moved his office to Chicago after he was appointed the superintendent of Mount Hope Cemetery. His disagreements with the cemetery company, however, led to his firing only three months later. In 1888, Weidenmann wrote *Modern Cemeteries*—an important work that examined the rural cemetery movement, stressed the need to hire a landscape architect to develop designs for cemeteries, and advocated the use of the landscape lawn plan, which by then had become the dominant cemetery landscape aesthetic in the United States.

Brief Profiles of Representative Rural Cemeteries

Albany Rural Cemetery, Menands, New York

Albany Rural Cemetery was incorporated April 2, 1841, in response to the rapid deterioration of crowded church cemeteries within the city of Albany, New York, and was officially dedicated three years later. The chosen site is located north of the city on high ground overlooking the Hudson River. Designed by Maj. David Bates Douglass, the cemetery includes thirty-five miles of romantically named roadways that wind through the rolling terrain of the 467-acre site (originally 240 acres). The cemetery is divided into three areas, known as the South Ridge, the Middle Ridge, and the North Ridge, with two creeks running through the ravines in the landscape. Elaborate mausoleums and monuments, often incorporating Gothic, Greek, and Egyptian Revival motifs, occupy positions of visual prominence in the landscape. Concentrations of sculptural monuments are often juxtaposed with open vistas, infusing the site with a picturesque quality. Meanwhile, a medieval-inspired gatehouse, designed by Albany architect Marcus Reynolds, greets visitors at the South Gate. The cemetery was listed in the National Register of Historic Places in 1979. www
.albanyruralcemetery.org.

Allegheny Cemetery, Pittsburgh, Pennsylvania

Founded in 1844, Allegheny Cemetery originally encompassed one hundred acres of former farmland in Lawrenceville, Pennsylvania, and served the residents of both Pittsburgh and Allegheny. Located along the southern slope of the Allegheny River, the gently undulating, heavily wooded site chosen for the cemetery included two small lakes fed by a natural spring. Architect John Chislett Sr. served as the cemetery's first superintendent and laid out the site's circuitous circulation system. In 1849, he also designed the Butler Street Gateway and Gothic Lodge, which has since undergone sensitive additions. Later, Henry A. Macomb designed the Penn Avenue gate complex—a Richardsonian Romanesque–style entrance with a chapel and 135-foot bell tower—which was completed in 1888.

Meanwhile, the memorial architecture of the cemetery was inspired by various styles including Greek Revival, Gothic Revival, and Egyptian Revival. Allegheny Cemetery, which now embraces three hundred acres, was listed in the National Register in 1980. www.alleghenycemetery.com.

Bayside Cemetery, Potsdam, New York

Bayside Cemetery was established in 1865 on twenty-one acres of hilly terrain three-quarters of a mile south of the village of Potsdam, New York. The site, which has grown to encompass eighty-four acres, is bounded on the north and east by the Raquette River. L. R. Briggs, a Boston architect and engineer, and H. T. Whitman, an engineer and surveyor, originally laid out the cemetery's narrow, winding roadways to separate the undulating site into distinctive sections and juxtapose open space with areas of hardwoods. The cemetery's oldest interments generally bordered the Raquette River. Many of the early, distinctive monuments were constructed of red Potsdam sandstone taken from nearby Raquette River quarries. Also constructed of Potsdam sandstone, the cemetery's gatehouse was designed in 1867 by New York architect Edgar A. Josselyn in the French Vernacular Revival style. Standing adjacent to the gatehouse, the cemetery's first gateway was constructed in 1884 with four archways with iron-grilled gates—two in the center for vehicles flanked on each side by an entrance for pedestrians. The cemetery was listed in the National Register of Historic Places in 2004.

Bellefontaine Cemetery, St. Louis, Missouri

Bellefontaine Cemetery was founded in 1849 in St. Louis, Missouri, on the rolling, tree-covered hills of the former Hempstead family farm along the old military road leading to Fort Bellefontaine. It was the first large-scale rural cemetery designed west of the Mississippi River. Almerin Hotchkiss, the cemetery's first superintendent, was responsible for designing the site, which included laying out four miles of broad avenues and curving roadways to present picturesque views of the surrounding land and

Mississippi River. He preserved existing mature trees and sited many unusual species to consciously contrast areas of light and shade in the overall composition of the landscape. Gothic Revival, Greek Revival, and Egyptian Revival monuments and mausoleums soon scattered over the site's gently sloping terrain. In 1892, Louis Sullivan designed the cemetery's most famous tomb—the oriental-inspired mausoleum of Charlotte Dickson Wainwright, which was listed in the National Register of Historic Places in 1970. Today, the cemetery encompasses approximately 330 acres, includes fourteen miles of roadways, and contains two lakes—Cascade Lake and Cypress Lake. www.bellefontaine cemetery.org.

Bellevue Cemetery, Lawrence and Methuen, Massachusetts

In 1847, Bellevue Cemetery was established by the Town of Lawrence, Massachusetts, on five acres of elevated terrain overlooking the Spicket River and the town's textile mills. One of the town's selectman, John M. Smith, laid out the cemetery's first lots. The earliest part of the cemetery, known as the "Old Yard," is characterized by curvilinear roads and pathways, terraced hillsides, and granite retaining walls. Wall crypts and granite and marble headstones intermingle with oak, cedar, and linden trees across the landscape. At the main entrance, the Hearse House, a Second Empire–style building constructed in 1873, serves as the cemetery's office. An elaborate entryway with brick pillars and iron gates was later added in 1922. In 1894, George G. Adams, the most prominent architect in Lawrence during the nineteenth century, designed the Bellevue Brick Stable. Built to quarter the cemetery's horses and wagons, the imposing Classical Revival–style building features numerous large windows that flood the interior with light. Bellevue Cemetery expanded in 1853, shortly after its establishment, and several times thereafter to accommodate the town's burial needs. Today, Bellevue Cemetery encompasses approximately ninety-six acres.

Bonaventure Cemetery, Savannah, Georgia

Bonaventure Cemetery—originally known as the Evergreen Cemetery of Bonaventure—was established by Capt. Peter Wiltberger after he purchased seventy acres of land once owned and operated by the Tatnall family as a rice plantation. The land, located on a high bluff east of the city of Savannah, Georgia, overlooking the Wilmington River, included the Tatnall family burial ground and the ruins of the family's mansion. The cemetery opened in 1849 and was formally laid out a year later by James Henry Rion, whose design was likely influenced by the existing landscape features of the site, including terraces, groves of live oaks, and straight avenues lined with trees. Rion's design, however, was also influenced by the philosophy of the rural cemetery movement. In 1907, the City of Savannah acquired the cemetery and today continues to maintain the site, which has grown to encompass 160 acres. Bonaventure Cemetery was listed in the National Register of Historic Places in 2001. www .bonaventurehistorical.org.

Cave Hill Cemetery, Louisville, Kentucky

Cave Hill Cemetery was established in 1848 on the former farm of William Johnston, east of Louisville, Kentucky. Edmund Francis Lee, a civil engineer from Connecticut, laid out the cemetery's grounds, which are roughly bisected east to west by the Springs Branch of Beargrass Creek, which flows from the cave that gave the property its name. Roads, which follow the gentle contours of the land, rise to hilltops that serve as burial grounds. Meanwhile, tree reserves and lakes occupy the site's valleys. The Japanese pagoda tree, willow oak, Southern magnolia, weeping beech, pond cypress, weeping balsam fir, and numerous other species provide backdrops for monumental art that augment the Picturesque landscape. In 1892, the Baxter Avenue entrance was completed; it features a monumental clock tower that was one of the tallest structures in the area at the time of its construction. Cave Hill was listed in the National Register of Historic Places in 1979. www .cavehillcemetery.com.

Easton Cemetery, Easton, Pennsylvania

Easton Cemetery was founded in 1849 after Trail Green, one of the leading citizens of Easton, Pennsylvania, took a tour of the state to learn how other communities cared for their dead. Subsequently, twelve prominent citizens of Easton, including Green, joined together to incorporate the Easton Cemetery. They retained Philadelphia civil engineer and architect James C. Sidney to assist with the endeavor. It was Sidney who recommended the acquisition of the thirty-four-acre site overlooking Bushkill Creek for the public burial ground. Sidney then laid out curving lanes between irregularly shaped burial plots on the cemetery's plateau and likely added red oaks, red maples, and white pines to the grounds. In the 1870s, the cemetery began to plant horse chestnuts and sugar maples along the main roadways. Over time, the interiors of the cemetery's older burial plots have been embellished with shapely ornamental trees, like red cedar, Japanese maple, and Norway spruce. Decorative cast iron urns, benches, and settees were added throughout the earliest sections of the cemetery until the 1880s when the landscape lawn aesthetic began to influence the site's design. New sections were added to the cemetery beginning in 1870 to accommodate the burial needs of the community; today, Easton Cemetery encompasses ninety-nine acres. The earliest sections of the cemetery were listed in the National Register of Historic Places in 1990.

Edgell Grove Cemetery, Framingham, Massachusetts

In 1846, Col. Moses Edgell donated approximately ten acres of his land in Framingham, Massachusetts, to a committee formed for the purpose of establishing a new rural cemetery. The committee solicited the expertise of Gen. Henry A. S. Dearborn—the principal designer of Mount Auburn Cemetery—to lay out the site. Dearborn charged $5.50 for his services. Warren Nixon surveyed the property and Nathaniel Swift Bennett supervised the site's construction. The cemetery was consecrated in 1848, and its first burial followed shortly thereafter. In 1875, Boston architect Alexander R. Estey designed the cemetery's granite gateway—it stands along Grove Street at the head of a natural ridge that extends to the interior of the cemetery and divides the cemetery's entrance and exit drives. Meanwhile, oaks, white pines, hemlocks, birches, and spruces dot the rolling landscape and provide a backdrop for funerary monuments. Edgell Grove has grown to encompass nearly fifty acres of picturesque landscape. www.edgellgrove.com.

Elm Grove Cemetery, Mystic, Connecticut

Elm Grove Cemetery was established in 1853 on twenty-two acres of land overlooking the Mystic River in Mystic, Connecticut. The trustees of the Elm Grove Cemetery Association hired engineer Niles Bierragaard Schubarth to lay out the site. Schubarth designed the cemetery in the shape of an elm tree, with a twenty-foot-wide main thoroughfare commencing at the front gate, stretching in a straight path to form the tree's trunk and then winding along the outskirts of the site following the contours of the tree's broad crown before returning back to the entrance. Meanwhile, other curvilinear avenues within the cemetery's interior measured eighteen feet wide, while footpaths measured only six feet in width. Relatively simple monuments were built over time on the cemetery's burial plots in comparison with those built in other rural cemeteries of the era. Obelisks dominate the landscape, while only three mausoleums stand within the cemetery's walls. The main entrance, which was built in 1892, is marked by a stone gate of three arches with double wrought iron gates in each one. The central arch serves as a driveway for vehicles, while the flanking arches are reserved for pedestrian use. www.elmgrovecemetery.org.

Elmwood Cemetery, Columbia, South Carolina

Founded in 1854, Elmwood Cemetery was established on approximately two hundred acres of uneven land just north of the city limits of Columbia, South Carolina. The cemetery was established by a group of prominent local citizens in response to overcrowding in the city's urban churchyards and in its Potters Field. The southern section of the cemetery was developed first and exhibits characteristics of the early rural cemetery movement including winding drives and ornately carved monuments. Cedar, magnolia, and oak trees dominate this section. Meanwhile, family plots, frequently enclosed by iron fencing or low stone retaining walls, often contain flowering plants and ornamental trees and shrubs. The southern portion of the cemetery also contains a section of Confederate dead enclosed by low stone retaining walls and featuring rows of simple, uniform marble tablets. The northern section, which was developed after 1921, exhibits open lawns, smaller and more standardized monuments, and fewer trees, reflecting a nationwide evolution in cemetery design. Elmwood Cemetery, which now encompasses only about 168 acres, was listed in the National Register of Historic Places in 1996.

Elmwood Cemetery, Memphis, Tennessee

Elmwood Cemetery was founded in 1852 by a corporation composed of fifty prominent citizens of Memphis, Tennessee, and was established on forty acres of land about two-and-a-half miles southeast of the city. The land selected for the cemetery featured a stream running through one of its valleys and stands of native oaks shading the site's numerous knolls. Ironically, elm trees were imported from New York and planted on the site only after the name Elmwood was chosen for the cemetery. Winding drives that respected the curvature of the land and showed off sweeping vistas were added to the site. Both elaborate and simple monuments, including draped urns, broken columns, and graceful flowers of marble and granite, were added to burial plots, enhancing the picturesque quality of the site. After the Civil War, the cemetery significantly increased its "underground population" when more than a thousand Confederate soldiers and veterans were buried in Confederate Soldiers Rest. Elmwood Cemetery was listed in the National Register of Historic Places in 2002. www.elmwoodcemetery.org.

Evergreen Cemetery, Oswego, New York

Evergreen Cemetery was founded in 1851 on eleven acres of land on a hillside overlooking the Susquehanna River and Oswego, New York, approximately one mile from the town's center. The town's trustees—who had established the cemetery as a nondenominational resting place open to all the town's residents—hired well-known local engineer Stephen Dexter to survey and lay out the site. Dexter designed a system of curvilinear avenues that divided the cemetery into irregular sections and created level terraces for burial lots. Egyptian Revival obelisks were common monuments built within the cemetery as were statues of classical young maidens motioning toward heaven. Today, visitors reach the cemetery by a steep, narrow winding road that approaches the site's unpretentious entrance gateway—two large posts topped with decorative urns. Evergreen Cemetery, which now encompasses approximately fifty-one acres, was listed in the National Register of Historic Places in 2002.

Evergreen Cemetery, Portland, Maine

Consecrated in 1854, Evergreen Cemetery was originally located on fifty-five acres of rolling property about two-and-one-half miles from downtown Portland, Maine. The land chosen by the city for the establishment of the cemetery was heavily forested in parts and open in others. It also encompassed a swampy area ideal for creating ponds. Charles H. Howe, a civil engineer, was chosen to lay out the cemetery's family burial plots and the system of roadways; he combined curving and grid-like avenues as necessitated by the existing topography. Howe's plan also established circular intersections, which served as focal points. In addition, Howe added two informal, irregularly shaped ponds to the property and one formal circular fountain. Although the property features four ponds today, none of them match those originally created. Evergreen Cemetery, which now encompasses 239 acres, was listed in the National Register of Historic Places in 1992. http://friendsof evergreen.org.

Evergreens Cemetery, Brooklyn and Queens, New York

The Evergreens Cemetery was founded in 1849 on approximately 183 acres of varied land bordering Brooklyn and Queens, New York. The acreage boasted views of Manhattan to the north and Jamaica Bay and the Atlantic Ocean to the south and encompassed large expanses of rolling lawns alternating with groves of native trees such as black oaks, maples, sweet gums, tulip trees, and hickories. Few evergreen trees initially grew on the site, so one of the cemetery's trustees and a local pastor journeyed to the Catskill Mountains and brought back a wide variety of evergreens to plant throughout the grounds. Meanwhile, Andrew Jackson Downing, who served as one of the cemetery's officers and as the site's "rural architect and landscape gardener", likely influenced the layout of more than eight miles of winding roadways that, at frequent intervals, provided panoramic views of the surrounding picturesque landscape. In 1852, renowned architect Alexander Jackson Davis designed the cemetery's Norman–style chapel. Evergreens Cemetery, which now encompasses 225 acres, was listed in the National Register of Historic Places in 2007. www.theevergreenscemetery.com.

Forest Hills Cemetery, Boston, Massachusetts

Forest Hills Cemetery, located in the Jamaica Plain neighborhood of Boston, Massachusetts, was established in 1848 as a rural municipal cemetery by Henry A. S. Dearborn, then mayor of Roxbury (the municipality with jurisdiction over the land at the time). Dearborn also designed the cemetery—which measured seventy-two acres in size within its first year—to incorporate large winding avenues and smaller connecting pathways. In 1852, Lake Hibiscus, a four-acre artificial pond, was added to the grounds. Over time, the cemetery's scenic views were punctuated by elaborate mausoleums and monuments, including six original works by famed sculptor Daniel Chester French. In 1868, the cemetery became a private, nonprofit corporation. In the late nineteenth century, an elaborate Gothic Revival gateway (which replaced an earlier Egyptian Revival structure) was constructed to mark the entrance to the cemetery, which today serves as a park, arboretum, and outdoor sculpture museum. Forest Hills Cemetery, now encompassing over 250 acres, was listed in the National Register of Historic Places in 2004. www.foresthillscemetery.com.

Forest Home Cemetery, Milwaukee, Wisconsin

Forest Home Cemetery was founded in 1850 on seventy-two gently rolling and forested acres nearly two miles outside the city limits of Milwaukee, Wisconsin. Realizing the need for a large, public burial ground for the growing city, the parish leaders of St. Paul's Episcopal Church established the cemetery and consciously opened it to all religious groups. Portions of the site chosen for the cemetery were originally dotted with Paleo Indian burial mounds known to settlers as the Indian Fields. Increase Allen Lapham, a pioneer scientist and surveyor who had studied the Fields, was enlisted to lay out the winding lanes of the cemetery. His original plan respected the archaeological features of the site. However, under the subsequent direction of George West, crews graded the landscape and ultimately destroyed the Indian mounds. In 1890, architects George Ferry and Alfred Clas designed the cemetery's Gothic Revival—style chapel. It includes a leaded glass conservatory that extends from the north and south sides of the nave and houses decades-old tropical plants. Forest Home Cemetery, which now encompasses two hundred acres, was listed in the National Register of Historic Places in 1980. www.foresthomecemetery.com.

Forest Lawn Cemetery, Buffalo, New York

In 1849, Forest Lawn Cemetery was founded by attorney Charles E. Clark on eighty acres of pastoral land located on Scajaquada Creek two-and-a-half miles from downtown Buffalo, New York. The chosen site featured variable terrain with a succession of knolls running parallel to the creek as well as valleys with broad expanses of lawn stretching between the bluffs. To provide visitors with captivating views of this picturesque landscape, Clark laid out wide, curving roadways snaking through the site. He also thinned out the groves of oak trees on the hills to make room for graves while planting trees in the valleys to provide shade for burial plots there. In addition, Clark adopted a policy to provide interesting sculpture to enhance the natural setting, and in 1851 he commissioned a statue of the Seneca Indian chief Red Jacket to become the first piece of public art to beautify the grounds. In 1865, the trustees of Forest Lawn invited Adolph Strauch from Spring Grove Cemetery to visit the site and subsequently adopted policies that favored the landscape lawn plan, including restrictions on internal fences. Forest Lawn was listed in the National Register of Historic Places in 1990. www.forest-lawn.com.

Frankfort Cemetery, Frankfort, Kentucky

The Frankfort Cemetery Company, which was incorporated by the Kentucky Legislature in 1844, acquired thirty-two acres of land on a high bluff overlooking the state's capital city in 1845 for the establishment of a rural cemetery. The cemetery company hired the Scottish-born landscape gardener Robert Carmichael to lay out and embellish the grounds. He subsequently became the cemetery's first superintendent. In 1847, the Kentucky State Legislature chose Frankfort Cemetery as the state's most suitable site for the burial of its most famous sons as well as for the construction of a monument to the country's fallen soldiers. The following year, a military memorial measuring sixty-five feet high was erected on a mound at the center of the grounds. Designed by sculptor Robert E. Launitz, it features a granite base with an eagle at each corner and an Italian marble column topped by the *Statue of Victory*. Over time, elaborate monuments were also added to mark the gravesites of governors, US senators and representatives, artists, educators, and pioneers including Daniel Boone. Frankfort's rural cemetery, which now encompasses one hundred acres, was listed in the National Register of Historic Places in 1974.

Graceland Cemetery, Chicago, Illinois

Graceland Cemetery was established in 1860 by Thomas Bryan, a successful Chicago lawyer, as a private cemetery on eighty-six acres of land that was two miles outside the city limits of Chicago, Illinois, at the time of its founding. The earliest part of the cemetery, located in the southwestern part of the site, was designed and executed by Swain Nelson under the direction of William Saunders and reflected the tenets of the early rural cemetery movement. In 1870, H. W. S. Cleveland was hired to design the first major expansion to the site. Then, beginning in 1878, William LeBaron Jenney and Ossian Cole Simonds oversaw the northeast expansion, which included elements of the landscape lawn plan such as the uniform sodding of paths and burial plots and the elimination of fencing and curbing around distinct family lots. In 1888, the local firm of Holabird & Roche designed the Arts and Crafts—style chapel, which was sited to complement the natural contours of the surrounding terrain. The firm also designed the entrance gate and administration building. Graceland Cemetery, which now encompasses 119 acres, was listed in the National Register of Historic Places in 2001. http://gracelandcemetery.org.

Green Hill Cemetery, Amsterdam, New York

Green Hill Cemetery was established by a nonprofit cemetery association in 1858 on a plateau overlooking the Mohawk River in Amsterdam, New York. Surveyor and landscape gardener Burton A. Thomas designed the cemetery's layout to take advantage of the site's natural topography—generally flat, but occasionally interspersed with knolls and hillocks—as well as the sweeping vistas of the Mohawk Valley to the south and west. He planned unpaved roadways and footpaths to wind around the site. He also incorporated mature native trees, particularly oaks, into the design scheme and added ornamental plantings. He positioned and trimmed vegetation to construct breathtaking views of the city and valley below. A rusticated stone and wrought iron gate was built on the northern edge of the cemetery along Church Street. Meanwhile, at the center of the cemetery, a circular plot marked by a tall, stone shaft was dedicated for the graves of the city's Civil War dead. The cemetery, which was initially fifteen acres in size, has grown to encompass forty-one acres. The site was listed in the National Register of Historic Places in 2005.

Green Mount Cemetery, Baltimore, Maryland

Green Mount was founded as a nonprofit, nonsectarian cemetery in 1838 on the northern edge of Baltimore, Maryland, on the former country estate of the late merchant Robert Oliver. Benjamin Henry Latrobe Jr., a civil engineer, laid out winding drives to highlight the prominent prospects inherent in the sixty-acre site. Latrobe also shaped irregular burial sections with his meandering roadways, which were given names such as hickory, cypress, oak, willow, cedar, maple, and walnut, reflecting the emphasis placed on horticulture by the site's organizers. Soon after its founding, the cemetery evolved into a sculpture garden with obelisks, raised sarcophagi, and elaborate monuments juxtaposed against the sylvan landscape. In addition, prominent local architect Robert Carey Long Jr. designed a grandiose Gothic Revival gateway to mark the entrance to the cemetery within a couple of years of its dedication. The architectural firm of Niernsee and Nielson later designed a Gothic Revival chapel to stand atop a gentle hill immediately inside the front gate. Green Mount Cemetery was listed in the National Register of Historic Places in 1980. www.greenmountcemetery.com.

Green-Wood Cemetery, Brooklyn, New York

The Green-Wood Cemetery was officially established in 1838 on 175 acres of elevated land east of Gowanus Creek in Brooklyn, New York. Maj. David Bates Douglass designed the layout of the cemetery, incorporating broad carriage roads that twisted around the graceful curvature of the land and hundreds of footpaths that made every glade, hill, and dell accessible to the visitor. Meanwhile, Richard Upjohn served as the cemetery's architect and, with his son, designed and constructed most of the original buildings during the cemetery's first three decades of existence. In the meantime, almost every variety of weeping tree that was available at the time was planted on the site during its first twenty years of development, including weeping mulberries inside the imposing Upjohn-designed main gate. Green-Wood, which now encompasses 478 acres, was listed as a National Historic Landmark in 2006. www.green-wood.com.

Harmony Grove Cemetery, Salem, Massachusetts

Harmony Grove Cemetery was established in 1839 on approximately thirty-five acres of picturesque land in Danvers, Massachusetts. A year later, the city limits of Danvers changed and the cemetery became part of the town of Salem. The land chosen for the cemetery was diverse, encompassing rocky cliffs, woody knolls, open plains, shady valleys with stands of mature trees, and a small river along the site's southwest boundary. Alexander Wadsworth of Boston was engaged to prepare the topographical plan for the cemetery; he laid out the grounds with winding avenues and walkways. Meanwhile, Francis Peabody, one of the cemetery's founders, designed a rustic stone gateway at the cemetery's eastern entrance off Grove Street. A rustic bridge was also installed from the main entrance to the superintendent's lodge. Early on, burial plots featuring marble monuments were frequently surrounded by fences or enclosures in the traditional rural cemetery style.

Hillside Cemetery, Middletown, New York

In 1860, the Hillside Cemetery Association was formed in Middletown, New York, to establish a rural cemetery. It subsequently purchased fifty acres of land on a hillside southeast of the city center. The site was characterized by sharp undulations in topography, which created a series of bluffs separated by valleys with broad lawns. The association hired architect Calvert Vaux to create a plan for the cemetery that would complement its existing picturesque landscape. Vaux's plan included winding roadways that created lobular burial plots that were crisscrossed by pedestrian pathways. The circulation system followed the contours of the natural topography and presented a series of stunning vistas. In addition, two ponds were created on the site. Over time, a wide variety of funerary art was added to the cemetery, including Egyptian-inspired obelisks, female allegorical figures, and stylized sarcophagi. Hillside Cemetery was listed in the National Register of Historic Places in 1994.

Hollywood Cemetery, Richmond, Virginia

Hollywood Cemetery was first conceived in 1847 and finally dedicated in 1849 on forty-two acres of land known as Harvie's Woods that was positioned on a bluff overlooking the falls of the James River approximately a quarter mile from the city of Richmond, Virginia. The site's gently rolling topography was punctuated by stands of holly, poplar, elm, and other hardwood trees. The cemetery's board of trustees chose well-known architect John Notman to design the grounds. It was Notman who suggested the cemetery be named Hollywood because of the prevalence of holly trees on the site. Notman's plan for the cemetery included countless winding roads that created numerous burial lots that fronted the thoroughfares. He also proposed that the central valley, which was traversed by a wide stream and two creeks, be reserved as an ornamental feature beautified by magnolias and other flowering shrubs. Hollywood Cemetery was listed in the National Register of Historic Places in 1969. www.hollywoodcemetery.org.

Hope Cemetery, Worcester, Massachusetts

Established on approximately fifty acres of rolling land overlooking the Middle River on its northern boundary, Hope Cemetery was dedicated by the City of Worcester, Massachusetts, in 1852. The city had hired local surveyor Gill Valentine to survey and create the initial plan for the site, which included winding roads that revealed stunning views and vistas. The roadways—including Chestnut Avenue, Elm Avenue, Linden Avenue, Maple Avenue, Pine Avenue, and Sycamore Avenue—took the names of trees found in the cemetery. Beech trees were also particularly abundant on the grounds. Over time, numerous mausoleums were erected throughout the cemetery in various revival styles, including Classical, Gothic, and Egyptian. The stone walls along Webster Street were added in two phases: the northern section at the time of the cemetery's establishment and the southern section in 1936 as a result of the Works Progress Administration. The twin-arched granite gates on Webster Street were added in 1917. Hope Cemetery, which encompasses 168 acres, was listed in the National Register of Historic Places in 1997.

Laurel Grove Cemetery, Savannah, Georgia

Laurel Grove Cemetery, designed in 1850 by James Otis Morse, is located in Savannah, Georgia, on a former rice plantation. Originally encompassing one hundred acres, Laurel Grove was established as a public cemetery by the City of Savannah and named after the native laurel oak trees that inhabited the site. The design incorporated typical Picturesque elements including curvilinear roadways winding around alternately high and low ground. From its inception, Laurel Grove was segregated into two main sections—the Northern section for whites and the Southern section for blacks. In 1963, the 37th Street Connector to Interstate 16 was built through an unused portion of the cemetery creating a physical boundary between the two sections. Today, the cemeteries are referred to as Laurel Grove North and Laurel Grove South and are maintained as two distinct cemeteries by the City of Savannah. Laurel Grove South was listed in the National Register of Historic Places in 1978; Laurel Grove North was listed in the Register in 1983.

Laurel Hill Cemetery, Philadelphia, Pennsylvania

Laurel Hill Cemetery was established in 1836 on rolling acreage overlooking the Schuylkill River outside of Philadelphia, Pennsylvania. Architect John Notman created the landscape design for the original twenty acres, which featured a three-tiered circulation system with a main carriage loop, secondary roads, and pathways all coming together near the center. Notman also carved out terraces overlooking the river that summoned visitors toward picturesque, panoramic vistas. In addition, he designed the classically inspired gatehouse on Ridge Avenue. In the midst of the cemetery's romantic landscape, he also created one geometrical section near the main entrance. Meanwhile, John Jay Smith, the cemetery's founder, advised Notman on the planting scheme for the grounds, which included the addition of cedars of Lebanon, hollies, rhododendrons, and mountain laurels to the site. The southern section, added in 1849, incorporated Picturesque design elements similar to those of the original northern section. However, the central section, added in 1861, was more formally arranged with symmetrical burial plots flanking straight pathways. Laurel Hill, which now encompasses seventy-four acres, became a National Historic Landmark in 1998. www.the laurelhillcemetery.org.

Lexington Cemetery, Lexington, Kentucky

The Lexington Cemetery Company was incorporated by the Kentucky General Assembly in 1848. The following year, the company purchased a forty-acre tract of land known as Boswell's Woods. The cemetery's board of trustees then hired horticulturist Charles S. Bell as the site's first superintendent. With the assistance of civil engineer John Lutz, Bell laid out the cemetery's curvilinear roadways and discrete burial sections in typical Picturesque fashion. Unlike superintendents of traditional rural cemeteries, however, Bell discouraged lot owners from erecting fences or curbing around burial plots. In 1890, a new iron gateway, office, and chapel, designed by architect Herman L. Rowe, replaced the gateway that had been built soon after the cemetery's establishment. The cemetery—which has grown to encompass 170 acres—includes two lakes and over two hundred species of trees including Southern magnolia, European hornbeam, Eastern redbud, common hackberry, Osage orange, American basswood, and Kentucky coffee tree. It also contains a National Cemetery within its grounds, where both Union and Confederate veterans are buried. Lexington Cemetery was listed in the National Register of Historic Places in 1976. www.lexcem .org.

Linden Grove Cemetery, Covington, Kentucky

Linden Grove Cemetery was officially consecrated in 1843. It was sited on twenty-two acres of land west of Covington, Kentucky, originally owned by the Western Baptist Theological Institute. The Institute had made plans under the guidance of Ephraim Robbins, a prominent Cincinnati insurance broker, to establish a public cemetery.

Under Robbins's direction, the relatively flat southern portion of the new cemetery site was laid out with formal linear roadways and pathways. The roadways arranged in the northern section, however, respected the principles of the rural cemetery movement. They followed the irregular topography of the section's gently rolling hills and skirted the multi-fingered ravine that punctuated the landscape. A small pond was also created on the site from a natural spring located in the ravine. Meanwhile, the entrance to the cemetery featured a Porter's House (no longer extant) that incorporated an arched, brick gateway at its center. In 1900, ornamental iron gates replaced the original entrance. Linden Grove Cemetery was listed in the National Register of Historic Places in 2000.

Loudon Park Cemetery, Baltimore, Maryland

Loudon Park Cemetery was founded in 1853 in the western portion of Baltimore, Maryland, on one hundred acres of the former country estate of James Carey. Winding avenues were added to the site of rolling hills to form burial sections of varied shapes and sizes. Bridges were also built to span a small creek called Maiden Choice Run that traversed the site. Over time, mausoleums and monuments of varied intricacy filled the Picturesque grounds. During the Civil War, the federal government purchased a section of the cemetery for Union dead, while southerners acquired a portion of the site that became known as Confederate Hill. In the twentieth century, the cemetery's management installed its own street car line through the site to accommodate the growing number of visitors to the cemetery; the line operated from 1905 to 1931. Today, the cemetery encompasses 350 acres and is the only extensive green space in west Baltimore. www.loudon-park.com.

Machpelah Cemetery, LeRoy, New York

Machpelah Cemetery was founded by George Blodgett in 1858 in northwest LeRoy, New York, on an eight-acre site bounded on one side by Oatka Creek. Blodgett added curvilinear drives to the undulating terrain to reveal picturesque vistas to visitors. Over time, a variety of funerary art was added to the cemetery including obelisks, columns, urns, and statuary in an array of materials including marble, limestone, sandstone, and granite. Meanwhile, the entrances to the cemetery were marked by massive limestone-block pillars topped by large stone orbs. The southern, relatively flat portion of the cemetery was a later addition. On this portion of the site, in the early twentieth century, Alling DeForest, drawing inspiration from the City Beautiful Movement, laid out a system of axial roadways radiating from a circle surrounding the classically inspired Woodward mausoleum. Machpelah Cemetery, which now encompasses approximately twenty-seven acres, was listed in the National Register of Historic Places in 2007.

Machpelah Cemetery, Mount Sterling, Kentucky

Machpelah Cemetery was established in 1855 at the summit of a hill on the eastern outskirts of Mount Sterling, Kentucky, as a joint venture by the Independent Order of Odd Fellows (IOOF) Watson Lodge #32 and the Masons. However, the IOOF eventually became the sole trustee of the site. As in other rural cemeteries of the period, winding roadways were laid out to follow the rolling terrain of the grounds. Originally, the roads were narrow; however, the main arteries have been widened to accommodate vehicular traffic. Funerary monuments including those in the shapes of obelisks, urns, and angels, are scattered throughout the cemetery, while only a few mausoleums exist. Mature trees—including spruce, cedar, cherry, mulberry, maple, walnut, sweet gum, and ash—stand in groups throughout the site. Machpelah Cemetery was listed in the National Register of Historic Places in 1991.

Magnolia Cemetery, Charleston, South Carolina

Magnolia Cemetery was established in 1850 on land that had been part of the Magnolia Umbra rice plantation on the northern outskirts of Charleston, South Carolina. Local architect Edward C. Jones surveyed and designed approximately 50 percent the cemetery's grounds. Jones laid out drives and pathways to meander around small ponds and a lake. He also designed the original receiving tomb—a small stucco-over-brick structure with an arched entrance—that remains extant. Today, undisturbed marshland along the cemetery's eastern and northeastern boundary encompasses nearly 40 percent of the property and offers open vistas toward the Cooper River. Magnolias and live oaks intermingle with the cemetery's funerary art, which includes popular nineteenth-century motifs like obelisks, urns, mourning figures, and reversed torches. A burial section dedicated to both known and unknown Confederate soldiers contains more than 1,700 graves. Magnolia Cemetery, which encompasses approximately ninety-two acres, was listed in the National Register of Historic Places in 1978. www.magnoliacemetery.net.

Mount Adnah Cemetery, Fulton, New York

In 1851, the Mount Adnah Cemetery Association was formed for the purpose of creating a rural cemetery in Fulton, New York. The following year, the organization purchased thirty-six acres of land on the eastern edge of town. The acreage encompassed the highest rise in the immediate area, varied terrain including two ridges and their corresponding valleys, and a grove of young oaks, including red oaks—the most prevalent species on the site. Moses Lindley Lee, one of the cemetery's trustees, and Peter Schenck, a local surveyor, laid out the grounds in 1853. They created three main circuitous carriage paths that followed the natural contours of the land as well as two smaller paths that further divided the grounds into distinct burial sections. The highest elevation in the cemetery, however, was not divided into burial lots; instead, it was set aside as a place for contemplation. Mount Adnah Cemetery was listed in the National Register of Historic Places in 2001.

Mount Albion Cemetery, Albion, New York

Mount Albion Cemetery was founded in 1842 on twenty-five acres of land on the eastern edge of Albion, New York. Marvin Porter, a former engineer on the Erie Canal, is generally credited with the layout of the cemetery's original northern section. There, pathways were sited to meander through a series of terraces in the hillside. Later, local Medina sandstone—a unifying element in the landscape—was used in the construction of a Gothic Revival–style chapel in 1875, the arch at the main entrance in 1881, as well as many of the cemetery's monuments and mausoleums. At the highest point in the cemetery, a red Medina sandstone monument rising fifty-eight feet high was constructed to memorialize the soldiers and sailors of the Civil War. In the northwest corner of the cemetery, a man-made pond was constructed in 1908 and surrounded by white granite and Medina sandstone. Mount Albion Cemetery, which now encompasses seventy acres, was listed in the National Register of Historic Places in 1976.

Mount Auburn Cemetery, Cambridge/Watertown, Massachusetts

Founded in 1831 by members of the Massachusetts Horticultural Society on an extramural site four miles from Boston, Mount Auburn Cemetery was the first rural cemetery established in the United States. Designed largely by Henry A. S. Dearborn with assistance from Jacob Bigelow and Alexander Wadsworth, Mount Auburn was a large-scale landscape of originally seventy-two acres that struck a balance between nature and art. The original plan retained many of the existing landscape features of the site, including the natural contours of the rolling topography and numerous native trees. Curvilinear roadways were originally laid out to emphasize focal points in both the natural and man-made landscape. Over time, permanent family lots were embellished by monuments of varied architectural styles as well as granite curbing, iron fencing, and mausoleums. Mount Auburn was established as a

nonprofit corporation and opened its gates to the general public who flocked to the naturalistic setting for recreation and repose. Mount Auburn Cemetery, which now includes 175 acres, was named a National Historic Landmark in 2003. www.mountauburn.org.

Mount Hope Cemetery, Bangor, Maine

Mount Hope Cemetery, the second-oldest rural cemetery in the United States, was founded in 1834 in Bangor, Maine, which had been incorporated as a city the same year. Mount Hope was largely established in an effort by civic leaders to rival the city of Boston, where the nation's first rural cemetery had been founded in 1831. Mount Hope was laid out by local architect Charles G. Bryant following the principles employed at Mount Auburn. The site chosen for the new cemetery was fifty acres of elevated land above the Penobscot River about two-and-one-half miles from Bangor's city center. Over time, narrow, curving carriage roads, which were named for trees or landscape features, were added to the site, which expanded in 1869 and again in the 1880s. In 1864, the Soldier's Monument—the country's oldest Civil War memorial—was dedicated at Mount Hope. The cemetery, which now encompasses 264 acres, was listed in the National Register of Historic Places in 1974. www.mthopebgr.com.

Mount Hope Cemetery, Boston, Massachusetts

Mount Hope Cemetery was established in 1852 on eighty-five acres of rocky, irregular ground in the Mattapan neighborhood of Dorchester, Massachusetts (later annexed by the City of Boston). In 1857, the City of Boston purchased the cemetery to fulfill its need for additional public burial options, including plots for paupers. David Haggerston, a horticulturist who had served as the superintendent of Mount Auburn's early experimental garden, created the original plan for Mount Hope. Haggerston fashioned a system of curvilinear roadways that responded to the natural topography of the site. This design divided the cemetery into irregularly shaped burial sections that would be used for family lots, civic lots, military lots, pauper lots, and lots to accommodate single and double graves. Shortly after the cemetery's establishment, Meadow Vale Pond—a picturesque landscape element with several islands—was created to help solve drainage issues in the northern part of the site. In 1900, the cemetery's Gothic Revival–style chapel was designed by the firm of Wood and White and built adjacent to the main entrance gate. A Gothic Revival–style administration building, designed by architect James Mulcahy, was constructed just three years later. Mount Hope Cemetery, which now encompasses approximately 125 acres, was listed in the National Register of Historic Places in 2009.

Mount Hope Cemetery, Rochester, New York

Dedicated in 1838, Mount Hope Cemetery was the first rural cemetery sponsored by a municipality—Rochester, New York. Two years earlier, the city had chosen Silas Andrus's fifty-four-acre tract of land on the east side of the Genesee River, south of the city, for the establishment of the cemetery. Silas Cornell was appointed to lay out the cemetery grounds, which were naturally enhanced by undulating topography, picturesque ponds, and a commanding view of the entire city. The first entrance gate to the cemetery, erected in 1839, was heavily influenced by the Egyptian Revival style; however, the Romanesque Revival stone gatehouse that survives today was designed by famous Rochester architect Andrew Jackson Warner in 1874. In 1862, Henry Robinson Searle designed the Gothic Revival–style chapel that stands near the northern entrance. Over time, numerous monuments and mausoleums were added to this sylvan landscape, which today encompasses over two hundred acres. www.fomh.org.

Mount Pleasant Cemetery, Taunton, Massachusetts

Mount Pleasant Cemetery was established by a nonprofit corporation in 1836 on the former homestead of John King about a mile from the center of Taunton, Massachusetts. The ten-acre parcel of land acquired by the corporation included the John King Family Burial Ground, which had seen its first interment in 1710. Local land surveyor John Wilbar designed the new rural cemetery to sensitively encompass this existing burial ground at the heart of the site. The family burying ground was enclosed on four sides by granite posts and metal stringers. Wilbar also laid out a system of curvilinear roadways and footpaths that followed the natural variations in the site's topography. He named the paths with both geographical and botanical monikers. Over time, both simple gravestones and highly ornate memorials were added throughout the site. They were shaded by a variety of trees including beeches, sugar maples, American basswoods, white cedars, Eastern hemlocks, and black maples. In 1986, the ownership of the cemetery was transferred to the City of Taunton. Mount Pleasant Cemetery was listed in the National Register of Historic Places in 2002.

Mountain View Cemetery, Oakland, California

Mountain View Cemetery, located in Oakland, California, was designed by renowned landscape architect Frederick Law Olmsted, with his partner Calvert Vaux, in 1863. The site chosen for the cemetery—220 acres of hilly, originally treeless terrain—overlooks the San Francisco Bay. The arid climate at the site forced Olmsted to deviate from plant species typically associated with rural cemeteries; instead, he planted cedar of Lebanon, Italian stone pine, and native California live oaks, which flourish in the dry, windy hills of Oakland. Olmsted chose the Italian cypress to line a long central avenue that he divided into three sections by rond-points, punctuated with monuments and fountains. He planned curvilinear pathways to branch off this main axis toward the burial plots, which were surrounded by hedges to create a sense of seclusion and protection around gravesites. Throughout the cemetery, Olmstead separated public park-like areas from private mourning areas with trees and shrubs. Over time, elaborate monuments and mausoleums have been added to the cemetery, which continues to be maintained by the Mountain View Cemetery Association. www.mountainviewcemetery.org.

Myrtle Hill Cemetery, Rome, Georgia

Founded in 1857, Myrtle Hill Cemetery is situated on one of Rome, Georgia's, seven hills overlooking the point where the Etowah and Oostanaula rivers converge to form the Coosa River. The cemetery was named for the *Vinca minor*, commonly known as myrtle or the Flower of Death, which grew wild on the hill. Crepe myrtle shrubs were later additions by a local garden club. The original plan for the cemetery, which only encompassed eleven of the original twenty-nine acres, was laid out by local citizen and surveyor Cunningham Pennington. The design incorporated curvilinear roadways, irregularly shaped burial sections, and terraces cut into the steep terrain of the site to form level ground for burials. Both Rome's elite and common citizens are buried here along with 377 Confederate and Union soldiers. Meanwhile, Rome's prominent African American citizens and their descendants rest in the Freedman's section, which was created when the cemetery was still segregated. Myrtle Hill was listed in the National Register of Historic Places in 1983.

Oak Hill Cemetery, Washington, D.C.

Oak Hill Cemetery was established on the highest ground in Georgetown, within the District of Columbia, in 1849 on fifteen acres of land purchased for burial purposes by banker William Wilson Corcoran. In 1851, civil engineer Capt. George F. de la Roche was commissioned to survey and design the layout of the cemetery. He created miles of serpentine drives that followed the hilly topography of the grounds and revealed long views across the landscape at the top of each natural rise. In rural cemetery fashion, the pathways bore names with botanical associations, such as

"Primrose" and "Violet." The captain also created a grand bank of terraces that descended down into the valley formed by Rock Creek. Famed architect James Renwick Jr. designed the one-story, Gothic Revival-style chapel on the highest ridge of the cemetery. Renwick's chapel was listed in the National Register of Historic Places in 1972.

Oakdale Cemetery, Wilmington, North Carolina

Oakdale Cemetery was founded in 1852 as the first municipal burial ground in Wilmington, North Carolina. The sixty-five-acre site chosen for the cemetery was five blocks beyond the town limits on the east side of Burnt Mill Creek. The grounds offered picturesque topography, streams, and native vegetation including dogwoods, magnolias, and oak trees. Surveyor Louis C. Turner, who laid out sections A through H, added a maze of winding drives to the hilly site. He generally depressed the drives within the landscape, while raising the burial plots, which were often encircled by masonry walls. Elaborate monuments, iron fencing, and benches were also added to the site over time. In 1867, the Ladies' Memorial Association was given charge of section K for the interment of Confederate veterans, the reinterment of unknown soldiers, and the construction of the Confederate Memorial Monument upon the crown of a hill. The cemetery, which has grown to encompass 165 acres, is now a privately funded and managed organization. www.oakdalecemetery.org.

Oakwood Cemetery, Syracuse, New York

In 1859, a group of prominent citizens in Syracuse, New York, purchased ninety-two acres of land approximately a mile-and-a-half from the city's central business district to establish a rural cemetery. The elevated land they chose for the site overlooked both the city and Onondaga Lake and comprised rounded hillocks, sweeping slopes, wide valleys, deep ravines, and a natural spring. Originally, the acreage was covered with an oak forest, interspersed with a few pine, ash, maple, and hickory trees. The board of trustees soon hired Howard Daniels, a New York City landscape gardener, to lay out the grounds. He added rare varieties of nonnative trees and plants as well as curvilinear drives to reveal open views at each turn. These controlled internal scenes were enhanced over time with elaborately carved monuments and mausoleums of granite and marble. The cemetery was dedicated in 1859; many schools and public offices were closed for the occasion so members of the community could attend the ceremony. Today, Oakwood Cemetery encompasses 160 acres. It was listed in the National Register of Historic Places in 1998. www.shadesofoakwood.com.

Oakwood Cemetery, Troy, New York

Oakwood Cemetery was founded in 1848 northeast of Troy, New York, on undulating terrain that rose steeply toward its northern boundary and afforded spectacular views of the city, the Hudson River, and the Catskill Mountains. James C. Sidney, a Philadelphia architect and engineer, was employed to design the grounds. He laid out broad avenues and smaller footpaths that wound their way through the site and divided the land into irregular sections. He created conifer groves and picturesque ponds by damning mountain streams. Over time, twenty-four mausoleums in the Greek Revival–, Egyptian Revival–, and Gothic Revival–styles were built throughout the cemetery. From 1871 to 1898, John Boetcher, who had studied under acclaimed landscape gardener Adolph Strauch, acted as the cemetery's superintendent. Boetcher is credited with much of the work that beautified the grounds including the addition of numerous exotic specimens to the site. Oakwood Cemetery was listed in the National Register of Historic Places in 1984. www.oakwoodcemetery.org.

Oconee Hill Cemetery, Athens, Georgia

Oconee Hill Cemetery, established in 1855 on seventeen acres along the North Oconee River in Athens, Georgia, was the successor to the Old Athens Cemetery, which had become gravely overcrowded by that time. The City of Athens established the new public cemetery—which was initially open to all races and classes—and later created a self-perpetuating board of trustees to manage its operations. The original sections of the cemetery, known as West Hill and East Hill, were laid out in 1856 in the tradition of the rural cemetery movement by James Camak, editor of the *Southern Cultivator*. In his scheme, he juxtaposed stands of trees against sweeping vistas. Over time, clearly delineated family plots incorporated sculptural monuments of granite or marble. Numerous war veterans were also interred here; graves of Confederate veterans were often marked by iron crosses. In 1898, as the original acreage was becoming crowded, the trustees purchased an additional ninety acres across the river to extend the life of the cemetery. http://oconeehillcemetery.com.

Pittsfield Rural Cemetery, Pittsfield, Massachusetts

Pittsfield Rural Cemetery was founded in 1850 on 130 acres of land approximately one mile northwest of the village of Pittsfield, Massachusetts. The land was purchased by the city to address concerns regarding overcrowded urban burial grounds. The city subsequently sold the acreage to a private, nonprofit organization for one dollar to develop it. The site chosen for the cemetery was varied with wooded knolls, broad lawns, and a small stream winding through the landscape. Beech, elm, hemlock, maple, mountain ash, oak, pine, spruce, and willow trees shaded the site. Horatio Stone of New York was hired to design the cemetery and afterward act as its superintendent. Stone laid out roadways that meandered through the contoured grounds and divided the burial sections into irregularly shaped spaces. Within each family's burial plot, a central monument was typically erected, with smaller gravestones encircling it and marking the plots of individual family members. Climbing roses, creeping ivy, flowering alder, and mountain laurel were often chosen to embellish the gravesites. Pittsfield Rural was listed in the National Register of Historic Places in 2007.

Riverside Cemetery, Oswego, New York

Riverside Cemetery was established in 1855 by the Oswego Rural Cemetery Association on 140 acres of hilly terrain about one-half mile south of Oswego, New York. The cemetery was designed by New York surveyor and landscape gardener Burton A. Thomas. In his plan, Thomas preserved distinct wooded areas, added strategically placed groupings of trees in open spaces, and thinned out vegetation in other sections. He did this to provide both striking internal views of two man-made lakes on the site and dramatic external views of the nearby Oswego River from the curvilinear roadways and footpaths he laid out. Thomas used primarily species indigenous to the site to create his framed views and lined many of the main roadways with maple, beech, oak, and cedar trees. The small stone Gothic Revival–style chapel on a knoll near the main entrance was a later addition designed by Pennsylvania architect Fielding Mantel; it was completed in 1906. Riverside Cemetery, which now encompasses approximately 112 acres, was listed in the National Register of Historic Places in 1993.

Riverside Cemetery, Waterbury, Connecticut

Riverside Cemetery was established in 1850 on approximately thirty-one acres of land one-half mile southwest of the city center of Waterbury, Connecticut. Located on the west bank of the Naugatuck River, the chosen cemetery site featured rolling topography with four primary hills, the highest of which rose over one hundred feet above the river below. A small, spring-fed stream ran through the center of the site. Willow and Fountain Ponds were later created from its water. New York architect and landscape gardener Howard Daniels was employed to design the layout of the site; work to implement his plan began

under the direction of Bridgeport landscape gardener John North in 1852. Narrow avenues were arranged to respect the site's existing topography, curve through the wooded landscape, and reveal picturesque vistas at strategic locations. Over subsequent years, the cemetery's monuments were arranged in varying patterns in response to the layout of adjacent roadways. Between 1884 and 1885, Hall Memorial Chapel—an irregularly massed, granite structure designed by architect Robert W. Hall in the late Victorian Gothic style —was built. Riverside Cemetery was listed in the National Register of Historic Places in 1988.

Rockland Cemetery, Sparkill, New York

Rockland Cemetery was established in 1847 on a gentle mountain slope adjacent to Sparkill, New York, near the Hudson River. The slanting site was chosen, in part, to protect it in perpetuity from the incursion of the modern railroad. From the site's highest elevations, visitors could see surrounding countryside thirty miles away or more. The cemetery's land was varied, with open dells, shaded niches, small valleys, and stands of cedars, elms, hemlocks, maples, oaks, and pines. To create winding avenues, numerous cedar trees were removed; however, the wood from the trees was reused to construct rustic gateways, arbors, and seats throughout the cemetery. Over time, burial plots were embellished with multiple monuments and enclosed by fences. New cemetery rules in 1881, however, prevented the construction of enclosures and the placement of more than one monument per lot in the newer sections of the cemetery.

Rose Hill Cemetery, Macon, Georgia

Founded in 1840, Rose Hill Cemetery is located north of the city of Macon, Georgia, on elevated land adjacent to the rocky banks of the Ocmulgee River. Simri Rose, a well-known Macon newspaper editor and horticulturist, designed the layout of the fifty-acre site and included a wide avenue stretching from the gated archway at the entrance to the rocky bluffs near the river. Meanwhile, he planned carriage drives that twisted around hills and valleys to provide striking views of the surrounding scenery. Two rustic, rocky bridges were built to span the deep, narrow dell that divided the grounds almost in half. Rose also supervised the planting of rare and exotic specimens, such as oriental cypress, to complement native species already on the site. Both elaborate and simple monuments were set against this Picturesque landscape over time. Meanwhile, distinct family plots were often encompassed by brick enclosures or iron fences. Rose Hill Cemetery was listed in the National Register of Historic Places in 1973. http://rosehill cemetery.org.

New Bedford Rural Cemetery, New Bedford, Massachusetts

In 1832, just one year after the establishment of Mount Auburn Cemetery, Timothy I. Dyre purchased land west of New Bedford, Massachusetts, for the eventual establishment of a rural cemetery. Dyre began clearing and laying out the site himself, but was later joined in the effort by local land surveyor Henry Howland Crapo. New Bedford's Rural Cemetery was incorporated in 1837. Dyre endeavored to emulate Mount Auburn. However, his project was influenced by earlier burial ground models; he had chosen, for instance, a flat parcel of land for the site and laid out the roadways on a grid pattern. Over time, the site became gradually more picturesque with the addition of varied headstones of marble and granite. In 1848, the proprietors of Rural Cemetery deeded the site to the City of New Bedford, which in 1868 acquired seventy acres of land adjacent to the site to substantially expand the cemetery. Curvilinear roadways, a pond, and picturesque groupings of trees were incorporated into this section, reflecting more closely the rural cemetery ideal. Today, New Bedford Rural Cemetery encompasses approximately ninety-two acres.

Sleepy Hollow Cemetery, Concord, Massachusetts

Designed by H. W. S. Cleveland and Robert Copeland and dedicated in 1855, Sleepy Hollow Cemetery was established on twenty-five acres of secluded land in Concord, Massachusetts. Cleveland and Copeland, who were paid $75 for their work, laid out the cemetery's walks and avenues to conform to the site's natural amphitheater. They also purposely left much of the site's native vegetation in place to create a picturesque effect with familiar trees and shrubs. Cleveland also provided the specifications for Cat's Pond, which was completed in 1860. Over the years, the memorials added to the grounds served to emphasize the site's natural advantages. For instance, Authors Ridge was established on the highest hill in the cemetery, where the graves of Henry David Thoreau, Louise May Alcott, Ralph Waldo Emerson, and other literary notables were marked by modest headstones. Sleepy Hollow Cemetery was listed in the National Register of Historic Places in 1998.

Sleepy Hollow Cemetery, Tarrytown, New York

Washington Irving (1783–1859), the author of *The Legend of Sleepy Hollow* (1820), was a vocal advocate for the establishment of a rural cemetery adjacent to Tarrytown's Old Dutch Burying Ground, which had been featured in Irving's legendary story but had since become overcrowded.

In 1849, Sleepy Hollow Cemetery was founded as Tarrytown Cemetery on undulating land adjoining the old burial place. The acreage, not far removed from the Hudson River, encompassed woody hills and part of the Pocantico River. Roadways were laid out through the site to snake around hills and gently curve through glens. The thoroughfares also divided the cemetery into marketable sections that were named to evoke sylvan imagery: Woodland Hill, Forest Shade, Shady Dell, and Mount Hope. Meanwhile, other sections were named to highlight the area's heritage: Irving Ridge, Hudson Hill, Battle Hill, and Tarry Grove. The cemetery was renamed Sleepy Hollow five years after Irving's death, and in 1922, the Washington Irving Memorial Chapel was built, which included stained glass windows depicting the author and scenes from his famous short story. http://sleepyhollowcemetery.org.

Spring Grove Cemetery, Cincinnati, Ohio

After having been granted a charter in 1845, the Proprietors of the Cemetery of Spring Grove purchased 166 acres of farmland outside of Cincinnati, Ohio, for a new cemetery. Spring Grove was initially designed based on the traditional rural cemetery aesthetic by architect and landscape gardener Howard Daniels with the aid of surveyor Thomas Earnshaw. However, in October of 1854, Adolph Strauch was appointed the cemetery's landscape gardener and was eventually given the authority to implement what became known as the landscape lawn plan. He convinced the cemetery's directors that his plan would rectify the problems inherent in traditional rural cemeteries, which, he argued, had become cluttered with "useless appendages." He urged the removal of cast iron fences, concrete curbing, and frivolous ornamentation from individual lots. He also instituted a policy that restricted all future gravestones to a height of only a few inches above the grass and allowed only one major monument to occupy the center of a family lot. Moreover, Strauch refused to plant flower beds on common grounds because he felt they distracted from the unity of the naturalistic landscape he was striving to create—one that featured large expanses of lawns and carefully sited groves of trees. As a result of Strauch's principles, Spring Grove became a less cluttered, more cohesive landscape. It was named a National Historic Landmark in 2007. www.springgrove.org.

Swan Point Cemetery, Providence, Rhode Island

Swan Point Cemetery was founded in 1846 in Providence, Rhode Island, on sixty acres of land overlooking the Seekonk River—a landscape where the steep banks along the waterway provided a striking contrast to the rolling topography of the surrounding countryside. Niles Bierragaard Schubarth designed the cemetery's initial acreage. He laid out winding avenues and pathways that crossed ridges and snaked through valleys and woodland. He also planted specimen trees and flowering shrubs such as laurels, rhododendrons, and azaleas to showcase and enhance the natural contours of the land. Over time, spaciously placed monuments were added to the cemetery, while most of the site's mausoleums were sited to encircle the Rock Pond, which was added to the grounds in the late nineteenth century. In 1899, large granite boulders were gathered from the grounds and arranged naturalistically to create a dignified and impressive main entrance on Blackstone Boulevard. Swan Point Cemetery, which has grown to encompass two hundred acres, was listed in the National Register of Historic Places in 1977. http://swanpoint cemetery.com.

Upper Middleburgh Cemetery, Middleburgh, New York

In 1865, the Middleburgh Cemetery Association acquired approximately sixteen acres of land about one mile southeast of the historic center of Middleburgh, New York, for the purpose of establishing a public cemetery. The "Upper Cemetery" was established on a steep hillside overlooking the village with striking views of Onistagrawan Mountain to the west and Schoharie Valley to the north and to the south. The entrance to the cemetery was sited at the center of the base of the hillside. The site was divided into ten distinct sections by unpaved carriage roads that followed the contours of the land. Over time, a range of funerary art—from simple, uninscribed slabs to ornate monuments and mausoleums featuring popular period motifs—was added to the terraced landscape. The cemetery also features ornamental plantings, including arborvitae, throughout. Upper Middleburgh Cemetery, which now encompasses twenty-one acres, was listed in the National Register of Historic Places in 2003.

Vale Cemetery, Schenectady, New York

Vale Cemetery was founded in 1857 on the outskirts of Schenectady, New York, on the former farm of Nott Terrace. City government had spearheaded the establishment of the new public cemetery, but by 1858, the city abandoned the project and deeded the thirty-eight-acre site to the Vale Cemetery Association, a private organization created by fourteen lot holders. The grounds were subsequently designed by surveyor and landscape gardener Burton A. Thomas, who laid out winding pathways throughout the site, and landscape gardener John Doyle, who directed the planting of over a thousand trees. Those that lined the main entrance from State Street became known as the Cathedral of Trees. A superintendent's house was built within the State Street entrance between 1889 and 1890 by Odgen and Wright, well-known architects from Albany. In addition, Cowhorn Creek, a large stream that ran through the site, was damned to create a lake within the cemetery grounds. Vale Cemetery, which now encompasses one hundred acres in the heart of Schenectady, was listed in the National Register of Historic Places in 2004.

West Laurel Hill Cemetery, Bala Cynwyd, Pennsylvania

West Laurel Hill Cemetery was incorporated in 1869 as a nonprofit, nondenominational cemetery outside of Philadelphia, Pennsylvania. When the three-decade-old Laurel Hill Cemetery no longer had room to expand its boundaries, John Jay Smith and other members of its board of directors purchased 150 acres of land on the west side of the Schuylkill River for the establishment of a new cemetery—West Laurel Hill. The site chosen for the new burial ground was situated on a plateau between two deep ravines to the north and south. Over time, beautifully carved monuments and imposing mausoleums were placed within the sylvan setting, which included sugar maples, red oaks, ginkgos, Japanese white pines, weeping white pines, and purple European beeches. In 1886, a Gothic Revival–style bell tower was designed by Walter Cope and John Stewardson to stand atop the highest point of the site. West Laurel Hill Cemetery, which now encompasses 187 acres, was listed in the National Register of Historic Places in 1992. www.forever-care.com.

White Plains Rural Cemetery, White Plains, New York

White Plains Rural Cemetery was established in 1854 on about thirty-five acres of undulating land near the northern boundary of the city of White Plains, New York. An eighteenth-century Methodist Meeting House and adjacent graveyard at the southeastern corner of the property were incorporated into the new public, nondenominational cemetery. The meeting house later became the cemetery's office building. John F. Jenkins, a little-known surveyor and civil engineer, laid out the site including several miles of narrow, winding roads that divided the burial sections into irregularly shaped spaces. The sections were given romantic names, a common practice in rural cemeteries at the time. In addition, both native and exotic species of trees were planted; today, pines, spruces, lindens, catalpas, cedars, beeches, Japanese maples, weeping cherries, and dogwoods can be seen throughout the grounds. White Plains Rural Cemetery, which now encompasses twenty-six acres (the cemetery sold nearly ten acres of undeveloped land to the New York and Harlem Railroad in 1906), was listed in the National Register of Historic Places in 2003. www.whiteplainsruralcemetery.com.

Wildwood Cemetery, Winchester, Massachusetts

In 1851, the City of Winchester, Massachusetts, purchased a ten-acre site for the purpose of establishing a cemetery. The graveyard that the town owned in conjunction with the First Congregational Church was no longer adequate for Winchester's burial needs. The site chosen for the new cemetery was adjacent to Wedge Pond, contained a large hill covered with pine trees, and exhibited varied topography, thus affording striking views and vistas. Amasa Farrier, the town surveyor of nearby Stoneham, Massachusetts, was employed to lay out the site. He created winding roadways and footpaths and added numerous ornamental trees to enhance the inherent picturesque qualities of the site. Wildwood Cemetery, which now encompasses approximately seventy acres, was added to the National Register of Historic Places in 1989.

The Woodlands Cemetery, Philadelphia, Pennsylvania

In 1840, the Woodlands Cemetery Company purchased approximately ninety-two acres of land west of Philadelphia, Pennsylvania, along the Schuylkill River for the establishment of a rural cemetery. The land had belonged to the distinguished botanist and plant collector William Hamilton and still retained Hamilton's famous late-eighteenth-century, Neo-classical mansion. In the early 1840s, surveyor Philip M. Price designed the overall layout of the cemetery, including the major serpentine roadways. Meanwhile, his brother Eli Price, a prominent lawyer, employed his horticultural knowledge to establish a planting plan that was both appropriate for the site's new use and respectful of the rich landscape legacy left by Hamilton. Price saved as many of the original plantings as possible, while adding species such as cedar and balm of Gilead to create screens along roadways and boundary lines to foster a sense of enclosure and privacy in cemetery lots. The Woodlands—which now encompasses approximately fifty-four acres and includes the cemetery as well as Hamilton's original mansion—is a National Historic Landmark.

Woodlawn Cemetery, Bronx, New York

The Woodlawn Cemetery was founded in 1863 on 313 acres of the Bussing family farm in the Bronx, New York. The Reverend Absalom Peters, who had gathered together eight prominent New Yorkers to finance the purchase and development of the new rural cemetery, likely selected its site—land straddling the crest separating the watersheds of the Hudson and Bronx Rivers. The cemetery was initially designed by Philadelphia architect James C. Sidney following the Picturesque style characteristic of the early rural cemetery movement. Notably, Sidney added an astonishing variety of native and exotic trees to the site; today, the cemetery is also considered an arboretum and bird sanctuary. As the 1860s progressed, however, the Woodlawn Trustees elected to emulate the design aesthetic implemented by Adolph Strauch at the Cemetery of Spring Grove, which was growing increasingly popular. Today, Woodlawn is particularly well-known for its impressive diversity of cemetery art and sculpture, including ornately carved mausoleums belonging to some of New York's most famous former citizens. Woodlawn Cemetery, which now encompasses four hundred acres, was designated a National Historic Landmark in 2011. www.the woodlawncemetery.org.

Woodlawn Cemetery, Elmira, New York

Woodlawn Cemetery was established in 1858 on a natural ridge overlooking the city of Elmira, New York. The cemetery's original fifty acres incorporated design elements typical of the rural cemetery movement including curvilinear roadways that showcased scenic vistas as strategic points. Well-placed trees and plantings added to the picturesque quality of the site by framing stunning views and creating enclosures around glens and dells. Meanwhile, family plots were often delineated by decorative ironwork fencing and granite curbing. The cemetery's two entrance gateways of rusticated stone and ornamental ironwork were designed in 1890 by the local architectural firm of Pierce and Bickford. The firm also designed the Gothic Revival–style mortuary chapel near the Walnut Street entrance in 1905. Woodlawn Cemetery, which now encompasses approximately 104 acres, was listed in the National Register of Historic Places in 2004. www.friendsofwoodlawnelmira.org.

APPENDIX C

Select Rural Cemeteries by Name, Date, and State

In 1849, Andrew Jackson Downing noted that "at the present moment, there is scarcely a city of note in the whole country that has not its rural cemetery." During the middle part of the nineteenth century, hundreds of rural cemeteries were founded in the United States, particularly in the Northeast. The following list of 175 examples is by no means a comprehensive list of those established during the rural cemetery movement. It is a list of those identified by the authors by consulting the National Register of Historic Places, state historic resource survey records (particularly for Massachusetts), and both historic and contemporary published sources. In short, it is a list of rural cemeteries for which ample documentation was found. The list includes many more examples than the ones chosen for examination in the main narrative and in Appendix B; it is meant to help illuminate the prevalence of the landscape type.

CEMETERIES BY NAME

Cemetery Name	City	State	Year	Designer, if known	Acreage, Original if known	National Register listed?
Albany Rural	Menands	N.Y.	1841	David Bates Douglass	240	Yes
Allegheny	Pittsburgh	Pa.	1844	John Chislett, Sr. (later altered by William Falconer)	100	Yes
Bay View–New York Bay	Jersey City	N.J.	1850			
Bayside	Potsdam	N.Y.	1865	L. R. Briggs and H. T. Whitman	21	Yes
Beechwoods	New Rochelle	N.Y.	1854			
Bellefontaine	St. Louis	Mo.	1849	Almerin Hotchkiss	138	
Bellevue	Lawrence	Mass.	1847	John M. Smith	5	Yes
Bonaventure	Savannah	Ga.	1849	James Henry Rion; John Postell (1869)	70	Yes
Brookside	Watertown	N.Y.	1853	Howard Daniels		
Calvary	Queens	N.Y.	1848			
Cave Hill	Louisville	Ky.	1848	Edmund Francis Lee; David Ross	47	Yes
Cedar Grove	New London	Conn.	1851	Horatio Stone	39	
Chester Rural	Chester	Pa.	1863		36	
Chippiannock	Rock Island	Ill.	1855	Almerin Hotchkiss	62	Yes
Clinton	Clinton	N.Y.	1856			
Cortland Rural	Cortland	N.Y.	1853		12	
Cypress Hills	Brooklyn	N.Y.	1848		25	Yes
Dale	Ossining	N.Y.	1851	Howard Daniels		
Easton	Easton	Pa.	1849	James C. Sidney	34	Yes
Edgell Grove	Framingham	Mass.	1846	Henry A. S. Dearborn	10	
Elm Grove	Mystic	Conn.	1853	Niles Bierragaard Schubarth	22	
Elmwood	Charlotte	N.C.	1853			

Cemetery Name	City	State	Year	Designer, if known	Acreage, Original if known	National Register listed?
Elmwood	Columbia	S.C.	1854		200	Yes
Elmwood	Detroit	Mich.	1849		42	
Elmwood	Memphis	Tenn.	1852		40	Yes
Elmwood	Norfolk	Va.	1853			
Erie	Erie	Pa.	1851	Capt. Samuel Low & Howard Daniels	75	
Evergreen	Brighton	Mass.	1850		14	
Evergreen	Camden	N.J.	1848			
Evergreen	Hillside	N.J.	1853			Yes
Evergreen	New Haven	Conn.	1848			
Evergreen	Oswego	N.Y.	1851	Stephen Dexter	11.2	Yes
Evergreen	Portland	Maine	1854	Charles H. Howe	55	Yes
Evergreen	Rutland	Vt.	1861			
Evergreens	Brooklyn	N.Y.	1849	Andrew Jackson Downing (rural architect and landscape gardener); Alexander Jackson Davis (architect)	183.5	Yes
Fair View	Red Bank	N.J.	1855	Ezra A. Osborn (surveyor)		
Fairmount	Newark	N.J.	1855		60	
Fishkill Rural	Fishkill	N.Y.	1866		27	
Forest Hill	Utica	N.Y.	1850	Almerin Hotchkiss		
Forest Hills	Boston	Mass.	1848	Henry A. S. Dearborn	56	Yes
Forest Home	Milwaukee	Wis.	1850	Increase Lapham (surveyor); George West	72	Yes
Forest Lawn	Buffalo	N.Y.	1849	Charles E. Clark	80	Yes
Fort Hill	Auburn	N.Y.	1851		22	
Frankfort	Frankfort	Ky.	1844	Robert Carmichael	32	Yes
Georgetown	Georgetown	Ky.	1850		30	
Glendale	Akron	Ohio	1839			Yes
Glenwood	Houston	Tex.	1871			
Glenwood	Washington	D.C.	1854			Chapel only
Graceland	Chicago	Ill.	1860	Swain Nelson & William Sanders (1860); H. W. S. Cleveland (1870); William LeBaron Jenney & O. C. Simonds (1878)	86	Yes
Green Hill	Amsterdam	N.Y.	1858	Burton A. Thomas (surveyor)	15	Yes
Green Lawn	Columbus	Ohio	1848	Howard Daniels	83	
Green Mount	Baltimore	Md.	1838	Robert Cary Long Jr. (architect); Benjamin Henry Latrobe Jr.	~60	Yes
Green Mount	Montpelier	Vt.	1854			
Green River	Greenfield	Mass.	1851	Albert R. Field		
Green-Wood	Brooklyn	N.Y.	1838	David Bates Douglass (engineer); Richard Upjohn (architect); Almerin Hotchkiss (superintendent)	175	Yes—National Historic Landmark
Greenwood	Hamilton	Ohio	1848	Adolph Strauch (later design)		Yes
Harmony Grove	Salem	Mass.	1839	Alexander Wadsworth	35	
Harrisburg	Harrisburg	Pa.	1845			Yes
Hazelwood	Rahway	N.J.	1859	William Saunders	40	

Cemetery Name	City	State	Year	Designer, if known	Acreage, Original if known	National Register listed?
Hillside	Middletown	N.Y.	1860	Calvert Vaux	50	Yes
Hollywood	Richmond	Va.	1847	John Notman (with assistance from Heinrich Adolph Engelhardt)	42	Yes
Holyhood	Brookline	Mass.	1857		31	Yes
Hope	Worcester	Mass.	1852	Gill Valentine	50	Yes
Huntington Rural	Huntington	N.Y.	1851		10	
Indian Hill	Middletown	Conn.	1850			
Island	Newport	R.I.	1848			Yes
Ivy Hill	Philadelphia	Pa.	1867			
Juniper Hill	Bristol	R.I.	1857	Niles Bierragaard Schubarth	22	Yes
Lake Forest	Lake Forest	Ill.	1857	Samuel F. Miller; A. M. Hirsch; later, William LeBaron Jenney; then O. C. Simonds	32	Yes
Lakewood	Cooperstown	N.Y.	1856			
Laurel Grove North	Savannah	Ga.	1850	James Otis Morse; Sholl & Fay		Yes
Laurel Grove South	Savannah	Ga.	1850	James Otis Morse; William George		Yes
Laurel Hill	Philadelphia	Pa.	1836	John Notman (later addition by civil engineer James C. Sidney and architect James P. W. Neff)	20	Yes—National Historic Landmark
Lexington	Lexington	Ky.	1848	Charles S. Bell & John Lutz	40	Yes
Linden Grove	Covington	Ky.	1843	Ephraim Robbins (superintendent)	21	Yes
Lone Mountain (later Laurel Hill)	San Francisco	Calif.	1853			54
Loudon Park	Baltimore	Md.	1853		100	
Lowell	Lowell	Mass.	1841	George P. Worcester		Yes
Lutheran (later All Faiths) (Queens)	Middle Village	N.Y.	1850		225	
Machpelah	LeRoy	N.Y.	1858	George Blodgett	8	Yes
Machpelah	Mount Sterling	Ky.	1855			Yes
Magnolia	Charleston	S.C.	1850	Edward C. Jones	92	Yes
Mount Adnah	Fulton	N.Y.	1851	Moses Lindley Lee & Peter Schenck; John Hopkins Shepard	36	Yes
Mount Albion	Albion	N.Y.	1842	Marvin Porter	25	Yes
Mount Auburn	Cambridge	Mass.	1831	Henry A. S. Dearborn, Alexander Wadsworth, and Jacob Bigelow	72	Yes—National Historic Landmark
Mount Feake	Waltham	Mass.	1857	Robert Morris Copeland	46	Yes
Mount Hope	Bangor	Maine	1834	Charles G. Bryant	50	Yes
Mount Hope	Dorchester/ Boston	Mass.	1852	David Haggerston	85	Yes
Mount Hope	Rochester	N.Y.	1838	John McConnell; Silas Cornell (surveyor)	50	
Mount Moriah	Philadelphia	Pa.	1855		54	
Mount Olivet	Hanover	Pa.	1859	Joseph S. Gitt	15	
Mount Olivet	Nashville	Tenn.	1856			Yes
Mount Pleasant	Newark	N.J.	1844			Yes
Mount Pleasant	Taunton	Mass.	1836	Joseph Wilbar	10	
Mount Vernon	Philadelphia	Pa.	1856			
Mount Wollaston	Quincy	Mass.	1855	Daniel Brims & Luther Briggs	25	Yes

Cemetery Name	City	State	Year	Designer, if known	Acreage, Original if known	National Register listed?
Mountain Grove	Bridgeport	Conn.	1849	Phineas Taylor "P. T." Barnum		
Mountain View	Oakland	Calif.	1863	Frederick Law Olmsted; Calvert Vaux; Edward C. Miller (civil engineer)	200	
Myrtle Hill	Rome	Ga.	1857	Cunningham Pennington	29	Yes
New Bedford Rural	New Bedford	Mass.	1837	Timothy I. Dyre & Henry Howland Crapo	7	
New Paltz Rural	New Paltz	N.Y.	1861		20	
Newton	Newton	Mass.	1855			
Oak Grove	Fall River	Mass.	1855	Josiah Brown	47	Yes
Oak Grove	Gloucester	Mass.	1855	H. W. S. Cleveland; Robert Copeland		Yes
Oak Hill	Birmingham	Ala.	1873		21.5	Yes
Oak Hill	Cedar Rapids	Iowa	1854	H. W. S. Cleveland		
Oak Hill	Evansville	Ind.	1852	John S. Goodge	56	Yes
Oak Hill	Newburyport	Mass.	1842		4.5	Yes
Oak Hill	Washington	D.C.	1849	Capt. George F. de la Roche & possibly A. J. Downing	15	Chapel only
Oak Hill	Woonsocket	R.I.	1856	Niles Bierragaard Schubarth		
Oak Ridge	Springfield	Ill.	1855	Williams Saunders	29	Yes
Oakdale	Wilmington	N.C.	1852	Louis C. Turner	65	
Oakland	St. Paul	Minn.	1853	(later design by H. W. S. Cleveland in the 1870s)	40	
Oakland	Yonkers	N.Y.	1866			
Oaklands	West Chester	Pa.	1854	Sidney & Neff	22	
Oakwood	Niagara Falls	N.Y.	1852	T. D. Judah		
Oakwood	Raleigh	N.C.	1869	Heinrich Adolph Englehardt		Yes—part of a district
Oakwood	Syracuse	N.Y.	1859	Howard Daniels	92	Yes
Oakwood	Troy	N.Y.	1848	J. C. Sidney	150	Yes
Oconee Hill	Athens	Ga.	1855	James Camak	17	
Old Gray	Knoxville	Tenn.	1850	Frederick Douglass	8	Yes
Paris	Paris	Ky.	1847			Gatehouse only
Pine Grove	Lynn	Mass.	1850	Henry A. S. Dearborn		
Pine Grove	Waterville	Maine	1851			
Pittsfield Rural	Pittsfield	Mass.	1850	Horatio Stone	132	Yes
Poughkeepsie Rural	Poughkeepsie	N.Y.	1853	Howard Daniels	54	
Prospect Hill	York	Pa.	1849			
River Bend	Westerly	R.I.	1849	Niles Bierragaard Schubarth		
Riverside	Oswego	N.Y.	1855	Burton A. Thomas	140	Yes
Riverside	Waterbury	Conn.	1850	Howard Daniels & John North	31	Yes
Rockland	Sparkill	N.Y.	1847			
Rome Rural	Rome	N.Y.	1851	Howard Daniels	25	
Rose Hill	Macon	Ga.	1840	Simri Rose	50	Yes
Rosehill	Chicago	Ill.	1859	Williams Saunders		Adm. Bldg. & Gate only
Rural	Johnstown	N.Y.	1849			
Rural	Southborough	Mass.	1842			
Salem Fields	Brooklyn	N.Y.	1850			

Cemetery Name	City	State	Year	Designer, if known	Acreage, Original if known	National Register listed?
Santa Rosa Rural	Santa Rosa	Calif.	1867			17
Sleepy Hollow	Concord	Mass.	1855	H. W. S. Cleveland & Robert Morris Copeland	25	Yes
Sleepy Hollow	Tarrytown	N.Y.	1849			
Spring Forest	Binghamton	N.Y.	1853	Howard Daniels		
Spring Grove	Cincinnati	Ohio	1845	Howard Daniels & Thomas Earnshaw; later altered by Adolph Strauch	166	Yes–National Historic Landmark
Spring Grove	Hartford	Conn.	1845		55	
Spring Hill	Charleston	W.Va.	1869	A. J. Vosburg (civil engineer)	20	Yes–part of a district
Spring Hill	Danville	Ill.	1864	Alexander Bowman	50	
Spring Hill	Harrodsburg	Ky.	1849			
Spring Hill	Lynchburg	Va.	1855	John Notman		
Springdale	Peoria	Ill.	1855			Yes
Swan Point	Providence	R.I.	1846	Niles Bierragaard Schubarth	60	Yes
Union	Kansas City	Mo.	1858		40	
Union	Steubenville	Ohio	1854			Yes
Union Dale	Pittsburgh	Pa.	1846		10	
Upper Middleburgh	Middleburgh	N.Y.	1865		16	Yes
Vale	Schenectady	N.Y.	1857	Burton A. Thomas (surveyor); John Doyle (landscape gardener)	38	Yes
Valley	Manchester	N.H.	1840		20	
Walnut Grove	Boonville	Mo.	1852			
Walnut Grove	Danvers	Mass.	1844			
Weedsport Rural	Weedsport	N.Y.	1860	Burton A. Thomas	8.75	
West Laurel Hill	Bala Cynwyd	Pa.	1869	John Jay Smith	150	Yes
Westwood	Oberlin	Ohio	1861	H. B. Allen	27.5	
White Plains Rural	White Plains	N.Y.	1854	John F. Jenkins (surveyor & engineer)	36	Yes
Wildwood	Winchester	Mass.	1851	Amasa Farrier	10	Yes
Wiltwyck Rural	Kingston	N.Y.	1850			
Woodland	Cleveland	Ohio	1853	Howard Daniels		Yes
Woodland	Dayton	Ohio	1841		40	Gate, chapel, office only
Woodland	Stamford	Conn.	1859			Yes
Woodland	Xenia	Ohio	1845	Howard Daniels		
Woodlands	Cambridge	N.Y.	1858	J. C. Sidney	15	
Woodlands	Philadelphia	Pa.	1840	Philip M. Price	92	Yes-part of National Historic Landmark district
Woodlawn	Bronx	N.Y.	1863	James C. Sidney	313	
Woodlawn	Chelsea	Mass.	1851	H. Weld Fuller	100	
Woodlawn	Elmira	N.Y.	1858	"Mr. Daniels"	50	Yes
Woodward Hill	Lancaster	Pa.	ca. 1850		Yes	
Worcester Rural	Worcester	Mass.	1838	James Barnes (topographical survey & plan); C. H. Hill (lot layout)	24	
Wyoming	Melrose	Mass.	1857		21	

Year	Cemetery Name	City	State
1831	Mount Auburn	Cambridge	Mass.
1834	Mount Hope	Bangor	Maine
1836	Laurel Hill	Philadelphia	Pa.
1836	Mount Pleasant	Taunton	Mass.
1837	New Bedford Rural	New Bedford	Mass.
1838	Green Mount	Baltimore	Md.
1838	Green-Wood	Brooklyn	N.Y.
1838	Mount Hope	Rochester	N.Y.
1838	Worcester Rural	Worcester	Mass.
1839	Glendale	Akron	Ohio
1839	Harmony Grove	Salem	Mass.
1840	Rose Hill	Macon	Ga.
1840	Valley	Manchester	N.H.
1840	Woodlands	Philadelphia	Pa.
1841	Albany Rural	Menands	N.Y.
1841	Lowell	Lowell	Mass.
1841	Woodland	Dayton	Ohio
1842	Mount Albion	Albion	N.Y.
1842	Oak Hill	Newburyport	Mass.
1842	Rural	Southborough	Mass.
1843	Linden Grove	Covington	Ky.
1844	Allegheny	Pittsburgh	Pa.
1844	Frankfort	Frankfort	Ky.
1844	Mount Pleasant	Newark	N.J.
1844	Spring Grove	Cincinnati	Ohio
1844	Walnut Grove	Danvers	Mass.
1845	Harrisburg	Harrisburg	Pa.
1845	Spring Grove	Hartford	Conn.
1845	Woodland	Xenia	Ohio
1846	Edgell Grove	Framingham	Mass.
1846	Swan Point	Providence	R.I.
1846	Union Dale	Pittsburgh	Pa.
1847	Bellevue	Lawrence	Mass.
1847	Hollywood	Richmond	Va.
1847	Paris	Paris	Ky.
1847	Rockland	Sparkill	N.Y.
1848	Calvary	Queens	N.Y.
1848	Cave Hill	Louisville	Ky.
1848	Cypress Hills	Brooklyn	N.Y.
1848	Evergreen	Brighton	Mass.
1848	Evergreen	Camden	N.J.
1848	Evergreen	New Haven	Conn.
1848	Forest Hills	Boston	Mass.
1848	Green Lawn	Columbus	Ohio
1848	Greenwood	Hamilton	Ohio
1848	Island	Newport	R.I.

Year	Cemetery Name	City	State
1848	Lexington	Lexington	Ky.
1848	Oakwood	Troy	N.Y.
1849	Bellefontaine	St. Louis	Mo.
1849	Bonaventure	Savannah	Ga.
1849	Easton	Easton	Pa.
1849	Elmwood	Detroit	Mich.
1849	Evergreens	Brooklyn	N.Y.
1849	Forest Lawn	Buffalo	N.Y.
1849	Mountain Grove	Bridgeport	Conn.
1849	Oak Hill	Washington	D. C.
1849	Prospect Hill	York	Pa.
1849	River Bend	Westerly	R.I.
1849	Rural	Johnstown	N.Y.
1849	Sleepy Hollow	Tarrytown	N.Y.
1849	Spring Hill	Harrodsburg	Ky.
1850	Bay View–New York Bay	Jersey City	N.J.
1850	Forest Hill	Utica	N.Y.
1850	Forest Home	Milwaukee	Wis.
1850	Georgetown	Georgetown	Ky.
1850	Indian Hill	Middletown	Conn.
1850	Laurel Grove North	Savannah	Ga.
1850	Laurel Grove South	Savannah	Ga.
1850	Lutheran (later All Faiths)	Middle Village	N.Y.
1850	Magnolia	Charleston	S.C.
1850	Old Gray	Knoxville	Tenn.
1850	Pine Grove	Lynn	Mass.
1850	Pittsfield Rural	Pittsfield	Mass.
1850	Riverside	Waterbury	Conn.
1850	Salem Fields	Brooklyn	N.Y.
1850	Wiltwyck Rural	Kingston	N.Y.
1850	Woodward	Lancaster	Pa.
1851	Cedar Grove	New London	Conn.
1851	Dale	Ossining	N.Y.
1851	Erie	Erie	Pa.
1851	Evergreen	Oswego	N.Y.
1851	Fort Hill	Auburn	N.Y.
1851	Green River	Greenfield	Mass.
1851	Huntington Rural	Huntington	N.Y.
1851	Mount Adnah	Fulton	N.Y.
1851	Pine Grove	Waterville	Maine
1851	Rome Rural	Rome	N.Y.
1851	Wildwood	Winchester	Mass.
1851	Woodlawn	Chelsea	Mass.
1852	Elmwood	Memphis	Tenn.
1852	Hope	Worcester	Mass.
1852	Mount Hope	Dorchester/ Boston	Mass.
1852	Oak Hill	Evansville	Ind.

Year	Cemetery Name	City	State	Year	Cemetery Name	City	State
1852	Oakdale	Wilmington	N.C.	1856	Mount Olivet	Nashville	Tenn.
1852	Oakwood	Niagara Falls	N.Y.	1856	Mount Vernon	Philadelphia	Pa.
1852	Walnut Grove	Boonville	Mo.	1856	Oak Hill	Woonsocket	R.I.
1853	Brookside	Watertown	N.Y.	1857	Holyhood	Brookline	Mass.
1853	Cortland Rural	Cortland	N.Y.	1857	Juniper Hill	Bristol	R.I.
1853	Elm Grove	Mystic	Conn.	1857	Lake Forest	Lake Forest	Ill.
1853	Elmwood	Charlotte	N.C.	1857	Mount Feake	Waltham	Mass.
1853	Elmwood	Norfolk	Va.	1857	Myrtle Hill	Rome	Ga.
1853	Evergreen	Hillside	N.J.	1857	Vale	Schenectady	N.Y.
1853	Lone Mountain (later Laurel Hill)	San Francisco	Calif.	1857	Wyoming	Melrose	Mass.
				1858	Green Hill	Amsterdam	N.Y.
1853	Loudon Park	Baltimore	Md.	1858	Machpelah	LeRoy	N.Y.
1853	Oakland	St. Paul	Minn.	1858	Union	Kansas City	Mo.
1853	Poughkeepsie Rural	Poughkeepsie	N.Y.	1858	Woodlands	Cambridge	N.Y.
1853	Spring Forest	Binghamton	N.Y.	1858	Woodlawn	Elmira	N.Y.
1853	Woodland	Cleveland	Ohio	1859	Hazelwood	Clark	N.J.
1854	Beechwoods	New Rochelle	N.Y.	1859	Mount Olivet	Hanover	Pa.
1854	Elmwood	Columbia	S.C.	1859	Oakwood	Syracuse	N.Y.
1854	Evergreen	Portland	Maine	1859	Rosehill	Chicago	Ill.
1854	Glenwood	Washington	D. C.	1859	Woodland	Stamford	Conn.
1854	Green Mount	Montpelier	Vt.	1860	Graceland	Chicago	Ill.
1854	Oak Hill	Cedar Rapids	Iowa	1860	Hillside	Middletown	N.Y.
1854	Oaklands	West Chester	Pa.	1860	Weedsport	Weedsport	N.Y.
1854	Union	Steubenville	Ohio	1861	Evergreen	Rutland	Vt.
1854	White Plains Rural	White Plains	N.Y.	1861	New Paltz Rural	New Paltz	N.Y.
1855	Chippiannock	Rock Island	Ill.	1861	Westwood	Oberlin	Ohio
1855	Fairmount	Newark	N.J.	1863	Chester Rural	Chester	Pa.
1855	Machpelah	Mount Sterling	Ky.	1863	Mountain View	Oakland	Calif.
1855	Mount Moriah	Philadelphia	Pa.	1863	Woodlawn	Bronx	N.Y.
1855	Mount Wollaston	Quincy	Mass.	1864	Spring Hill	Danville	Ill.
1855	Newton	Newton	Mass.	1865	Upper Middleburgh	Middleburgh	N.Y.
1855	Oak Grove	Fall River	Mass.	1866	Bayside Cemetery	Potsdam	N.Y.
1855	Oak Grove	Gloucester	Mass.	1866	Fishkill Rural	Fishkill	N.Y.
1855	Oak Ridge	Springfield	Ill.	1866	Oakland	Yonkers	N.Y.
1855	Oconee Hill	Athens	Ga.	1867	Ivy Hill	Philadelphia	Pa.
1855	Red Bank	Fair View	N.J.	1867	Santa Rosa Rural	Santa Rosa	Calif.
1855	Riverside	Oswego	N.Y.	1869	Oakwood	Raleigh	N.C.
1855	Sleepy Hollow	Concord	Mass.	1869	Spring Hill	Charleston	W.Va.
1855	Spring Hill	Lynchburg	Va.	1869	West Laurel Hill	Bala Cynwyd	Pa.
1855	Springdale	Peoria	Ill.	1871	Glenwood	Houston	Tex.
1856	Clinton	Clinton	N.Y.	1873	Oak Hill	Birmingham	Ala.
1856	Lakewood	Cooperstown	N.Y.				

LIST OF RURAL CEMETERIES BY STATE

State	City	Cemetery Name
Ala.	Birmingham	Oak Hill
Calif.	San Francisco	Lone Mountain (later Laurel Hill)
Calif.	Oakland	Mountain View
Calif.	Santa Rosa	Santa Rosa
Conn.	New London	Cedar Grove
Conn.	Mystic	Elm Grove
Conn.	New Haven	Evergreen
Conn.	Middletown	Indian Hill
Conn.	Bridgeport	Mountain Grove
Conn.	Waterbury	Riverside
Conn.	Hartford	Spring Grove
Conn.	Stamford	Woodland
D.C.	Washington	Glenwood
D.C.	Washington	Oak Hill
Ga.	Savannah	Bonaventure
Ga.	Savannah	Laurel Grove North
Ga.	Savannah	Laurel Grove South
Ga.	Rome	Myrtle Hill
Ga.	Athens	Oconee Hill
Ga.	Macon	Rose Hill
Iowa	Cedar Rapids	Oak Hill
Ill.	Rock Island	Chippiannock
Ill.	Chicago	Graceland
Ill.	Lake Forest	Lake Forest
Ill.	Springfield	Oak Ridge
Ill.	Chicago	Rosehill
Ill.	Danville	Spring Hill
Ill.	Peoria	Springdale
Ind.	Evansville	Oak Hill
Ky.	Louisville	Cave Hill
Ky.	Frankfort	Frankfort
Ky.	Georgetown	Georgetown
Ky.	Lexington	Lexington
Ky.	Covington	Linden Grove
Ky.	Mount Sterling	Machpelah
Ky.	Paris	Paris
Ky.	Harrodsburg	Spring Hill
Mass.	Lawrence	Bellevue
Mass.	Framingham	Edgell
Mass.	Brighton	Evergreen
Mass.	Boston	Forest Hills
Mass.	Greenfield	Green River
Mass.	Salem	Harmony Grove
Mass.	Brookline	Holyhood
Mass.	Worchester	Hope
Mass.	Lowell	Lowell
Mass.	Cambridge	Mount Auburn
Mass.	Waltham	Mount Feake
Mass.	Dorchester/ Boston	Mount Hope
Mass.	Taunton	Mount Pleasant
Mass.	Quincy	Mount Wollaston
Mass.	New Bedford	New Bedford Rural
Mass.	Newton	Newton
Mass.	Fall River	Oak Grove
Mass.	Gloucester	Oak Grove
Mass.	Newburyport	Oak Hill
Mass.	Lynn	Pine Grove
Mass.	Pittsfield	Pittsfield Rural
Mass.	Southborough	Rural
Mass.	Concord	Sleepy Hollow
Mass.	Danvers	Walnut Grove
Mass.	Winchester	Wildwood
Mass.	Chelsea	Woodlawn
Mass.	Worchester	Worcester Rural
Mass.	Melrose	Wyoming
Md.	Baltimore	Green Mount
Md.	Baltimore	Loudon Park
Maine	Portland	Evergreen
Maine	Bangor	Mount Hope
Maine	Waterville	Pine Grove
Mich.	Detroit	Elmwood
Minn.	St. Paul	Oakland
Mo.	St. Louis	Bellefontaine
Mo.	Kansas City	Union
Mo.	Boonville	Walnut Grove
N.C.	Charlotte	Elmwood
N.C.	Wilmington	Oakdale
N.C.	Raleigh	Oakwood
N.H.	Manchester	Valley
N.J.	Jersey City	Bay View-New York Bay
N.J.	Camden	Evergreen
N.J.	Hillside	Evergreen
N.J.	Red Bank	Fair View
N.J.	Newark	Fairmount
N.J.	Rahway	Hazelwood
N.J.	Newark	Mount Pleasant
N.Y.	Menands	Albany Rural
N.Y.	Potsdam	Bayside
N.Y.	New Rochelle	Beechwoods
N.Y.	Watertown	Brookside
N.Y.	Queens	Calvary
N.Y.	Clinton	Clinton
N.Y.	Cortland	Cortland Rural

State	City	Cemetery Name	State	City	Cemetery Name
N.Y.	Brooklyn	Cypress Hills	Ohio	Hamilton	Greenwood
N.Y.	Ossining	Dale	Ohio	Cincinnati	Spring Grove
N.Y.	Oswego	Evergreen	Ohio	Steubenville	Union
N.Y.	Brooklyn	Evergreens	Ohio	Oberlin	Westwood
N.Y.	Fishkill	Fishkill Rural	Ohio	Cleveland	Woodland
N.Y.	Utica	Forest Hill	Ohio	Dayton	Woodland
N.Y.	Buffalo	Forest Lawn	Ohio	Xenia	Woodland
N.Y.	Auburn	Fort Hill	Pa.	Pittsburgh	Allegheny
N.Y.	Amsterdam	Green Hill	Pa.	Chester	Chester Rural
N.Y.	Brooklyn	Green-Wood	Pa.	Easton	Easton
N.Y.	Middletown	Hillside	Pa.	Erie	Erie
N.Y.	Huntington	Huntington Rural	Pa.	Harrisburg	Harrisburg
N.Y.	Cooperstown	Lakewood	Pa.	Philadelphia	Ivy Hill
N.Y.	Middle Village	Lutheran (later All Faiths)	Pa.	Philadelphia	Laurel Hill
N.Y.	LeRoy	Machpelah	Pa.	Philadelphia	Mount Moriah
N.Y.	Fulton	Mount Adnah	Pa.	Hanover	Mount Olivet
N.Y.	Albion	Mount Albion	Pa.	Philadelphia	Mount Vernon
N.Y.	Rochester	Mount Hope	Pa.	West Chester	Oaklands
N.Y.	New Paltz	New Paltz Rural	Pa.	York	Prospect Hill
N.Y.	Yonkers	Oakland	Pa.	Pittsburgh	Union Dale
N.Y.	Niagara Falls	Oakwood	Pa.	Bala Cynwyd	West Laurel Hill
N.Y.	Syracuse	Oakwood	Pa.	Philadelphia	Woodlands
N.Y.	Troy	Oakwood	Pa.	Lancaster	Woodward Hill
N.Y.	Poughkeepsie	Poughkeepsie Rural	R.I.	Newport	Island
N.Y.	Oswego	Riverside	R.I.	Bristol	Juniper Hill
N.Y.	Sparkill	Rockland	R.I.	Woonsocket	Oak Hill
N.Y.	Rome	Rome Rural	R.I.	Westerly	River Bend
N.Y.	Johnstown	Rural	R.I.	Providence	Swan Point
N.Y.	Brooklyn	Salem Fields	S.C.	Columbia	Elmwood
N.Y.	Tarrytown	Sleepy Hollow	S.C.	Charleston	Magnolia
N.Y.	Binghamton	Spring Forest	Tenn.	Memphis	Elmwood
N.Y.	Middleburgh	Upper Middleburgh	Tenn.	Nashville	Mount Olivet
N.Y.	Schenectady	Vale	Tenn.	Knoxville	Old Gray
N.Y.	Weedsport	Weedsport Rural	Tex.	Houston	Glenwood
N.Y.	White Plains	White Plains Rural	Va.	Norfolk	Elmwood
N.Y.	Kingston	Wiltwyck Rural	Va.	Richmond	Hollywood
N.Y.	Cambridge	Woodlands	Va.	Lynchburg	Spring Hill
N.Y.	Bronx	Woodlawn	Vt.	Rutland	Evergreen
N.Y.	Elmira	Woodlawn	Vt.	Montpelier	Green Mount
Ohio	Akron	Glendale	Wis.	Milwaukee	Forest Home
Ohio	Columbus	Green Lawn	W.Va.	Charleston	Spring Hill

NOTES

Chapter 1: A Brief History of Common Burial Landscapes Prior to the Nineteenth Century

1. Ariès, *The Hour of Our Death*, 29.
2. Smith, *Smith's Illustrated Guide to and Through Laurel Hill Cemetery*, 10.
3. Ariès, *The Hour of Our Death*, 202.
4. Ibid.
5. *The Picturesque Pocket Companion*, 70–71.
6. Ibid., 70.
7. Ibid.
8. Quoted in Notman and Strauch, *The Cincinnati Cemetery of Spring Grove*, 82.
9. *The Picturesque Pocket Companion*, 70.
10. Seymer, *The Romance of Ancient Egypt*, 72.
11. Sloane, *The Last Great Necessity*, 18.
12. Smith, *Smith's Illustrated Guide to and Through Laurel Hill Cemetery*, 11.
13. *Remarks on the Dangers and Duties of Sepulture*, 9.
14. Ariès, *The Hour of Our Death*, 47.
15. Ibid., 79.
16. Smith, *Smith's Illustrated Guide to and Through Laurel Hill Cemetery*, 13.
17. Ariès, *The Hour of Our Death*, 30.
18. Ibid., 207.
19. Ibid., 213.
20. Stannard, *The Puritan Way of Death*, 15.
21. Linden, *Silent City on a Hill*, 15–19, 25.
22. Ibid., 16.
23. Ibid., 18.
24. Ibid., 17–18.
25. Ibid., 24.
26. Sloane, *The Last Great Necessity*, 19.
27. Ariès, *The Hour of Our Death*, 338–39.
28. Ibid., 339.
29. Linden, *Silent City on a Hill*, 23.
30. Ibid., 25.
31. Pollock, *History of Trinity Church and Its Grave Yard*, 9.
32. Ibid., 11.
33. Sloane, *The Last Great Necessity*, 19–20.
34. Ariès, *The Hour of Our Death*, 340.
35. Ibid.
36. Ibid., 338–41.
37. Stannard, *The Puritan Way of Death*, 157.
38. Farrell, *Inventing the American Way of Death*, 18.
39. Stannard, *The Puritan Way of Death*, 27.
40. Ibid., 41, 75–79.
41. Ibid., 41.
42. Ibid.
43. Ibid., 41, 77, 83.
44. Ibid., 174.
45. Ariès, *The Hour of Our Death*, 473.
46. Ibid., 340.
47. Stannard, *The Puritan Way of Death*, 157.
48. *Historical Sketch and Matters Appertaining to the Granary Burial-Ground*, 11.
49. Ibid.
50. Ibid., 12.
51. Ibid.

Chapter 2: Changing Attitudes toward Nature and Death

1. Draper, *The Funeral Elegy and the Rise of English Romanticism*, 255.
2. Ibid., 80–81, 91.
3. Ibid., 119.
4. Stannard, *The Puritan Way of Death*, 147.
5. Draper, *The Funeral Elegy and the Rise of English Romanticism*, 267.
6. Ibid., 17, 250–51.
7. Ibid., 261.
8. Ibid., 191.
9. Quoted in Draper, *The Funeral Elegy and the Rise of English Romanticism*, 191.
10. Evelyn, *Silva, or, a Discourse of Forest-Trees*, book 4, chapter 1, 295.
11. Ibid.
12. Ibid.
13. Ibid., 296.

14. Ibid.
15. Ibid., 295.
16. Ibid.
17. Etlin, *The Architecture of Death*, 171.
18. Ibid., 163.
19. Favretti and Favretti, *Landscapes and Gardens for Historic Buildings*, 21.
20. Hadfield, *The English Landscape Garden*, 32.
21. Curl, *The Victorian Celebration of Death*, 2.
22. Ibid., 11.
23. Ibid.
24. Cothran, *Gardens and Historic Plants of the Antebellum South*, 47.
25. Favretti and Favretti, *Landscapes and Gardens for Historic Buildings*, 21–24.
26. Walpole, *Essay on Modern Gardening*, 57.
27. Ibid., 59.
28. Ibid., 57.
29. Hadfield, *The English Landscape Garden*, 32.
30. Etlin, *The Architecture of Death*, 190.
31. Curl, *The Victorian Celebration of Death*, 13.
32. Ibid.
33. Linden, *Silent City on a Hill*, 34.
34. Ibid.
35. Ibid., 35.
36. Quoted in Etlin, *The Architecture of Death*, 172.
37. Linden, *Silent City on a Hill*, 47.
38. Curl, *The Victorian Celebration of Death*, 3.
39. Ariès, *The Hour of Our Death*, 524.
40. Ibid.
41. Gray, *Elegy Written in a Country Church-Yard*, lines 77–84.
42. Curl, *The Victorian Celebration of Death*, 5.
43. Young, *The Complaint: or Night Thoughts on Life, Death & Immortality-Night the Third*, lines 533–36.
44. Curl, *The Victorian Celebration of Death*, 8–10.
45. Favretti and Favretti, *Landscapes and Gardens for Historic Buildings*, 24.
46. Otis, *Grounds for Pleasure*, 116.
47. Hadfield, *The English Landscape Garden*, 63.
48. Gilpin, *An Essay Upon Prints Containing Remarks Upon the Principles of Picturesque Beauty*, x.
49. Quoted in Hadfield, *The English Landscape Garden*, 66.
50. Price, *An Essay on the Picturesque*, 18.
51. Curl, *The Victorian Celebration of Death*, 7.
52. Ibid., 5, 7.
53. Ibid., 8.
54. Etlin, *The Architecture of Death*, 200.
55. Ibid.
56. Curl, *The Victorian Celebration of Death*, 13.
57. Girardin, *An Essay on Landscape*, 14–15.
58. Curl, *The Victorian Celebration of Death*, 16.
59. Etlin, *The Architecture of Death*, 209.
60. Curl, *The Victorian Celebration of Death*, 16.
61. Etlin, *The Architecture of Death*, 216.
62. Ibid., 209.
63. Ibid., 214.
64. Quoted in Etlin, *The Architecture of Death*, 215.
65. Ibid., 214.
66. Etlin, *The Architecture of Death*, 215
67. Rogers, Eustis, and Bidwell, *Romantic Gardens*, 12.
68. Ibid., 31.
69. Ibid., 71.
70. Ariès, *The Hour of Our Death*, 409.
71. Stannard, *The Puritan Way of Death*, 167–68, 174.
72. Ariès, *The Hour of Our Death*, 452.
73. Ibid. See also 507.
74. Ibid., 471.
75. Wordsworth, *The Prose Works of William Wordsworth*, 32.
76. Ibid., 31–32.
77. Ibid., 39.
78. Ibid., 31.
79. Ibid., 32.
80. Linden, *Silent City on a Hill*, 51.
81. Davis, *Bradford's History of Plymouth Plantation*, 96.
82. Linden, "The Willow Tree and Urn Motif," 151.
83. Rogers, Eustis, and Bidwell, *Romantic Gardens*, 55.
84. Sloane, *The Last Great Necessity*, 51.
85. Stilgoe, *Common Landscape of America*, 53.
86. Clifford, *A History of Garden Design*, 198–99.
87. Otis, *Grounds for Pleasure*, 20.
88. Ibid., 111.
89. Stilgoe, *Common Landscape of America*, 6.
90. Sweeting, *Reading Houses and Building Books*, 16.
91. Downing, *A Treatise on the Theory and Practice of Landscape Gardening*, 41.
92. Downing, *Rural Essays*, 101–2.
93. Rogers, Eustis, and Bidwell, *Romantic Gardens*, 14.
94. Ibid., 55.
95. Farrell, *Inventing the American Way of Death*, 33.
96. Ariès, *The Hour of Our Death*, 511.
97. Bryant, "Thanatopsis," lines 24–26.
98. Ibid., line 37.
99. Ibid., lines 37–42.
100. Ibid., lines 77–81.
101. Bryant, "The Old Man's Funeral," lines 19–22.
102. Ibid., lines 23–24.
103. Irving, *The Sketch Book*, 268.
104. Ibid.
105. Ibid.
106. Ibid., 269.
107. Ibid., 279.
108. Linden, *Silent City on a Hill*, 97.
109. Warren, *The History of the Bunker Hill Monument*

Association During the First Century of the United States of America, 42.

110. Laderman, *The Sacred Remains,* 60.
111. Channing, "Unitarian Christianity," 287.
112. Linden, *Silent City on a Hill,* 138.
113. Quoted in Linden, *Silent City on a Hill,* 138.
114. Quoted in Farrell, *Inventing the American Way of Death,* 28.
115. Linden, *Silent City on a Hill,* 137.
116. Channing, "Likeness to God," 233.
117. Laderman, *The Sacred Remains,* 44.
118. Linden, *Silent City on a Hill,* 22.
119. Ibid., 312. In a note, Linden attributes authorship of the pamphlet to Coffin based on a close reading of the report. The pamphlet is attributed to Jacob Bigelow in other published references.
120. *Remarks on the Dangers and Duties of Sepulture,* 11.
121. Ibid., 24.
122. Ibid., 20.
123. Smith, *Smith's Illustrated Guide to and Through Laurel Hill Cemetery,* 18.
124. Etlin, *The Architecture of Death,* 238.
125. Ibid., 272.

Chapter 3: The Rural Cemetery Movement

1. Etlin, *The Architecture of Death,* 300.
2. Ibid., 301.
3. Sloane, *The Last Great Necessity,* 3.
4. Etlin, *The Architecture of Death,* 343–44.
5. Carter, *Letters from Europe,* 394.
6. Strang, *Necropolis Glasguensis,* 29.
7. Ibid.
8. Ibid., 31.
9. Ariès, *The Hour of Our Death,* 534.
10. Carter, *Letters from Europe,* 392–93.
11. Sloane, *The Last Great Necessity,* 32.
12. Ibid.
13. Hall, *Travels in North America,* 201.
14. Ibid.
15. Ibid.
16. Massachusetts Horticultural Society and Manning, *History of the Massachusetts Horticultural Society,* 69.
17. Bigelow, *A History of Mt. Auburn Cemetery,* 2.
18. Quoted in Massachusetts Horticultural Society and Manning, *History of the Massachusetts Horticultural Society,* 75.
19. Massachusetts Horticultural Society and Manning, *History of the Massachusetts Horticultural Society,* 76.
20. Ibid., 77.
21. Rotundo, "Mount Auburn: Fortunate Coincidences and an Ideal Solution," 257.
22. Quoted in *The Picturesque Pocket Companion,* 10–11.
23. *The Picturesque Pocket Companion,* 78.
24. Ibid., 72.
25. Ibid., 74.
26. Ibid., 68.
27. Ibid., 75.
28. Ibid.
29. Ibid., 69.
30. Ibid., 70.
31. Ibid.
32. Ibid., 40.
33. Wines, *A Trip to Boston,* 45.
34. Bigelow, *A History of Mt. Auburn Cemetery,* 172.
35. Linden, *Silent City on a Hill,* 147.
36. Wines, *A Trip to Boston,* 45.
37. Dearborn, *A Concise History of and Guide Through Mount Auburn,* 5.
38. Ibid.
39. Massachusetts Horticultural Society and Manning, *History of the Massachusetts Horticultural Society,* 93.
40. Linden, *Silent City on a Hill,* 145.
41. *The Picturesque Pocket Companion,* 39.
42. Massachusetts Horticultural Society and Manning, *History of the Massachusetts Horticultural Society,* 96.
43. Ibid.
44. Ibid., 101–2.
45. Channing, "Unitarian Christianity," 287.
46. Bigelow, *A History of Mt. Auburn Cemetery,* 197.
47. Rotundo, "Mount Auburn: Fortunate Coincidences and an Ideal Solution," 259.
48. North, "The Proper Expression of a Rural Cemetery," 254.
49. Dearborn, *A Concise History of and Guide Through Mount Auburn,* 16.
50. Linden, *Silent City on a Hill,* 261.
51. Bigelow, *A History of Mt. Auburn Cemetery,* 197.
52. Linden, *Silent City on a Hill,* 210.
53. Bigelow, *A History of Mt. Auburn Cemetery,* 26.
54. Ibid.
55. Dearborn, *Dearborn's Guide Through Mount Auburn,* [13].
56. Dearborn, *A Concise History of and Guide Through Mount Auburn,* 6.
57. Linden, *Silent City on a Hill,* 144.
58. *The Picturesque Pocket Companion,* 76.
59. Linden, *Silent City on a Hill,* 187.
60. Ibid., 194.
61. Ibid., 193.
62. Bigelow, *A History of Mt. Auburn Cemetery,* 65.
63. French, "The Cemetery as Cultural Institution," 49.
64. Ciregna, "Museum in the Garden," 105.
65. Ibid., 130.
66. *The Picturesque Pocket Companion,* 48.
67. Flagg, *Mount Auburn,* 37.

68. Ibid., 35–36.

69. Arfwedson, *The United States and Canada, in 1832, 1833 and 1834*, 210-11.

70. Wines, *A Trip to Boston*, 45-45.

71. Buckingham, *America: Historical, Statistical & Descriptive*, 379.

72. Hayward, *A Gazetteer of Massachusetts*, 119.

73. Lyell, *A Second Visit to the United States of North America*, 171.

74. Hall, *Appletons' Hand-book of American Travel*, 88.

75. Medley, *An Autumn Tour in the United States and Canada*, 124.

76. Bigelow, *A History of Mt. Auburn Cemetery*, 29.

77. Ibid., 27.

78. Downing, *Rural Essays*, 154.

79. Cleaveland, *Green-Wood Cemetary*, 6–7.

80. Henderson, "What is the grass?," 90.

81. Ibid.

82. Ibid., 91.

83. Rousmaniere, *Green Oasis in Brooklyn*, 41.

84. Hedrick, *A History of Horticulture in America*, 256.

85. Downing, *Rural Essays*, 154–55.

86. Kern, "The Cemetery," 267.

87. MacDonald, *Old Copp's Hill and Burial Ground*, 31.

88. Meinwald, "Memento Mori," 26.

89. Stannard, *The Puritan Way of Death*, 187.

90. Scee, *The Mount Hope Cemetery of Bangor*, 134.

91. Quoted in Scee, *The Mount Hope Cemetery of Bangor*, 25.

92. Mattor and Teegarden, "Rural Cemeteries," 121–24.

93. Ibid., 124

94. Quoted in Scee, *The Mount Hope Cemetery of Bangor*, 61.

95. Quoted in National Register of Historic Places Registration Form, Laurel Hill Cemetery, 19.

96. National Register of Historic Places Registration Form, Laurel Hill Cemetery, 4.

97. Laurel Hill Cemetery, *Guide to Laurel Hill Cemetery*, 90.

98. Ibid., 90–91.

99. Morgan, "The emergence of the American landscape professional," 280.

100. See Chapter 5 for a complete list of the catalogue.

101. Laurel Hill Cemetery, *Guide to Laurel Hill Cemetery*, 74.

102. Smith, *Smith's Illustrated Guide to and Through Laurel Hill Cemetery*, 45.

103. Quoted in Cleaveland, *Green-Wood: a Directory for Visitors*, 244.

104. Richman, *Brooklyn's Green-Wood Cemetery*, 4.

105. Cleaveland, *Green-Wood: a Directory for Visitors*, 245–46.

106. Green-Wood Cemetery and Cleaveland, *Rules and Regulations of the Green-Wood Cemetery*, 5.

107. Cleaveland, *Green-Wood Illustrated*, 3.

108. Cleaveland, *Green-Wood: a Directory for Visitors*, 5.

109. *Baedeker's United States, 1893*, 53.

110. Richman, *Brooklyn's Green-Wood Cemetery*, 16.

111. Bremer, *America of the Fifties: Letters of Fredrika Bremer*, 3–4.

112. Ibid, 4.

113. Quoted in National Register of Historic Places Registration Form, Green-Wood Cemetery, 41.

114. Howard, *The Monumental City*, 89.

115. Quoted in *Green Mount Cemetery: One Hundredth Anniversary*, 19–20.

116. *Green Mount Cemetery: One Hundredth Anniversary*, 30.

117. Hall, *Appletons' Hand-Book of American Travel*, 296.

118. Wilson, *The Very Quiet Baltimoreans*, 20.

119. *Green Mount Cemetery: One Hundredth Anniversary*, 11.

120. Ibid.

121. Church, *An Address Delivered at the Dedication of Mount Hope Cemetery*, 16–17.

122. Reisem and Gillespie, *Mount Hope, Rochester*, 10.

123. Angevine, *A Guide or Handbook for Mount Hope Cemetery*, 5.

124. Ibid., 47.

125. Ibid, 50–51.

126. National Register of Historic Places Inventory-Nomination Form, Rose Hill Cemetery, [4].

127. Quoted in National Register of Historic Places Inventory-Nomination Form, Rose Hill Cemetery, [2].

128. Ibid.

129. Bremer, *The Homes of the New World*, 324.

130. Earnheart, *Rose Hill Cemetery*, 83.

131. Quoted in National Register of Historic Places Inventory-Nomination Form, Rose Hill Cemetery, [2].

132. Schwaab, *Travels in the Old South*, 534.

133. Ibid.

134. Quoted in National Register of Historic Places Inventory-Nomination Form, Rose Hill Cemetery, [2].

135. Ibid, [3].

136. Earnheart, *Rose Hill Cemetery*, 91.

137. *Allegheny Cemetery*, 22.

138. Ibid., 40.

139. Ibid., 84.

140. Ibid.

141. Ibid., 126. See chapter 5 for a list of trees and shrubs available for purchase at the cemetery at the time.

142. "Holly-Wood Cemetery," *Richmond Enquirer*, June 12, 1849.

143. Bryant, *Picturesque America or the Land We Live In*, 1:73.

144. Morgan, "The emergence of the American landscape professional," 281.

145. Quoted in Greiff, *John Notman, Architect*, 142.

146. Ibid, 143–45.

147. Quoted in Mitchell, *Hollywood Cemetery*, 79.

148. Bryant, *Picturesque America or the Land We Live In*, 1:73.

149. Mitchell, *Hollywood Cemetery*, 4.

150. Marion, *Famous and Curious Cemeteries*, 167.

151. Peters, *Richmond's Hollywood Cemetery*, 64.

152. National Register of Historic Places Inventory—Nomination Form, Cave Hill Cemetery, [n.p].

153. *Louisville Daily Ledger*, August 11, 1873.

154. *Louisville Daily Courier*, July 11, 1849.

155. Thomas, *Cave Hill Cemetery*, 35.

156. Quoted in Thomas, *Cave Hill Cemetery*, 14.

157. Putnam, *An Address Delivered Before the City Government and Citizens of Roxbury*, 5.

158. Crafts, *Forest Hills Cemetery*, 46.

159. Wilson, *Garden of Memories*, 9.

160. Ibid., 61.

161. National Register of Historic Places Registration Form, Forest Hills, [13].

162. Wilson, *Garden of Memories*, 12.

163. Quoted in "The Bellefontaine Cemetery," *Daily Missouri Republican*, May 16, 1850.

164. Muir, *A Thousand-Mile Walk to the Gulf*, 69.

165. Rousmaniere, *Green Oasis in Brooklyn*, 37.

166. Ibid, 236.

167. Quoted in "Dead Chinamen," *New York Herald*, August 15, 1880.

168. Gurda, *Silent City*, 4.

169. Quoted in Gurda, *Silent City*, 6.

170. Ibid., 6–7.

171. Chapman, *The Forest Home Cemetery*, 7–8.

172. Gurda, *Silent City*, 26.

173. Leland and Smith, *The Pioneers of Cemetery Administration in America*, [n.p.].

174. Quoted in Gurda, *Silent City*, 31.

175. Pinckney, *Remarks Addressed to the Citizens of Charleston*, 24.

176. Bryant and Bunce, *Picturesque America*, 1:210.

177. Baedeker, *The United States*, 349.

178. Fraser, *Address Delivered on the Dedication of Magnolia Cemetery*, 3.

179. Mazÿck, *Guide to Charleston Illustrated*, 118–19.

180. Elwell, *Portland and Vicinity*, 123.

181. Quoted in National Register of Historic Places Registration Form, Evergreen Cemetery, Portland, [6].

182. Quoted in Mattor and Teegarden, "Rural Cemeteries," 132.

183. Mattor and Teegarden, "Rural Cemeteries," 132

184. Halvorson Co. and Friends of Evergreen Cemetery, *Evergreen Cemetery, Portland Maine: Master Plan*, 4.

185. Elwell, *Portland and Vicinity*, 124.

186. Ibid., 126.

187. Ibid.

188. Halvorson Co. and Friends of Evergreen Cemetery, *Evergreen Cemetery, Portland Maine: Master Plan*, 8.

189. Ibid., 1.

190. "The Proposed Rural Cemetery," *Standard*, August 11, 1857.

191. National Register of Historic Places Registration Form, Oakwood Cemetery, Syracuse, 26.

192. Maltbie, *Picturesque Oakwood*, 211.

193. Ibid., 240.

194. Ibid.

195. Ibid., 59.

196. Oakwood Cemetery, *The History, Incorporation, Rules and Regulations of Oakwood Cemetery*, 43.

197. Ibid, 53.

198. Quoted in Oakwood Cemetery, *The History, Incorporation, Rules and Regulations of Oakwood Cemetery*, 54.

199. Ibid.

200. Maltbie, *Picturesque Oakwood*, 163.

201. Ibid.

202. Beveridge, "The California Origins of Olmsted's Landscape Design Principles for the Semiarid American West," 453.

203. Olmsted, "To Calvert Vaux," 325.

204. Beveridge, "The California Origins of Olmsted's Landscape Design Principles for the Semiarid American West," 454.

205. Olmsted and Vaux, "Preface to the Plan for Mountain View Cemetery," 482.

206. Ibid, 480.

207. Ibid.

208. Ibid, 482.

209. Ibid, 481.

210. Ibid, 475.

211. Shinn, "A California Cemetery," 207.

212. Ibid., 206.

213. Ibid.

214. Spring Grove Cemetery Association, *Spring Grove Cemetery*, 26.

215. Notman and Strauch, *The Cincinnati Cemetery of Spring Grove*, 23.

216. Rattermann, *Spring Grove and Its Creator*, 13–14.

217. Linden, "Spring Grove: Celebrating 150 Years," 16.

218. Ibid., 18.

219. Notman and Strauch, *The Cincinnati Cemetery of Spring Grove*, 31.

220. Ibid., 32.

221. Ibid.

222. Ibid.

223. Ibid.

224. Ibid., 34–35.

225. Ibid, 35.

226. Ibid., 31.

227. Ibid.

228. Quoted in Linden, "Spring Grove: Celebrating 150 Years," 34.

229. Spring Grove Cemetery Association, *Spring Grove Cemetery*, 66.

230. Ibid., vi.

231. Hall, *Appletons' Hand-Book of American Travel*, 176.

232. Spring Grove Cemetery Association, *Spring Grove Cemetery*, 9.

233. Ibid.

234. Linden, "Spring Grove: Celebrating 150 Years," 41.

235. Notman and Strauch, *The Cincinnati Cemetery of Spring Grove*, 23. See chapter 5 for reprint of the catalogue.

236. Ibid.

237. Linden, "Spring Grove: Celebrating 150 Years," 48.

238. Notman and Strauch, *The Cincinnati Cemetery of Spring Grove*, 31.

239. Ibid.

240. Farrell, *Inventing the American Way of Death*, 120.

241. Notman and Strauch, *The Cincinnati Cemetery of Spring Grove*, 22.

242. Linden, "Spring Grove: Celebrating 150 Years," 55.

243. Quoted in Linden, "Spring Grove: Celebrating 150 Years," 51.

244. "Spring Grove," *Cincinnati Commercial Tribune*, December 19, 1870.

245. "Spring Grove Cemetery to be Copied After," *Cincinnati Commercial Tribune*, September 9, 1880.

246. Quoted in Vernon, *Graceland Cemetery: A Design History*, 28.

247. Ibid., 80.

248. Vernon, *Graceland Cemetery: A Design History*, 159.

249. Ibid.

250. Ibid., 165.

251. Ibid., 170.

252. National Register of Historic Places Registration Form, Graceland Cemetery, 119.

253. National Register of Historic Places Registration Form, Crown Hill National Cemetery, 4.

254. Quoted in Nicholas, *The Story of Crown Hill*, 14.

255. "Crown Hill Cemetery," *Indiana State Sentinel*, October 22, 1863.

256. Quoted in Nicholas, *The Story of Crown Hill*, 20.

257. Quoted in Wissing, Davis, and Fields, *Crown Hill: History, Spirit, Sanctuary*, 80.

258. *Crown Hill Cemetery*, 17.

259. Wissing, Davis, and Fields, *Crown Hill: History, Spirit, Sanctuary*, 39.

260. Quoted in "Woodlawn Cemetery," *Evening Post*, August 30, 1865.

261. "Woodlawn: Growth and Beauty of the New Cemetery," *Evening Post*, July 6, 1871.

262. "The Woodlawn Cemetery," *Evening Post*, October 24, 1868.

263. "Improvements at Woodlawn," *Evening Post*, May 29, 1874.

264. National Register of Historic Places Registration Form, Draft, Woodlawn Cemetery, 4.

265. Cedar Hill Cemetery, *Cedar Hill Cemetery*, 9.

266. Ibid., 10.

267. Ibid., 16.

268. Bigelow, *A History of Mount Auburn Cemetery*, 91.

269. Ibid., 121.

270. Ibid.

271. Flagg, *Mount Auburn*, 77.

272. Berg, "Mount Auburn Cemetery," 13.

273. Ibid.

274. Quoted in Berg, "Mount Auburn Cemetery," 13.

Chapter 4: Physical and Design
Characteristics of Rural Cemeteries

1. Quoted in Michaels, Reisem, and Rupp, *Forest Lawn Cemetery*, 40.

2. Putnam, *An Address Delivered Before the City Government and Citizens of Roxbury*, 6.

3. Cleaveland, *Green-Wood Illustrated*, 12.

4. Notman and Strauch, *The Cincinnati Cemetery of Spring Grove*, 5.

5. Phelps, *The Albany Rural Cemetery*, 65–66.

6. Linden, *Spring Grove: Celebrating 150 Years*, 9.

7. Downing, *A Treatise on the Theory and Practice of Landscape Gardening*, 74.

8. Quoted in National Register of Historic Places Inventory—Nomination Form, Rose Hill Cemetery, [3].

9. Downing, *A Treatise on the Theory and Practice of Landscape Gardening*, 75.

10. Roth, *A Concise History of American Architecture*, 108.

11. Fitzgerald, *A Hand Book for the Albany Rural Cemetery*, 3.

12. Laderman, *The Sacred Remains*, 81.

13. Cleaveland, *Green-Wood Illustrated*, 2.

14. Ibid., 56.

15. Notman and Strauch, *The Cincinnati Cemetery of Spring Grove*, 24.

16. Linden, *Silent City on a Hill*, 180.

17. Fitzgerald, *A Hand Book for the Albany Rural Cemetery*, 6.

18. Smith, *Smith's Illustrated Guide to and Through Laurel Hill Cemetery*, 39.

19. Ibid., 38.

20. Ibid., 140.

21. Ibid.

22. Roark, "Embodying Immortality: Angels in America's Rural Cemeteries," 69.

23. Carmack, *Your Guide to Cemetery Research*, 130.

24. Ibid.

25. Ariès, *The Hour of Our Death*, 529–30.

26. Linden, *Silent City on a Hill*, 83.

27. Keister, *Going Out in Style*, 1.

28. Ibid.

29. Sears, "Prisons, Asylums, Cemeteries, Parks," 106–7.

30. Linden-Ward, "The Fencing Mania," 39–42.

31. "Reviews," 230.

32. Ibid.

33. Cleaveland, *Green-wood Cemetery*, 143.

34. Quoted in Richman, *Brooklyn's Green-Wood Cemetery*, 22.

35. Richman, *Brooklyn's Green-Wood Cemetery*, 23.

36. Smith, *Smith's Illustrated Guide to and Through Laurel Hill Cemetery*, 145.

37. Sloane, *The Last Great Necessity*, 83–84.

38. Quoted in Duer and Smith, *Cypress Hills Cemetery*, 8.

39. Magness, *Elmwood 2002*, 117.

40. Muir, *A Thousand-Mile Walk to the Gulf*, 67.

41. Ibid., 70–71.

42. Ibid., 67.

43. Ibid., 69.

44. Linden-Ward, "Putting the Past in Place," 189.

45. Simonds, "Landscape Cemeteries," 879.

46. Farrell, *Inventing the American Way of Death*, 116.

Chapter 5: Plants in Rural Cemeteries

1. *The Picturesque Pocket Companion*, 44.

2. Ibid., 45.

3. Notman and Strauch, *The Cincinnati Cemetery of Spring Grove*, 23.

4. *The Picturesque Pocket Companion*, 47.

5. Flagg, *Mount Auburn*, 244.

6. Sloane, *The Last Great Necessity*, 73.

7. Smith, "Rural Cemeteries," 347.

8. Ibid., 346.

9. Buckingham, *America: Historical, Statistical and Descriptive*, 379.

10. Hall, *Appletons' Hand-Book of American Travel*, 176.

11. Cleaveland, *Green-wood Cemetery*, 136.

12. Ibid., 135.

13. Smith, "Rural Cemeteries," 347.

14. Laurel Hill Cemetery, *Guide to Laurel Hill Cemetery*, 53.

15. Downing, *Rural Essays*, 155–56.

16. Notman and Strauch, *The Cincinnati Cemetery of Spring Grove*, 23.

17. "Trees for Rural Cemeteries," 153.

18. Loudon, *On the Laying Out, Planting, and Managing of Cemeteries and on the Improvement of Churchyards*, 13.

19. Ovid, *Metamorphoses*, 10.191–99.

20. Shoberl, *The Language of Flowers*, 222.

21. Flagg, *Mount Auburn*, 244.

22. "Trees for Rural Cemeteries," 153–57.

23. Barry, "Drooping Trees," 123.

24. Ibid.

25. Ibid.

26. "Drooping Deciduous Trees," 73.

27. Barry, "Drooping Trees," 124.

28. "Drooping Deciduous Trees," 69.

29. "Trees for Rural Cemeteries," 155.

30. Notman and Strauch. *The Cincinnati Cemetery of Spring Grove*, 31.

31. Stuart-Wortley, *Travels in the United States*, 77.

32. Oakwood Cemetery (Syracuse, N.Y.), *The History, Incorporation, Rules and Regulations of Oakwood Cemetery*, 37.

33. Laurel Hill Cemetery, *Guide to Laurel Hill Cemetery*, 129.

34. Flagg, *Mount Auburn*, 54.

35. Notman and Strauch, *The Cincinnati Cemetery of Spring Grove*, 4.

36. Quoted in Walter, *Mount Auburn Illustrated*, 118–19.

37. "Trees for Rural Cemeteries," 155.

38. Ibid., 154.

39. "Rural Cemeteries, No. 2 Planting, &c.," 395.

40. "Trees for Rural Cemeteries," 156.

41. "Rural Cemeteries, No. 2 Planting, &c.," 394.

42. "Planting in Cemeteries," 479.

43. Ibid.

44. Flagg, *Mount Auburn*, 245.

45. "Planting in Cemeteries," 531.

46. Loudon, *On the Laying Out, Planting, and Managing of Cemeteries and on the Improvement of Churchyards*, 21.

47. Flagg, *Mount Auburn*, 247.

48. Gilpin, *Remarks on Forest Scenery*, 29.

49. Crafts, *Forest Hills Cemetery*, 32.

50. *Allegheny Cemetery*, 126–28.

51. Cleaveland, *Green-wood Cemetery*, 137.

52. Ibid.

53. Flagg, *Mount Auburn*, 55.

54. Cleaveland, *Hints Concerning Green-Wood*, 13.

55. Crafts, *Forest Hills Cemetery*, 101.

Chapter 6: Symbolism in Rural Cemeteries

1. Cleaveland, *Green-Wood Illustrated*, 48.

2. Hijiya, "American Gravestones and Attitudes toward Death," 339–40.

3. Sloane, *The Last Great Necessity*, 77.

4. M'Carty, *Inside the Gates*, 13–15.

5. Hijiya, "American Gravestones and Attitudes toward Death," 352.

6. Linden, *Silent City on a Hill*, 84.

7. Keister, *Stories in Stone*, 137.

8. Ibid.

9. Cleaveland, *Green-Wood Illustrated*, 50–51.

10. Smith, *Smith's Illustrated Guide to and Through Laurel Hill Cemetery*, 9.

11. Crafts, *Forest Hills Cemetery*, 79–80.

12. Roark, "Embodying Immortality," 64.

13. Cleaveland, *Green-Wood Illustrated*, 49.

14. Roark, "Embodying Immortality," 70.

15. Ibid., 66.

16. Ibid., 70.

17. Cleaveland, *Green-Wood Illustrated*, 7.

18. Keister, *Stories in Stone*, 102–5.

19. Wallace, *The Loved and the Lost*, 80.

20. Shoberl, *The Language of Flowers*, 13.

21. Ibid., vi.

22. Linden, *Silent City on a Hill*, 84.

23. Keister, *Stories in Stone*, 49.

24. Ibid., 50.

25. Ibid.

26. Quoted in Shoberl, *The Language of Flowers*, 242–43.

27. Ibid., 242.

28. Snyder, "Innocents in a Worldly World," 11–14.

29. Ibid., 25.

30. Gabel, "Ritual, Regalia and Remembrance," 4.

31. Keister provides an extensive list of "Acronyms of Societies, Clubs, and Organizations" in *Stories in Stone: A Field Guide to Cemetery Symbolism and Iconography*.

32. Gabel, "Ritual, Regalia and Remembrance," 15.

33. Sources of lists include Richman's *Brooklyn's Green-Wood Cemetery*; Reisem and Gillespie's *Buried Treasures in Mount Hope Cemetery*; Wilson's *Garden of Memories*; Keister's *Stories in Stone*; Carmack's *Your Guide to Cemetery Research*; and the Association of Gravestone Studies' *Symbolism in the Carvings on Old Gravestones*.

Chapter 7: Impact of Rural Cemeteries on the American Landscape and the Profession of Landscape Architecture

1. Woolsey, "Cemeteries and Monuments," 491.

2. Sears, "Prisons, Asylums, Cemeteries, Parks," 100.

3. Gilman, *The Poetry of Travelling in the United States*, 163.

4. "A Talk About Public Parks and Gardens," 157.

5. Ibid.

6. "Public Cemeteries and Public Gardens," 9–11.

7. "A Talk About Public Parks and Gardens," 157.

8. Hedrick, *A History of Horticulture in America to 1860*, 257–58.

9. "A Talk About Public Parks and Gardens," 157.

10. "Public Cemeteries and Public Gardens," 12.

11. Ibid., 11.

12. Hedrick, *A History of Horticulture in America to 1860*, 258.

13. Ibid.

14. "The New York Park," 347.

15. Ibid., 345.

16. [Board of Commissioners of the Central Park], "Description of Central Park," 213.

17. Cook, *A Description of the New York Central Park*, 107.

18. Sears, "Prisons, Asylums, Cemeteries, Parks," 117.

19. [Board of Commissioners of the Central Park], "Description of Central Park," 213.

20. Ibid., 214.

21. Cook, *A Description of the New York Central Park*, 201.

22. [Olmsted and Vaux], "Description of a Plan for the Improvement of the Central Park," 119.

23. National Register of Historic Places Inventory-Nomination Form, Central Park, [9].

24. Cook, *A Description of the New York Central Park*, 131.

25. Ibid.

26. Ibid., 140.

27. National Register of Historic Places Inventory-Nomination Form, Central Park, [8].

28. "The New York Park," 347.

29. Alden, "Editor's Easy Chair," 455.

30. Sloane, *The Last Great Necessity*, 116.

31. Reps, *The Making of Urban America*, 336.

32. Quoted in Reps, *The Making of Urban America*, 336.

33. Sloane, *The Last Great Necessity*, 117.

34. Baltimore (Md.) City Department of Recreation and Parks, *Renewing Druid Hill Park*, 10.

35. National Register of Historic Places Inventory—Nomination Form, Prospect Park, [n.p.].

36. *Allegheny Cemetery*, 149.

37. Ibid., 150–51.

38. "Llewellyn Park," *Independent*, April 23, 1865.

39. Quoted in Jackson, *Crabgrass Frontier*, 93.

40. National Register of Historic Places Inventory—Nomination Form, Llewellyn Park Historic District," [24].

41. Reps, *The Making of Urban America*, 348.

42. Mann, *Landscape Architecture*, xiii.

43. Morgan, "The emergence of the American landscape professional," 269, 287.

44. Rotundo, "Mount Auburn," 264.

45. Cleveland, *Landscape Architecture*, 11.

46. Quoted in Linden, *Silent City on a Hill*, 208.

47. "The Great Central Park," *New York Times*, February 6, 1856.

48. Morgan, "The emergence of the American landscape professional," 270.

49. Ibid., 271.

50. Ibid., 284.

51. Ibid.

52. Ibid.

53. Ibid., 287.

54. Ibid., 269, 287.

55. "Rural Cemeteries," 298.

56. Ibid., 298–99.

57. Sloane, *The Last Great Necessity*, 106.

58. Ibid., 105–7.

59. Ibid., 109.

60. Spring Grove Cemetery Association, *Spring Grove Cemetery*, 74.

61. Sloane, *The Last Great Necessity*, 110.

62. Ibid., 111.

63. Eurich, "Life of Adolph Strauch," 134.

64. Quoted in Eurich, "Life of Adolph Strauch," 134.

65. Vernon, "Adolph Strauch," 5.

66. Quoted in Vernon, "Adolph Strauch," 5.

67. Ibid.

68. Cleveland, *Landscape Architecture*, ix.

69. Ibid., 17.

70. Newton, *Design on the Land*, 312.

71. Cleveland, *Landscape Architecture*, 82.

72. Newton, *Design on the Land*, 312.

Contemporary Resources

National Register Nominations

Nearly 50 percent of the rural cemeteries identified as part of this study (see appendix C) have been listed in the National Register of Historic Places, which is America's official list of buildings, sites, districts, structures, and objects worthy of preservation. Rural cemeteries were included in the National Register shortly after its creation in 1966. One of the first to be included was Hollywood Cemetery in Richmond, Virginia, which was listed in 1969. Rural cemeteries continue to be added to this celebrated list today. The depth of information provided by the National Register nomination forms generally correlates to when the cemetery was nominated. The earliest nominations tend to be more succinct than more recent ones. The level of documentation provided in the nomination forms for Forest Hills Cemetery (2004) and Graceland Cemetery (2000), for instance, is much more extensive than that provided for Hollywood. However, National Register nominations are an excellent resource to consult in the process of researching any rural cemetery that has already been listed in the National Register.

For each of the listed cemeteries, National Register nomination forms provide a contemporary description of the property as well as a description of the physical evolution of the site. The nominations also evaluate the significance of the property. Although some rural cemeteries are evaluated under multiple areas of significance including architecture, art, urban planning, and even entertainment/recreation, landscape architecture tends to be the focus of the discussion of the statement of significance. Therefore, the process of site selection, involvement of land surveyors and landscapes designers, and creation of early landscape plans are documented, if known. National Register nominations are, therefore, one of the best contemporary sources to consult for information on the landscape characteristics of rural cemeteries.

National Register nomination forms also provide bibliographies of source material on the property and photographs taken at the time of the nomination.

Websites

More than half of the rural cemeteries identified as part of this study (see appendix C) have a website either created by the cemetery's governing authority or by an official "Friends" group. The type and depth of information differs from one site to another, however. Although most have a history page or an about us page with historical information, the articles vary significantly. For instance, the website for Mount Olivet in Nashville relays the cemetery's founding date and references its "celebrated history." But the primary goal of the website for Mount Olivet—an active cemetery that is administered by a national funeral provider—is to supply details about the cemetery's burial services. In sharp contrast, Laurel Hill Cemetery provides much more extensive information about its history—the motivation for its founding, its design by John Notman, and its role as a rural retreat for the citizens of Philadelphia. Although still an active cemetery, Laurel Hill is a major tourist attraction and educational resource in the city. It is also a National Historic Landmark. As such, it offers guided walking tours and special events highlighting the history of the site. This is reflected in the content of its website. Most of the rural cemetery websites do offer contemporary maps and photographs of the property. This documentation can be particularly useful if historic maps and photographs are either available on the website as well or from another source. Researchers can then compare the layout and landscape features from different time periods to obtain a better understanding of the physical evolution of the property.

Cemetery Publications—Books and Brochures

Cemetery associations, foundations, and friends groups often produce contemporary publications that promote and educate the public about the history of the site and the people interred there. Just as website content varies widely, so too does the type and depth of information in these contemporary accounts.

Many rural cemeteries are attractions for heritage tourists, and numerous cemeteries have produced self-guided tour brochures to satisfy the curiosity of their guests. These guides often provide a brief historical overview of the cemetery and a map keyed to specific buildings, structures, and monuments of interest, which are then concisely described. Oakwood Cemetery in Syracuse, New York, has a particularly informative walking-tour brochure. It provides a short account of the rural cemetery movement and descriptions of features that the site's designer Howard Daniels created. The brochure presents information on the cemetery's entry area, its main avenues, several of its main monuments, as well as the landform and vegetation of Dedication Valley. It also includes several historic photographs so visitors can compare the cemetery's contemporary landscape to its historic one. Most cemetery brochures, however, emphasize the individuals buried in the cemetery with brief biographies provided and the location of their monuments indicated on a map. Cemetery brochures are, in fact, a good source of contemporary maps that can reveal landscape elements such as circulation patterns; these can be compared to historic maps to reveal changes in the cemetery's layout over time.

A few of the largest and most well-known rural cemeteries have published books about the history and inhabitants of their site. As with tour brochures, cemetery histories place a particular emphasis on individual grave markers and the life stories of those interred there. The overwhelming majority of *Woodlawn Remembers: Cemetery of American History*, for instance, focuses on notable people buried there and their monuments. The book does, however, begin with a historical overview of cemetery precedents and the development of the rural cemetery movement as well as the motivation for Woodlawn's founding and details regarding its establishment. The depth of information in this regard varies widely from publication to publication. Although contemporary photographs (not surprisingly) outnumber historic images in these publications, the books are generally valuable compilations of images that make research of visual documentation of cemetery sites efficient.

Historic Resources

Historic Guidebooks and Travel Accounts

Rural cemeteries were the precursors of American parks, and during the nineteenth century, they attracted visitors to enjoy "refined outdoor recreation amidst art and sculpture previously available only for the wealthy." Visitors enjoyed picnics in wooded glades and spectacular views from their carriages as they rode along winding avenues. Rural cemeteries became such popular attractions that travel guidebooks often featured them as must-see destinations and frequently offered glimpses of what the visitor would and *should* see as well as directions on how to reach the sites. *Appletons' Handbook of American Travel* from 1857, for instance, informed tourists that Mount Auburn Cemetery's "walks, and lanes, and lawns make it the most delightful of all the resorts in the vicinage of the city" and that "cars run from the station in Bowdoin square, every 15 minutes, during the day, and until half-past eleven o'clock at night."

Some cemetery sightseers recorded their impressions of the rural burial places they visited that can be found in published form today. The accounts often provide both sentimental reactions to these "cities of the dead" as well as landscape details at a particular moment in time. A visitor to Magnolia Cemetery in 1859, for example, described it as being "situated some mile or more from the city, on low and broken ground, intersected by a winding creek, whose banks are sunny and pleasant. Here and there may be seen a gray old rock, standing erect like a sentinel, within the precincts of this consecrated inclosure, in company with groups of native trees, hung with trailing moss, and looking like gray nuns." This account was contemporaneously published in the *Great Republic Monthly*, and later republished as part of a compilation of accounts of *Travels in the Old South*.

Historic Newspaper Accounts

Not only did Boston's newspapers report on the founding of the ground-breaking cemetery at Mount Auburn but newspapers from as far away as Washington, D.C., did as well. The creation of this new type of civic institution was, indeed, newsworthy during the period.

Local newspapers often reported on the founding of rural cemeteries in their own communities. They also frequently reported on dedication ceremonies, which were notable events worthy of coverage. For instance, in its September 12, 1850, edition, the *Sun* reported on the dedication of the Pittsfield Rural Cemetery in Pittsfield, Massachusetts, and relayed that "between 3 and 4000, participated in the exercises of the deeply interesting occasion." Such newspaper accounts were often accompanied by descriptions of the new cemeteries and details surrounding the development of the site. The Pittsfield paper, for instance, gave the following details: "The spot selected for the Cemetery is the farm formerly owned by Geo. W. Campbell, Esq., and previously by the late Dr. Timothy Childs, about 1 ½ mile northwest of the village, and consisting of about 140 acres. Only about 70 acres, for the purposes of immediate burial, have been laid out by Dr. Horatio Stone, a gentleman whose skill and refined taste in this particular department is unsurpassed." Newspapers even commented more broadly on the impetus for the development of the new landscape aesthetic and trends in the evolution of the design ideal.

Dedicatory Addresses and Cemetery Histories

Numerous rural cemeteries published contemporary accounts of the founding of their cemetery corporation and its regulations and often included transcripts of the cemetery's dedicatory address. These accounts frequently reported on site selection and landscape planning as well. Although undoubtedly self-aggrandizing, these cemetery publications often provide details of the early history of the cemeteries difficult to obtain from other sources. The publications also speak more broadly to the motivations behind the establishment of such institutions, particularly through the text of the dedicatory addresses themselves. The addresses are often lyrical and laced with dramatic language, but at their heart the speeches reflect the mindset of the period. For instance, Prof. C. Mason, in his introductory address at Dale Cemetery in New York, stated that "the Cemetery will be an important source of social welfare because of the rural and sculptural art which will be here displayed. These arts will instruct the eyes of the people to appreciate what is beautiful." The dedication address for the same cemetery suggested that "the multitudes of trees and shrubs which are found in Rural Cemeteries, while they beautify and adorn the ground, tend to purify the air and neutralize, in a measure, the influence of the miasma." Overall, these contemporary accounts reveal the general sentiment of the period toward the establishment of these institutions.

Maps, Plans, and Bird's-Eye Views

Historic maps and plans are an important source of information about the landscape characteristics and layouts of rural cemeteries. Maps not only illustrate road patterns and names but may also reveal topographical details of the site at a particular moment in time. For instance, a map of Green-Wood Cemetery produced by engraver William Lawrence reveals the layout of the curvilinear roadways, the location and names of hills and dells, and the size and location of three water features in the cemetery around 1846. Comparing maps produced at different times for the same cemetery can help illuminate the evolution of the property. A map produced by surveyor Edward Boyle of Green-Wood in 1850 clearly reveals, for example, how the cemetery had expanded southward when compared to the earlier plan of the grounds. State and local historical societies, public libraries, and the Library of Congress are all excellent sources for early maps and plans of rural cemeteries. Many of these institutions have begun to digitize their collections, and many historic cemetery maps can be accessed online. The Library of Congress and the New York Public Library have particularly valuable online collections.

Historic Photographs, Postcards, and Other Visual Material

Historic photographs, as well as other visual material, are important sources of information about the early landscape character of rural cemeteries. The photographic medium was introduced to the public with the daguerreotype in 1839, within the first decade of the establishment of Mount Auburn Cemetery. Jacob Bigelow, reflecting the enthusiasm for the new technique, commented in his *Useful Arts* on the "perfection of M. Daguerre's process, by which the external picture is depicted in miniature, light for light, and shade for shade, to the minutest gradation of each." At mid-century, stereographs and stereoscopes helped fuel the popularity of photography. Stereographs were two almost identical photographic images of a scene mounted side-by-side on a stiff support. When viewed through a binocular device called a stereoscope, the image appeared three-dimensional to the viewer. The technology was first introduced to the public at the Crystal Palace Exhibition of 1851 in England. It became exceedingly popular in the United States beginning in the 1860s and continued to be used extensively into the 1910s. Stereographs are, therefore, an excellent source of documentation on the evolving rural cemetery of the late nineteenth century.

Many historic cemeteries have adopted new landscape trends over time. What a visitor to a rural cemetery sees today might not reflect the original design intent of the cemetery's founders. Historic images can often reveal whether the early landscape character was Picturesque or Beautiful. And a series of historic images can depict the maturation of a particular landscape aesthetic at the site or the transformation of the site based on more "modern" landscape principles. For instance, the side-by-side comparison of early engravings of Mount Auburn Cemetery with stereographs from the early twentieth century reveals a dramatic change from a Picturesque, woodsy landscape with widely dispersed monuments to a much more manicured scene with ornamental shrubs, closely cropped grass, and numerous memorials.

Cemetery associations are an excellent source of historic photographs; many of these institutions maintain their own archives of historical documentation. Local and state historical societies, such as the Filson Historical Society in Louisville, Kentucky, and the Maine Historical Society, are also good sources of photographs, postcards, and other visual materials. Public libraries should not be overlooked. The New York Public Library has an online digital gallery that is particularly valuable; it has images not only of cemeteries in New York but also cemeteries in other states, such as Bonaventure Cemetery in Savannah, Georgia. In addition, the Prints and Photographs Division of the Library of Congress is a significant repository of cemetery images from across the country.

A. D. G. "Rural Cemeteries." *Horticulturist and Journal of Rural Art and Rural Taste* 5, no. 6 (June 1855): 1278–82.

An Address by Rev. Henry Neill, and a Poem by Oliver Wendell Holmes: Delivered at the Dedication of the Pittsfield (Rural) Cemetery, September 9th, 1850, With Other Matter, and a Map of the Grounds. Pittsfield, Mass.: Axtel, Bull and Marsh, printers, 1850.

Alden, Henry Mills. "Editor's Easy Chair." *Harper's New Monthly Magazine* 46 (February 1873): 452–56.

Allegheny Cemetery: Historical Account of Incidents and Events Connected with Its Establishment. Charter and Supplemental Acts of Legislation. Reports of 1848 and 1857. Proceedings of Corporators, June 21, 1873 . . . Remarks on the Ornamentation and Arrangement of Cemeteries. Funeral Oration of Wilson McCandless . . . on Commodore Barney and Lieut. Parker. Pittsburgh: Bakewell & Marthens, 1873.

"American Cemeteries." *Garden and Forest* 1, no. 10 (May 2, 1888): 109.

Angevine, Edward. *A Guide or Handbook for Mount Hope Cemetery With Photo-Engravings and Diagram.* Rochester, N.Y.: Democrat and Chronicle Book and Job Print, 1885.

Arfwedson, Carl David. *The United States and Canada, in 1832, 1833 and 1834.* Vol. 1. London: Richard Bentley, 1834.

Ariès, Philippe. *The Hour of Our Death: The Classic History of Western Attitudes Toward Death Over the Last One Thousand Years.* Translated by Helen Weaver. New York: Vintage Books, 2008. First published 1981 by Alfred A. Knopf, Inc.

Baltimore (Md.) City Department of Recreation and Parks, People & Parks Foundation (Baltimore, Md.), Druid Hill Advisory Committee (Baltimore, Md.), and LANDSCAPES. *Renewing Druid Hill Park: A Vision for the Future of Baltimore's Great Park.* 1995.

Barry, P. "Drooping Trees." *Horticulturist and Journal of Rural Art and Rural Taste* 5, no. 3 (September 1850): 123–26.

Bender, Thomas. "The 'Rural' Cemetery Movement: Urban Travail and the Appeal of Nature." *The New England Quarterly* 47, no. 2 (June 1974): 196–211.

Berendt, John. *Midnight in the Garden of Good and Evil.* New York: Random House, 1994.

Berg, Shary Page. "Mount Auburn Cemetery: An Evolving Legacy of Public Horticulture." *Journal of the New England Garden History Society* 5 (Fall 1997): 9–16.

Bergman, Edward F. *Woodlawn Remembers: Cemetery of American History.* Utica, N.Y.: North Country Books, 1988.

Beveridge, Charles E. "The California Origins of Olmsted's Landscape Design Principles for the Semiarid American West." In *The Papers of Frederick Law Olmsted: The California Frontier, 1863–1865.* Vol. 5, edited by Victoria Post Ranney, 449–73. Baltimore: Johns Hopkins University Press, 1977.

Bigelow, Jacob. *A History of Mount Auburn Cemetery.* Boston and Cambridge: James Munroe and Company, 1860. Reprint, Cambridge: Published in cooperation with the Mount Auburn Cemetery, Applewood Books, 1988.

———. *The Useful Arts: Considered in Connexion with the Application of Science.* Vol. 1. New York: Harper & Brothers, Publishers, 1853.

Birnbaum, Charles A., and Lisa E. Crowder, eds. *Pioneers of American Landscape Design: An Annotated Bibliography.* Washington, D.C.: US Department of the Interior, National Park Service, Cultural Resources, 1993.

Birnbaum, Charles A., and Stephanie S. Foell, eds. *Shaping the American Landscape: New Profiles from the Pioneers of American Landscape Design Project.* Charlottesville: University of Virginia Press, 2009.

[Board of Commissioners of the Central Park.] "Description of the Central Park, With an Explanation of the Purposes of the Work Already Done Upon the Site, and of That in Immediate Contemplation, January 1859." In *The Papers of Frederick Law Olmsted,* Vol. 3, *Creating Central Park, 1857–1861,* edited by Charles E. Beveridge and David Schuyler, 204–19. Baltimore: Johns Hopkins University Press, 1983.

Bremer, Fredrika. *America of the Fifties: Letters of Fredrika Bremer.* Selected and edited by Adolph B. Benson. New York: American-Scandinavian Foundation, 1924.

———. *The Homes of the New World, Impressions of America, by Fredrika Bremer.* Translated by Mary Howitt. Vol. 1. New York: Harper & Brothers, 1853.

Bryant, William Cullen. "The Old Man's Funeral." In *Poetical Works of William Cullen Bryant,* 53–55. New York: D. Appleton and Company, 1883.

———. "Thanatopsis." In *Poetical Works of William Cullen Bryant,* 24–26. New York: D. Appleton and Company, 1883.

Bryant, William Cullen, ed. *Picturesque America, or, The Land We Live In: A Delineation by Pen and Pencil of the Mountains, Rivers, Lakes, Forests, Water-Falls, Shores, Cañons, Valleys, Cities, and Other Picturesque Features of Our Country.* 2 vols. New York: D. Appleton and Co., 1872.

Buckingham, James Silk. *America: Historical, Statistical and Descriptive.* Vol. 2. New York: Harper & Brothers, 1841.

Carmack, Sharon DeBartolo. *Your Guide to Cemetery Research.* Cincinnati, Ohio: Betterway Books, 2002.

Carter, Nathaniel H. *Letters from Europe: Comprising the Journal of a Tour Through Ireland, England, Scotland, France, Italy, and Switzerland in the Years 1825, '26, and '27.* Vol. 1. New York: G. & C. Carvill, 1827.

Cedar Hill Cemetery (Hartford, Conn.). *Cedar Hill Cemetery, Hartford Connecticut, 1863–1903.* Hartford, Conn.: The Cemetery, 1903.

Channing, William Ellery. "Likeness to God: Discourse at the Ordination of the Rev. F. A. Farley, Providence, R.I., 1828." In *The Complete Works of William Ellery Channing, D.D.: Including the Perfect Life, and Containing a Copious General Index and a Table of Scripture References,* 230–37. London: "Christian Life" Publishing Co., 1884.

———. "Unitarian Christianity: Discourse at the Ordination of the Rev. Jared Sparks, Baltimore, 1819." In *The Complete Works of William Ellery Channing, D.D.: Including the Perfect Life, and Containing a Copious General Index and a Table of Scripture References,* 278–88. London: "Christian Life" Publishing Co., 1884.

Chapman, Silas. *The Forest Home Cemetery, Milwaukee, Wis.: With a Map of the Grounds.* Milwaukee, Wis.: Godfrey & Crandall's Book Printing House, 1871.

Church, Pharcellus. *An Address Delivered at the Dedication of Mount Hope Cemetery, Rochester, Oct. 2, 1838; And Repeated, by Request, Before the Rochester Athenæ and Young Men's Association.* Rochester, N.Y.: David Hoyt, printer, 1839.

Ciregna, Elise Madeleine. "Museum in the Garden: Mount Auburn Cemetery and American Sculpture, 1840–1860." *Markers* 21 (2004): 100–47.

City of Boston. "Report of the Joint Special Committee on Intramural Interments." Document 96—1879. Boston, 1879.

Cleveland, H. W. S. *A Few Words on the Arrangement of Rural Cemeteries.* Chicago: Geo. K. Hazlitt & Co., 1881.

———. *Landscape Architecture, As Applied to the Wants of the West: With an Essay on Forest Planting on the Great Plains.* Chicago: Jansen, McClurg & Co., 1873. Reprinted with preface by Robin Karson and introduction by Daniel J. Nadenicek and Lance M. Neckar. Amherst: University of Massachusetts Press in association with Library of American Landscape History, 2002.

Cleaveland, N. *Green-wood Cemetery: A History of the Institution from 1838–1864 . . . With Illustrations.* New York: Anderson & Archer, 1866.

———. *Green-Wood: A Directory for Visitors.* New York: Pudney & Russell, Printers, 1850.

———. *Green-Wood Illustrated. In Highly Finished Line Engraving, from Drawings Taken on the Spot, by James Smillie. With Descriptive Notices, by Nehemiah Cleaveland.* The Rural Cemeteries of America. New York: R. Martin, 1847.

———. *Hints Concerning Green-Wood: Its Monuments and Improvements.* New York: Pudney & Russell, Printers, 1853.

Clifford, Derek Plint. *A History of Garden Design.* Rev. ed. New York: Praeger, 1966.

Clinton Cemetery Association (Clinton, N.Y.). *Addresses Delivered at the Dedication of the Clinton Cemetery: With a Copy of the Act Authorizing the Formation of Rural Cemetery Associations: Together with the Rules and Regulations, Dedicatory Proceedings, &C., Clinton, N.Y., 1857.* Utica: Roberts, printer, 1857.

Cook, Clarence. *A Description of the New York Central Park.* New York: F. J. Huntington and Co., 1869.

Cothran, James R. *Gardens and Historic Plants of the Antebellum South.* Columbia: University of South Carolina Press, 2003.

Crafts, William A. *Forest Hills Cemetery: Its Establishment, Progress, Scenery, Monuments, Etc.* Roxbury: John Backup, 1855.

Crown Hill Cemetery. Indianapolis: Journal Job Printing Company, 1896.

Curl, James Stevens. *The Victorian Celebration of Death.* Stroud: Sutton Publishing, 2000.

Dale Cemetery (Ossining, N.Y.). *The Dale Cemetery, (at Claremont, Near Sing-Sing,) Its Incorporation, Rules and Regulations, and the Dedication Addresses.* New York: C. C. Childs, printer, 1852.

Dall, Caroline Wells Healey. *In Memoriam, Alexander Wadsworth.* Washington, D.C., 1898.

Darnall, Margaretta. "The American Cemetery as Picturesque Landscape: Bellefontaine Cemetery, St. Louis." *Winterthur Portfolio* 18, no. 4 (Winter 1983): 249–69.

Davis, William T., ed. *Bradford's History of Plymouth Plantation, 1606–1646.* New York: C. Scribner's Sons, 1908.

Dearborn, Nathaniel. *A Concise History of and Guide Through Mount Auburn With a Catalogue of Lots Laid Out in That Cemetery, a Map of the Grounds, and Terms of Subscription, Regulations Concerning Visitors, Interments, &C., &C.* Boston: Nathaniel Dearborn, 1843.

———. *Dearborn's Guide Through Mount Auburn: With Eighty Engravings for the Benefit of Strangers, Desirous of Seeing the Clusters of Monuments with the Least Trouble: With the Established Rules for the Preservation of the Cemetery, Purchase of Lots, and Other Concerns.* 11th ed. Boston: Nathaniel S. Dearborn, 1857.

Downing, Andrew Jackson. *Rural Essays.* Edited, with a Memoir of the Author, by George William Curtis; and A Letter to His Friends, by Fredrika Bremer. New York: George P. Putnam and Company, 1853.

———. *A Treatise on the Theory and Practice of Landscape Gardening: Adapted to North America.* 4th ed. New York: Putnam, 1850. Reprinted with an introduction by Therese O'Malley. Washington, D.C.: Dumbarton Oaks Research Library and Collection, 1991.

Draper, John William. *The Funeral Elegy and the Rise of English Romanticism.* New York: Phaeton Press, 1967.

"Drooping Deciduous Trees." *Horticulturist and Journal of Rural Art and Rural Taste* 22 (March 1967): 69–73.

Duer, Stephen C., and Allan B. Smith. *Cypress Hills Cemetery.* Charleston, S.C.: Arcadia Publishing, 2010.

Earnheart, Bruce W. "Rose Hill Cemetery: Derivation, Development, Degeneration." MLA thesis, University of Georgia, 1989.

Edgell Grove Cemetery (Framingham, Mass.). *Edgell Grove Cemetery, Framingham, Mass.* Framingham, Mass.: The Cemetery, 1938.

Ellis, George Edward. *An Address Delivered at the Consecration of the Woodlawn Cemetery In Chelsea and Malden. On July 2, 1851.* Boston: Printed by John Wilson & Son, 1851.

Elmwood Cemetery Association (Memphis, Tenn.). *Elmwood: Charter, Rules, Regulations and By-Laws of Elmwood Cemetery Association of Memphis.* Memphis, Tenn.: Boyle & Chapman Printers, Publishers and Binders, 1874.

Elwell, Edward H. *Portland and Vicinity, With a Sketch of Old Orchard Beach and Other Maine Resorts.* Rev. ed. Portland: Loring, Short & Harmon, 1881.

Erie Cemetery (Erie, Pa.). *Erie Cemetery: A Hand Book, Historical, Biographical and Descriptive, Containing Also the Charter and Laws, Rules and Regulations, and Other Matters of General Information.* Erie, Pa.: Herald Printing and Publishing Co., 1903.

Etlin, Richard A. *The Architecture of Death: The Transformation of the Cemetery in Eighteenth-Century Paris.* Cambridge, Mass.: MIT Press, 1984.

———. "Père Lachaise and the Garden Cemetery." *Journal of Garden History* 4, no. 3 (1984): 211–22.

Eurich, Frank. "Life of Adolph Strauch." In *Modern Cemeteries: A Selection of Papers Read Before the Annual Meetings of the Association of American Cemetery Superintendents, 1887–1897,* 132–35. Chicago: The AACS, 1898.

Evelyn, John. *Silva Or, A Discourse of Forest-Trees, and the Propagation of Timber in His Majesty's Dominions: As It Was Delivered in the Royal Society the 15th of October, 1662, Upon Occasion of Certain Quaeries Propounded to That Illustrious Assembly, by the Honourable and Principal Officers and Commissioners of the Navy. In Two Books.* 5th ed. London: Printed for J. Walthoe, J. Knapton, D. Midwinter, A. Bettesworth, J. Tonson, W. Innys, R. Robinson, J. Wilford, J. Osborn and T. Longman, B. Motte, A. Ward, 1729.

Farber, Jessie Lie. *The Association for Gravestone Studies: Symbolism in the Carvings of Old Gravestones.* Greenfield, Mass.: The Association for Gravestone Studies, 1986.

Farrell, James J. *Inventing the American Way of Death, 1830–1920.* Philadelphia: Temple University Press, 1980.

Favretti, Rudy J. *Jacob Weidenmann: Pioneer Landscape Architect.* Hartford, Conn.: Cedar Hill Cemetery Foundation, 2007.

Favretti, Rudy J., and Joy P. Favretti. *Landscapes and Gardens for Historic Buildings: A Handbook for Reproducing and Creating Authentic Landscape Settings.* 2nd ed., rev. Walnut Creek: Altamira Press, 1997.

Fitzgerald, Edward. *A Hand Book for the Albany Rural Cemetery With an Appendix on Emblems.* Albany: Van Benthuysen Printing House, 1871.

Flagg, Wilson. *Mount Auburn: Its Scenes, Its Beauties, and Its Lessons.* Boston: James Munroe and Co., 1861.

Frankfort Cemetery Company (Frankfort, Ky.). *Charter and By-Laws of the Frankfort Cemetery Co. With the Revised Rules and Regulations Adopted A.D., 1936.* Frankfort, Ky.: Roberts Printing Co., 1936.

Fraser, Charles. *Address Delivered on the Dedication of Magnolia Cemetery, On the 19th November, 1850.* Charleston, S.C.: Walker and James, 1850.

French, Stanley. "The Cemetery as Cultural Institution: The Establishment of Mount Auburn and the 'Rural Cemetery' Movement." *American Quarterly* 26, no. 1 (March 1974): 37–59.

Gabel, Laurel K. "Ritual, Regalia and Remembrance: Fraternal Symbolism and Gravestones." *Markers* 16 (1994): 1–27.

Gado, Frank. "William Cullen Bryant." Poetry Foundation. *From Gado, Frank, ed. William Cullen Bryant: An American Voice.* Hartford, Vt.: Antoca Press, 2006. http://www.poetryfoundation.org/bio/william-cullen-bryant (accessed January 2, 2015).

Gibson, Campbell. "Population of the 100 Largest Cities and Other Urban Places in the United States: 1790 to 1990." Population Division Working Paper No. 27, Population Division, US Bureau of the Census, Washington, D.C., June 1998. https://www.census.gov/population/www/documentation/twps0027/twps0027.html (accessed June 6, 2014).

Gilman, Caroline Howard. *An Essay Upon Prints Containing Remarks Upon the Principles of Picturesque Beauty, the Different Kinds of Prints, and the Characters of the Most Noted Masters, Illustrated by Criticisms Upon Particular Pieces, to Which Are Added Some Cautions That May Be Useful in Collecting Prints.* 2nd ed. London: Printed by G. Scott, 1768.

———. *The Poetry of Travelling in the United States.* New York: S. Colman, 1838.

Gilpin, William. *Remarks on Forest Scenery And Other Woodland Views, (Relative Chiefly to Picturesque Beauty) Illustrated by the Scenes of New-Forest in Hampshire: In Three Books.* Vol. 1. London: Printed for R. Blamire, Strand., 1791.

Girardin, René. *An Essay on Landscape; Or, the Means of Improving and Embellishing the Country Round Our Habitations. Translated from the French of R. L. Gérardin Victe D'Ermenonville.* London: Printed for J. Dodsley, Pall-Mall, 1783.

Gray, Thomas. *Elegy Written in a Country Church-Yard.* London, John Van Voorst, 1834. First published 1751 by R. Dodsley.

Green Mount Cemetery: One Hundredth Anniversary, 1838–1938. Baltimore: The Proprietors of the Green Mount Cemetery, 1938.

Green-Wood Cemetery (New York, N.Y.), and N. Cleaveland. *Rules and Regulations of the Green-Wood Cemetery; With a Catalogue of Proprietors.* New York, 1853.

Greiff, Constance M. *John Notman, Architect, 1810–1865.* Philadelphia: Athenaeum of Philadelphia, 1979.

Gurda, John. *Silent City: A History of Forest Home Cemetery.* Milwaukee, Wis.: Forest Home Cemetery, 2000.

Hadfield, Miles. *The English Landscape Garden.* Aylesbury: Shire Publications, 1977.

Hall, Basil. *Travels in North America, in the Years 1827 and 1828.* 3rd ed. Vol. 2. Edinburgh: Printed for Robert Cadell, 1830.

Hall, Edward H., ed. *Appletons' Hand-Book of American Travel: Containing a Full Description of the Principal Cities, Towns, and Places of Interest: Together with the Routes of Travel, and Leading Hotels Throughout the United States and British Provinces.* 9th ed. New York: D. Appleton & Co, 1869.

Halvorson Co., Portland (Me.), and Friends of Evergreen Cemetery. *Evergreen Cemetery, Portland Maine: Master Plan.* Boston, Mass.: Halvorson Co., 1994.

Harkness, Rosa, and Stewart B. Harkness. *A History of West Laurel Hill Cemetery.* Bala Cynwyd, Pa., 1990.

Harmony Grove Cemetery, Salem, Mass. Salem, Mass.: G. M. Whipple and A. A. Smith, 1866.

Hayward, John. *A Gazetteer of Massachusetts Containing Descriptions of All the Counties, Towns, and Districts, in the Commonwealth, Also, of Its Principal Mountains, Rivers, Capes, Bays, Harbours, Islands, and Fashionable Resorts; To Which Are Added, Statistical Accounts of Its Agriculture, Commerce, and Manufactures, with a Great Variety of Other Useful Information.* Rev. ed. Boston: John P. Jewett & Co., 1849.

Hedrick, U. P. *A History of Horticulture in America to 1860.* New York: Oxford University Press, 1950. Reprint, *A History of Horticulture in America to 1860 with an Addendum of Books Published 1861–1920 by Elisabeth Woodburn.*, Portland, Oregon: Timber Press, 1988.

Henderson, Desirée. "'What is the grass?': The Roots of Walt Whitman's Cemetery Meditation." *Walt Whitman Quarterly Review* 25, no. 3 (Winter 2008): 89–107.

Hijiya, James A. "American Gravestones and Attitudes toward Death: A Brief History." *Proceedings of the American Philosophical Society* 127, no. 5 (Oct. 14, 1983), 339–63.

Historical Sketch and Matters Appertaining to the Granary Burial-Ground. Boston: Municipal Printing Office, 1902.

The Holy Bible. Revised Standard Version Containing the Old and New Testaments, Translated from the Original Tongues; Being the Version Set Forth A.D. 1611, Revised A.D. 1881–1885 and A.D. 1901; Compared with the Most Ancient Authorities and Revised A.D. 1946–1952. New York: World Publishing Company, 1962.

Howard, George W. *The Monumental City: Its Past History and Present Resources.* Baltimore: J. D. Ehlers & Co., Engravers and Steam Book Printers, 1873.

Howett, Catherine. "Living Landscapes for the Dead." *Landscape* 21, no. 3 (Spring–Summer 1977): 9–17.

Inventory of the Historic and Archaeological Assets of the Commonwealth Form, Hope Cemetery, Worcester, Massachusetts, 1995.

Inventory of the Historic and Archaeological Assets of the Commonwealth Form, Mount Wollaston, Quincy, Massachusetts, 1986.

Inventory of the Historic and Archaeological Assets of the Commonwealth Form, Rural Cemetery, New Bedford, Massachusetts, 2009.

Inventory of the Historic and Archaeological Assets of the Commonwealth Form, Rural Cemetery, Southborough, Massachusetts, 2000.

Inventory of the Historic and Archaeological Assets of the Commonwealth Form, Wildwood Cemetery, Winchester, Massachusetts, 1987.

Irving, Washington. *The Sketch Book of Geoffrey Crayon, Gent.* In *The Complete Works of Washington Irving in One Volume, With a Memoir of the Author*, 225–344. Frankfort on the Main: Sold by Sigismond Schmerber, 1835.

Jackson, Kenneth T. *Crabgrass Frontier: The Suburbanization of the United States.* New York: Oxford University Press, 1985.

Jackson, Kenneth T., and Camilo Jose Vergara. *Silent Cities: The Evolution of the American Cemetery.* New York: Princeton Architectural Press, 1989.

Karl Baedeker (Firm). *The United States: With an Excursion into Mexico: A Handbook for Travellers, 1893.* Reprint, New York: Da Capo Press, 1971.

Karson, Robin. "Layers of Invention at Graceland Cemetery." *View*, Summer 2010, 5–7.

Keister, Douglas. *Forever Dixie: A Field Guide to Southern Cemeteries & Their Residents.* Salt Lake City, Utah: Gibbs Smith, Publisher, 2008.

———. *Going Out in Style: The Architecture of Eternity.* New York: Facts On File, 1997.

———. *Stories in Stone: A Field Guide to Cemetery Symbolism and Iconography.* Salt Lake City, Utah: Gibbs Smith, Publisher, 2004.

Kern, G. M. "The Cemetery." In *Practical Landscape Gardening: With Reference to the Improvement of Rural Residences, Giving the General Principles of the Art; with Full Directions for Planting Shade Trees, Shrubbery and Flowers, and Laying Out Grounds*, 258–67. 3rd. ed. Cincinnati: Moore, Wilstach, Keys & Co., 1855.

Kidney, Walter C. *Allegheny Cemetery: A Romantic Landscape in Pittsburgh.* Pittsburgh: Pittsburgh History & Landmarks Foundation, 1990.

Laderman, Gary. *The Sacred Remains: American Attitudes Toward Death, 1799–1883.* New Haven: Yale University Press, 1996.

Lanctot, Barbara. *A Walk Through Graceland Cemetery.* Chicago: Chicago School of Architecture Foundation, 1977.

Laurel Hill Cemetery (Philadelphia, Pa.). *Guide to Laurel Hill Cemetery, Near Philadelphia: With a List of Lotholders.* Philadelphia: T. K. and P. G. Collins, Printers, [1857?].

Ledent, Sabra Bissette. *A Tribute to Oakdale, 1852–1991.* Wilmington, N.C.: Oakdale Cemetery Co., 1991.

Leland, Ernest Stevens, and Donald W. Smith. *The Pioneers of Cemetery Administration in America, A Collection of Biographical Essays.* New York: Printed by the Sterling Press, 1941.

Lincoln, Levi. *An Address Delivered on the Consecration of the Worcester Rural Cemetery, September 8, 1838.* Boston: Dutton and Wentworth, printers, 1838.

Linden, Blanche M. G. *Death and the Garden: The Cult of the Melancholy and the "Rural" Cemetery.* PhD thesis, Harvard University, 1981.

———. *Silent City on a Hill: Picturesque Landscapes of Memory and Boston's Mount Auburn Cemetery.* Amherst: University of Massachusetts Press in association with Library of American Landscape History, 2007.

———. *Spring Grove: Celebrating 150 Years.* Cincinnati: Cincinnati Historical Society, 1995.

———. "The Willow Tree and Urn Motif." *Markers* 1 (1979/80): 149–55.

Linden-Ward, Blanche. "The Fencing Mania': The Rise and Fall of Nineteenth Century Funerary Enclosures." *Markers* 7 (1990): 35–58.

———. "Putting the Past in Place: The Making of Mount Auburn Cemetery." *Cambridge Historical Society Proceedings* 44 (1976–79): 171–96.

Loudon, J. C. "Reviews." *Gardener's Magazine* 8 (1832): 698–720.

———. *On the Laying Out, Planting, and Managing of Cemeteries and on the Improvement of Churchyards, with Sixty Engravings.* London, 1843. Reprinted with an introduction by James Stevens Curl. Redhill, Surrey: Ivelet Books, 1981.

Lyell, Charles. *A Second Visit to the United States of North America.* Vol. 1. London: John Murray, 1849.

M'Carty, J. Hendrickson. *Inside the Gates.* Cincinnati: Hitchcock and Walden, 1876.

MacDonald, E. *Old Copp's Hill and Burial Ground: With Historical Sketches.* Boston: Industrial School Press, 1895.

Madden, W. C. *Crown Hill Cemetery.* Charleston, S.C.: Arcadia Publishing, 2004.

Magness, Perre. *Elmwood 2002: In the Shadows of the Elms.* Memphis, Tenn.: Elmwood Cemetery, 2001.

Magnolia Cemetery Company (Charleston, S.C.). *Magnolia Cemetery: The Proceedings at the Dedication of the Grounds, To Which Are Appended the Rules, Regulations and Charter of the Company: With a List of Officers and Members of the Board.* Charleston, S.C.: Steam Power-Press of Walker & James, 1851.

Maltbie, Annie C. *Picturesque Oakwood: Its Past and Present Associations.* Syracuse, N.Y.: Fred. S. Hills, Publisher, 1894.

Mann, William A. *Landscape Architecture: An Illustrated History in Timelines, Site Planning, and Biography.* New York: John Wiley and Sons, Inc., 1993.

Marion, John Francis. *Famous and Curious Cemeteries: A Pictorial, Historical, and Anecdotal View of American and European Cemeteries and the Famous and Infamous People Who Are Buried There.* New York: Crown Publishers, Inc., 1977.

Marshall, Charlotte Thomas. "Oconee Hill Cemetery." *Athens Historian* 2, no. 1 (October 1997): 33–40.

Martineau, Harriet. *Retrospect of Western Travel.* Vol. 3. London: Saunders and Otley, 1838.

Massachusetts Horticultural Society (Boston, Mass.), and Robert Manning. *History of the Massachusetts Horticultural Society. 1829–1878.* Boston: The Society, 1880.

Mattor, Theresa, and Lucie Teegarden. "Rural Cemeteries: Landscapes for the Living and the Dead." In *Designing the Maine Landscape,* 119–35. [Camden, Maine]: Down East Books, 2009.

Mazÿck, Arthur. *Guide to Charleston Illustrated: Being a Sketch of the History of Charleston, S. C., With Some Account of Its Present Condition, With Numerous Engravings.* Charleston: Walker, Evans & Cogswell, 1875.

McCoy-Massey, Debra P. "The Life of Mary Catherine Rion." *Magnolia* 17, no. 2 (Winter 2001–2002): 10–13.

Medley, Julius George. *An Autumn Tour in the United States and Canada.* London: Henry S. King & Co., 1873.

Meinwald, Dan. "Memento Mori: Death in Nineteenth Century Photography." *CMP Bulletin* 9, no. 4 (1990): 1–26.

Michaels, Albert L., Richard O. Reisem, and Bette A. Rupp. *Forest Lawn Cemetery: Buffalo History Preserved.* Buffalo, N.Y.: Forest Lawn Heritage Foundation, 1996.

Mitchell, Mary H. *Hollywood Cemetery: The History of a Southern Shrine.* Richmond: Virginia State Library, 1985.

Morgan, Keith N. "The Emergence of the American Landscape Professional: John Notman and the Design of Rural Cemeteries." *Journal of Garden History* 4, no. 3 (July–September 1984): 267–90.

Moss, Roger W., and Sandra L. Tatman. "Notman, John." American Architects and Buildings, The Athenaeum of Philadelphia. http://americanbuildings.org (accessed May 4, 2013).

———. "Sidney, James Charles." American Architects and Buildings, the Athenaeum of Philadelphia. http://americanbuildings.org (accessed May 4, 2013).

Mount Auburn Cemetery (Cambridge, Mass.). *Visitor's Reference Book.* Mount Auburn: W. H. Safford & Jas. Derby, Jr., 1864.

Mountain View Cemetery Association (Oakland, Calif.). *By-Laws and Rules of Mountain View Cemetery Association with History and Appendix.* 1889.

Muir, John. *A Thousand-Mile Walk to the Gulf.* Edited by William Frederic Badè. Boston: Houghton Mifflin Company, 1916.

Muncy Cemetery (Muncy, Pa.). *History, Condition, Rules, Regulations, Etc. of the Muncy Cemetery at Muncy, Penna.* Muncy, Pa.: Luminary Print, 1896.

National Register of Historic Places Inventory—Nomination Form, Albany Rural Cemetery, Menands, Albany County, New York, 2002.

National Register of Historic Places Inventory—Nomination Form, Allegheny Cemetery, Pittsburgh, Allegheny County, Pennsylvania, 1980.

National Register of Historic Places Registration Form. Bayside Cemetery and Gatehouse Complex, Potsdam, St. Lawrence County, New York, 2002.

National Register of Historic Places Registration Form, Bellevue Cemetery, Lawrence and Methuen, Essex County, Massachusetts, 2003.

National Register of Historic Places Inventory—Nomination Form, Cave Hill Cemetery, Louisville, Jefferson County, Kentucky, 1979.

National Register of Historic Places Registration Form, Cedar Hill Cemetery, Hartford, Hartford County, Connecticut, 1996.

National Register of Historic Places Inventory—Nomination Form, Central Park, New York, New York County, New York, 1975.

National Register of Historic Places Registration Form, Crown Hill National Cemetery, Indianapolis, Marion County, Indiana, 1999.

National Register of Historic Places Registration Form, Easton Cemetery, Easton, Northampton County, Pennsylvania, 1990.

National Register of Historic Places Registration Form, Elmwood Cemetery, Columbia, Richland County, South Carolina, 1995.

National Register of Historic Places Registration Form, Evergreen Cemetery, Oswego, Tioga County, New York, 2002.

National Register of Historic Places Registration Form, Evergreen Cemetery, Portland, Cumberland County, Maine, 1992.

National Register of Historic Places Registration Form, the Evergreens Cemetery, Brooklyn and Queens, Kings and Queens Counties, New York, 2007.

National Register of Historic Places Registration Form, Forest Hills Cemetery, Boston, Suffolk County, Massachusetts, 2004.

National Register of Historic Places Inventory—Nomination Form, Forest Home Cemetery and Chapel, Milwaukee, Milwaukee County, Wisconsin, 1979.

National Register of Historic Places Registration Form, Forest Lawn Cemetery, Buffalo, Erie County, New York, 1990.

National Register of Historic Places Inventory—Nomination Form. Frankfort Cemetery, Frankfort, Franklin County, Kentucky, 1973.

National Register of Historic Places Registration Form, Graceland Cemetery, Chicago, Cook County, Illinois, 2000.

National Register of Historic Places Registration Form, Green-Wood Cemetery, Brooklyn, Kings County, New York, 2006.

National Register of Historic Places Nomination Form, Green Hill Cemetery, Amsterdam, Montgomery County, New York, 2004.

National Register of Historic Places Inventory—Nomination Form, Green Mount Cemetery, Baltimore, Baltimore City County, Maryland, 1979.

National Register of Historic Places Registration Form, Grove Street Cemetery, New Haven, New Haven County, Connecticut, 1997.

National Register of Historic Places Registration Form, Hillside Cemetery, Middletown, Orange County, New York, 1994.

National Register of Historic Places Inventory—Registration Form, Hollywood Cemetery, Richmond, Richmond County, Virginia, 1969.

National Register of Historic Places Registration Form, Laurel Hill Cemetery, Philadelphia, Philadelphia County, Pennsylvania, 1998.

National Register of Historic Places Registration Form, Linden Grove Cemetery, Covington, Kenton County, Kentucky, 2000.

National Register of Historic Places Inventory—Nomination Form, Llewellyn Park Historic District, West Orange, Essex County, New Jersey, 1984.

National Register of Historic Places Registration Form, Machpelah Cemetery, LeRoy, Genesee County, New York, 2007.

National Register of Historic Places Registration Form. Machpelah Cemetery, Mount Sterling, Montgomery County, Kentucky, 1990.

National Register of Historic Places Inventory—Nomination Form. Magnolia Cemetery, Charleston, Charleston County, South Carolina, 1976.

National Register of Historic Places Registration Form, Mount Adnah, Fulton, Oswego County, New York, 2000.

National Register of Historic Places Inventory—Nomination Form, Mount Albion, Albion, Orleans County, New York, 1976.

National Register of Historic Places Registration Form, Mount Auburn, Watertown and Cambridge, Middlesex County, Massachusetts, 2001.

National Register of Historic Places Inventory—Nomination Form, Mount Hope Cemetery, Bangor, Penobscot County, Maine, 1979.

National Register of Historic Places Registration Form, Mount Hope Cemetery, Boston, (Mattapan), Suffolk County, Massachusetts, 2009.

National Register of Historic Places Registration Form, Mount Pleasant Cemetery, Taunton, Bristol County, Massachusetts, 2002.

National Register of Historic Places Registration Form, Oakwood Cemetery, Syracuse, Onondaga County, New York, 1990.

National Register of Historic Places Inventory—Nomination Form, Oakwood Cemetery, Troy, Rensselaer County, New York, 1984.

National Register of Historic Places Registration Form, Pittsfield Rural Cemetery, Pittsfield, Birkshire County, Massachusetts, 2007.

National Register of Historic Places Inventory—Nomination Form, Prospect Park, Brooklyn, Kings County, New York, 1978.

National Register of Historic Places Registration Form, Riverside Cemetery, Oswego, Oswego County, New York, 1993.

National Register of Historic Places Registration Form, Riverside Cemetery, Waterbury, New Haven County, Connecticut, 1988.

National Register of Historic Places Inventory—Nomination Form, Rose Hill Cemetery, Macon, Bibb County, Georgia, 1973.

National Register of Historic Places Inventory—Nomination Form, the Spring Grove Cemetery, Cincinnati, Hamilton County, Ohio, 1975.

National Register of Historic Places Registration Form, Upper Middleburgh Cemetery, Middleburgh, Schoharie County, New York, 2003.

National Register of Historic Places Registration Form, White Plains Rural Cemetery, White Plains, Westchester County, New York, 2003.

National Register of Historic Places Registration Form, the Woodlands, Philadelphia, Philadelphia County, Pennsylvania, 2004.

National Register of Historic Places Registration Form, Draft, Woodlawn Cemetery, Bronx, Bronx County, New York, 2009.

National Register of Historic Places Registration Form, Woodlawn Cemetery, Elmira, Chemung County, New York, 2004.

"The New York Park." *Horticulturist: Journal of Rural Art and Rural Taste* 6, no. 8 (August 1, 1851): 345–49.

Newton, Norman T. *Design on the Land; The Development of Landscape Architecture.* Cambridge, Mass.: Belknap Press of Harvard University Press, 1971.

Nicholas, Anna. *The Story of Crown Hill.* Indianapolis: Crown Hill Association, 1928.

North, Edward. "The Proper Expression of a Rural Cemetery." *Horticulturist: Journal of Rural Art and Rural Taste* 7 (June 1857): 253–56.

Notman, John, and Adolph Strauch. *The Cincinnati Cemetery of Spring Grove: Report for 1857.* Cincinnati: C. F. Bradley & Co., printers, 1857.

Nuxhall, Phillip J., Randall Lee Schieber, Charles Gast, and Robert A. Flischel. *Beauty in the Grove: Spring Grove Cemetery & Arboretum.* Wilmington, Ohio: Orange Frazer Press, 2009.

Oakwood Cemetery (Syracuse, N.Y.). *The History, Incorporation, Rules and Regulations of Oakwood Cemetery, at Syracuse, N.Y.: Together with the Dedication Odes and Addresses, with Other Papers.* Syracuse: J. G. K. Truair & Co., printers, 1860.

Olmsted, Frederick Law. "To Calvert Vaux, March 12th, 1865." In *The Papers of Frederick Law Olmsted: The California Frontier, 1863–1865.* Vol. 5, edited by Victoria Post Ranney, 324–26. Baltimore: Johns Hopkins University Press, 1977.

[Olmsted, Frederick Law, and Calvert Vaux.] "Description of a Plan for the Improvement of Central Park "Greensward."" In *The Papers of Frederick Law Olmsted*, Vol. 3, *Creating Central Park, 1857–1861*, edited by Charles E. Beveridge and David Schuyler, 119–51. Baltimore: Johns Hopkins University Press, 1983.

Olmsted, Frederick Law, and Calvert Vaux. "Preface to the Plan for Mountain View Cemetery, Oakland, California." May 1865. In *The Papers of Frederick Law Olmsted: The California Frontier, 1863–1865.* Vol. 5, edited by Victoria Post Ranney, 473–88. Baltimore: Johns Hopkins University Press, 1977.

Orr, J. Robert. "Tomb with a View: Mount Auburn, Oak Hill and the Rise of the Rural Landscape Cemeteries in America." *Smithsonian Preservation Quarterly,* Summer/Fall 1995, 12–16.

Osteen, Mame. *Haven in the Heart of the City: The History of Lakewood Cemetery.* Minneapolis, Minn.: Lakewood Cemetery, 1992.

Otis, Denise. *Grounds for Pleasure: Four Centuries of the American Garden.* New York: Harry N. Abrams, 2002.

Ovid. *Metamorphoses.* Translated by Horace Gregory with a new introduction by Sara Myers. New York: Signet Classics, 2009.

Payne, Calder W. *Rose Hill Rambles in Rose Hill Cemetery, Macon, Georgia.* Macon: The Middle Georgia Historical Society, 1985.

Peters, John O. *Richmond's Hollywood Cemetery.* Richmond, Va.: Valentine Richmond History Center, 2010.

Phelps, Henry P. *The Albany Rural Cemetery: Its Beauties, Its Memories.* Albany: Phelps and Kellogg, 1893.

Phillips, Ted, and Thomas J. Brown. *City of the Silent: The Charlestonians of Magnolia Cemetery.* Columbia: University of South Carolina Press, 2010.

The Picturesque Pocket Companion, and Visitor's Guide, Through Mount Auburn: Illustrated with Upwards of Sixty Engravings on Wood. Boston: Otis, Broaders and Co., 1839.

Pinckney, Henry Laurens. *Remarks Addressed to the Citizens of Charleston, on the Subject of Interments, and the Policy of Establishing a Public Cemetery, Beyond the Precincts of the City.* Charleston: Printed by Steam Power Press of Walker Evans & Co., 1858.

"Planting in Cemeteries." *Horticulturist: Journal of Rural Art and Rural Taste* 1, no. 10 (April 1847): 479.

"Planting in Cemeteries." *Horticulturist: Journal of Rural Art and Rural Taste* 1, no. 11 (May 1847): 531.

Pollock, Allan. *History of Trinity Church and Its Grave Yard.* New York: Allan Pollock, 1880.

Poughkeepsie Rural Cemetery (Poughkeepsie, N.Y.). *The Poughkeepsie Rural Cemetery, Its by-Laws, Rules and Regulations and the Dedication Ceremonies, with an Appendix.* Poughkeepsie: Platt & Schram's Steam Printing Establishment, 1854.

Price, Uvedale. *An Essay on the Picturesque, As Compared with the Sublime and the Beautiful; and, on the Use of Studying Pictures, for the Purpose of Improving Real Landscape, by Uvedale Price, Esq.* London: Printed for J. Robson, 1794.

"Public Cemeteries and Public Gardens." *Horticulturist and Journal of Rural Art and Rural Taste* 4, no. 1 (July 1849): 9–12.

Putnam, George. *An Address Delivered Before the City Government and Citizens of Roxbury: At the Consecration of the Cemetery at Forest Hills, June 28, 1848.* Roxbury, [Mass.]: Joseph G. Torrey, city printer, 1848.

Rattermann, H. A. *Spring Grove and Its Creator: H.A. Rattermann's Biography of Adolph Strauch.* [1905]. Edited by Don Heinrich Tolzmann. Cincinnati, Ohio: Ohio Book Store, 1988.

Reisem, Richard O., and Frank A. Gillespie. *Buried Treasures in Mount Hope Cemetery, Rochester, New York: A Pictorial Field Guide.* Rochester: Friends of Mount Hope Cemetery, 2002.

———. *Mount Hope, Rochester, New York: America's First Municipal Victorian Cemetery.* Rochester: Printed by Printing Methods, Inc., 1994.

Remarks on the Dangers and Duties of Sepulture; or Security for the Living with Respect and Repose for the Dead, By a Fellow of the Massachusetts Medical Society. Boston: Phelps and Farnham, 1823.

Reps, John William. *The Making of Urban America: A History of City Planning in the United States.* Princeton, N.J.: Princeton University Press, 1992. First published 1965.

"Reviews." *Horticulturist: Journal of Rural Art and Rural Taste* 1, no. 5 (November 1846): 228–30.

Richards, T. Addison, ed. *Appletons' Illustrated Hand-Book of American Travel: A Full and Reliable Guide by Railway, Steamboat, and Stage to the Cities, . . . the United States and the British Provinces.* New York: D. Appleton & Co, 1857.

Richman, Jeffrey I. *Brooklyn's Green-Wood Cemetery: New York's Buried Treasure.* Brooklyn: The Green-Wood Cemetery, 1998.

Risk, John Kevin. *Shadow, Memory, Inscription: Interpreting Multiple Layers of History in Savannah's Bonaventure Cemetery.* MLA thesis, University of Georgia, 1997.

Roark, Elizabeth. "Embodying Immortality: Angels in America's Rural Cemeteries, 1850–1900." *Markers* 24 (2007): 56–111.

Rogers, Elizabeth Barlow. *Landscape Design: A Cultural and Architectural History.* New York: Harry N. Abrams, 2001.

Rogers, Elizabeth Barlow, Elizabeth S. Eustis, and John Bidwell. *Romantic Gardens: Nature, Art, and Landscape Design.* New York: Morgan Library & Museum, 2010.

Rosell, Lydia J. *Auburn's Fort Hill Cemetery.* Charleston, S.C.: Arcadia Publishing, 2001.

Roth, Leland M. *A Concise History of American Architecture.* New York: Harper & Row, Publishers, 1979.

Rotundo, Barbara. "Mount Auburn: Fortunate Coincidences and an Ideal Solution." *Journal of Garden History* 4, no. 3 (July-September 1984): 255–67.

Rousmaniere, John. *Green Oasis in Brooklyn: The Evergreens Cemetery, 1849–2008.* Kittery Point, Maine: Seapoint Books, Smith/Kerr Associates, 2008.

"Rural Cemeteries." *Horticulturist and Journal of Rural Art and Rural Taste* 6, no. 7 (July 1, 1853): 297–300.

"Rural Cemeteries." *North American Review* 53, no. 113 (October 1841): 385–412.

"Rural Cemeteries, No. 2 Planting, &c." *Horticulturist: Journal of Rural Art and Rural Taste* 7, no. 6 (September 1856): 393–96.

Rural Cemetery Association (St. Louis, Mo.). *Dedication of the Bellefontaine Cemetery, Address of Professor Post, and Other Proceedings on That Occasion: Also, the Rules and Regulations, and Charter of the Rural Cemetery Association, &C.: with an Appendix Containing the Proceedings of the Second Annual Meeting and Report of the Secretary and Treasurer of the Association.* St. Louis: Printed by T. W. Ustick, 1851.

Scee, Trudy Irene. *The Mount Hope Cemetery of Bangor, Maine: The Complete History.* Charleston, S.C.: History Press, 2012.

Schwaab, Eugene L, comp. *Travels in the Old South, Selected from Periodicals of the Times.* Edited by Eugene L. Schwaab, with the collaboration of Jacqueline Bull.

Vol. 2. [Lexington]: University Press of Kentucky, [1973].

Sears, John F. "Prisons, Asylums, Cemeteries, Parks." In *Sacred Places: American Tourist Attractions in the Nineteenth Century,* 87–121. Amherst: University of Massachusetts Press, 1998. First published 1989 by Oxford University Press.

Seymer, John Gunning. *The Romance of Ancient Egypt: Second Series of the Romance of Ancient History.* Vol. 1. London: Printed for Whittaker & Co., 1835.

Shaw, Terry. "Peter Wiltberger: Creator of a Cemetery at Bonaventure." *Bonaventure Historical Society* 3, no. 11 (August 1997): 1–3.

Shinn, Charles Howard. "A California Cemetery." *Garden and Forest,* 4, no. 167 (May 6, 1891): 206–7.

Shoberl, Frederic, ed. *The Language of Flowers, With Illustrative Poetry; to Which Are Now Added the Calendar of Flowers and the Dial of Flowers.* 8th American, from the 10th London ed. Philadelphia: Lea & Blanchard, 1848.

Simonds, O. C. "Landscape Cemeteries." In *Cyclopedia of American Horticulture: Comprising Suggestions for Cultivation of Horticultural Plants, Descriptions of the Species of Fruits, Vegetables, Flowers, and Ornamental Plants Sold in the United States and Canada, Together with Geographical and Biographical Sketches,* 879–83. E-M. New York: Macmillan, 1901.

Sloane, David Charles. *The Last Great Necessity: Cemeteries in American History.* Baltimore: Johns Hopkins University Press, 1991.

Smith, Henry Perry. *History of Oakwood Cemetery.* Syracuse: H. P. Smith & Co., 1871.

Smith, John Jay. "Rural Cemeteries." *Horticulturist and Journal of Rural Art and Rural Taste* 6 (August 1856): 345–47.

Smith, R. A. *Smith's Illustrated Guide to and Through Laurel Hill Cemetery, With a Glance at Celebrated Tombs and Burying Places, Ancient and Modern, an Historical Sketch of the Cemeteries of Philadelphia, an Essay on Monumental Architecture, and a Tour Up the Schuylkill.* Philadelphia: Willis P. Hazard, 1852.

Snyder, Ellen Marie. "Innocents in a Worldly World: Victorian Children's Gravemarkers." In *Cemeteries and Gravemarkers: Voices of American Culture,* edited by Richard E. Meyer, 11–29. Logan, Utah: Utah State University Press, 1992.

Spring Grove Cemetery Association (Cincinnati, Ohio). *Spring Grove Cemetery, Its History and Improvements: With Observations on Ancient and Modern Places of Sepulture.* Cincinnati: Robert Clarke & Co., 1869.

Stannard, David E. *The Puritan Way of Death: A Study in Religion, Culture, and Social Change.* New York: Oxford University Press, 1977.

Stevens, Levi Merriam. *Guide Through Mount Auburn; A Hand-Book for Passengers Over the Cambridge Railroad.* 5th ed. Boston: Bricher & Russell, 1860.

Stilgoe, John R. *Common Landscape of America, 1580 to 1845.* New Haven, Conn.: Yale University Press, 1982.

Strang, John. *Necropolis Glasguensis; With Observations on Ancient and Modern Tombs and Sepulture.* Glasgow: Atkinson and Company, 1831.

Stuart-Wortley, Emmeline. *Travels in the United States, Etc., During 1849 and 1850.* Vol. 1. New York: Harper & Brothers, Publishers, 1851.

Sweeting, Adam W. *Reading Houses and Building Books: Andrew Jackson Downing and the Architecture of Popular Antebellum Literature, 1835–1855.* Hanover: University Press of New England, 1996.

Taliaferro, Tevi. *Historic Oakland Cemetery.* Charleston, S.C.: Arcadia Publishing, 2001.

"A Talk About Public Parks and Gardens." *Horticulturist and Journal of Rural Art and Rural Taste* 3, no. 4 (October 1848): 153–58.

Thomas, Samuel W. *Cave Hill Cemetery: A Pictorial Guide and Its History.* Louisville, Ky.: Cave Hill Cemetery Co., 1985.

Thomas, W. Stephen, and Ruth Rosenberg-Naparsteck. "Sleeper's City: The Sesquicentennial History of Mt. Hope Cemetery." *Rochester History* 50, no. 4 (October 1988): 3–23.

TRC, City of Rome, Georgia: Cemetery Department, and Historic Preservation Office. *Myrtle Hill Cemetery Education Handbook,* 2007.

"Trees for Rural Cemeteries." *Horticulturist: Journal of Rural Art and Rural Taste* 7, no. 4 (April 1, 1854): 153–58.

Vernon, Christopher. *Graceland Cemetery: A Design History.* Amherst: University of Massachusetts Press, 2011.

Vernon, Nöel Dorsey. "Adolph Strauch: Cincinnati and the Legacy of Spring Grove Cemetery." In *Midwestern Landscape Architecture,* edited by William H. Tishler, 5–24. Urbana: University of Illinois Press, 2000.

Wales, William. *Rockland Cemetery Illustrated: Suggestions and Associations Connected With It and a Brief Statement of the Superior Advantages Presented to Those Who Desire Beautiful Resting Places for Their Dead.* New York: A. D. F. Randolph, 1881.

Wallace, William Ross. *The Loved and the Lost.* New York: Richards & Jones, Printers, 1856.

Walpole, Horace. *Essay on Modern Gardening.* 1785. A facsimile of the edition printed by Mr. Walpole at Strawberry Hill, with an introductory note by Alice Morse Earle. Canton, Pa.: Lewis Buddy III, The Kirgate Press, 1904.

Walter, Cornelia W. *Mount Auburn Illustrated: In Highly Finished Line Engraving, from Drawings Taken on the Spot, by James Smillie, with Descriptive Notices by Cornelia W. Walter.* The Rural Cemeteries of America. New York: R. Martin, 1851.

Wansley, James Hoyt. *Rose Hill Cemetery and the Ocmulgee Heritage Greenway: The Impact of Integration.* MLA thesis, University of Georgia, 2000.

Warren, George Washington. *The History of the Bunker Hill Monument Association During the First Century of the United States of America.* Boston: J. R. Osgood, 1877.

Weedsport Rural Cemetery Association (Weedsport, N.Y.) *Hand-Book of Weedsport Rural Cemetery Containing a Brief History of the Association; Also the Ordinances of the Board of Trustees and Suggestions As to Improvements.* Weedsport, N.Y.: The Association, 1895.

Weidenmann, Jacob. *Beautifying Country Homes. A Handbook of Landscape Gardening. Illustrated by Plans of Places Already Improved.* New York: Orange Judd & Co., 1870.

Wilson, Aime Marie, and Mandi Dale Johnson. *Historic Bonaventure Cemetery: Photographs from the Collection of the Georgia Historical Society.* Charleston, S.C.: Arcadia Publishing, 1998.

Wilson, Jane Bromley. *The Very Quiet Baltimoreans: A Guide to the Historic Cemeteries and Burial Sites of Baltimore.* Shippensburg, Pa.: White Mane Publishing Co., 1991.

Wilson, Susan. *Garden of Memories: A Guide to Historic Forest Hills.* [Boston, Mass.]: Forest Hills Educational Trust, 1998.

Wines, E. C. *A Trip to Boston, In a Series of Letters to the Editor of the United States Gazette.* Boston: Charles C. Little and James Brown, 1838.

Wissing, Douglas A., Marty N. Davis, and Richard Fields. *Crown Hill: History, Spirit, and Sanctuary.* Indianapolis: Indiana Historical Society Press, 2013.

Woodlands Cemetery Association (Cambridge, N.Y.), and A. D. Gillette. *The Woodlands Cemetery, at Cambridge, N.Y., with Historical Sketches, and an Address of Rev. A. D. Gillette, D.D., Delivered at the Dedication, June 2, 1858.* Troy, N.Y.: A.W. Scribner and Co., 1858.

Woolsey, T. D. "Cemeteries and Monuments." *New Englander* 7, no. 28 (November 1849): 489–501.

Wordsworth, William. *The Prose Works of William Wordsworth.* Aesthetical and Literary, edited by Alexander Balloch Grosart, 2. London: E. Moxon, Son, and Co., 1876. Reprint, New York: AMS Press, Inc., 1967.

Young, Edward. *The Complaint: or Night Thoughts on Life, Death & Immortality.* 6th ed. London: R. Dodsley, 1743.

INDEX

Cemetery of Père Lachaise (Paris, France): design of, 34; family lots in, 35; founding of, 33; as inspiration for rural cemeteries, 39, 42, 47, 54, 68, 144; monuments in, 35; and perpetual burial rights, 34–35; plantings in, 35; popularity of, 35; as tourist attraction, 35–36

Cemetery of Spring Grove (Cincinnati, Ohio): and Adolph Strauch, 59, 110–11, 113–14, 150, 158, 204–6, 227; dedicatory address of, 3; family lots in, 110, 150, 227; founding of, 57, 108; influence of, on other cemeteries, 104, 114, 118, 121, 126, 206–7; and landscape lawn plan, 59–60, 110–11, 113–14, 150, 227; lot enclosures in, 109, 110–11; and maintenance fees, 206; monuments in, 110, 227; original design of, 108–9, 209, 227; site selection of, 108, 132, 133; trees and shrubs in, 108, 110, 111, 113–14, 153–54, 158–61

cemetery superintendent, 55, 206

Central Burying Ground (Boston, Mass.), 10, 38

Central Park (New York, N.Y.), 189, 191–97

Channing, William Ellery, 30, 45

chapels, 138–39; in Crown Hill Cemetery, 119; in Evergreens Cemetery, 95; in Forest Home Cemetery, 98, 219; in Graceland Cemetery, 118, 219; in Green Mount Cemetery, 70–71, 220; in Mount Albion Cemetery, 223; in Mount Auburn Cemetery, 51–52, 54; in Mount Hope Cemetery (Boston, Mass.), 223; in Mount Hope Cemetery (Rochester, N.Y.), 72, 224; in Oak Hill Cemetery, 139, 225; in Riverside Cemetery (Oswego, N.Y.), 226; in Riverside Cemetery (Waterbury, Conn.), 226; in Sleepy Hollow Cemetery (Tarrytown, N.Y.), 227; in Woodlawn Cemetery (Elmira, N.Y.), 229

charnel house, 4, 6, 34

Chislett, Frederick W., 118

Chislett, John, Jr., 78

Chislett, John, Sr., 76, 77–78, 118, 215

Christian's Defence Against the Fears of Death, The (Drelincourt), 11

churchyards: in Colonial America, 6–7; in France, 31, 32; in Medieval Christendom, 4–5; observations of, by Washington Irving, 27; origins of burial in, 3–4; in Protestant England, 5–6

Cincinnati Horticultural Society, 108

Citizen Soldier (Milmore), 87

Civil War burial lots, 148; at Crown Hill Cemetery, 119; at Elmwood Cemetery (Columbia, S.C.), 217; at Elmwood Cemetery (Memphis, Tenn.), 148, 217; at Green Hill Cemetery, 219; at Hollywood Cemetery, 81; at Lexington Cemetery, 221; at Loudon Park Cemetery, 222; at Magnolia Cemetery, 101, 222; at Mount Hope Cemetery (Bangor, Maine), 60; at Oakdale Cemetery, 225; at Rose Hill Cemetery, 75

Clark, Charles E., 219

Clarke, James Freeman, 30

Classical Revival architecture, 123, 216

Cleveland, H. W. S., 116, 201, 207, 209, 219, 227

Cobham, Richard, 16

Coffin, John Gorham, 32

Complaint: or Night-Thoughts on Life, Death & Immortality, The (Young), 18, 21

Congreve's monument (Stowe), 16

Cook, Zebedee, Jr., 39

Cope, Walter, 228

Copeland, Robert Morris, 207, 209, 227

Copp's Hill Burying Ground (Boston, Mass.), 38, 59

Cornell, Silas, 71, 224

Cowley, Abraham, 13

Crapo, Henry Howland, 227

Crawford, Thomas, 52

Crouse, James, 106

Crown Hill Cemetery (Indianapolis, Ind.), 59, 118–21

cult of melancholy, 11–12, 17–18

Currie, James, 97–98

cypress trees: symbolism of, 2–3, 161; use of, in ancient burial grounds, 12, 153, 161; use of, at Cemetery of Père Lachaise, 35; use of, at Mount Auburn Cemetery, 39, 54; use of, at Mountain View Cemetery, 106–7, 161; use of, at Twickenham, 17

Cypress Hills Cemetery (Brooklyn, N.Y.), 57, 148

Daniels, Howard, 105, 108–9, 197, 209–10, 226, 227

Davis, Alexander Jackson, 95, 200, 218

Davis, Jefferson, 81

Davis, Varina Anne, 81, 83

de la Roche, George F., 224–25

Dearborn, Henry A. S.: biographical sketch of, 203, 210; and Bunker Hill Monument, 29; and Edgell Grove Cemetery, 217; and Forest Hills Cemetery, 85, 86, 218; and Mount Auburn Cemetery, 40, 41, 42, 44, 53, 201, 203; on use of trees in rural cemeteries, 151, 153

Dearborn, Nathaniel, 53–54

Dearborn's Guide Through Mount Auburn (Dearborn), 53–54

death: American attitude toward, 26–28, 30, 40, 60, 142, 172; English attitude toward, 11, 17–18, 23; and Romanticism, 23–24, 26–28, 40, 60, 142; and Unitarianism, 30

Death and the Sculptor (French), 87

DeForest, Alling, 222

Dexter, Henry, 52

Dexter, Stephen, 218

Dimmock, Charles H., 81

Directory for Visitors (Cleaveland), 65, 67

Douglass, David Bates, 65, 71, 210, 215

Downing, Andrew Jackson: as advocate for public parks, 187–89; biographical sketch of, 210; and Calvert Vaux, 213; on cemetery lot enclosures, 144–45; on Central Park, 189, 195; and Evergreens Cemetery, 94, 218; on Gothic Revival-style architecture, 51, 139; on influence of horticulture, 153; and John Notman, 211; on Laurel Hill Cemetery as arboretum, 154; on Picturesque landscape design, 26, 133, 134, 189; on spread of rural cemeteries, 55, 57

Doyle, John, 228

Drelincourt, Charles, 11

granite, 139

grave robbing, 48

gravestones: in churchyards, 6, 7; Puritanism's influence on, 7–9. *See also* iconography; monuments; symbolism

graveyards. *See* burial grounds; churchyards

Gray, Thomas, 18

Green, Charles E., 61

Green Hill Cemetery (Amsterdam, N.Y.), 219

Green Lawn Cemetery (Columbus, Ohio), 57

Green Mount Cemetery (Baltimore, Md.), 69–71, 220

greenhouses, 67, 86

Greenough, Richard S., 52

Greensward Plan, 189, 191, 194, 200

Green-Wood Cemetery (Brooklyn, N.Y.): as attraction, 67–68, 187, 188; cemetery enclosure around, 136–37; family lots in, 147; founding of, 55–56, 65; grand Gothic Arch in, 68–69; landscape design of, 65, 220; lot enclosures in, 145, 146; mausoleums in, 67, 144; as nonprofit organization, 47; original landscape features of, 65; publications about, 56, 65, 67, 68, 163; receiving tomb in, 139; trees in, 154, 163, 170, 220

Greenwood Cemetery (Hamilton, Ohio), 57

Green-Wood Illustrated, 56, 132, 136–37, 138–39, 172, 174, 177, 179

group lots, 46, 95, 144, 147–48. *See also* Civil War burial lots

Grove Street Cemetery. *See* New Burying Ground

Guide to Laurel Hill Cemetery, 28, 64, 65, 154–58, 164

Guide for Mount Hope Cemetery, 73

guidebooks, 56, 136, 140, 141; and Albany Rural Cemetery, 136; and Cemetery of Père Lachaise, 35; and Cemetery of Spring Grove, 111; and Evergreen Cemetery (Portland, Maine), 103; and Green Mount Cemetery, 71; and Green-Wood Cemetery, 65, 67; and Laurel Hill Cemetery, 64, 65, 140; and Magnolia Cemetery, 101; and Mount Auburn Cemetery, 53–54, 55, 56; and Mount Hope Cemetery (Rochester, N.Y.), 73. *See also* names of individual guidebooks; travel accounts

H. Searle & Son, 72, 224

Haggerston, David, 44, 223

Hall, Robert W., 226

Hamilton, William, 229

Hand Book for the Albany Rural Cemetery, A (Fitzgerald), 136, 140, 172, 184

Harmony Grove Cemetery (Salem, Mass.), 220

Haskell, Llewellyn S., 198, 200, 201

Highland Park (Ill.), 207

Hillhouse, James, 36–37

Hillside Cemetery (Middletown, N.Y.), 220

Hirschfeld, Christian, 21, 23, 35

Holabird & Roche, 118, 219

Hollywood Cemetery (Richmond, Va.), 78–83, 204, 220

Hollywood Memorial Association of the Ladies of Richmond, 81

Holy Innocents' Cemetery (Paris, France), 32

Hope Cemetery (Worcester, Mass.), 221

Horticulturist, The, 45, 144, 153, 154, 161–63, 165–68, 188–89, 195, 204

Hosmer, Harriet, 87

Hotchkiss, Almerin, 90, 201, 210–11, 215–16

Howe, Charles H., 102–3, 218

Hughes, Robert Ball, 51

iconography: evolution of, in Colonial New England, 10; influence of Puritanism on, 7–9; use of Classical, 30; use of Egyptian, 47; use of macabre, 4, 9, 27–28. *See also* symbolism

Idylls (Gessner), 21, 22, 35

Île de Peupliers. *See* Isle of Poplars

Imperial Decree on Burials, 33

Improved Order of the Red Men, 183

Independent Order of the Odd Fellows (IOOF), 183, 222

inscriptions: in ancient times, 1–2; in Colonial America, 142; in English elegiac landscapes, 17; in graveyard poetry, 18; influence of Puritanism on, 7–9, 142; influence of Romanticism on, 24, 142; in Medieval Christendom, 4; in rural cemeteries, 142

International Cemetery, Cremation and Funeral Association. *See* Association of American Cemetery Superintendents

Irving, Washington, 27–28, 227

Isle of Poplars, 22

Jenkins, John F., 228

Jenney, William LeBaron, 116, 219

John on the Isle of Patmos (Cantalamessa-Papotti), 140

Joint Committee on Urban Interments, 38

Jones, Edward C., 100–101, 222

Josselyn, Edgar A., 215

Kennedy, John Pendleton, 69–70

Kensal Green Cemetery (London, England), 63

Kent, William, 15–16

King's Chapel Burying Ground (Boston, Mass.), 7, 10, 38

Knights of Pythias, 183

Lake Forest (Ill.), 201

Lakewood Cemetery (Minneapolis, Minn.), 59–60

landscape architect, 201, 207

landscape architecture, 201, 207

Landscape Architecture, as Applied to the Wants of the West (Cleveland), 201, 207, 209

landscape gardener, 94, 110, 117, 150, 201, 204–6

landscape gardening, 201, 203, 204–6

landscape lawn plan, 59–60, 150; use of, at Cedar Hill Cemetery, 59–60, 126; use of, at Cemetery of Spring Grove, 59–60, 110–11, 113–14, 150, 227; use of, at Crown Hill Cemetery, 59–60, 118–19; use of, at Evergreen Cemetery (Portland, Maine), 104; use of, at Graceland Cemetery, 116–17, 219; use of, at Mount Auburn Cemetery, 128; use of, at Woodlawn Cemetery, 121, 123